Entrepreneurship and Small Firms

4th edition

Entrepreneurship and Small Firms

4th edition

David Deakins and Mark Freel

The **McGraw·Hill** Companies

London   Boston   Burr Ridge, IL   Dubuque, IA   Madison, WI   New York   San Francisco
St Louis   Bangkok   Bogotá   Caracas   Kuala Lumpur   Lisbon   Madrid   Mexico City
Milan   Montreal   New Delhi   Santiago   Seoul   Singapore   Sydney   Taipei   Toronto

Entrepreneurship and Small Firms
David Deakins & Mark Freel
ISBN-13 978-007710-826-7
ISBN-10 0-07-710826-4

 **Education**

Published by McGraw-Hill Education
Shoppenhangers Road
Maidenhead
Berkshire
SL6 2QL
Telephone: 44 (0) 1628 502 500
Fax: 44 (0) 1628 770 224
Website: www.mcgraw-hill.co.uk

British Library Cataloguing in Publication Data
A catalogue record for this book is available from the British Library

Library of Congress Cataloging in Publication Data
The Library of Congress data for this book has been applied for from the
Library of Congress

Acquisitions Editor: Kirsty Reade
Editorial Assistant: Natalie Jacobs
Senior Marketing Manager: Marca Wosoba
Senior Production Editor: Beverley Shields and Eleanor Hayes

Text design by Ken Vail Design
Cover design by Ego Creative
Typeset by Thomson Press India
Printed and bound in Finland by WS Bookwell

ISBN-13 978-007710-826-7
ISBN-10 0-07-710826-4

Brief Table of Contents

Detailed Table of Contents

Detailed Table of Contents

Preface

This fourth edition *Entrepreneurship and Small Firms* continues our policy with this text of using the new editions as an opportunity to revise all the chapters and to introduce new material, reflecting current issues, research and academic debate on entrepreneurship and small firms. For example, in this edition, the reader will find new chapters on 'Diversity in Entrepreneurship' and 'Family Businesses', reflecting the increased importance that has been given to these areas in research, academic study and policy. In addition, a number of chapters have either been re-written or extensively revised, such as the chapter entitled 'Entrepreneurial Activity, the Economy and the Importance of Small Firms', which has been rewritten to take a more European and international approach to this material. Other changes include the removal of a specific chapter on enterprise support; following reviews and feedback on the third edition, it was felt that this could be accommodated in other chapters, where appropriate. Thus a section in Chapter 3, for example, examines the role of support agencies in supporting women and ethnic minority entrepreneurs and supporting diversity in entrepreneurship. A further section, in Chapter 11, focuses on the role of support agencies in assisting business creation.

Readers familiar with previous editions will also find that the chapters have been restructured with some changes in sequence, but of course the overall style has been retained, with many of the features introduced in the third edition, such as 'Entrepreneurship in Action' boxes, case studies and suggested assignments. In order to accommodate some of the new material for this edition, some of the in-depth case material has been moved to the online student resource centre. To get the most benefit from this edition, students should consult this online resource material, which now contains a significant amount of additional material to supplement the case material. We have, of course, retained and revised the tutors' online resource material, which contains lecture slides and additional material not available to students.

The introduction to the third edition discussed the policy commitment of the UK Government as expressed in the following statement:[1]

Government is committed to making the UK the best place in the world to start and grow a business. (p. 4)

Taken from the Small Business Service's (SBS's) recent publication of *A Government Action Plan*, it represents a continuing emphasis for government policy on the importance of entrepreneurship and small firms for the vitality of the UK economy. As discussed in Chapter 2, this is something that has become a characteristic of policy for the EU member nations, embodied in the publication of the EU Green Paper on entrepreneurship.[2] This paper focuses on creating the right conditions and environment for entrepreneurship to flourish. Of course, placing the importance of entrepreneurship and small firms at the 'heart of policy'[3] is one thing, creating an environment in which entrepreneurship can thrive is another matter. The publication of the SBS's Action Plan[1] is a welcome attempt to identify some of the barriers to increased entrepreneurial activity in the UK, and the role that support bodies (such as the SBS) and the network of support agencies can take in encouraging entrepreneurial activity and improving the environment, especially in deprived areas, where entrepreneurial activity is more difficult.

Having an integrated approach is something that will be important at all levels in society, hence we have seen the development of enterprise initiatives in education, in deprived areas and with targeted groups, such as women and ethnic minorities, and related policy measures such as changes in taxation, incentives and regulation. Some of these initiatives are discussed in the text, especially in Chapters 3 and 11. However, as mentioned in our Introduction to the previous edition, such initiatives eventually affect us. For example, the government has stated previously that:[3]

The Government's direct interactions with SMEs form part of the overall picture but they are by no means the whole story. People may be put off starting a business if the environment in schools, further and higher education is discouraging and there are no effective role models available . . . Media stereotypes of business may cumulatively be discouraging. (p. 7)

The increased attention given to education, through a number of enterprise initiatives is something that is taken up in Chapter 11. The discussion of the importance of the financial environment is taken up in Chapters 4 and 5, technology, innovation and e-business is covered in Chapters 6 and 7, and Chapters 8 and 9 focus on growth and international entrepreneurship. All these topics reflect the importance of creating an appropriate infrastructure at all levels of society if the government is eventually going to achieve the aim of making the UK the best place in the world for entrepreneurship and small firms.

As mentioned, this fourth edition has retained the learning and pedagogical features that were introduced with the previous edition. Learning outcomes are given at the start of each chapter; boxed examples, titled 'Entrepreneurship in Action', are provided throughout the text, and Review Questions are also incorporated to review the material and to allow the reader to reflect upon the material and develop alternative concepts. However, the reader familiar with the previous edition will notice that the sets of review questions are now grouped at the end of each chapter. Suggested Assignments are given for each chapter; some of these incorporate or draw upon the additional material available in the student online material. Finally, the reader should find that the references have been completely updated, reflecting recent changes and the policy agenda discussed briefly above, and also that the Recommended Reading sections have been updated and are included at the end of each chapter.

Using the Text

This text is aimed at undergraduate and postgraduate students of entrepreneurship, enterprise, small firms and business venturing. Comments on using the text are provided here for students and lecturers.

Students will find that the text has been designed to be read in digestible sections. Chapters are broken up with highlights such as the 'Entrepreneurship in Action' features and with Review Questions at the end of the chapter. These questions do not treat each of these sections in isolation; rather they try to encourage the student to consider some of the implications raised in the chapter's content and material and attempt to get them to think further and perhaps link the material to that in other chapters of the text. Hints are given to enable them to do this. Suggested answers to the Review Questions are provided in the student's online resources material. These are not meant to be prescriptive, but provide an indication of the ways to think about the questions set, which may be in a discussion form.

The text is designed to cover entrepreneurial and small firm theory, concepts, evidence, policy and practice. It is designed to link these areas together. For example, discussion of entrepreneurial concepts is followed by practical mini-case examples or discussion of theoretical issues in small firm development; discussion of the growth of small firms is followed by a discussion of evidence; discussion of business creation is followed by discussion of some of the policy implications and policy measures, as well as practical examples. You are encouraged to link these distinct elements together through the Review Questions and Suggested Assignments. For example, you may be asked to relate entrepreneurial concepts to a practical case study.

The detailed case studies, most of which are in the online student resources for this edition, are all real entrepreneurial cases. In some of them, names have been changed to preserve anonymity. They are designed to take you to a decision point in the case study, to put you in the place of the entrepreneur. This may form part of a class group discussion in which you discuss the different paths the entrepreneur(s) may take and give a recommended course of action. It is important to realise that there is ambiguity in entrepreneurial decision-making. An ability to recognise different options can be as important as the actual decision made. A number of options can be equally valid courses of action, in other words, there is not necessarily one right answer. However, there are, for some of the detailed case studies, further sections provided in the online student learning material and further information in the online tutors' material (some of this information is available for registered tutors only).

While much of the material in this text is designed to enable you to understand entrepreneurship and small firm and enterprise development, to apply concepts, to understand case studies and to understand new policy developments, Chapter 12 also provides a guide to preparing *for* entrepreneurship through the coverage of research, design and writing of business plans. Of course, other chapters of the book also provide an opportunity to develop skills and to prepare for entrepreneurship through the discussion of case material and practical examples, but Chapter 12 focuses specifically on sources of information, research methods and the planning process. Throughout the text, we combine a focus on *understanding* with *doing*; a combination of enterprise skills should be developed if you use the review questions, material, case studies and assignments in the book throughout your course. These enterprise skills include problem-solving, creative thinking, research and information gathering, presentation and strategic planning. The value of developing these enterprise skills is that they are *transferable*, whatever career is undertaken. Increasingly employers are seeking graduates with transferable enterprise skills, who can think entrepreneurially, be creative and innovative and communicate new ideas. This is part of the reason for the increased emphasis governments are placing on enterprise education initiatives. We believe that this book will help you to develop those skills and apply them in different problem-solving situations, whether you decide to follow an entrepreneurial career or not. More important, research indicates that most entrepreneurial students do not wish to enter entrepreneurship when they graduate, rather they intend to enter entrepreneurship or self-employment after a period of employment,[4] but having undertaken study of entrepreneurship and small firms they are better prepared for such a change of career.

Lecturers will able to use this text for undergraduate and postgraduate courses in entrepreneurship and small firms. As discussed above, it combines concepts and theory with practical entrepreneurial case studies and examples, although the more detailed in-depth cases have now been placed in the student online resources to create additional room in this edition for the discussion of concepts and content on additional topics, such as the new chapter on family businesses (Chapter 10). It also has policy-related sections, where these are relevant, so that the material is placed in the context of recent developments in entrepreneurship and economic development. As indicated above, additional case material and suggested answers to the Review Questions are available to students through the online student resources.

For this fourth edition, we have retained the tutor online material, originally written by Margaret Fletcher, but revised for this edition. This provides additional course lecture slides and material for teaching purposes, which can be used in teaching alongside this text. The online resource for tutors also contains further information on using the case material in the text. Apart from these additional features, lecturers familiar with the third edition should find that we have rewritten the text to take account of new developments, new research and new policy initiatives in this area.

Other users should find that they are able to use this text for a variety of purposes. For example, for training courses for new entrepreneurs, for an understanding of new developments in entrepreneurship and for an appreciation of concepts applied to practical examples. We hope that this new text will continue to appeal and be of use to a large and varied audience, including potential entrepreneurs, trainers, policy-makers and other users with an interest in entrepreneurship and small firms.

Chapter Content

The first two chapters are foundation chapters, covering entrepreneurship (Chapter 1) and small firms (Chapter 2); they provide the underlying theory and concepts for much of the material presented in the text. Chapter 1 provides a foundation for many of the concepts on entrepreneurship. It examines the three approaches to entrepreneurship: from economic writers, from a psychological perspective and the socio-behavioural view. Alternative paradigms are also considered. Although the emphasis of the chapter is on different conceptual approaches, underlying evidence to support these approaches is considered with a critical review that emphasises the importance of entrepreneurial learning and entrepreneurship as a process. Chapter 2 builds upon this foundation by covering the importance of small firms and entrepreneurial activity for European economies, with comparisons of importance in different European countries, including those of eastern Europe. Measures of entrepreneurial activity are considered with a critical examination of the relationship between entrepreneurial activity and economic performance.

Chapter 3 provides an assessment of the importance of diversity of entrepreneurship. The chapter has been revised and updated to cover the issues of women's enterprise and ethnic minority entrepreneurship and examines some of the factors that affect the participation of women and ethnic minorities in entrepreneurial activity. Diversity is a theme running through much of the material of the text and, therefore, this chapter provides a further important step in understanding the nature and importance of entrepreneurship and small firms.

The next two chapters, 4 and 5, discuss the nature of the financial environment for entrepreneurs and small firms, focusing on the UK, although with some international comparisons. As with previous editions, the first of these chapters focuses mainly on debt finance – that is, the banks – and the latter on equity finance – that is, formal and informal venture finance.

Chapters 6 and 7 discuss the nature of rapidly changing environments and concepts in entrepreneurship and small firms concerned with innovation and e-business. Chapter 6 discusses the relationship between innovation and entrepreneurship, building on and developing many of the concepts that were introduced in Chapter 1. The chapter develops additional concepts in innovation and examines the advantages of small firms in the innovation process. Chapter 7 has been revised to update material on e-business, an increasingly important dimension for all entrepreneurs and small firms. The chapter examines the role of information and communications technologies (ICT) in small firms and examines how entrepreneurs can take advantage of ICT and e-business.

Two entrepreneurial processes are examined in Chapters 8 and 9, those of growth and internationalisation. The nature and process of entrepreneurial growth firms is discussed in Chapter 8, with discussion of both theory and evidence on growth firms. Chapter 9 examines the process of internationalisation of firms, again with discussion of theory and evidence. The two chapters draw out some of the similarities to be found in models of the two processes, which, of course, are not mutually exclusive.

Chapter 10, on family businesses, is a new innovation for the fourth edition. This chapter examines the nature of relationships in family businesses, which are now an important part of modern entrepreneurial economies. The chapter also examines specific issues in this area, notably succession planning, with a discussion of general principles applied to specific case studies.

The last two chapters focus on business start-up and creation. Chapter 11 discusses issues in business start-up, including creativity, opportunity recognition and business development. This chapter provides the basis for the more practical approach of Chapter 12, which focuses on the planning process for business start-up, including the design, writing and implementation of business plans. The material in the final two chapters has been revised and updated for the fourth edition.

David Deakins
2005

References

1   Small Business Service (2004) *A Government Action Plan for Small Businesses: The Evidence Base*, SBS/DTI, London.
2   European Commission (2003) *Entrepreneurship in Europe*, Green Paper, Brussels http://europa.eu.int/comm/enterprise/entrepreneurship/green_paper/.
3   Small Business Service (2001) *Think Small First: Supporting Smaller Businesses in the UK: A Challenge for the Government*, SBS/DTI, London.
4   Anderson, M., Galloway, L., Brown, W. and Wilson, L. (2003) 'Skills Development for the Modern Economy', paper presented at the 23rd ISBA National Small Firms Conference, Guildford.

Guided Tour

Learning Objectives

Identify the abilities and skills the student should be able to demonstrate after reading the chapter.

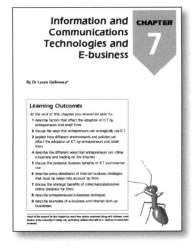

Boxed Features

These are highlighted throughout the chapter to aid the understanding of the concepts and theories developed.

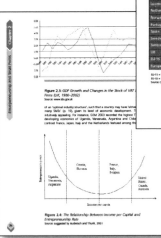

Figures and Tables

Each chapter provides a number of figures and tables to help you to visualise the information, and to illustrate and summarise important concepts.

Entrepreneurship in Action

Throughout the book these boxes provide practical examples demonstrating the application of concepts, followed by discussion questions to encourage students to analyse and discuss real issues.

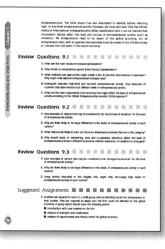

Review Questions

These questions encourage you to review and apply the knowledge you have acquired from each chapter. They are pitched at different levels.

Suggested Assignments

This end-of-chapter feature provides tasks or discussions to reinforce the subjects covered and enable students to gain the most benefit from each chapter.

Case Studies

These provide up-to-date examples, which give students the opportunity to apply what they have learnt to real-life problems.

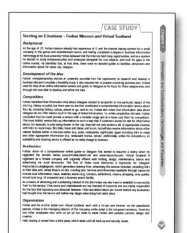

References and Recommended Reading

These provide students with the opportunity to research the subject further.

Technology to Enhance Learning and Teaching

Visit www.mcgraw-hill.co.uk/textbooks/deakins today

Online Learning Centre (OLC)

After completing each chapter, log on to the supporting Online Learning Centre website. Take advantage of the study tools offered to reinforce the material you have read in the text, and to develop your knowledge of entreprenerurship in a fun and effective way.

Resources for students include:
- Multiple Choice Questions
- True or False Questions
- Weblinks
- Suggested Answers

Also available for lecturers:
- Lecturer Manual
- Power Point Slides

For lecturers: Primis Content Centre

If you need to supplement your course with additional cases or content, create a personalised e-book for your students. Visit

www.primiscontentcenter.com

or e-mail

primis_euro@mcgraw-hill.com

for more information.

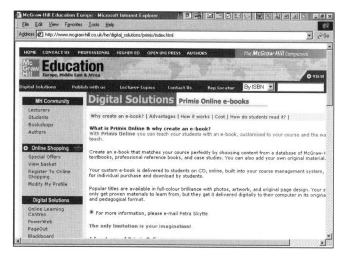

Study Skills

We publish guides to help you study, research, pass exams and write essays, all the way through your university studies. Visit

www.openup.co.uk/ss/

to see the full selection and get £2 discount by entering promotional code **study** when buying online!

Computing Skills

If you'd like to brush up on your computing skills, we have a range of titles covering MS Office applications such as Word, Excel, PowerPoint, Access and more.

Get a £2 discount on these titles by entering the promotional code **app** when ordering online at

www.mcgraw-hill.co.uk/cit

Acknowledgements

We would like to thank all the reviewers that have contributed to the review process for the fourth edition:

Maggie Anderson, Napier University
Richard Blundel, Oxford Brookes University
David Butler, University of Kent
David Douglas, Staffordshire University
Nerys Fuller-Love, The University of Wales, Aberystwyth
Catherine Gurling, Kingston University
Sarah Ingle, Dublin City University
Ossie Jones, Manchester Metropolitan University
Claire Leitch, Queen's University, Belfast
George Lodorfos, Leeds Metropolitan
Frank Martin, University of Stirling
Susan Moult, Robert Gordon University
Yong Wang, University of Wolverhampton

The text has benefited enormously from their insightful and constructive suggestions.

The Entrepreneur:
Concepts and Evidence

Learning Outcomes

At the end of this chapter you should be able to:

1 describe the main theories and concepts of the entrepreneur

2 compare and contrast different theories and concepts connected with the role of the entrepreneur

3 discuss the application of these theories and concepts to attempts to research the personality of the entrepreneur

4 describe some of the problems and limitations of research into the personality of the entrepreneur

5 discuss some of the social and environmental factors that influence the extent of entrepreneurship

6 distinguish between personality of owners and the management skills of small firm owner-managers, and the importance of the distinction between ownership and management of a small firm.

■ ■ ■ ■ Introduction

■ What makes an entrepreneur or small business owner?

■ Is an entrepreneur different from other individuals or can anyone be an entrepreneur given sufficient resources?

■ Can anyone set up in business or do you need to have special skills and characteristics?

These are questions that have occupied researchers and theorists for some time; indeed theories on what makes an entrepreneur date from the early Industrial Revolution. We will attempt to answer some of these questions later when we examine factors that can encourage successful new business creation and entrepreneurial success. However, it is useful to review the contribution of the major theorists on entrepreneurship first. It is only when these have been examined that we can understand the characteristics, traits and factors that researchers have sought to find in the modern entrepreneur. Later we question much of this research effort into the characteristics of the entrepreneur; it may, for example, be better to concentrate on the management skills and competencies that are required of business owners.

This chapter will be concerned with three approaches to entrepreneurship. These are illustrated in Figure 1.1.

The three approaches shown in Figure 1.1 are associated with the following sources:

■ the contributions of economic writers and theorists on the role of the entrepreneur in economic development and the application of economic theory

■ the psychological trait approach to personality characteristics of the entrepreneur, which is examined critically later

■ a social-behavioural approach, which stresses the influence of the social environment as well as personality traits.

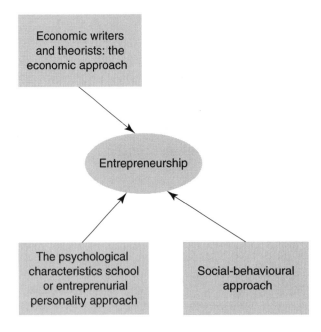

Figure 1.1: *Approaches to Entrepreneurship*

Each approach is considered in this chapter, and it can be claimed that all three have something to contribute to our understanding of the entrepreneurship process. However, it will be seen that the psychological trait and social-behavioural approaches are more controversial. Indeed there is some dispute over whether 'entrepreneurial' traits or characteristics can be identified at all.

There are many writers who have contributed to theories about the entrepreneur, but there is insufficient space in this text to consider more than the major contributors. For a detailed analysis of other theorists and contributors, the student is advised to consult the recommended reading listed at the end of this chapter.

■ ■ ■ ■ ■ The Entrepreneur

If we examine conventional economic theory, the term 'entrepreneur' is noticeable only by its absence. In mainstream or neo-classical economic theory, the entrepreneur can be viewed as someone who co-ordinates different factors of production, but the important distinction is that this role is viewed as a non-important one. The entrepreneur becomes merged with the capitalist employer, the owner-manager, who has the wealth to enable production to take place, but otherwise does not possess any special attributes. The entrepreneur, if recognised at all, is a pure risk-taker, the reward being the ability to appropriate profits. It is a remarkable fact that the main body of conventional economic theory has developed without a place for the entrepreneur, yet there is no shortage of writers who have contributed to the development of views on the role and concept of the entrepreneur.

The idea that the entrepreneur has a significant role in economic development has been developed by writers outside mainstream economic thinking. Their contributions now have an important place, but it is only relatively recently that the importance of these contributions has been recognised. As attention has become more focused on the importance of the small and medium-sized enterprise (SME) sector for economic development and job creation, so greater attention has also been directed at theories of entrepreneurship. We examine the most important of those theories that are accepted today; they are summarised in Table 1.1 by their key insights.

The term 'entrepreneur' is French in origin and a literal meaning might translate as 'one who takes between'. Some important French writers have contributed views on the role of the entrepreneur; the most important of these are Cantillon and Say.

Table 1.1: *Key Contributions of Economic Writers on the Role of the Entrepreneur*

Writer	Key role of entrepreneur	Additional insights
Say	Organiser of factors of production	Catalyst for economic change
Cantillon	Organiser of factors of production	Catalyst for economic change
Kirzner	Ability to spot opportunity	Entrepreneur's key ability is 'creative' alertness
Schumpeter	Innovator	Entrepreneur as 'hero' figure
Knight	Risk-taker	Profit is reward for risk-taking
Casson	Organiser of resources	Key influence of the environment
Shackle	Creativity	Uncertainty creates opportunities for profit

■ Cantillon was the first to recognise the crucial role of the entrepreneur in economic development, which was founded on individual property rights. Of the three classes in society recognised by Cantillon, entrepreneurs were the important class and were the central economic actors. The other two classes were landowners and workers.

■ Say also made the entrepreneur the pivot of the economy, and a catalyst for economic change and development. The entrepreneur provided a commercial stage in three stages of production. In this way, the entrepreneur could be seen as close to the traditional mainstream, as someone willing to take the risk of bringing different factors of production together.

Both Cantillon and Say belonged to a French school of thought known as the 'physiocrats', so called because of the physical nature of the agrarian economy that dominated their thinking. It could be because of this view that developments in the concept of the entrepreneur were not seen as being relevant to the nineteenth-century industrial economy. It was much later before more modern concepts of the entrepreneur were developed. Some of these views have been developed within the 'Austrian School' of thought; however, this is such a wide-ranging term that there is no one particular view associated with this school for the entrepreneur. What is different, however, is that the entrepreneur is seen as being crucial to economic development and a catalyst for dynamic change. We turn now to these Austrian School writers, who underpin much of the current theory of the entrepreneur and hence much of modern-day research into the characteristics of the entrepreneur.

Kirzner

For Kirzner, the entrepreneur is someone who is *alert* to profitable opportunities for exchange. Recognising the possibilities for exchange enables the entrepreneur to benefit by acting as a 'middleman' who facilities the exchange. The Kirznerian entrepreneur is alert to opportunities for trade. He or she is able to identify suppliers and customers and act as the intermediary. Note that there is no necessity to own resources, and profit arises out of the intermediary function.

These possibilities for profitable exchange exist because of imperfect knowledge. The entrepreneur has some additional knowledge, which is not possessed by others, and this permits the entrepreneur to take advantage of profitable opportunities. The information is costless – it arises when someone notices an opportunity that may have been available all the time. It can often seem obvious after the service or product has been provided, but it still takes someone with additional knowledge to recognise and exploit the opportunity.

The role of information in the marketplace is important for the Kirznerian entrepreneur. Market exchange is itself an entrepreneurial process, but people can profit from exchange because of information gaps in the market. In this view, the entrepreneur may be seen as little more than a market trader taking advantage of opportunities to trade; yet for Kirzner the entrepreneur is someone who is still creative. The possession of additional knowledge provides opportunities for creative discoveries. However, in contrast to the Schumpeterian view below, anyone could potentially possess the additional knowledge and be alert to opportunities for exchange and trade.

Schumpeter

By contrast, Schumpeter's entrepreneur is a special person. Although Schumpeter is a writer classified in the 'Austrian School', his views on the entrepreneurial functional are quite different from those of Kirzner.

The Schumpeterian entrepreneur is an *innovator*. The entrepreneur brings about change through the introduction of new technological processes or products. For Kirzner, anyone has the potential to be an entrepreneur and they operate within set production constraints. For Schumpeter, only certain extraordinary people have the ability to be entrepreneurs and they bring about extraordinary events. The Schumpeterian entrepreneur changes technological possibilities, alters convention through innovative activity and, hence, moves production constraints. He or she develops new technology, whereas the Kirznerian entrepreneur operates on opportunities that arise out of new technology.

Although the entrepreneur is again an important catalyst for economic change, the entrepreneur is essentially temporary for Schumpeter. Schumpeter predicted the demise of the function of the entrepreneur, that technological advance and change would be carried out by teams of workers and scientists operating in large organisations. This is because, for Schumpeter, large monopolistic firms have distinct advantages over small firms in the technological process.

The Internet Boom and the Relevance of Schumpeter

The dotcom 'boom and bust' situation bears comparison to Schumpeter's cycles of 'creative destruction'. In 1999 and 2000 explosive growth in the use of the Internet created opportunities for many dotcom enterprises and e-entrepreneurs, among the most famous, in the UK, being lastminute.com, established by Martha Lane-Fox and Brent Hoberman. Internet technology had made new ways of trading possible and there was a rush of money from institutions and small shareholders into such new e-entrepreneurial firms at vastly inflated share prices. At the height of the boom, lastminute.com shares were issued at a price of £ 3.20 and briefly reached £ 3.80. When the dotcom bubble burst after March 2000, the shares in such companies collapsed and many (such as boo.com) ceased trading, although lastminute.com is now one of the more successful dotcom companies, having established a trading base across Europe. Schumpeter predicted that such new technology waves would occur from time to time in the economy but that the life of many such new entrepreneurs would be short-lived; in order to create change it was necessary to have creative destruction – brought by new technology – but out of this, new opportunities would be available.

Such dotcom entrepreneurs could be seen to be innovative – they were pioneering new ways of trading, using new technology and, in some cases, revolutionised ways of trading (such as the low-cost airlines' ticketing policies and booking through the Internet).

For a full discussion of the implications of e-commerce see Chapter 7.

The concept that large firms are more successful than small firms in new-technology-based industries is more correctly attributable to Galbraith. However, this concept has come to be associated with Schumpeter, even though he was more concerned with the advantages of monopolistic market structure than firm size. The small-firm entrepreneur faces considerable disadvantages in research and development (R&D); for example, R&D is expensive; it has long development times and teams of researchers are able to benefit by feeding off one another's ideas. If the entrepreneur is an innovator then this argument suggests that he or she will find it difficult to establish new small firms. Technological change is carried out by large firms. The entrepreneur may still exist in large firms and is sometimes termed an 'intrapreneur', an individual who is capable of initiating change in large firms.

The concept that the entrepreneur is someone who is different, someone who is an innovator, is important. Some writers have carried this forward to distinguish entrepreneurs (business owners who wish to develop and expand their businesses) from other small-business owners who have no ambition to expand their business or wish to remain merely self-employed. The essential distinguishing feature for such writers is that the entrepreneur is a Schumpeterian innovator, although here the term 'innovator' would be more loosely defined to include a person who wishes to manage or initiate change in some way. For example, Curran and Stanworth[1] state that:

Entrepreneurship, rigorously defined, refers to the creation of a new economic entity centred on a novel product or service or, at the very least, one which differs significantly from products or services offered elsewhere in the market. (p. 12)

Knight

The commonly held view of the entrepreneur as a calculated risk-taker comes close to the view of Knight. For Knight, the entrepreneur is an individual who is prepared to undertake risk, and the reward – profit – is the return for bearing uncertainty, which is an uninsurable risk.

The opportunity for profit arises out of the uncertainty surrounding change. If change is perfectly predictable then no opportunity for profit exists. The entrepreneur is someone who is prepared to undertake risk in an uncertain world.

Knight made an important distinction between risk and uncertainty. Risk exists when we have uncertain outcomes, but those outcomes can be predicted with a certain degree of probability. For example, the outcome that your car will be stolen or not stolen is uncertain, but the risk that your car will be stolen can be calculated with some degree of probability and this risk can be insured against. True uncertainty arises when the probability of outcomes cannot be calculated. Thus, anyone can set up in business, but that person cannot insure against business failure because that particular outcome cannot be predicted with any degree of probability. The entrepreneur is someone who is willing to accept the remaining risk that cannot be transferred through insurance. This important distinction, established by Knight, has not so far been explored in small firms research. We include some research on risk management and insurance in a later section in this chapter; however, issues such as the extent to which the entrepreneur assesses, accepts and transfers risk have yet to be properly explored.

This distinction helps to distinguish a small firm manager from the entrepreneur/owner. One of the characteristics of entrepreneurs (following Knight) could be considered to be the responsibility for one's own actions. If a manager assumes this, then he or she is performing some entrepreneurial functions. We can also use this distinction as a criticism of some research into entrepreneurship that concentrates solely on personality traits and ignores management skills.

These distinctions are unfortunately rarely discussed in the small firms literature. However, for a good discussion of the extent of the different meanings of entrepreneurship in the literature see Galloway and Wilson.[2] An exception is also provided by Shailer.[3] For example, Shailer considers that:

[The] entrepreneur is now a widely used term, with considerable contemporary diversity in meaning associated with the intended interests of its users. . . . Owner-managers do not necessarily fit any of the current popular definitions of 'entrepreneur'. (p. 34)

Shailer prefers to adopt the view of entrepreneurship as a process and refers to a stage of the firm when it is in owner-management. Again we have the important concept of management of the firm, the willingness to accept risks and responsibilities. If the firm grows, it is possible to transfer this entrepreneurial function, but still retain part-ownership through the issue of shares. The manager, as opposed to the owner, now takes on the function of the entrepreneur. The fact that the behaviour of the previous owner-entrepreneur is likely to alter has been established (theoretically) by writers such as Jensen and Meckling[4] by applying agency theory. The concept of the importance of small business management skills is also discussed by Ray.[5] He considers that the search for the prototype (entrepreneur) has been ill conceived and considers that, 'There is no empirical evidence or conceptual base to say much, if anything, about entrepreneurs and risk taking' (p. 347).

Ray considers that we should concentrate on the development of skills and how managers acquire them. These concepts are too frequently ignored and this entrepreneurial and learning process has not been adequately researched, although, as we shall note, there has been recent progress.

The concept of entrepreneurship as a process has also been highlighted by Stevenson and Jarillo,[6] who suggest that: 'entrepreneurship is a process by which individuals ... pursue opportunities without regard to the resources they control' (p. 23). Stevenson and Jarillo usefully denote the approach of economic writers to entrepreneurship as being concerned with what happens when entrepreneurs act, or with the results and consequences of entrepreneurship, whereas they view the psychological characteristics approach as being concerned with how entrepreneurs act, or with the study of entrepreneurial management.[6]

We could say, then, that the Knightian entrepreneur is anyone who is prepared to undertake the risk of setting up their own business. However, equally, it could be any risk-taker (and this is a source of criticism). The entrepreneur is someone who has the confidence and is venturesome enough to make judgements about the uncertain future, and the reward for this is profit.

Shackle

Shackle's entrepreneur is someone who is creative and imaginative. Whereas Kirzner's entrepreneur *perceives* opportunities, Shackle's *imagines* opportunities. Everyone potentially has this creative ability, which is exercised in making choices.

The role of uncertainty and imperfect information is crucial for the view of the role of the entrepreneur by Shackle. Uncertainty gives rise to opportunities for certain individuals to imagine opportunities for profit. Shackle's entrepreneur is creative and original. The act of imagination is important for identifying the potential of opportunities. This potential is compared to resources available, which can lead to the decision to produce, hence the act of entrepreneurship. Shackle's creative entrepreneur indicates that *creativity* is an important element in the entrepreneurship process. However, how this creative process occurs, and the factors that might influence it, remain areas that are only just beginning to be explored. A host of factors will influence an individual's ability to be creative, including personal background, education and attitudes; but it is likely that such influences will combine to affect the extent to which that individual is prepared to recognise and exploit opportunities. It is only recently that pre-entrepreneurial experiences (including education, employment and learning) are beginning to be recognised as important influences on nascent (pre-start) entrepreneurs.[7] In fact the neglect of the study of important influencing factors pre-start – or the process of nascent entrepreneurship – is surprising, given its potential importance for modern economies.[8]

Casson

Casson attempts to synthesise some of the entrepreneurial attributes and concepts that have been discussed by the major writers. Casson recognises that the entrepreneur will have different skills from others. These skills enable the entrepreneur to make judgements, to co-ordinate scarce resources. The entrepreneur makes judgemental decisions that involve the reallocation or organisation of resources.

Casson emphasises that entrepreneurs require command over resources if they are to back their judgements and that this is likely to imply that they will have personal wealth. Lack of capital would thus be a barrier to successful entrepreneurship.

Casson's view is closer to that of Knight than other writers. The entrepreneur operates within a set of technological conditions; by making difficult judgemental decisions they are able to enjoy the reward of profit (for bearing uninsurable risk). This enables the entrepreneur to co-ordinate demand and supply under uncertainty.

In Figure 1.2 the demand curve represents the return to each entrepreneur as their numbers increase and is part of a map of such curves. The supply curve of entrepreneurs depends on access to resources and, thus, depends on the local economy and environment. Casson's analysis attempts to explain why in some economies entrepreneurs can flourish, yet in others there are low participation rates for people who own their own businesses. For example, in the UK, the South-East has higher participation rates of people in small business ownership than the Midlands, which in turn has higher participation rates than Scotland. The low participation rates in Scotland have been partly attributed to, for example, relatively low home ownership, which limits the amount of equity that a nascent entrepreneur might have to invest in a start-up firm.[9] Thus Casson's point about access to resources would appear to be an important one. The clear implication, when we examine such participation rates, is that the environment can be a more powerful influence than any predilection among the local population for entrepreneurship.

Casson's insight is to view change as an accompaniment to entrepreneurship. The pace of change provides opportunities, and the entrepreneur chooses which one to back. Entrepreneurs can vie with each other as their numbers increase, the supply of

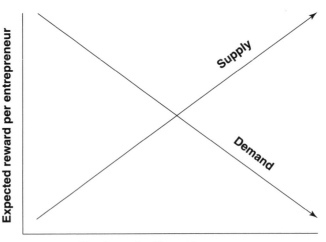

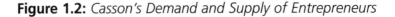

Figure 1.2: *Casson's Demand and Supply of Entrepreneurs*

entrepreneurs depending on their access to resources. The supply curve shown in Figure 1.2 will thus depend on the propensity of any given set of circumstances and the extent to which potential entrepreneurs have access to resources. This will depend on factors such as social mobility, as well as institutional factors such as the ability to access capital. An equilibrium position will result from the interaction of these factors, as shown in Figure 1.2.

A number of other economic writers and theorists have considered the development of the role of the entrepreneur. These include, for example, Thünen, who could be seen as a forerunner of Knight. Thünen recognised the function of the entrepreneur as a risk-taker, involving risks that cannot be transferred through insurance, a theme we will return to later in this chapter. For Thünen, however, the entrepreneur was also concerned with innovation and problem-solving.

It would be untrue to say that the Neo-classical School of economists added little to the concept of the entrepreneur. For example, Marshall recognised a distinction between the capitalist and the entrepreneur through his 'undertaker', who was alert to opportunities but also innovative in devising new methods of production.

Section Summary and Review

A consensus has emerged that, in conditions of uncertainty and change, the entrepreneur is a key actor in the economy. The different views on the role of the entrepreneur are summarised in Table 1.1, but two major lines of thinking have developed: the Knightian approach, which highlights the risk-bearing and uncertainty-reducing role of entrepreneurs; and the Schumpeterian approach in which the entrepreneur is an innovator.

Other perspectives highlight the knowledge and insight of the entrepreneur to new possibilities. This co-ordinating role has been developed and emphasised by Casson, but in addition it is thought that there are other factors that influence participation in entrepreneurship, such as access to resources and facilities in the local environment. The entrepreneurial act of business creation is part of a process that will be affected by many historical factors as well as the opportunities arising from economic change, such as the example of the dotcom boom. As the pace of economic change increases, so opportunities increase; yet our understanding of the complete entrepreneurship process, and why participation rates (of different groups in society) are far from equitable, remains quite limited.

▪ ▪ ▪ ▪ ▪ The Entrepreneurial Personality

The second approach to entrepreneurship is to identify certain personality characteristics or 'traits' in individuals that appear to be possessed by successful entrepreneurs. The characteristics literature has been concerned with testing and applying some perceived characteristics in individuals. From this approach, it is possible to argue that the supply of potential entrepreneurs is limited to a finite number of people that have innate abilities, that have a set of characteristics that marks them out as special, and have particular insights not possessed by others. This has led to some controversy and, in terms of policy, it has significant implications. Obviously, if entrepreneurial characteristics are inherent then there is little to be gained from direct interventions to encourage new entrepreneurs to start new businesses, although interventions into improving the infrastructure or environment may still have an effect.

We will examine some of these personality 'traits', although, as will become apparent, we do not accept the hypothesis that there is a fixed limit to the supply of potential entrepreneurs. For example, many of the characteristics that are often said to be peculiar to successful entrepreneurs are the same abilities and skills that could be applied to most successful managers; it is therefore difficult to separate out specific characteristics of entrepreneurs.

Some of this research stems from the original work carried out by McClelland,[10] who identified the historical role model influence of heroes on subsequent generations. Such influence induced a high need for achievement on the population of the subsequent generations. McClellend, however, is also associated with identifying the key competencies of successful entrepreneurs shown in the accompanying box.

Proposed Key Competencies of Successful Entrepreneurs

- ■ Proactivity: initiative and assertiveness
- ■ Achievement orientation: ability to see and act on opportunities
- ■ Commitment to others

Much has been made of the need for achievement trait, as though this was the one characteristic that set potential budding entrepreneurs apart from others. An implicit assumption with this approach is that the individual bears responsibility for his or her lack of entrepreneurial activity and this proposition could be used by policy-makers to divert interventions away from regions that have low rates of participation in small firm ownership.

Considering the work of writers on the entrepreneurship personality and those who might subscribe to the characteristics approach, we can identify certain key characteristics that have been identified in the literature as being important abilities for any entrepreneur (see the accompanying box).

The Entrepreneurial Personality – Key Characteristics

- ■ McClelland's need for achievement
- ■ Calculated risk-taker
- ■ High internal locus of control
- ■ Creativity
- ■ Innovative
- ■ Need for autonomy
- ■ Ambiguity tolerance
- ■ Vision
- ■ Self-efficacy

Some writers subscribe to the view of McClelland – that the key characteristic is achievement motivation, or a high need for achievement, which can be described as a desire to excel, to achieve a goal in relation to a set of standards. High achievers are those that accept responsibility for decisions and for achieving solutions to problems, but standards will be set carefully so that they can be achieved. Satisfaction is gained from finding the solution to a problem rather than with monetary reward. Yet, partly because such a characteristic is difficult to measure, the evidence has proved to be contradictory. A high need for achievement can also be an important characteristic for success for people in many occupations, not just entrepreneurs.

Another characteristic that has been advocated is the internal locus of control. Individuals with a high internal locus of control like to be in charge of their environment and of their own destiny. Again, as with the need for achievement trait, it has not been possible to reconcile conflicting evidence on entrepreneurs with this approach to one or two important personality traits. For a critique of the characteristics literature see Chell et al.[11] In a review of this approach, Delmar[12] comments that 'the [research] results have been poor and it has been difficult to [discern] any specific traits to entrepreneurial behaviour' (p. 145).

A further example is provided by Meredith et al.[13] who give five core traits:

1. self-confidence
2. risk-taking activity
3. flexibility
4. need for achievement
5. strong desire to be independent.

Perceived self-confidence or self-efficacy has been advocated by some writers as an important concept in entrepreneurship. High self-confidence in entrepreneurship translates into self-belief in one's capabilities to mobilise resources, motivate others and produce change (business start-up). Although there is some evidence that perceived self-efficacy is related to business performance,[12] researchers have been concerned with whether successful entrepreneurs display psychological traits that separate them out as individuals from others, and this approach can be criticised in a number of ways.

Criticisms of the Personality Characteristics Approach

- ■ It is inappropriate to search for a significant single trait.
- ■ It ignores environmental factors that may be more important than personality.
- ■ It comprises an essentially static analysis approach to the dynamic process of entrepreneurship.
- ■ It ignores the role of learning, preparation and serendipity in the process of entrepreneurship (these factors are discussed in later in this chapter).

A more negative characteristic, that of the deviant (non-conformist) personality is associated with Kets de Vries.[14] The deviant personality is associated with the third approach to the entrepreneur, that of the social-behavioural school. A deviant character is associated with individuals who do not easily fit in with their existing employment – for instance, someone who is out of place in a large firm. The non-conformist behaviour precipitates a desire to start their own business, rather than operate within the regulations of a large organisation. However, this would seem to rule out the possibility of the dynamic employee wishing to create change in the large firm, the intrapreneur.

Writers such as Timmons[15] have attempted to summarise the personality characteristics of successful entrepreneurs and to categorise characteristics that can be acquired and those that are more innate. While Timmons does admit that many of these characteristics can be acquired, through learning or from experience, Timmons also considers that there are some attributes that cannot be acquired, that are innate, and perhaps mark out 'born entrepreneurs' from 'made entrepreneurs'.

Timmons considers that both need for achievement and locus of control can be acquired along with other leadership abilities and competencies such as the ability to take responsibility for actions/decisions. Many of these characteristics are management skills. Entrepreneurs obviously need to be ambitious but need to be satisfied that they have achieved personal goals and ambitions.

We can assume that profit or monetary reward is not the only driving force behind entrepreneurs. There is also the need to build and achieve personally set goals, hence implying that entrepreneurs have a high need for achievement in order to establish a growing business or 'entrepreneurial' firm (this is discussed in more detail in Chapter 8). Similarly, the internal locus of control has been identified as an important characteristic of potential entrepreneurs. A high internal locus of control means that the person needs to be in control of their own environment, to be their own boss. Timmons considers that these characteristics can be acquired; many of these abilities can be taught or, at the very least, scenarios can be provided that stimulate the acquisition of these skills and abilities.

In practice, many of the entrepreneurial characteristics are those associated with any successful manager or indeed with any successful individual. It is therefore difficult to justify a separate set of characteristics for a successful career in entrepreneurship.

Timmons also gives additional attributes that are more innate. These are listed as:

- high energy coupled with emotional stability
- creative and innovative ability
- conceptual ability
- vision combined with a capacity to inspire.

Although it may be claimed that this set of characteristics is more innate in terms of identifying people who are potential entrepreneurs, it is difficult to justify that these abilities mark people out for entrepreneurship. It also does not mean that they cannot be acquired. By the use of planning scenarios and problem-solving it is still possible to demonstrate how opportunities can be exploited, how resources can be acquired and how creative solutions can be developed.

Some institutions and writers have attempted to develop tests of potential entrepreneurial ability or enterprise. Caird, for example, has developed a measure of enterprising traits (or entrepreneurial abilities) called the General Enterprise Tendency (GET),[16] as used by the Durham Business School. It consists of a scale of different questions within the following categories:

- 12 questions that measure need for achievement
- 12 that assess internal locus of control
- 12 to determine creative tendency
- 12 to gauge calculated risk-taking
- six to measure need for autonomy.

Entrepreneurial or enterprise tendency tests, however, suffer from the same limitations as the characteristics approach. Not surprisingly, these tests have been found not to be consistent in their application or selection. However, more recent work at Durham, carried out by Johnson and Suet Fan Ma,[17] with an expanded scaled test with nine dimensions, appears to claim more promising results as an enterprise tendency test.

Problems arise whenever attempts are made to measure these characteristics. Here are some examples.

- Characteristics are not stable and change over time.
- In many cases they are subjective judgements that do not lend themselves to objective measurement. For example, how do we define being innovative? It can simply be the ability to deal with change and the ability to cope with new processes

and solutions. How do we measure the calculated risk-taker? In many respects there are unsatisfactory definitions of these concepts, which makes their measurement difficult to justify.

- Concentrating on personality characteristics means that we are in danger of ignoring environmental and cultural influences, which can be just as, if not more, important than any set of personality traits.

- Placing too much importance on an inherent set of personality characteristics reduces the role of education and training. Learning is a very valuable process that allows potential entrepreneurs to acquire skills, to develop methods of business planning. While we would agree that many people are not suited to entrepreneurship, there is still much that can be learned and acquired by potential entrepreneurs and this process is far from understood.

There is a danger that these approaches can influence and dominate approaches to small firm ownership and entrepreneurship so that important influences on entrepreneurship, such as quality of the infrastructure provided in the environment, are ignored. There are a number of problems with these approaches and they include ignoring issues such as gender, age, social class and education, all of which can have a bearing on the propensity of an individual to enter entrepreneurship.

Socio-behavioural Approaches

Socio-behavioural approaches recognise the importance of some of these factors, but especially the environment and the influence of culture on individuals. It can be argued that a society's culture is a more powerful influence on the extent to which individuals can successfully pursue entrepreneurship. An example is provided by a nation's tolerance of failure.

Dealing with Failure

Timmons considers that dealing with failure can be an important attribute of entrepreneurs. However, the ability to tolerate failure depends on the culture. In the USA, failure is viewed as a learning experience and people can benefit from it, can learn from their experience and can go on to form successful companies as a result. In Britain, the culture is less tolerant of failure and, too often, highly talented individuals have not been able to recover from it. According to a recent report, in the EU as many as 40 per cent of people would not start a business due to fear of failure, whereas the equivalent in the USA is 26 per cent.[18] The culture and environment is crucial to tolerance of failure. There is little doubt that Britain has lost many potentially successful entrepreneurs because, having failed once, they have not been allowed to recover from that failure, perhaps in the shape of an inability to raise capital following bankruptcy. Failure is a very valuable learning experience, as many entrepreneurs have admitted. It is a pity that, in Britain, new entrepreneurs are often not allowed a further opportunity so that they can benefit from their experience, apply lessons learned and build a successful business.

The Influence of the Environment: Different Entrepreneurship Participation Rates

We turn now to consider some of the empirical evidence on the factors that influence entrepreneurship. As we have suggested much research effort has gone into discovering the personality traits of the entrepreneur; some of this literature is controversial, since some of it assumes that an entrepreneur must have some special ability that distinguishes him or her from other people. Unfortunately, this does not explain why there are low participation rates in entrepreneurship by women and by African-Caribbeans in the UK. As Ram[19] has pointed out, the Asian community has high rates of participation in small business ownership/entrepreneurship, yet this has had more to do with negative factors of barriers to employment elsewhere than any predisposition for entrepreneurship.

The ideas and concepts surrounding the entrepreneur, which have been outlined above, are used as a basis by researchers for detecting traits in successful small business owners and entrepreneurs. As in any scientific method, theory can be used for developing hypotheses about the behaviour of successful entrepreneurs. These hypotheses are then tested against the observed characteristics of entrepreneurs and small business owners in the real world. However, there are a number of problems with this approach, among which is the assumption that additional factors affecting participation rates will be constant.

Entrepreneurial Participation Rates Vary

- Different participation rates in different regions
- Different participation rates by gender
- Active inter-firm networks vary by region

1. Some regions are more favoured than others at establishing successful small businesses and entrepreneurs, and hence their economic development is more successful. The question of whether this is due to characteristics in the population, or due to certain aspects of the environment and infrastructure that enable potential entrepreneurs to more easily exploit their skills and opportunities, remains, at this stage, an open one.

   Research undertaken for Scottish Enterprise,[9] after concern with low participation rates in entrepreneurship, showed that a complex series of factors contributed to low participation rates in Scotland. For example, the historical dependence on a limited number of large employers, coupled with inward investment (North Sea oil) had produced a 'dependency culture' – that is, people were used to depending on large firms for employment. Thus, the thought of going into business on their own account did not come easily to them. Other factors were found to be important as well, such as difficulties in accessing finance. Scottish Enterprise introduced a Business Birth Rate Strategy in 1993[20] with a raft of measures designed to improve access to environmental factors affecting entrepreneurship; after seven years a comprehensive review of the strategy[21] concluded that although the environment had been improved, little difference had been made to the business birth rate. This example shows that participation rates can vary in different geographical areas, but explanations of such spatial variations involve complex reasons.

2. Concern has been expressed at the existence of latent entrepreneurial talent. For example, why are there so few successful female entrepreneurs? In Scotland, a compilation and promotion of over 400 recent high-growth entrepreneurs (conducted by Scottish Enterprise[22] in an attempt to provide

more role models that might influence possible or potential nascent entrepreneurs) contained only 16 per cent who were female. Why is the participation rate of African-Caribbeans in entrepreneurship low? Again these remain open questions that appear to have no simple solution but rather are caused by a complex combination of social and economic reasons.

Limited research has been conducted specifically on these groups, in the UK, although, a UK study involving the author[23] with African-Caribbean and the other main ethnic-minority entrepreneurs in the UK has provided more information on motivation, aspirations and the issues facing these groups (for a more detailed discussion of ethnic-minority entrepreneurship, see Chapter 3).

3. Attention has focused on the role of networks in successful entrepreneurial development. For example, some research suggests that inter-firm networks contribute to successful entrepreneurship.

Official statistics indicate that a high proportion of new firms fail within three years of start-up. For example, in the UK, 30 per cent of new firms appear to cease trading by the third year and 50 per cent by the fifth year.[24] Official statistics need to be treated with caution and are likely to overstate the true failure rate; for example, a successful start-up firm may cease to exist when taken over by another firm; some business owners leave and re-enter self-employment, dependent on labour market conditions. However, it is accepted that only a small proportion of new firms grow to employ 50 or more workers. One of the factors that might affect such limited numbers of high-growth firms is the potential loss of control faced by the entrepreneur as the firm grows. New small firms and entrepreneurs that are successful are predominantly located in the South-East in the UK, which suggests that the environment and infrastructure are at least as important as the characteristics of the entrepreneur. It is also likely that the development of inter-firm networks is more advanced in the South-East than in other regions of the UK.

The inter-organisational networks that link firms after they are established have been found to be important to the ongoing success of firms.[25] Efficient networks that foster good communications between firms contribute to entrepreneurial behaviour and success.[26]

The Ability to Learn

Much research effort has gone into identifying entrepreneurial characteristics and this has diverted research effort away from important areas concerning the entrepreneur's ability to learn from problem-solving and gain from their business experience. Although there have been recent advances in understanding – for example, following work by Cope and Watts[27] and Rae[28] – there is still a need to improve our knowledge of how entrepreneurs learn, yet it is accepted that there is a learning experience from merely establishing a new enterprise. The learning process that is involved in business and enterprise development is still imperfectly understood, yet programmes have been designed and interventions are made in business development. The problem with these interventions (at least in the past) is that they were often task-orientated. They were built around particular tasks and skills in terms of business planning – for example, book-keeping or financial skills, liquidity or controlling for debt. As such, they concentrated on the specific tasks involved in running a business. A failing of such interventions is that they do little to alter the approach of the entrepreneur to solving business problems and learning from dealing with those problems. However, in recent years, in the UK, there has been evidence of the introduction of more mentoring-style assistance. Overall, though, it is not surprising that Storey and Westhead,[29] from a survey of the literature, found that there was little evidence of a link between formal training and improved performance of small firms, indicating that formal personal management development and training of the entrepreneur appears, paradoxically, to have no impact on improved performance. Gibb,[30] however, proposes that development of the entrepreneur is affected by the extent of interaction with 'stakeholders' in the small firm environment (for example, customers, bankers, creditors and supply chain relationships), thus implying that intervening to improve learning from interaction and experience should improve entrepreneurial ability and performance. According to Gibb:

Learning better from experience implies bringing knowledge, skills, values and attitudes together to interact upon the learning process; it therefore fundamentally demands an action-learning approach. (p. 16)

Gibb's 'stakeholder' model of entrepreneurial learning places importance on small firms' relationships with the external environment. This can be contrasted with an alternative approach based on an evolutionary theory of learning and entrepreneurial behaviour. Drawing on evolutionary theories, Costello,[31] for example, has shown that, with high-technology small firms, entrepreneurs learn to adapt behaviour into 'routines' that enable knowledge to be acquired and it is the routine (a set of rules) that enables learning to evolve. This, however, also implies that such learning becomes 'path dependent',[32] taking a critical event to change a routine.

Entrepreneurs who become task-orientated are those that are more likely to fail. Entrepreneurship involves a learning process, an ability to cope with problems and to learn from those problems. An ability to recognise why problems occur and be able to deal with them, and, more importantly, understand why they occur, will ensure that the entrepreneur will be able not only to deal with those problems, but also to learn from the experience and ensure that processes are put in place within the firm to ensure that either the problem does not occur again or that the firm can deal with the problem. As shown in Figure 1.3, this ability to learn from experiences involves the concept of double-loop learning,[33] a process that involves examining why the problem occurred and learning from that process. It is a process of learning 'how to learn'.

Despite recent improvements, our limited knowledge and understanding of the interaction of learning and the entrepreneurship process remains one of the more neglected areas of entrepreneurial research and, thus, understanding. This is surprising

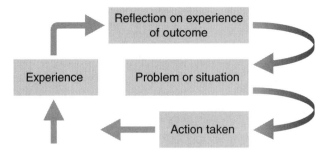

Figure 1.3: *Double-Loop Learning*

given the attention that has been paid to areas such as 'the learning organisation'. Case studies of the features of learning organisations have been developed in some detail,[34] yet little equivalent research has been undertaken within small firms, partly because of the lack of appropriate ethnographic and case study approaches that are capable of revealing the complex and often subtle mix of factors that will affect entrepreneurial learning. At the same time, we need developments of theories and concepts that are appropriate to entrepreneurship. Learning organisation concepts are derived from large organisations; more promising are developments in evolutionary approaches to learning and the entrepreneur. In part, these stem from a Schumpeterian dynamics analysis of the forces of change, and attempt to explain how the entrepreneur can adapt, change and thus learn from dealing with uncertainty.[35] The interaction between learning and the entrepreneurship process has been highlighted by Levinthal,[36] who stresses the adaptive role of the entrepreneur as they adjust to their environment, to their learning experience and, as a result, change behaviour. The nature of learning may follow a trial-and-error and discovery activity; entrepreneurial behaviour becomes adapted in an evolutionary way to the discovery of information from trial and error. It is suggested that such evolutionary theories may be able to model the nature of entrepreneurial behaviour and development, although there is a need for further work in this area.

The ability of the entrepreneur, or entrepreneurial team, to learn is crucial to their behaviour and ability to succeed. To be successful, entrepreneurs must be able to learn from decisions, from mistakes, from experience and from their networks. It is a process that is characterised by significant and critical *learning events*. To be able to maximise knowledge as a result of experiencing these learning events will determine how successful their firm eventually becomes. There seems little doubt that there are methods of enhancing the learning activity, such as the careful choice of an entrepreneurial team with complementary skills. We have suggested, however, that at present there is a need for further theoretical development, which will help to guide policy-makers and, thus, interventions. Entrepreneurial behaviour is a dynamic response to a constantly changing environment. Large firm organisational theory does not capture the dynamics of learning in such an environment. Approaches that attempt to model the nature of such dynamic interaction stem from a Schumpeterian dynamic modelling of entrepreneurial response to their experience.

The author's view is that these dichotomous approaches to entrepreneurial learning (as represented by Gibb and Costello) have something to offer in understanding the nature of entrepreneurial learning. The author has suggested that entrepreneurial learning occurs as a result of a combination of the processes involved in these two approaches.[37] The important contribution of these theories is that entrepreneurial behaviour is a dynamic process, where the entrepreneur learns to adjust decision-making, and consequently we cannot view the ability of the entrepreneur as something that is static; rather it is continually evolving.

Risk Management

In this section we return to Knight's concepts of risk and uncertainty, and of the entrepreneur as risk-taker and manager. It has sometimes been expressed that an entrepreneur is a risk-taker but 'not a gambler'; that is, that he or she will take calculated risks, not gambles (which are seen as uncalculated risks). However, a gambler can just as easily be described as someone who does take calculated risks – a gambler knows the odds against winning, has calculated the chances of beating those odds and hence takes a calculated risk with a financial stake. It is possible to argue that there is little difference between this approach and that of the entrepreneur who has made a calculated risk by putting up a financial stake and has worked out the odds against success. We can describe first attempts to enter business, by definition, as a form of calculated gamble. The entrepreneur can minimise those risks but there is always an element of luck, of right timing. There are always things that can go wrong – after all, the entrepreneur is dealing with uncertainty. This is the key insight of Knight: that the entrepreneur is dealing with uncertainty and takes risks that can be calculated.

It is more helpful to see the entrepreneur as a risk manager, as this identifies one of the key concepts to understanding the process of entrepreneurship. In dealing with uncertainty, the entrepreneur has to identify, assess, evaluate, manage and transfer risk. Knight saw risk as a subset of uncertainty. Events that are truly uncertain cannot be predicted with any degree of probability. However, most events are risky; their probability of occurrence can be predicted with a degree of probability. Some events have a greater degree of probability of occurrence than others. For example, insurance premiums in the inner city are high because the probability of damage to premises is higher than in other locations. A successful entrepreneur is someone who is able to identify, assess and evaluate the importance of the risk, say, of trading in the inner city. They are able to manage this risk through preventive measures or through the transfer of risk with insurance, and hence make decisions about trading and market opportunities weighed against the risk of operating in a particular location. Chapter 3 examines ethnic-minority entrepreneurs. In the UK they have been successful entrepreneurs in marginal economic environments; they have successfully managed the risk of operating in such environments by being resourceful, by developing coping strategies, by learning to manage within a limited ethnic market, and by developing policies that enable them to break out into mainstream markets. Understanding the process of entrepreneurship in the context of the environment, and the degree of risk imposed by that environment, gives us a greater degree of understanding of what contributes to entrepreneurial success.

A successful entrepreneur is someone who can minimise risks either through the limitation of his or her financial stake or by reducing the degree of uncertainty, so that the risks can be calculated accurately and decisions made with more reliability. Entrepreneurs will want to know what their potential market is, who their competitors are, and what strategy would be best in the marketplace. By assessing different risks in the process of production, which includes buying materials and supplies, and assessing risks in the market, the entrepreneur engages in uncertainty-reducing behaviour that will maximise his or her probability of success. An example of risk-taking and risk management is provided by our first case, Hullachan (see the accompanying 'Entrepreneurship in Action' box). Hullachan is, in some ways, typical of many start-ups where an individual leaves employment to invest their life savings in a start-up venture that has previously been a hobby. But what is the risk involved? The subsequent development of Hullachan and further discussion is available in the online learning centre resource materials for students and tutors.

ENTREPRENEURSHIP IN ACTION

Risk-taking and the Hullachan Case

Craig Coussins had been in employment for 20 years, but had a life-long interest in dance; his mother had been a successful Celtic dancer, and he was acutely aware of the type and extent to which injury to dancers' feet can occur. He had been a salesman, selling sports and dance products and, ultimately, due to his interest in and experience of the market, he sold dance products worldwide for a large international company.

During his time with this company Craig's interest in designing dance shoes developed. He was taught design by the chief pattern-cutter of the company and, eventually, he sold his designs to the company's MD. His designs were successful because of their focus on minimising injury. For 10 years Craig had studied anatomy and physiology privately in order to better his knowledge and understanding of the nature and causes of dance injury; in fact, he became something of an authority on the subject, writing articles for trade magazines and presenting to specialists.

With his understanding of the issues concerning dance injury Craig was able to produce innovative injury-reducing designs for dance shoes. It was this knowledge and experience of the subject, alongside his career as a salesman, that prompted him to identify a market.

His view was that a design such as his had not been implemented before in the Celtic dance market, despite the fact that Celtic dancers are extremely susceptible to both long- and short-term injuries, such as Achilles tendonitis and impact injury. He was also aware that, throughout the world, Celtic dance is very popular (for example in the USA, Canada and Australia); therefore, Craig had a potential worldwide market for his product.

Craig decided that he would eventually start up in business, designing, manufacturing and selling Celtic dance shoes.

Start-up

Craig knew that to start up in business he would have to raise between £40,000 and £50,000, a high figure, mainly due to the necessity to patent his designs. He felt it was unlikely that he could attract external investment because of the specialist nature of the market he intended to enter, so he set about raising the money himself. After years of saving and planning Craig arranged a large overdraft from the bank (£50,000), by pledging his house as security, and decided to leave his job and start Hullachan.

Review Questions for Discussion

1. Is Craig Coussins a calculated risk-taker?
2. What is his financial risk in starting Hullachan?
3. How would his perception of risk differ if Craig was at the start of his career?
4. What about if he was approaching retirement?

The discussion generated by the Review Questions in the box should reveal that our perception of risk can change over time and depends on individual circumstances. Like entrepreneurship, risk-taking is not a static concept; rather, it changes with individual circumstances over time. One person's perception may be high risk and another's low risk.

Risk Management and the Use of Insurance

Although Knight identified the importance of risk-taking, the entrepreneur needs to be able to assess which to accept and which to transfer. In this process, the entrepreneur may decide to accept some risk, reduce risk through risk management, or transfer risk through insurance. As indicated before, however, we know little of the extent to which an entrepreneur attempts to perform this function.

The availability of insurance is important because it enables the entrepreneur to transfer risk instead of accepting the full risk liability. For example, in the case of

Hullachan, Craig Coussins, with a manufacturing concern, was faced with a number of risks that could prevent the business operating successfully. These included theft of stocks, fire, damage to vehicles through motor accidents, personal injury from the product, and injury to employees and visitors on company premises. All of these risks can easily be transferred through insurance policies and, in some cases, such insurance is compulsory (for example, employer's liability). Some risks, of course, are not transferable. The risk of making losses cannot be transferred through any insurance policy, although it is possible to transfer subsequential losses from some other risk, such as fire. In addition, the management of risk can reduce the extent of insurance needed, and risk can also be reduced by taking a number of measures that prevent the possibility of accidents. For example, special training for employees in health and safety may reduce the risk of employee accidents and hence reduce the insurance premium required by the insurance company.

Some firms are faced with more risks than others. For example, Hullachan represents a case where risks are relatively high due to manufacturing a product where risks may exist in the product process (to employees and to customers); manufacturing small firms face greater risks than service-sector firms. They may have product liability risks and, if their product is protected by a patent, they face the risk that another firm could copy their product, thus incurring expensive legal action to defend their patent.

The extent to which entrepreneurs undertake both risk management and the transfer of risks through insurance is largely unknown, yet the ability to manage risk (of which insurance is part) is an important subset of management skills for small firm survival. Previous research in the West Midlands and Scotland provides comparisons in the use of insurance by technology-based firms.[38] The evidence suggested that the use of more specialised insurance is low, with only 8 per cent and 9 per cent (West Midlands/Scotland) of firms taking out cover for the protection of patents and copyright. The low take-up of patent protection may reflect a low application rate of high-technology-based and innovative entrepreneurs to take out patents, which are time-consuming, relatively complicated and expensive. Follow-up research in Scotland indicated that 38 per cent of firms were concerned with acquiring patents, which would suggest that the low take-up rates of cover were due to difficulties in the insurance environment. In the case of Hullachan, it was important for Craig Coussins to lodge applications for patents for his designs, but he did not take out patent insurance.

A follow-up study by Bentley and Sparrow,[39] focusing on technology-based entrepreneurs and their perception of risk, revealed that the low take-up of some forms of insurance was due to 'cost reasons' in relation to overall risks, with high premiums for specialised insurance accounting for low take-up rates. The study by Bentley and Sparrow recommended that more attention should be given to the education of entrepreneurs with regard to risk management, a potential area of intervention for support agencies. Clink[40] has suggested that small firms' approach to risk management can be segmented through a typology related to the proactiveness of planning and risk control within the firm, which may provide a framework for further analysis and support.

Further discussions with the insurance industry and small firm representatives, such as the Federation of Small Businesses (FSB), have indicated that risk management and the use of insurance was an important topic that suffered from a low profile in research. A paper by the FSB[41] indicated that insurance was seen as a particular problem by its members, especially in the inner city, where the difficulties in obtaining adequate insurance cover were seen as a significant constraint in small firm entrepreneurship, start-up and development. For example, insurance premiums in these areas are expensive, yet risk-management measures were difficult to impose due to local authority restrictions on the extent of security provisions.

■ ■ ■ ■ Conclusions

We can see that attempts to develop tests on entrepreneurial characteristics owe something to the development of theories of entrepreneurship. Shackle's creator and Schumpeter's innovator are included in the measures of creative tendency; there is Knight's calculated risk-taker; the role of co-ordinator of Casson and Kirzner is included by the need to have an internal locus of control and autonomy. These theories have been the guidelines for tests of entrepreneurial ability. Concern with the entrepreneurial personality has diverted attention away from the learning and development process in entrepreneurship and enterprise development, away from the recognition that the individual entrepreneur *acquires* skills and abilities, which are learned from the very process of entrepreneurship. Much of this learning process is not understood, although there have been recent advances following research into this learning process. However, there is still a need to refocus research away from the investigation of the entrepreneurial personality, which is effectively a cul-de-sac, towards identifying the important factors (of which the environment might be only one) that affect the process of learning and development in entrepreneurship. Support for entrepreneurship can then be better informed to enable individuals to acquire management skills that enable them to learn from their experience, from their solution of problems.

There is little doubt, however, that the environment can be just as important as personal management skills for successful entrepreneurship. This has important implications for policy and the support of SMEs. Some of these issues will reoccur when we examine small business support later in this book. If the environment is not conducive then entrepreneurial talent will lie dormant. The importance of identifying entrepreneurial characteristics lies in encouraging potential entrepreneurs to start their own businesses. Schemes that give blanket coverage run the risk of persuading people to enter business who are not suited to the task of controlling and running their own business (however good the business idea may be) and who eventually fail. There is evidence that policy has become more focused on start-ups and increasing the level of entrepreneurial activity,[18] but it is also important to ensure that policies encourage high-quality sustainable businesses.

Review Questions 1.1 ■ ■ ■ ■ ■ ■ ■ ■ ■ ■ ■ ■

1. Contrast the Schumpeterian view of the entrepreneur with that of Kirzner. Give examples.

2. List the key contributions to our understanding of entrepreneurial abilities from each of the following:

   ■ Knight

   ■ Casson

   ■ Kizner

   ■ Schumpeter.

3. Why is the environment important to our understanding of differing participation rates in entrepreneurship?

4. How does Schumpeter help to explain the dotcom bubble of 1999–2000 and the subsequent fallout of failing dotcom entrepreneurs?

Hint: see also Chapter 6.

Review Questions 1.2

1. Suggest key personality characteristics associated with successful entrepreneurs.

2. Suggest additional key personality characteristics that may be required to be a successful entrepreneur (for example, consider the perseverance required to overcome initial rejection of a new idea by funders).

3. Which of the personality characteristics you have listed in your answer to Question 1 could be acquired through learning?

4. Critically review the entrepreneurial personality approach with a series of bullet points.

Review Questions 1.3

1. Using case material in this chapter, why is risk management a key attribute of the entrepreneur?

2. Review the three approaches to entrepreneurship discussed in this chapter. Why do they each have something to contribute to our understanding of entrepreneurship?

3. Why is it important to treat entrepreneurship as a process?

Suggested Assignments

1. Students undertake a small research study by interviewing small-firm owner-managers about their concepts of management and entrepreneurship. For example, do they consider themselves entrepreneurs? Small groups of students can each interview one small-firm owner and discuss the results in class.

2. Students debate the skills of entrepreneurs. Students are each given one of two briefs indicating which case they have to argue:

■ entrepreneurs are special and have to be born

■ entrepreneurship skills can be acquired and the environment that fosters entrepreneurship is important.

3. Compare risk-taking by Craig Coussins in the Hullachan 'Entrepreneurship in Action' case to an individual who seeks to start a business with virtually no capital. The latter uses a number of personal credit cards (boot-strapping) to start the business and he opens a bank account. Against his new account, on a Friday, he is able to write a cheque to acquire stock over the weekend to sell at a market, hoping that he can make enough money to pay in the cash to the bank on the Monday. Who is taking the bigger risk?

Recommended Reading

Chell, E., Haworth, J. and Brearley, S. (1991) *The Entrepreneurial Personality, Concepts, Cases, and Categories*, Routledge, London.

Global Entrepreneurship Monitor (2003) *Executive Report*, Kauffman Center for Entrepreneurial Leadership, Babson College, Boston, USA.

Handy, C. (1999) *The New Alchemists*, Hutchinson, London.

Reynolds, P.D. and White, S.B. (1997) *The Entrepreneurial Process*: *Economic Growth, Men, Women and Minorities,* Quorum, Westport, USA.

References

1 Curran, J. and Stanworth, J. (1989) 'Education and Training for Enterprise: Some Problems of Classification, Evaluation, Policy and Research', *International Small Business Journal*, vol. 7, no. 2, pp. 11–22.

2 Galloway, L. and Wilson, L. (2003) 'The Use and Abuse of the Entrepreneur', Management School Working Paper, Heriot-Watt University, Edinburgh.

3 Shailer, G. (1994) 'Capitalists and Entrepreneurs in Owner-managed Firms', *International Small Business Journal*, vol. 12, no. 3, pp. 33–41.

4 Jensen, M.C. and Meckling, W.H. (1976) 'Theory of the Firm: Managerial Behaviour, Agency Costs and Ownership Structure', *Journal of Financial Economics*, vol. 3, no. 2, pp. 305–60.

5 Ray, D. (1993) 'Understanding the Entrepreneur: Entrepreneurial Attributes, Experience and Skills', *Entrepreneurship and Regional Development*, vol. 5, no. 4, pp. 345–57.

6 Stevenson, H.H. and Jarillo, J.C. (1990) 'A Paradigm of Entrepreneurship: Entrepreneurial Management', *Strategic Management Journal*, vol. 11, special issue, pp. 17–27.

7 Reynolds, P.D. and White, S.B. (1997) *The Entrepreneurial Process*: *Economic Growth, Men, Women and Minorities,* Quorum, Westport, USA.

8 Reynolds, P.D. and White, S.B. (1997) *The Entrepreneurial Process: Economic Growth, Men, Women and Minorities*, Quorum, Westport, USA.

9 Scottish Enterprise (1993) *Scotland's Business Birth Rate: A National Enquiry*, Scottish Enterprise, Glasgow.

10 McClelland, D.C. (1961) *The Achieving Society*, Van Nostrand, New Jersey.

11 Chell, E., Haworth, J. and Brearley, S. (1991) *The Entrepreneurial Personality, Concepts, Cases, and Categories*, Routledge, London.

12 Delmar, F. (2000) 'The Psychology of the Entrepreneur', in Carter, S. and Jones-Evans, D. (eds), *Enterprise and Small Business: Principles, Practice and Policy*, FT/Prentice Hall, London, pp. 132–154.

13 Meredith, G.G., Nelson, R.E. and Neck, P.A. (1982) *The Practice of Entrepreneurship*, International Labour Office, Geneva.

14 Kets de Vries, M. (1977) 'The Entrepreneurial Personality: A Person at the Crossroads', *Journal of Management Studies*, vol. 14, no. 1, pp. 34–57.

15 Timmons, J.A. (1994) *New Venture Creation: Entrepreneurship for the 21st Century*, 4th edn, Irwin, Illinois, USA.

16 Cromie, S. and O'Donoghue, J. (1992) 'Assessing Entrepreneurial Inclinations', *International Small Business Journal*, vol. 10, no. 2, pp. 66–71.

17 Johnson, D. and Suet Fan Ma, R. (1995) 'Research Note: A Method for Selecting and Training Entrants on New Business Start-up Programmes', *International Small Business Journal*, vol. 13, no. 3, pp. 80–4.

18 Small Business Service (2004) *A Government Action Plan for Small Business: The Evidence Base*, SBS/DTI, London.

19 Ram, M. (1993) *Managing to Survive: Working Lives in Small Firms*, Blackwell, Oxford.

20 Scottish Enterprise (1993) *A National Strategy for Scotland*, Scottish Enterprise, Glasgow.

21 Fraser of Allander Institute (2001) *Promoting Business Start-ups: A New Strategic Formula, Stage 1 Final Report*, Scottish Enterprise, Glasgow.

22 Scottish Enterprise (1997) *Local Heroes*, Scottish Enterprise, Glasgow.

23 Ram, M., Smallbone, D. and Deakins, D. (2002) *Ethnic Minority Businesses in the UK: Access to Finance and Business Support*, British Bankers' Association, London.

24 DTI (1997) *Small Firms in Britain Report 1996*, DTI, London.

25 Butler, J.E. and Hansen, G.S. (1991) 'Network Evolution, Entrepreneurial Success and Regional Development', *Entrepreneurship and Regional Development*, vol. 3, no. 1, pp. 1–16.

26 Greve, A. and Salaff, J.W. (2003) 'Social Networks and Entrepreneurship', *Entrepreneurship Theory and Practice*, vol. 28, no. 1, pp. 1–22.

27 Cope, J. and Watts, G. (2000) 'Learning by Doing: An Exploration of Experience, Critical Incidents and Reflection in Entrepreneurial Learning', *International Journal of Entrepreneurial Behaviour and Research*, vol. 6, no. 3, pp. 104–24.

28 Rae, D. (2003) *Entrepreneurial Identity and Capability: The Role of Learning*, PhD thesis, Nottingham Trent University, Nottingham.

29 Storey, D.J. and Westhead, P. (1996) 'Management Training and Small Firm Performance: Why is the Link so Weak?', *International Small Business Journal*, vol. 14, no. 4, pp. 13–24.

30 Gibb, A. (1997) 'Small Firms Training and Competitiveness. Building Upon the Small Business as a Learning Organisation', *International Small Business Journal*, vol. 15, no. 3, pp. 13–29.

31 Costello, N. (1996) 'Learning and Routines in High Tech SMEs: Analysing Rich Case Study Material', *Journal of Economic Issues*, vol. 30, no. 2, pp. 591–7.

32 Freel, M. (1998) 'Evolution, Innovation and Learning: Evidence from Case Studies', *Entrepreneurship and Regional Development*, vol. 10, no. 2, pp. 137–49.

33 Pedler, M., Burgoyne, J. and Boydell, T. (1991) *The Learning Company: A Strategy for Sustainable Development*, McGraw-Hill, Maidenhead.

34 Kline, P. and Saunders, B. (1993) *Ten Steps to a Learning Organisation*, Great Ocean, Virginia.

35 Nelson, R. and Winter, S. (1982) *An Evolutionary Theory of Economic Change*, Harvard University Press, Boston, Massachusetts.

36 Levinthal, D. (1996) 'Learning and Schumpeterian Dynamics', in Dosi, G. and Malerba, F. (eds), *Organisation and Strategy in the Evolution of Enterprise*, Macmillan, London.

37 Deakins, D. (1999) Editorial: 'Entrepreneurial Learning', *International Journal of Entrepreneurial Behaviour and Research*, vol. 5, no. 3.

38 Deakins, D., Paddison, A. and Bentley, P. (1997) 'Risk Management, Insurance and the High Technology Small Firm', *Small Business and Enterprise Development*, vol. 4, no. 1, pp. 21–30.

39 Bentley, P. and Sparrow, J. (1997) *Risk Perception and Management Responses in Small and Medium-sized Enterprises*, Enterprise Research and Development Centre, University of Central England, Birmingham.

40 Clink, S. (2001) 'Risk Management in Small Businesses', unpublished PhD thesis, Glasgow Caledonian University, Glasgow.

41 Goodman, F. (1994) 'Insurance and Small Firms: A Small Firm Perspective', paper presented to Insurance and Small Firms Seminar, University of Central England, Birmingham, April.

Entrepreneurial Activity, the Economy and the Importance of Small Firms

CHAPTER 2

Learning Outcomes

At the end of this chapter you should be able to:

1 discuss different approaches to the definitions of small firms

2 describe the importance of small firms in European economies

3 describe the importance of small firms for job creation

4 discuss the association between entrepreneurial activity and economic growth

5 discuss international comparisons on the importance of small firms

6 describe the factors that account for the increased importance of small firms in modern economies

7 discuss differences in the importance of small firms in European transition economies.

■ ■ ■ ■ Introduction

This chapter focuses on the importance of small firms in the UK and in other economies, particularly European economies. It includes a section on European transition economies for comparative purposes. The reader should also refer to Chapter 9, which covers additional material on international entrepreneurship and also considers entrepreneurship in transition economies. This chapter, however, focuses on data on the importance of small firms.

Texts of this type inevitably beg the question 'Why study entrepreneurship and small firms?' The simple answer is that they 'matter'. Indeed, there is an established consensus, at least within policy circles, that they matter a great deal. For instance, in a recent speech to an influential pan-European employer's group, Erkki Liikanen (Member of the European Commission, responsible for Enterprise and the Information Society), noted that:

entrepreneurship and small businesses are – particularly for the European economy – a key source of jobs, business dynamism and innovation. Some 25 million SMEs in Europe provide more than two-thirds of total jobs in the private sector. This means SMEs employ more than 100 million people. Our most dynamic SMEs account for around 80 per cent of new jobs created.[1]

In 2000 the European Council adopted a 'Charter for Small Enterprises',[2] which opens with the line 'Small enterprises are the backbone of the European economy', and goes on to outline key areas through which the environment for small businesses may be improved. In 2003, the European Commission published its Green Paper on Entrepreneurship in Europe,[3] noting that 'Europe . . . needs more new and thriving firms', with a clear implication that the bulk of these firms would be small. Within individual member states and further afield, the policy focus on small firms is clearer still. In the UK, for instance, the Department of Trade and Industry[4] has set itself the key target of helping to 'build an enterprise society in which small firms of all kinds thrive and achieve their potential' (p. 49). In a similar vein, the second OECD Small and Medium Enterprise Outlook[5] opens with the confident assertion that the 'role of SMEs in OECD economies continues to be crucial for strengthening economic performance, particularly in light of the recent slowdown in economic growth, the abrupt downturn in the technology sector and the shock to the business climate caused by the events of September 2001' (p. 7).

Undoubtedly, small firms matter and it is encouraging that policy-makers recognise this. But why do they matter? And why do they matter, or appear to matter, more now than, say, 30 or 40 years ago? Answering these supplementary questions is central to understanding why we study entrepreneurship and small firms, and why our attitudes towards the sector have changed in relatively recent times.

■ ■ ■ ■ Definitions and Measurement

Before attempting to answer these questions, it is important to clarify what we mean by 'small firms'. Intuitively most people will have a sense of what constitutes 'smallness' in any given context. However, it is this issue of context that leads to general ambiguity. For instance, a car manufacturer that employs 450 people (independent British specialist sports car manufacturer TVR is one example) is likely to be considered very small. Yet, in contrast, and with a similar number of staff, Manchester United is a public limited company and among the largest football clubs in the world. Clearly, the precise answer to the question 'What is a small firm?', should be 'it depends'. And it depends upon a number of factors. Among the most obvious of these are the industry sector and market in which a given firm operates. Taking our car manufacturer TVR, for example, it is clearly very small when compared to familiar industry names such as Ford or General Motors. However, in the market for specialist sports cars it is actually relatively large when compared with its key competitors, such as Caterham and Morgan.

Moreover, in addition to industry and market considerations, time also matters when discussing firm size – at least to the extent that size is measured by the number of employees. For instance, European labour productivity (measured as GDP per hours worked) has more than doubled since 1970.[6] Simplistically, one might reasonably suggest that the same amount may be produced today with less than half the number of employees required 35 years ago. Accordingly, our conception of small, medium and large must also be altered. Or, indeed, it may be that, in some instances (e.g. industries that experience persistently high productivity growth) measures of firm size that rely on staffing levels are simply less appropriate.

As a result of these difficulties in defining or classifying small firms, it is likely that no single objective or statistical measure will suit the purpose. Nonetheless, in light of its attempt to properly address the issues, a popular point of departure is provided by the UK Committee of Inquiry on Small Firms,[7] chaired by Sir John Bolton (hereafter termed the Bolton Committee). The Bolton Committee distinguished both 'statistical' and 'economic' definitions (see Table 2.1). In terms of its statistical definition, the committee

Table 2.1: *Bolton's Definitions of Small Firms*

The 'Statistical' Definitions	
Manufacturing	200 employees or less
Construction, mining and quarrying	25 employees or less
Retail and miscellaneous services	Turnover of £50,000 or less
Motor trades	Turnover of £100,000 or less
Wholesale trades	Turnover of £200,000 or less
Road transport	5 vehicles or less
Catering	All; excluding multiple and brewery managed houses
The 'Economic' Definitions	
Small firms are those which:	
1. Have a relatively small share of their marketplace	
2. Are managed by owners or part-owners in a personalised way, and not through the medium of a formalised management structure	
3. Are independent, in the sense of not being part of a large enterprise	

recognised that size is relative to sector. Moreover, it recognised that it may be appropriate to define size by the number of employees in some sectors but more appropriate to use turnover or assets in others. Clearly the sectors identified by the Bolton Committee are not exhaustive and are a function of both the time and the place in which the definitions were devised. Certainly, they are not comprehensive, nor have they been 'updated'. However, it is the principle of, and reasons for, employing multiple measures that are the important legacy.

More interesting than the statistical, quantitative measures offered by the Bolton Committee are the 'economic', qualitative measures. Indeed, these have enjoyed a certain durability, at least within UK policy circles. The UK Small Business Service website, for instance, notes that the 'best description of the key characteristics of a small firm remains that used by the *Bolton Committee* in its 1971 Report on Small Firms' (www.sbs.gov.uk). Undoubtedly, there is a comfortable, if a little superficial, underpinning logic, and firms that satisfy these criteria will, in all likelihood, be small. However, notwithstanding their enduring popularity, the Bolton Committee's 'economic' definitions have not been above criticism. Storey[8] for instance, notes that 'the Bolton criterion that a small business is "managed by its owners or part-owners and not through the medium of a formal management structure" is almost certainly incompatible with its "statistical" definition of small manufacturing firms which could have up to 200 employees' (p. 10). Indeed, there is evidence that managerial appointments are made when firm size reaches between 10 and 20 employees.[9] As such, it seems unlikely that a firm that employs over 100 staff will not have evolved some degree of managerial formality that involves substantial delegation of decision-making.

Storey[8] also questions the Bolton Committee's emphasis on the small firm's inability to influence its environment, and the implication that small firms are inevitably price-takers. Here he draws the distinction between the economic concept of perfect competition, which he believes influenced the Committee, and the reality of small firm competition as largely monopolistic, with many firms occupying market 'niches'. In this way, they 'provide a highly specialised service or product, possibly in a geographically isolated area, and often do not perceive themselves to have clear competitors' (p. 10).

In spite of these legitimate criticisms, the value of the Bolton Committee definition lies in its willingness to address the complexities involved in accurately defining small firms, and its engagement with the issue of context. Nonetheless, these strengths may also be the source of the definition's principal weakness – that is, an awareness of the specificities of context necessarily retards general and consistent application in practice: a sensible prerequisite for government schemes aimed at assisting small firms, in which it is necessary to have simple, unambiguous qualifying criteria to ensure that administration is not overly complex or costly.

As a result of problems in the practical application of Bolton's 'economic' definitions, and despite the difficulties in objectively defining small firms, the most commonly used measure of 'smallness' relates to employment levels. To this end, small firms are considered by the OECD[5] to be 'non-subsidiary independent firms which employ fewer than a given number of employees' (p. 7). Though the threshold number varies across countries (the USA, for example, includes firms with fewer than 500 employees, while the Netherlands collects data on firms with fewer than 100 employees), perhaps the most commonly adopted definition is provide by the European Commission (EC). With the intention of overcoming the identified problems of earlier statistical and economic definitions, the EC coined the phrase small and medium-sized enterprises (SMEs).

The SME sector itself was disaggregated into three subsets (see accompanying box).

EC Definitions of Small Firms

- Micro enterprises – those of between 0 and 9 employees
- Small enterprises – those of between 10 and 99 employees (11–50 as of February 1996)
- Medium enterprises – those of between 100 and 499 employees (51–250 as of February 1996)

Financial criteria are also used in the EC definition. For instance, in 2003, micro-firms were those employing fewer than 10 people whose annual turnover and/or balance sheet did not exceed €2 million. Small firms were those employing fewer than 50 people whose annual turnover and/or balance sheet did not exceed €10 million. Finally, medium-sized firms were those employing fewer than 250 people whose annual turnover and/or balance sheet did not exceed €50 million (EU, 2003). Nevertheless, it is employment size bands that are most commonly cited and that, to all intents and purposes, are used as the standard working definition. These definitions hold for all industries (except agriculture, hunting, forestry and fishing) and, having been explicitly adopted by most member states, form the basis for both domestic and EU policy development in the area. Accordingly, they are the definitions used in this text.

It is important to note, however, that none of the principal criticisms of the earlier definitions has been answered. The EC definition still treats the small firm sector as an homogeneous whole and will still be liable to significant misclassification errors. Essentially, it is a measure of convenience.

Small Firms in the Economy

Turning now to why small firms matter, perhaps the simplest way of illustrating this is to point to their prevalence and the contribution they make to common measures of economic well-being, such as employment and income. To this end, Tables 2.2–2.4 detail the absolute number of enterprises, and distributions of employment and value added, by firm-size class for all EU countries (plus Iceland, Norway and Switzerland). Addressing Table 2.2, in the first instance, it seems clear that most firms are small firms. In all European economies, SMEs represent in excess of 99 per cent of the total business stock. Moreover, the vast majority of these firms are micro-enterprises. While there is some minor variation, in terms of the distributions across size bands (Germany, for instance, appears to have proportionately more firms in the small and medium-sized categories), the picture is broadly consistent across Europe.[a] Simply put, one might argue that we should be interested in small firms because most firms are small. Indeed, recent evidence seems to suggest that the trend is towards a continued expansion of the numbers of small firms (Figure 2.1), so strengthening this observation.

However, merely remarking that the small business sector dominates the European business stock may, in itself, be insufficient to explain the current level of interest focused upon it. Rather, policy-makers and academics are inevitably more interested in the sector's contribution to employment and income – as more direct indicators of small firms' role in the economy. To that end, the data in Table 2.3 indicate the proportionate distribution of total employment, by firm-size band, for the European economies. Once again, it is clear that small firms 'matter'. SMEs account for in excess of 50 per cent of

[a] The available data rounds to the nearest thousand. Accordingly, it is difficult to generate accurate proportions in Table 2.2.

Table 2.2: *Number of Enterprises ('000s) by Size Class: 2000*

	micro	small	medium	*SME*	LSE	Total
Austria	195	26	5	*225*	1	**226**
Belgium	515	23	3	*542*	1	**543**
Denmark	161	15	3	*178*	1	**179**
Finland	199	11	2	*211*	1	**212**
France	2 318	142	24	*2 484*	5	**2 489**
Germany	3 127	363	45	*3 535*	13	**3 548**
Greece	778	17	2	*797*	0	**798**
Iceland	26	1	0	*27*	0	**27**
Ireland	79	11	2	*93*	0	**93**
Italy	3 938	168	16	*4 122*	3	**4 125**
Luxembourg	19	2	1	*22*	0	**22**
Netherlands	500	42	9	*551*	2	**553**
Norway	162	11	2	*175*	0	**175**
Portugal	638	38	6	*682*	1	**683**
Spain	2 555	124	16	*2 695*	3	**2 698**
Sweden	244	22	4	*270*	1	**271**
Switzerland	286	30	6	*321*	1	**322**
UK	3 301	158	25	*3 483*	7	**3 490**
EU-15	18 568	1 160	162	*19 889*	39	**19 928**
Europe-19	19 042	1 202	169	*20 413*	40	**20 453**

EU-15 = 15 member states of the European Union (excludes Iceland, Norway and Switzerland)
EU-19 = 18 members of the EEA plus Switzerland
Source: Observatory of European SMEs (2002)

total employment in all of the economies considered and, for instance, as much as 86.7 per cent in Greece. Indeed, there is considerably more between-country variation in the small firm contribution to employment than the data in Table 2.2 might have indicated. Moreover, this variation may be systematic. That is, small firms appear to be more important providers of jobs in the southern European economies of Greece, Italy, Spain and Portugal than they do in the northern European economies of the UK, Germany, Finland and Iceland.

Table 2.3: *Proportionate Contribution to Total Employment by Size Class: 2000*

	micro	small	medium	*SME*	LSE
Austria	24.0%	21.8%	19.6%	65.5%	34.5%
Belgium	42.8%	15.6%	10.5%	68.9%	31.1%
Denmark	28.3%	22.9%	17.6%	68.8%	31.3%
Finland	26.1%	17.2%	15.9%	59.2%	40.9%
France	33.8%	18.7%	14.2%	66.9%	33.1%
Germany	28.5%	20.3%	11.1%	59.8%	40.2%
Greece	56.8%	17.1%	12.8%	86.7%	13.3%
Iceland	25.9%	19.0%	8.6%	53.4%	47.4%
Ireland	25.4%	23.6%	20.7%	69.6%	30.4%
Italy	48.2%	21.1%	11.0%	80.3%	19.7%
Luxembourg	23.7%	24.2%	25.1%	72.5%	27.5%
Netherlands	24.9%	18.4%	19.1%	62.5%	37.5%
Norway	31.9%	20.9%	17.9%	70.8%	29.2%
Portugal	37.7%	23.0%	18.1%	78.9%	21.1%
Spain	46.8%	20.0%	12.6%	79.5%	20.5%
Sweden	27.3%	18.1%	15.9%	61.4%	38.6%
Switzerland	23.1%	22.0%	21.7%	66.8%	33.2%
UK	29.3%	14.2%	11.8%	55.3%	44.7%
EU-15	34.6%	18.9%	12.9%	66.3%	33.7%
Europe-19	34.3%	19.0%	13.1%	66.4%	33.6%

EU-15 = 15 member states of the European Union (excludes Iceland, Norway and Switzerland)
EU-19 = 18 members of the EEA plus Switzerland
Source: Observatory of European SMEs (2002)

The pattern is not perfect, but there is tentative evidenced of a north–south divide. Alas, identifying why this might be the case is not likely to be a simple matter, though one is tempted to suggest that enduring craft traditions, sectoral variations (such as the relative role of tourism) and culture, will feature in any account.

Unfortunately, this inchoate pattern does not appear as clearly in the data relating to value added (Table 2.4). Certainly, there is further evidence of the relatively more or less significant economic role of SMEs in some southern and northern European

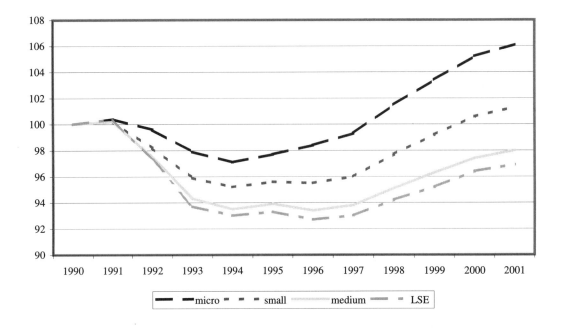

Figure 2.1: *Number of Enterprises by Size Class (EU-15): 1990–2001*
Source: Observatory of European SMEs (2002)

economies (compare, for example, Greece and the UK). However, if one considers the data for Germany and Ireland, for instance, it is obvious that the picture is more complicated. Nonetheless, one may be able to say, with reasonable confidence, that in those countries where both relatively high SME employment figures and relatively low SME value-added figures coincide (e.g. Ireland), labour productivity[b] in small firms is comparatively low (at least when compared with same-country large firms). By contrast, in countries recording relatively low SME employment, but a relatively high SME share in value added (e.g. Germany), small firm labour productivity appears to be comparatively high.

It may well be that variations in this crude indicator of labour productivity merely represent underlying sectoral variations. Certainly, it does not inevitably suggest poorer economic performance on the part of those countries where the SME share in value added is low. Interestingly, for those who would counsel expansion and support of the small business sector as some form of economic panacea, Ireland's growth during the 1990s was driven by successful inward direct investment by American and European multinationals and by strong export performance.[10]

Similarly, the Finnish economy is dominated by a large public sector, with state-owned enterprises and a few large, and successful, private-sector firms. For instance, past evidence suggests that Nokia and its first-tier suppliers were responsible for over a third of Finland's GDP growth during the late 1990s.[11] Indeed, with few exceptions, labour productivity across Europe appears to be positively correlated with firm size – as is, importantly, *growth* in labour productivity.[12] Larger firms are more productive and the gap is widening – driven by the increasing importance of export markets, faster technological change in large firms and a small-firms orientation towards services. Germany is the clearest exception to this observation, probably reflecting the strength

---

[b] Value added per person employed is a measure of labour productivity adopted by the European Observatory.

Table 2.4: *Proportionate Contribution to Value Added by Size Class: 2000*

	micro	small	medium	*SME*	LSE
Austria	14.4%	17.8%	18.6%	50.9%	49.1%
Belgium	28.7%	20.5%	15.4%	64.5%	35.5%
Denmark	21.8%	19.1%	17.8%	58.8%	41.2%
Finland	18.4%	14.2%	11.7%	44.3%	55.7%
France	17.7%	14.5%	13.5%	45.8%	54.2%
Germany	19.3%	21.4%	19.5%	60.2%	39.8%
Greece	34.1%	29.9%	18.9%	82.9%	17.1%
Iceland	5.8%	4.3%	2.2%	12.3%	87.7%
Ireland	6.5%	10.9%	15.6%	33.0%	67.0%
Italy	32.1%	23.8%	15.5%	71.4%	28.6%
Luxembourg	9.2%	13.9%	51.0%	74.2%	25.8%
Netherlands	15.5%	16.4%	24.1%	56.1%	43.9%
Norway	16.7%	15.9%	19.4%	52.0%	48.0%
Portugal	23.5%	22.4%	20.9%	66.8%	33.2%
Spain	20.3%	17.5%	17.5%	55.3%	44.7%
Sweden	18.7%	15.8%	17.0%	51.5%	48.5%
Switzerland	17.3%	15.4%	15.3%	47.9%	52.1%
UK	8.5%	12.7%	17.3%	38.4%	61.6%
EU-15	17.4%	17.2%	17.1%	51.7%	48.3%
Europe-19	17.4%	17.1%	17.1%	51.5%	48.5%

EU-15 = 15 member states of the European Union (excludes Iceland, Norway and Switzerland)
EU-19 = 18 members of the EEA plus Switzerland
Source: Observatory of European SMEs (2002)

of the Mittelstand (literally 'middle estate'). Historically, the relative size and strength of the German Mittelstand, in turn, rests largely on the higher proportion of start-ups that survive and grow.

Irrespective of these specific observations, what is clear from the data in Table 2.4 is that SMEs account for over 50 per cent of value added in 12 of the 18 countries considered. Only in Iceland do they account for less than one-third of value added. Clearly, on the basis of the raw data presented in Tables 2.2–2.4, small firms matter a great deal to employment, income and economic activity within Europe. Moreover, there is substantial evidence that these patterns are representative further afield [5;13].

■ ■ ■ ■ Linking Entrepreneurship and Economic Growth

Perhaps more important than the immediate contribution small firms make to employment and income is the widely held belief that there exists a positive link between entrepreneurship and economic growth. And, while entrepreneurship is not the exclusive province of small firms, the two are often conflated in policy and academic discussions. To this end, small firms are thought to act as agents of change and are the sources of considerable innovative activity.[14] A vibrant small firm sector stimulates industry evolution and generates a disproportionate share of new jobs. Accordingly, as Wennekers and Thurik[15] observe, 'Many economists and politicians now have an *intuition* that there is a positive impact of entrepreneurship on the growth of GDP and employment' (p. 29, emphasis added). Unfortunately, this 'intuition' has yet to be unequivocally supported by empirical evidence.

Among the foremost proponents of the positive entrepreneurship–economic growth link is the ambitious, and highly influential, annual Global Entrepreneurship Monitor (GEM). For an explanation of the underlying GEM model, see also Chapter 9. The GEM project undertakes surveys of the adult population in 40 countries[c] to establish a Total Entrepreneurial Activity (TEA) index for each country. The TEA[16] is a measure of 'the proportion of individuals in the working age population who are actively trying to start their own business, including self-employment, or running their own business that is less than $3^1/_2$ years old' (p. 4). In each of the GEM reports, starting in 1999,[17] 'the evidence was compelling' (p. 3). The GEM consortium is in no doubt that there is a strong positive correlation between entrepreneurial activity in a country and economic growth. On the evidence they present, this thesis is hard to resist. For instance, Figure 2.2,using data from GEM,[18] plots one-year lagged growth in GDP against TEA for the 40 countries studied.[d] While not perfect, there does seem to be evidence of the anticipated positive relationship. Moreover, this apparent relationship between TEA and GDP growth is statistically significant, with a strong correlation coefficient (R = 0.45). The policy conclusion that seems to flow from this may best be expressed as 'more entrepreneurship leads to higher economic growth'.

Certainly, in the face of the evidence presented by successive GEM reports, and notwithstanding some methodological concerns, one is happy to accept the existence of some form of positive relationship between entrepreneurship and economic growth.

However, it is not clear that the relationship is as simple as is intimated or, more importantly, that the arrow of causation is as described. While there is a comfortable logic in arguing that entrepreneurship 'causes' economic growth, it is equally plausible to argue the reverse. That is, as the economy grows and more money flows around the system, opportunities for entrepreneurship are created. Using data from the UK (because of its ready availability), Figure 2.3 plots changes in the stock of value-added tax (VAT) registered firms and GDP growth for the period 1980–2002 (with no lags).

The stock of VAT-registered firms is certainly different from the TEA used by GEM. However, they both crudely measure the same sort of thing and VAT data has the

[c] In 2003.
[d] Each point represents a country and year, though only the extremes of the distribution are labelled.

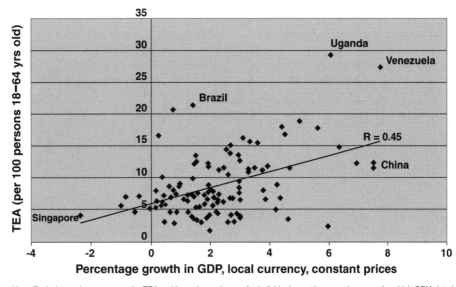

Note: Each data point represents the TEA and lagged growth rates for individual countries, covering years for which GEM data is available. Accordingly, some countries are represented by only one data point and others by up to four. Limited labels given are for illustration purposes.

Figure 2.2: *TEA Rates and National Economic Growth: One Year Lag (Pooled Data)*
Source: GEM (2004)

benefit of greater objectivity.[e] A cursory glance at the figure seems to suggest that entrepreneurial activity (i.e. changes in the stock of VAT registered firms) follows, rather than precedes changes in GDP growth rates. That is, entrepreneurial activity is a consequence, rather than a cause of, economic growth.

More formally, if one conducts a simple bivariate regression using the VAT data (and lagging GDP growth by one year, in line with GEM practice), one is able to generate similar results to the GEM project. That is, there appears to a statistically significant positive relationship between net business start-ups and GDP growth ($p = 0.027$ and $R = 0.466$). However, working in the opposite direction (i.e. lagging the VAT stock by two years as suggested by the data in Figure 2.3) increases both the explanatory power and the degree of statistical significance ($p = 0.015$ and $R = 0.524$).

Unsurprisingly, one can make the statistics tell both stories. However, on the basis of this very crude analysis, there does appear to be a stronger case for arguing that entrepreneurship is 'consequence', rather than 'cause' of growth. Nevertheless, the purpose of this exercise is not to suggest that entrepreneurship is an unimportant factor in generating economic growth. This would be both counter-intuitive and foolish. Rather, it is merely to note that the evidence remains patchy and the complexities of the relationship warrant considerably more attention, before 'more small firms' or 'more self-employment' is enshrined as some sort of economic development panacea.

To this end, two recent lines of academic enquiry warrant brief elaboration here. First, work by David Audretsch and Roy Thurik,[19] building on earlier work,[20] and ongoing work at the Dutch-based EIM, has tentatively suggested a U-shaped relationship between a country's stage of development (proxied by per capita GDP) and the level of entrepreneurial activity (Figure 2.4). These authors[19] suggest the concept

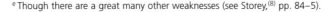

[e] Though there are a great many other weaknesses (see Storey,[8] pp. 84–5).

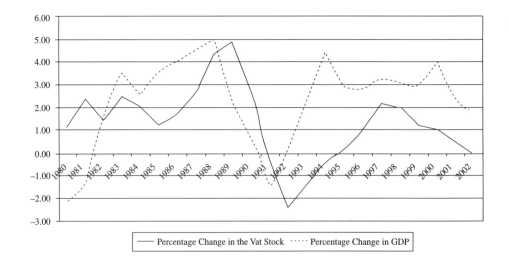

Figure 2.3: *GDP Growth and Changes in the Stock of VAT Registered Firms (UK, 1980–2002)*

Source: www.sbs.gov.uk

Crown copyright material is reproduced with the permission of the Controller of HMSO and the Queen's Printer for Scotland.

of an 'optimal industry structure', such that a country may have 'either too few or two many SMEs' (p. 19), given its level of economic development. This argument is intuitively appealing. For instance, GEM 2003 recorded the highest TEA rates for the developing economies of Uganda, Venezuela, Argentina and Chile respectively. In contrast France, Japan, Italy and the Netherlands featured among the lowest six TEA

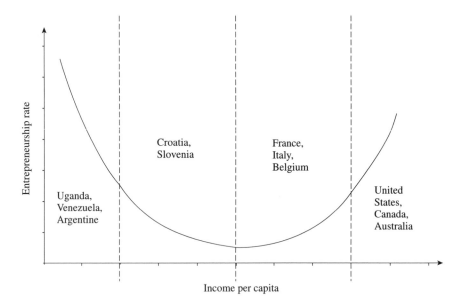

Figure 2.4: *The Relationship between Income per Capital and Entrepreneurship Rate*

Source: suggested by Audretsch and Thurik (2001)

rates recorded.[f] On this basis, and employing the GEM 2003 data, Figure 2.4 speculates on examples of countries that may appear at various points on the curve.

Regardless of this contingency, Audretsch and Thurik[19] do suggest that, for OECD economies at least, 'those countries that have experienced an increase in entrepreneurial activity have also enjoyed higher rates of growth and greater reductions in unemployment' (p. 26).

However, for the less developed economies outside the OECD, the standard small-firm prescription may be less appropriate. If one accepts that an equilibrium level of business ownership exists, given a country's level of economic development, this suggests that there are implications for deviations from this equilibrium. For instance, deviations above or below the equilibrium could mean either loss of economy of scale efficiencies, or underdeveloped or unexploited opportunities, respectively. Accordingly, the policy conclusion is conditional: if the level of entrepreneurship is too high, expanding business ownership would reduce economic growth; if the level is too low, then increasing the number of entrepreneurial firms would be rewarded by[19] 'growth dividends and reduced unemployment' (p. 29).

More specifically, Wennekers and Thurik[15] point to the importance of 'competition and selection amidst variety' (p. 51), with the clear allusion that policy should seek to keep both entry and exit barriers low as a means of finding the equilibrium number of firms. Indeed, it has long been recognised that high rates of both firm entry and exit are important factors influencing the dynamics of economic development.[21; 22] Economists term this phenomenon 'turbulence' and, as Audretsch et al.[23] note, 'high rates of innovation, growth and entry are characteristics of young industries with high levels of turbulence' (p. 10). Again, the UK figures clearly suggest that higher rates of entry are generally associated with higher rates of exit (Figure 2.5). This perspective sees economic development as an evolutionary process, wherein entry facilitates the

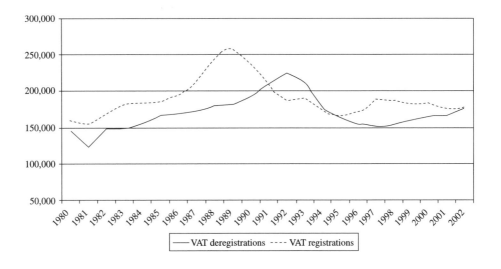

Figure 2.5: *VAT Registrations and Deregistrations (UK, 1980–2002)*
Source: www.sbs.gov.uk
Crown copyright material is reproduced with the permission of the Controller of HMSO and the Queen's Printer for Scotland.

---

[f]Along with Croatia and Hong Kong.

necessary variety, and market competition provides the 'rules' for selection, enabling[15] 'individuals (and firms) to learn from both their own and others' successes and failures' (p. 51).

Yet, despite their determined attempt to link entrepreneurship to economic growth, and the generally confirmatory conclusions they reach, Wenneker and Thurik[15] note that 'the importance of institutions for the development of entrepreneurship is paramount and deserves further study' (p. 51). This then leads to the second thesis worthy of elaboration.

This 'institutional' view regards relative levels of entrepreneurship as consequences of economic development rather than causes. Arguing from an Austrian perspective,[24] it is suggested that since 'entrepreneurship is an omnipresent aspect of human action such that all individuals are entrepreneurs . . . entrepreneurship cannot be the cause of economic development. Instead we must look at the rules of the game and determine the behaviours which those incentives encourage and discourage' (p. 23). In this way, entrepreneurship is a consequence of a country's economic development, and of the adoption and development of institutions that 'encourage the entrepreneurial aspect of human action'. Development is caused by the adoption of certain institutions, which in turn concentrates and promotes entrepreneurship and enterprising behaviour, which in turn spurs economic growth. Appropriate institutions may range from cultural attitudes to work and to risk, the structure of educational provision and skills training, the make-up of capital marks, and many more besides. However, Boettke and Coyne[24] believe that the 'two most important "core" institutions for encouraging entrepreneurship are well-defined property rights and the rule of law' (p. 17), with all others flowing from these. This is not an entirely new idea; 250 years ago, Adam Smith (1755) commented that:

Little else is requisite to carry a state to the highest degree of opulence from the lowest barbarism, but peace, easy taxes, and a tolerable administration of justice; all the rest being brought about by the natural course of things.

This may well overstate the case, but it serves as a useful reminder to policy-makers that, in encouraging entrepreneurship and economic development, the institutional infrastructure cannot be neglected. However, a great deal of work remains to be done to determine which institutional arrangements are causative and which are simply noise.

Notwithstanding these ongoing developments, the general view[25] remains that entrepreneurship is 'at the heart of national advantage' (p. 125). The role of the entrepreneur, most often through the medium of the small firm, in carrying through innovations and in enhancing competitive rivalry are thought to be central to economic growth. Less is known about quite how the mechanisms linking entrepreneurship and economic growth operate. Yet, most commentators appear to agree that some form of positive link exists, and the consensus has been sufficient to drive policy.

The Changing Role of Small Firms

Having discussed the contribution of small firms to the economy and to economic growth, it is worth considering why they feature more prominently in policy deliberations now than they did 30 years ago. To that end, it is commonplace, at least within the Anglo-Saxon economies of the UK and North America, to point to one or two landmark events. Unquestionably, the first of these was the publication, in 1979, of David Birch's *The Job Generation Process*.[26]

Birch's work undermined the established belief that large corporations were the principal drivers of growth in the economy.[27] Using Dun & Bradstreet data relating to over 5.6 million firms, Birch's research suggested that small firms (i.e. those with fewer than 100 employees) created over 80 per cent of net new jobs in the US economy between 1969 and 1976. Rather pithily, Birch[28] concluded that 'whatever else they are doing, large firms are no longer the major providers of new jobs for Americans' (p. 8). Such bold claims have inevitably drawn scrutiny and the work has since been subject to considerable criticism (principally relating to methodology). For example, Storey[29] suggests that, since jobs in small firms tend to have less permanency, if one concentrates solely on job generation and not 'job disappearance', one is likely to overstate the contribution of small firms to this measure of economic activity. However, notwithstanding the legitimacy of much of the critique, *The Job Generation Process* was, and continues to be, highly influential. The common acceptance of small business as the primary source of net new jobs has led to government commitment, in most industrialised countries, to a wide variety of programmes designed to foster small firms and entrepreneurship. In this sense, the influence of Birch's work has been truly global.

More or less coincidental to the publication of *The Job Generation Process*, both the UK and the USA witnessed the election of political administrations with markedly different economic philosophies to those they succeeded. Both the first Thatcher government in the UK (1979) and the Reagan administration in the USA (1981) were committed to: reducing the role of government; reducing the marginal tax rates on income from both labour and capital; reducing regulation; reducing inflation by controlling the growth of the money supply. Under these regimes, reliance upon social services and the welfare state was to be discouraged and a premium was placed upon personal enterprise.

In the UK, this philosophy was caricatured in Norman Tebbit's infamous 'get on your bike and look for work' speech at the Conservative Party conference in 1981. However, irrespective of the merits of the economic thesis and its political manifestation, there is little doubt that, since the respective elections, a great deal of emphasis has been placed, by government spokespersons on both sides of the Atlantic, on the virtues of an expanding small business sector.[30] Accordingly, there has been a natural temptation to view these events not only as landmarks in our attitudes towards small firms, but also as landmarks in the expansion of the small firm sector itself. Proponents of this latter argument would undoubtedly point to such factors as: the market-making opportunities afforded by privatisation and deregulation policies; the role of lower levels of income tax as an incentive to self-employment; falling real unemployment benefit rates as a means of lowering the opportunity cost to entrepreneurship; government fostering of an 'enterprise culture' and the myriad associated policy initiatives; greater labour market flexibility (see Storey[8] for a fuller discussion). However, notwithstanding the validity or otherwise of such an argument, it is unlikely that theories based upon local factors alone will be able to explain the more generalised shift towards smaller firm size experienced by every developed western economy (though with variations in timing and extent).[31]

In (the former Federal Republic of) Germany, for instance, Fritsch[32] noted a steadily increasing concentration of employment in large firms from 1907–1970, and a reversal of this trend thereafter. Similar patterns have been observed for countries as diverse as Italy,[33] the Netherlands[34] and the United States of America. Data for UK manufacturing[30] illustrates this general trend well (Figure 2.6). While the nadir for small firms comes a little earlier in the UK (mid-1960s rather than 1970s), the broad pattern is consistent with that observed elsewhere. In short, the small firm sector's role in the economy was at its least significant during the height of Fordist mass production,

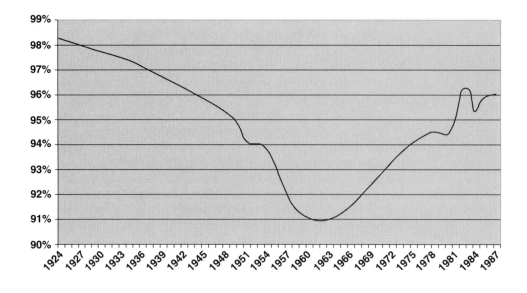

Figure 2.6: *Proportion of UK Manufacturing Establishments Employing Fewer than 200 (1924–87)*
Source: extrapolated from Hughes (1993)

preceding the oil crisis of the early 1970s, a time that allowed prominent economists, such as J.K. Galbraith,[35] to confidently predict that large firms would prevail in economic life, due to higher efficiency (through scale economies) and superior technology. However, by the 1980s it had become clear that the importance of Fordist mass production was on the decline and a new thesis of 'flexible specialisation'[36] was developed to explain the relative success of small firms in certain industries and locales.

There are a number of related explanations given for this widespread shift in firm-size distribution. However, the clearest starting point is probably to note the general shift from manufacturing to services witnessed throughout the industrialised West. In the UK, for instance, the manufacturing sector's contribution to GDP fell from 31 per cent in 1972 to 19 per cent in 2000. Similarly, employees in employment in UK manufacturing fell from 8 million to fewer than 4 million over the same period. By contrast, over the last three decades of the twentieth century, services contribution to UK GDP rose from 59 to 72 per cent and employment from less than 14 million to over 20 million.

For the former Federal Republic of Germany (FRG), Fritsch[32] noted that 'the main reason for the increasing share of small firm employment in the FRG is simply the change in the sectoral composition of employment during this period' (p. 44). Service firms tend, in the main, to be smaller than manufacturing firms. In the jargon of economics, they have a smaller minimum efficient scale. Accordingly, one would expect a shift from manufacturing to services to be accompanied by an apparent increasing role for small firms.

Perhaps the most obvious reason for the contraction of the manufacturing sectors of industrialised economies relates[37] to 'deagglomeration or specialisation: the selling off or disinvestment of non-core business in order to free up scarce resources (particularly management time) to defend and nurture core business activities' (p. 21) in the face of low unit labour cost competition from the developing world. As John

Travolta's President in the film *Primary Colors* tells a US shipyard, 'muscle jobs are going to go where muscle is cheap, and that's not here' (thought to be an indirect quote from former US President Bill Clinton).

However, the rise of small firms is not simply a result of the contraction of incumbent firms. Rather, two parallel processes appear to be in play. In addition to the decline in average size of existing firms, there is substantial evidence of a significant net inflow of new small firms.[33; 31] To explain this second phenomenon, Carlsson[37] points to 'the emergence of new computer-based technology which improves the productivity of small and medium-scaled production relative to standardised mass production techniques which dominated for the previous 150 years' (p. 21). The implementation of such flexible technologies has served to diminish the importance of scale economies over the last three decades and may account, in part, for changes in firm size distributions. According to Dosi:[38]

As an historical example, I suggest that we are currently observing, at least in the industrial countries, a process of change in the size distribution of plants and firms that is significantly influenced by the new flexibility-scale trade-offs associated with electronic production technologies . . . in mass production industries the higher flexibility of the new forms of automation is likely to allow the efficient survival of relatively smaller firms [as compared to the past]. (pp. 1155–6)

However, this final argument warrants a couple of qualifications. First, as Hughes[30] notes for the UK, 'new business formation in the 1980s . . . has led to a significant increase in the number of businesses in the service sector, but to a much less significant increase in manufacturing' (p. 35), suggesting that where there has been entry, there has also been exit. Second, while average firm size has been decreasing in the manufacturing sectors of most industrial economies, it has been increasing in the service and finance sectors.[31] The concentration of economic activity has increased in services at the same time as it has decreased in manufacturing, begging questions about the relative roles of scale economies. Notwithstanding these provisos, some things are clear. First, according to Acs and Audretsch,[31] 'a distinct and consistent shift away from large firms and towards small enterprises has occurred within the manufacturing sector of every developed western country' (p. 227). Second, there has been a contemporaneous shift in economic activity, from manufacturing towards services. Taken together, the result has been the increase in small firms' economic significance that is so evident in the data.

Importantly, this is not to suggest that such structural change was inevitable, at least to the extent witnessed, and that local factors have had no influence. Rather, policy action is likely to have facilitated and, perhaps, quickened the necessary restructuring, which may have taken longer in its absence. However, the evidence seems to suggest that the transformation in the fortunes of the small business sector was, and is, a continuation of long-run trends that predated the flurry of focused policy activity associated with the 1980s and 1990s.

■ ■ ■ ■ Entrepreneurship in European Transition Economies

Unsurprisingly, much of the preceding discussion has concentrated on data and trends in western industrialised economies. This is an inevitable consequence of both the majority readership and, more importantly, data availability. In particular, the discussion of long-term trends in entrepreneurship (above) is exclusively concerned with OECD economies. Indeed, a large part of the material that this section draws upon is to be found in a single edited text published in 1993.[39] Perhaps this may seem a little dated. Yet, for the OECD economies considered, the period of principal interest runs from around 1970–1990 and the text is admirably fit for purpose. Importantly, the text was also explicitly concerned with illuminating an 'East–West perspective', and includes chapters on (the former) Czechoslovakia, East Germany and Poland. The timing of the text is intriguingly coincidental. Most of the datasets used terminate in the late 1980s, immediately preceding the fall of the Berlin Wall (November 1989) and the disintegration of the former Soviet Union (December 1991). Up to this point, the picture painted of small firms in eastern Europe stood in stark contrast to its western equivalent. As Acs and Audretsch[31] noted:

There are two striking consistencies emerging from the country studies of Eastern Europe. First, the role of small firms throughout the Eastern European countries is remarkably small, especially when compared to that in Western nations . . . Second, while the developed Western economies all experienced a shift in economic activity in manufacturing away from large firms and towards small enterprises, the trend was exactly the opposite in Eastern Europe. (p. 228)

Undoubtedly, these trends reflected deliberate policies to centralise and concentrate economic assets under state planning. However, it is what has happened since that is of interest here. Following the collapse of the Warsaw Pact in 1991, many former Soviet republics and other eastern European nations began a process of transition from socialism to market capitalism. While much of the contemporaneous debate revolved around the importance of privatising existing firms, private-sector entrepreneurship (and, in particular, the creation of new firms), became central to the creation of wealth and economic development.[40] The greater flexibility in prices, wages and production decisions, which followed initial reforms, created profit opportunities for entrepreneurs. According to McMillan and Woodruff,[40] 'Entrepreneurs responded by starting enterprises at a rapid – though varying – rate in each of the transition economies' (p. 154). Over a period of around 10 years, private-sector enterprise rose from illegality to contributing 60–80 per cent of GDP in the transition economies of central Europe and the newly independent Baltic states.[41]

However, the process of transition has not been uniform (see also Chapter 9). For instance, there is some evidence that it has stalled in Russia, while Hungary and the Czech Republic are notable 'success stories'.[41] It is tempting to argue that transition progress is somehow a function of either an earlier start or closer proximity to western Europe, and simple consideration of the 'better' performers would seem to support this view. Yet, perhaps a more compelling rationalisation reflects upon the institutional arguments touched upon previously.[24]

In a recent study of a sample of European transition economies, Ovaska and Sobel[41] examined the policies and institutions most highly correlated with transition success – where success is equated with entrepreneurial activity and economic growth. These authors conclude that high rates of entrepreneurial activity were associated with credit availability, contract enforcement, low government corruption, high foreign direct investment, sound monetary policy and 'policies (such as low regulations and taxation) that are consistent with giving citizens a high degree of economic freedom' (p. 2). Of these, credit availability and lower levels of government corruption tended to be most important in encouraging new firm formation. Interestingly, however, these authors also suggest that policies that foster new firm formation do not, inevitably, also promote the higher rates of technological innovation thought central to economic growth:

To be successful, these countries not only need to institute policies consistent with fostering the creation of new businesses but also have to place policies conducive with fostering new high-tech innovation. One of the most important of these factors is the presence of economic freedom – low taxes, low regulation, and secure property rights. (pp. 3–4)

This seems to comfortably echo Adam Smith's 'peace, easy taxes, and a tolerable administration of justice'. That is, while, at the micro level, these imperatives may be manifest in a variety of managerial challenges, at the macro level creating the appropriate institutions may be the primary task. McMillan and Woodruff[40] provide a remarkable illustration of the importance of such institutions in providing incentives to entrepreneurship. Drawing upon data from a survey of start-up manufacturing firms in Russia, Poland, Slovakia, Ukraine and Romania,[42] these authors record that:

Managers were asked . . . whether they would invest $100 today if they expected to receive $200 in two years (an implied annual rate of return of 40 percent). The responses to this question give an indication of both the opportunity cost and the security of property. A striking 99 percent of the Russian managers said they would not, compared with 22 percent of the Polish managers. (p. 155)

■ ■ ■ ■ Conclusions

In this chapter we have tried to provide some answers to the question 'Why study entrepreneurship and small firms?' To this end, we began by pointing to the simple statistics illustrating the extent to which small firms dominate the business stock, and the contributions they make to both employment and income. In every European economy, over 99 per cent of all firms are small firms. Moreover, in most of these economies small firms account for over 60 per cent of total employment and over 50 per cent of value added. Clearly, on this basis small firms 'matter'.

However, the chapter was also concerned with the more dynamic contribution small firms may make to economic well-being. With this in mind, we outlined the widely held belief that entrepreneurship (most often embodied in small firms) positively impacts upon economic growth. Casual reading of the literature and attention to policy announcements would leave one in little doubt that, as expressed by Wennekers and Thurik[15] 'Entrepreneurship matters [and] In modern open economies it is more important for economic growth than it has ever been' (p. 51). Unfortunately, while one may share this intuition, the evidence to date is far from unequivocal. Nonetheless, this general view has already had considerable influence on policy.

Finally, the chapter tried to understand why small firms appear to matter more now than they have in the recent past or, at least, why our interest in them has grown. Here, the influence of David Birch's work and the coincidence of changing political circumstance in the UK and USA are acknowledged. However, the trends in the growth of the small firm sector appear to predate these landmark events. Moreover, the changes have not been limited to the Anglo-Saxon economies of the UK and North America. Rather, they have occurred in every developed western economy, though with some variations in timing and extent. Such a widespread phenomenon calls for more general explanations and the chapter suggests two: first, a structural shift from manufacturing towards services; and, second, the development of new flexible manufacturing technologies, which, in some sectors, have diminished the importance of scale economies. Numerous other factors are likely to have contributed to the pace of change; however, the power of these two alone is quite compelling.

Review Questions 2.1 ▪ ▪ ▪ ▪ ▪ ▪ ▪ ▪ ▪ ▪ ▪ ▪ ▪

1. What factors account for the increased policy attention given to entrepreneurial activity and the small firm sector?

2. What are the accepted definitions of:

■ micro firms

■ small firms

■ medium-sized firms?

3. Account for the growth in entrepreneurial activity in the last 20 years. Discuss, in your view, whether this constitutes an entrepreneurial revolution.

Review Questions 2.2 ▪ ▪ ▪ ▪ ▪ ▪ ▪ ▪ ▪ ▪ ▪ ▪ ▪

1. Should policy-makers focus merely on encouraging more entrepreneurial activity and new firm start-ups?

2. Why should an emphasis of policy on quality start-ups (rather than blanket support) be worthwhile?

3. Should under-represented groups (e.g. women) be targeted by policy-makers?

4. What factors might account for small firm volatility or stability?

Review Questions 2.3 ▪ ▪ ▪ ▪ ▪ ▪ ▪ ▪ ▪ ▪ ▪ ▪ ▪

1. Why is new entrepreneurial activity important to the health of a nation's economy?

2. Why are different views held on the volatility or otherwise of small firm formation and failure rates?

3. Why is it important to establish consistent definitions of small firms?

4. What is the EU definition of a small firm?

Suggested Assignments ■ ■ ■ ■ ■ ■ ■ ■ ■ ■ ■ ■ ■

1. Students are allocated to small working groups and are required to present and contrast the growth in the numbers of small firms in the UK compared to large firms. Student groups are required to discuss their definition adopted of a small firm and account for the differences shown.

2. Students are allocated to groups to discuss factors that have contributed to the growth in the numbers of small firms. Their task is to suggest why small business ownership has become an attractive alternative career for many people compared to large firm employment in the modern labour market.

3. Students select one economy in western Europe, one economy from eastern Europe and compare and contrast the importance of small firms. What factors will account for the differences?

Recommended Reading ■ ■ ■ ■ ■ ■ ■ ■ ■ ■ ■ ■ ■

Acs, Z. and Audretsch, D. (eds) (1993) *Small Firms and Entrepreneurship: An East–West Perspective*, Cambridge Univeristy Press, Cambridge.

European Commission (2003) *Entrepreneurship in Europe*, Green Paper, Brussels, http://europa.eu.int/comm/enterprise/entrepreneurship/green_paper/.

Reynolds, P., Hay, M. and Camp, S. (1999) *Global Entrepreneurship Monitor, 1999 Executive Report*, Babson College, Kauffman Foundation and London Business School.

References

1 Erkki Liikanen (2004) 'Entrepreneurship: An Integral and Vital Part of the EU Policy Mix', extraordinary meeting with the Employer's Group of the European Economic and Social Committee, Brussels, 25 May.

2 European Commission (2000) 'Charter for Small Enterprises', Brussels, http://europa.eu.int/comm/enterprise/enterprise_policy/charter/charter_en.pdf.

3 European Commission (2003) *Entrepreneurship in Europe*, Green Paper, Brussels, http://europa.eu.int/comm/enterprise/entrepreneurship/green_paper/.

4 Small Business Service (2002) *Small Business and Government – The Way Forward*, HMSO, London, http://www.sbs.gov.uk/content/whoweare/sbsstrategyfinalversion.pdf.

5 OECD (2002) *Small and Medium Enterprise Outlook*, 2002 edition, OECD, Paris.

6 Cotis, J.-P. (2004) 'Alternatives for Stable Economic Growth: Increasing Productivity, Greater Competitiveness and Entrepreneurial Innovation', paper presented at the Economist Conference, Madrid, 29 June.

7 Bolton, J. (1971) *Report of the Committee of Inquiry on Small Firms*, Cmnd 4811, HMSO, London.

8 Storey, D. (1994) *Understanding the Small Firm Sector*, Routledge, London.

9 Atkinson, J. and Meagre, N. (1994) 'Running to a Stand Still: The Small Business in the Labour Market', in Atkinson, J. and Storey, D. (eds), *Employment, the Small Firm and the Labour Market*, Routledge, London.

10 Stevenson, L. and Lundström, A. (2001) *Patterns and Trends in Entrepreneurship/SME Policy and Practice in Ten Economies*, vol. 3 of the 'Entrepreneurship Policy for the Future' series, Swedish Foundation for Small Business Research.

11 Reynolds, P., Hay, M. and Camp, S. (1999) *Global Entrepreneurship Monitor, 1999 Executive Report*, Babson College, Kauffman Foundation and London Business School.

12 EIM (2002) *Observatory of European SMEs 2002*, Zoetermeer, the Netherlands.

13 OECD (2000) *Small and Medium Enterprise Outlook*, 2000 edition, OECD, Paris.

14 Acs, Z. and Audretsch, D. (1990) *Innovation and Small Firms*, MIT Press, Cambridge, MA.

15 Wennekers, S. and Thurik, R. (1999) 'Linking Entrepreneurship and Economic Growth', *Small Business Economics* 13, pp. 27–55

16 Levie, J., Brown, W. and Cooper, S. (2003) *Global Entrepreneurship Monitor: Scotland 2003*, Hunter Centre for Entrepreneurship, University of Strathclyde.

17 GEM (1999) *Global Entrepreneurship Monitor, 1999 Executive Report*, Babson College, Kauffman Foundation and London Business School.

18 GEM (2003) *Global Entrepreneurship Monitor, 2003 Executive Report*, Babson College, Kauffman Foundation and London.

19 Audretsch, D. and Thurik, R. (2001) 'Linking Entrepreneurship to Growth', STI Working Papers 2001/2, OECD, Paris.

20 Acs, Z., Audretsch, D. and Evans, D. (1994) 'The Determinants of Variations in Self-employment Rates Across Countries and Over Time', Cambridge, MA (unpublished manuscript).

21 Audretsch, D. (1995) Innovation, growth and survival, *International Journal of Industrial Organisation* 13, pp. 441–57.

22 Geroski, P.A. (1995) 'What Do We Know About Entry?', *International Journal of Industrial Organisation* 13, pp. 441–57.

23 Audretsch, D., Houweling, P. and Thurik, R. (1997) 'New-firm Survival: Industry versus Firm Effects', DP 97-063, Tinbergen Institute, Rotterdam.

24 Boettke, P. and Coyne, C. (2002) 'Entrepreneurship and Development: Cause or Consequence?', Global Prosperity Initiative WP 6, George Mason University.

25 Porter, M. (1990) *The Competitive Advantage of Nations*, The Free Press, New York.

26 Birch, D. (1979) *The Job Generation Process*, MIT Programme on Neighborhood and Regional Change, Cambridge, MA.

27 Kirchhoff, B.A. and Greene, P.G. (1995) 'Response to Renewed Attacks on the Small Business Job Creation Hypothesis', in *Frontiers of Entrepreneurship Research*, Babson College, Boston, MA.

28 Birch, D. (1981) 'Who Creates Jobs?', *The Public Interest* 65, Fall, pp. 3–14.

29 Storey, D. (1990) 'Firm Performance and Size', in Acs, Z. and Audretsch, D. (eds), *The Economics of Small Firms: A European Challenge*, Kluwer, Dordrecht.

30 Hughes, A. (1993) 'Industrial Concentration and Small Firms in the United Kingdom: The 1980s in Historical Perspective', in Acs, Z. and Audretsch, D. (eds), *Small Firms and Entrepreneurship: An East–West Perspective*, Cambridge University Press, Cambridge, pp. 15–37.

31 Acs, Z. and Audretsch, D. (1993) 'Conclusion', in Acs, Z. and Audretsch, D. (eds), *Small Firms and Entrepreneurship: An East–West Perspective*, Cambridge University Press, Cambridge, pp. 227–32.

32 Fritsch, M. (1993) 'The Role of Small Firms in West Germany', in Acs, Z. and Audretsch, D. (eds), *Small Firms and Entrepreneurship: An East–West Perspective*, Cambridge University Press, Cambridge, pp. 38–54.

33 Invernizzi, B. and Revelli, R. (1993) 'Small Firms and the Italian Economy: Structural Changes and Evidence of Turbulence', in Acs, Z. and Audretsch, D. (eds), *Small Firms and Entrepreneurship: An East–West Perspective*, Cambridge University Press, Cambridge, pp. 123–54.

34 Thurik, R. (1993) 'Recent Development in the Firm-size Distribution and Economies of Scale in Dutch Manufacturing', in Acs, Z. and Audretsch, D. (eds), *Small Firms and Entrepreneurship: An East–West Perspective*, Cambridge University Press, Cambridge, pp. 78–109.

35 Galbraith, J.K. (1967) *The New Industrial State*, Houghton Mifflin, Boston, MA.

36 Piore, M. and Sabel, C. (1984) *Second Industrial Divide: Possibilities for Prosperity*, Basic Books, New York.

37 Carlsson, B. (1989) 'The Evolution of Manufacturing Technology and its Impact on Industrial Structure: an International Study', *Small Business Economics* 1, pp. 21–38.

38 Dosi, G. (1988) 'Sources, Procedures and Microeconomic Effects of Innovation', *Journal of Economic Literature* 26, pp. 1120–71.

39 Acs, Z. and Audretsch, D. (eds) (1993) *Small Firms and Entrepreneurship: An East–West Perspective*, Cambridge University Press, Cambridge.

40 McMillan, J. and Woodruff, C. (2002) 'The Central Role of Entrepreneurs in Transition Economies', *Journal of Economic Perspectives* 16, pp. 153–70.

41 Ovaska, T. and Sobel, R. (2004) 'Entrepreneurship in Post-socialist Economies', WP 04-06, Economics Department, University of West Virginia.

42 Johnson, S., McMillan, J. and Woodruff, C. (2002) 'Property Rights and Finance', *American Economic Review* 92, pp. 1335–56.

Diversity in Entrepreneurship: The Role of Women and Ethnic Minorities

CHAPTER 3

The material in this chapter is drawn from research undertaken by the author with a number of colleagues including, among others, Professor Monder Ram, de Montfort University, and Professor David Smallbone, Kingston University, concerning ethnic-minority entrepreneurship, Laura Wilson, University of Portsmouth, and Geoff Whittam, University of Paisley, concerning women's enterprise.

Learning Outcomes

At the end of this chapter you should be able to:

1 discuss the differing importance of men, women and ethnic minorities in entrepreneurship

2 discuss factors that might affect the importance and diversity of such roles

3 assess the impact of recent policies to support the role of women and ethnic minorities

4 discuss and account for the importance of Asian and African-Caribbean entrepreneurs

5 describe the untapped potential of development that still exists with African and Caribbean entrepreneurs

6 explain why ethnic-minority entrepreneurs are dependent on bank finance

7 discuss why the issue of 'break-out' has become an important issue for the future development of ethnic-minority entrepreneurs

8 describe recent policy initiatives to support women's enterprise in the UK.

■ ■ ■ ■ ■ Introduction

This chapter picks up some of the themes introduced in Chapter 1, where we noted that there are different rates of participation in entrepreneurial activity in different regions, in different environments and in different groups of society. For example, we have noted that some ethnic-minority groups have high rates of participation in entrepreneurship, despite operating in inner-city environments that might have limited resources and markets. Table 3.1 indicates the demographic importance of ethnic minorities in the UK; however, they have a greater importance in entrepreneurial activity than their relative importance by population might indicate. Taking self-employment as a proxy for participation in entrepreneurship, Figure 3.1 illustrates some of the variation and diversity in self-employment for men, women and ethnic-minority groups. Although UK national data is available on the number of small businesses,[1] a breakdown by gender or ethnicity is not available, therefore, self-employment data is

Table 3.1: *Population Size by Ethnic Minority Group*

	Population	Per cent of UK Population	Per cent of Ethnic Minority Population
White	54.15 million	92.1%	N/a
Mixed	6.77 million	1.2%	14.6%
All ethnic minorities	4.6 million	7.9%	100%
Indian	1.05 million	1.8%	22.7%
Pakistani	0.75 million	1.3%	16.1%
Bangladeshi	280,000	0.5%	6.1%
Other Asian	248,000	0.4%	5.3%
Caribbean	566,000	1.0%	12.2%
African	485,000	0.8%	10.5%
Other Black	98,000	0.2%	2.1%
Chinese	247,000	0.4%	5.3%
Other	231,000	0.4%	5.0%
All UK population	58.8 million		

Source: Office for National Statistics, London.

Crown copyright material is reproduced with the permission of the Controller of HMSO and the Queen's Printer for Scotland.

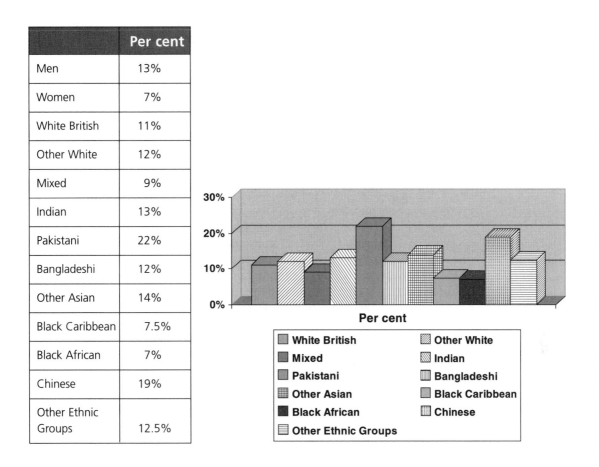

	Per cent
Men	13%
Women	7%
White British	11%
Other White	12%
Mixed	9%
Indian	13%
Pakistani	22%
Bangladeshi	12%
Other Asian	14%
Black Caribbean	7.5%
Black African	7%
Chinese	19%
Other Ethnic Groups	12.5%

Figure 3.1: *UK Self-Employment Rates for Men, Women and Ethnic Minorities*

Source: Office for National Statistics, London

Crown copyright material is reproduced with the permission of the Controller of HMSO and the Queen's Printer for Scotland.

used as proxy for gender and cultural diversity in entrepreneurship in the UK. Figure 3.1 shows that a number of sectors in society in the UK are under-represented, whereas others are over-represented. For example, women's rates are only around half those for men, and Africans and Caribbeans are also under-represented, whereas the highest rates of self-employment are attained by Pakistanis. This chapter reviews recent evidence on the barriers that such groups face in participation. Equality of opportunity in society should be available to all groups, yet, in certain cases, barriers may exist due to institutional practices that naturally favour men over women, or white business owners over ethnic-minority business owners. Access to resources, such as finance, or access to markets, may be more limited due to formal institutional practices that favour specific groups in society. For example, formal business networks such as local Chambers of Commerce may be male dominated, with an influence on agendas that reflects such a biased membership. This can limit women's abilities to access local business networks. We review recent evidence on the importance of such barriers in this chapter.

Women and Entrepreneurship

Participation rates for women in the UK are typical of rates in most advanced economies. For example, one study suggests that in most countries women's participation rates were around one-half of that of men.[3] It should be noted, however, that official statistics may underestimate the participation of women in business; for example, women may participate through involvement as partners or in family businesses as employees, but remain 'hidden' in official statistics. For example, a recent study for the Federation of Small Businesses (FSB) confirms higher rates of women's participation with mixed-gender ownership among its membership in the UK, at 35 per cent.[4] The same study indicated that the proportion of businesses wholly owned by women, who were members of the FSB was, on average, 15 per cent in the UK. Taking this study, then, women are therefore participating in business ownership, in some role, nationally at 50 per cent. The FSB study confirms an increasing rate of business ownership of about 5 per cent among women from its member base, as compared with a similar study in 2002.[5] These studies indicate that one of the information gaps is reliable data on women's participation in business and entrepreneurial activity.[6] However, overall, women still lag behind men in starting businesses in the UK and the Prowess membership initiative[7] states as its vision 'equal numbers of women and men starting businesses' (p. 2). Prowess is a UK government-supported networking and pressure group for women in business seeking to profile women in business and promote its members' interests.

Barriers, Networks and Women's Enterprise

Issues in the literature, on the nature and characteristics of women in business, focus on the nature of their performance and whether women face greater constraints in developing their business than do men.[6] Issues include cultural and social barriers that may exist in business start-up and development[8] – for example, whether women may be intimidated by institutional barriers such as attitudes affecting access to formal sources of finance. Shaw et al.[9] have claimed that women face particular distinct issues and potential barriers in developing their businesses, notably in pre-start experience, finance and in developing and accessing networks. There is evidence that women form different networks and place different values on them compared to men.[10; 11] Thus it can be more difficult for women in business to form mentoring relationships, suggesting that it can be important for women-only or woman-friendly networks to exist if women are to access the mentoring opportunities critical to business and career development.[12]

Previous research, in Scotland, suggested that women faced barriers in accessing finance and business support.[13] Carter et al.[6] claim that 'the majority of studies show that women find it more difficult to access resources . . . than do men', although a study by Read,[14] on the treatment of men and women by bank managers in England, found more similarities than differences between male and female clients of business bank managers. One of the problems with the literature is that robust and consistent methodology has not been adopted and that some of the studies are rather dated, making it difficult to establish the importance of barriers, in accessing finance and business support, to women's enterprise.

Overall there has been a lack of systematic evidence on the nature of barriers faced by women as business owners; this has not stopped policy-makers and policy initiatives such as the Small Business Services' Strategic Framework for Women's Enterprise assuming that the main barriers for women starting businesses are access to formal sources of finance, and access to formal and informal business networks.[15] However, we leave policy issues until later in this chapter, and consider the extent of distinctive issues and diversity of entrepreneurship in ethnic minorities in the UK.

There is little doubt that women are increasing their importance in entrepreneurship (confirmed by recent GEM surveys), although the nature of barriers can be subtle and difficult to identify. Some of these issues are illustrated through the case of Lawton Dancewear (see the 'Entrepreneurship in Action' box), an example of a woman-owned business, overcoming some difficulties to establish a successful business in a niche market. The information on Lawton Dancewear is based on a real case and real events, but the names of the people and the business concerned have been changed to preserve anonymity.

ENTREPRENEURSHIP IN ACTION

Lawton Dancewear

By Dr Laura Galloway, Heriot-Watt University

The Gradual Awareness of Opportunity

Six years ago Lesley Holland's daughter decided she wanted to be a dancer. Not an uncommon ambition for a nine-year-old girl. Her career started with ballet and tap classes, and included, eventually, Irish dancing. At this point Lesley, with a family to support noticed that her daughter's current passion was beginning to impact on the purse strings. Irish dancing costumes are expensive, and as Lesley's family was based in the rural Borders region between England and Scotland, had to be bought either by mail order from Ireland or via a visit to Coatbridge, near Glasgow — Scotland's only Irish dance dressmaker at that time. A keen hobby-seamstress, Lesley decided it would be easier and less expensive if she were to make her daughter's costumes herself.

Irish dancing dresses are not simple in design or formation. As an industry, Irish dressmakers are very protective of their designs and craft, and trade secrets are well kept. Lesley found that it would be no simple process of buying a pattern and making a dress, as patterns for Irish dancewear are almost non-existent. As a result, she began a process of research that involved contacting dressmakers in Ireland and studying photographs of dresses with a view to learning the nuances of the designs as well as how the dresses are made.

The first Irish dance dress Lesley made for her daughter was a huge success. Not only was her daughter delighted with it, but her friends and, more importantly, her friends' parents, were also impressed. Increasingly friends and neighbours in the Borders town of Galashiels who had children in Irish dancing classes asked Lesley if she could make their dresses too. Working from home, and with no industrial machinery, Lesley supplied local people with dresses for the cost of materials and pin money. When the volume of work increased Lesley was only too glad to be able to take on some help in the form of Lynn, a student of textiles at the Heriot-Watt Borders Campus, who first became involved during a part-time work-experience placement.

Realisation of a Venture

In early 2001, Lesley was told by Lynn's university supervisor of a new business incubator opening at the Borders Campus in Galashiels. While Lesley's motivation and interest in making Irish dance dresses had waned periodically due to other demands on her time, she felt that with her children now older, she would be able to devote herself fully to developing this hobby into a financially viable venture.

Lesley applied for funding through her local enterprise support agency, but was unsuccessful. Not to be put off, she invested £2500 of her own savings in buying equipment, and applied through the agency for a unit in the incubator. A major incentive the Galashiels Incubator offered at that time for new businesses was free rent for the first six months. Lesley also has the ongoing support of Lynn, who continues to help out part-time as she benefits from the work and business experience. Between Lesley and Lynn, start-up costs have been an estimated £10,000 much of which comprises equipment they already owned. By December 2002, upon entering the Galashiels Incubator, Lawton Dancewear was born.

The Product

Lesley believes that Lawton Dancewear can offer a quality of service and product not readily found elsewhere. While people in Scotland often purchase Irish dancewear from catalogues, Lawton Dancewear can offer a fully iterative design service. Customers are consulted on design and fitted for dresses throughout the design and production processes, and ultimately receive a fully bespoke product. While children's dresses in particular can be sold 'off the peg', Lesley believes that this relationship-building service with customers for individual dresses is her competitive advantage. Products made by Lawton Dancewear in this way are commonly several hundred pounds cheaper than equivalent products sold in Ireland and England.

The Market

The most common means of buying Irish dancewear is by purchasing direct from Ireland. The market is made up of children and adults in all parts of the UK, and in the 'new' countries to which Irish people and their customs have migrated in recent centuries. The market potential of these 'new' countries is massive. Notwithstanding the fact that children continuously grow out of costumes, the Irish dancewear industry has maintained and increased its popularity among adults too, particularly since the success of spectacular productions such as *Riverdance*. Scotland, with its historical and traditional links with Ireland, is a lucrative potential first market for Lawton Dancewear, as the number of Irish dance schools and classes, and associated shows and competitions is considerable.

Lesley was aware that one Irish-dance dressmaking company was trading in Scotland, and was actually having to turn work away. Lawton Dancewear aims to take advantage of this significant Scottish market and, with the advantage of trading from the Scottish Borders – the traditional home of the textile industry – to be able to offer its products to the wider UK and overseas markets too.

While the market for Lawton Dancewear's products is potentially huge, Irish dancing remains a niche sector. There would be limited benefit of promotion or advertising in mainstream media, particularly with start-up funding so tight. One dedicated Irish dancing publication exists and is widely referred to in Irish dance circles. Lesley has placed an advert for Lawton Dancewear within that publication and has already generated interest in the company and its products. A highly lucrative outcome from this might involve a parent or teacher connected with an Irish dance school using Lawton Dancewear for a 'class costume' either for general use or for a particular event.

As with any industry, but particularly with Irish dancing, word of mouth is one of the most effective methods of advertising and promoting your services and product. Not only does this mean that Lesley has to maintain the highest standard of quality of her products, but also that she must ensure that the company is known throughout the Irish dance network in Scotland. To this end Lesley attends various events to promote Lawton Dancewear. For example, last May she rented a stall at the Dunedin Feis in Musselburgh, an annual national competition, and generated from that enough orders to see the company through to the end of the year.

The Achievement

For Lesley, the motivation to start and build a sustainable venture was twofold. She had always wanted to work for herself, to have the independence and challenges associated with self-employment and business ownership. She also feels strongly that she is capable of contributing to employment and economic development in the Borders area – a region that has been blighted by industrial decline.

Lesley believes that Lawton Dancewear has the potential to be a successful Borders venture. She has been disappointed, however, in the lack of support she has received to launch it. She feels that the business support sector has essentially let her down, and questions the reasons for this.

Like many potential entrepreneurs operating in niche markets she has wondered if support agents have failed to understand the potential of her market, or the potential of her business within the local economy. She has also wondered if traditional and latent prejudices about female business potentiality have affected the level of support she has received. These questions are never likely to be answered, but the reality is that Lawton Dancewear has successfully started up and is positioning itself for sustainability and, potentially, growth.

It is to Lesley Holland's credit that this is the case, and that she, a mother, a divorcee, a seamstress, living in tranquil Galashiels has prevailed and succeeded in her ambition to gain independence through business ownership.

Discussion Questions

1. What difficulties or barriers do you consider that Lesley has overcome?

2. Would you agree that local support agencies have not understood her market or her business?

3. What are the qualities demonstrated by Lesley in this case?

■ ■ ■ ■ Ethnic-minority Entrepreneurship

In Britain's history, ethnic immigrants have traditionally been of crucial importance to economic development, a tradition that goes back to groups such as the Huguenots. These ethnic groups have been willing to accept new practices or bring new skills that facilitate significant economic developments. The tradition continues to be significant in the modern economy where Asian entrepreneurs were the first to open retail outlets on Sundays, pre-dating a modern movement towards Sunday opening in most retail sectors. Ethnic entrepreneurs have also been willing to develop in areas that are shunned by 'mainstream' or white entrepreneurs – for example, economically marginal inner-city areas. Location in these inner-city areas has significant implications for ethnic-minority entrepreneurs. Not only does location often limit the available market to the ethnic enclave, it also makes the acquisition and availability of resources (especially finance and insurance) difficult or (in the case of insurance) expensive.

Although Table 3.1 shows the demographic importance of the main ethnic groups in the UK, the potential of ethnic minorities in economic development can be highlighted further by statistical analysis of 2001 census data, which shows that one of the demographic features of ethnic minorities is their considerably younger age profile. For example, in 2001, the census showed that 32 per cent of the African minority population were under 16 years of age compared to less than 20 per cent of the white population.[16] By contrast, 9 per cent of the Caribbean minority were aged 65 and over, compared to 16 per cent for the white group (which was the largest proportion of any group). Further illustration of the dramatic differences in age profiles of minority ethnic groups for the UK is illustrated in Figure 3.2. This has indicated that the changing demographic profile and entrepreneurial potential of ethnic-minority groups is crucial to the future economic development of significant areas in Britain.[17]

Age Distribution of Ethnic Groups

Figure 3.1 indicates that the rates of self-employment in ethnic-minority groups in the UK, although high, do vary, indicating diversity in entrepreneurial activity. Taking the five main ethnic-minority groups in the UK, the highest rates are for South Asians, particularly Pakistanis and Bangladeshis, at 22 per cent and 13 per cent respectively,

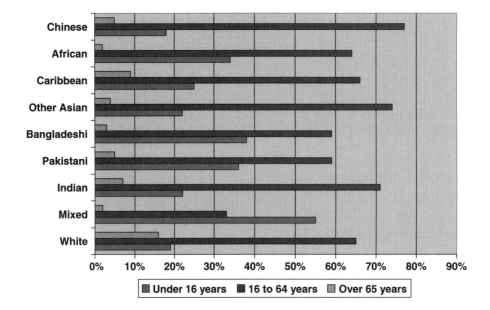

Figure 3.2: *UK Age Distribution by Ethnic Group*
Source: Office for National Statistics, London
Crown copyright material is reproduced with the permission of the Controller of HMSO and the
Queen's Printer for Scotland.

and for Chinese, who have self-employment rates of 19 per cent. However, the rates
for Africans and Caribbeans are much lower, being only 7 to 7.5 per cent, but as
indicated by the recent Small Business Service's Action Plan (SBS), the dynamics of these
patterns are changing, illustrating further diversity. For example, there are higher rates
of those who have recently become self-employed in African and Caribbeans compared
to South Asian ethnic groups.[18]

Issues in Ethnic-minority Entrepreneurship

The literature on ethnic-minority enterprise development has focused on three main
issues: *accessing resources*, notably finance and labour; *accessing markets*; and
motivation. Earlier literature focused on the cultural and additional forces that led
early-stage immigrant labour into self-employment and high rates of participation in
entrepreneurship. For example, Light stressed the importance of cultural minority
status that produced a strong sense of social solidarity in immigrant and ethnic
enterprise in North America.[19] Bonacich *et al.*'s study of Koreans in Los Angeles
identified access to resources and informal support networks as two of the key
factors that accounted for the success of this ethnic-minority group in
entrepreneurship.[20] Some writers have pointed to the success of ethnic groups
despite difficult trading conditions, with survival achieved through piecing together
a living from semi-legal activities.[21; 22] Light identified particularly the difficulties of
black entrepreneurs in North America due to limited access to resources.[19] Models
of such ethnic enterprise development – for example, those of Waldinger, and
Waldinger *et al.*[23; 24] – reflect these issues and focus on how the entrepreneurial

attributes of different ethnic groups determine their ability to access resources and markets to achieve entrepreneurial success.[25; 26]

Accessing Resources

The first of the three issues has concerned the ability of ethnic-minority entrepreneurs to generate or access resources. In some cases, writers have claimed that the advantages of informal networks have given ethnic minorities in business an advantage due to access to sources of finance and family labour.[27; 28; 29] Waldinger also pointed to the importance of informal networks as a key factor in successful entrepreneurial development of ethnic immigrants in New York.[23] Ethnic-minority entrepreneurs' relationship with banks has also attracted research. For example, Curran and Blackburn's study of Bangladeshis, Greek-Cypriots, and African and Caribbeans in the UK highlighted the problems of the latter ethnic group in accessing bank finance.[30]

Previous research by the author has supported the findings of Curran and Blackburn,[30; 31] which shows that small firms owned by ethnic-minority entrepreneurs are no different from white-owned small firms in being heavily dependent on the banks for external finance. However, they found that reliance on bank finance was much less significant for African and Caribbeans; a finding also confirmed by the author's research.[32] A Bank of England report,[33] which reviewed the previous research at the time, indicated that there was a perception by ethnic-minority entrepreneurs of prejudice by the banks, but concluded that problems perceived by ethnic-minority entrepreneurs may be due to sectoral concentration of ethnic groups rather than any discrimination, and called for more systematic research. For example, the report commented:

There are a number of possible explanations as to why ethnic minority businesses encounter difficulties, including risk aversion behaviour by lenders, sectoral concentration of ethnic businesses, failure rates and lack of business planning. (p. 7)

The largest UK study on ethnic-minority entrepreneurs and access to finance and business support, by Ram *et al.*,[34] was established as a result of the issues identified in the Bank of England report. This study suggests that reasons for differences in the pattern of access to finance are complex. For example, their report included in the conclusions that, 'The issue is complex, reflecting a preference for informal sources of finance in some cases, yet strong perceptions of discrimination on the part of the banks in others' (p. 116).

This study[34] involved a demand-side baseline survey of the five main ethnic groups with a white control group, longitudinal case studies and an extensive programme of supply-side interviews with bank mangers and support agencies. The demand-side research has confirmed particular problems of access to finance for African and Caribbeans.[35] The supply-side findings reflect variety in practice in bank managers' dealings with ethnic-minority applications, despite proactive policies towards ethnic-minority entrepreneurs by all the banks.[36]

There is evidence of diversity of experience of the business owners from different minority ethnic groups. In the Ram *et al.* study,[34] comment was made on different experience: 'The survey evidence in particular clearly demonstrates the diversity of experience that exists between ethnic minority groups with respect to raising external finance' (p. 7).

The study goes on to comment that the ability to raise formal sources of finance such as bank finance is significantly higher in Chinese-owned businesses, while significantly less in African- and Caribbean-owned businesses. Reliance on informal finance was more significant in South Asian-owned businesses. This diversity of experience will be further affected by differing experiences of ethnic-minority entrepreneurs in traditional and emergent sectors.

Diversity of experience is compounded by variety in practice with relationships between ethnic-minority entrepreneurs and their funders. Ram et al.[34] also comment that, 'There was variation in practice in the level and intensity of bank manager experience of ethnic-minority businesses' (p. 118). Good practice was evident where bank managers had built up trust through stable relationships and close involvement with their local minority community, leading to a better understanding of the way that ethnic-minority business owners conducted their business.

The importance to ethnic businesses of the use of family and co-ethnic labour has been highlighted by studies such as Wilson and Portes, whose research on Cubans in Miami pointed to the importance of ethnic preferences in hiring labour, which allowed this ethnic group to thrive where native whites did not; even where the native population had superior access to resources.[37]

Accessing Markets

The second issue has stressed the reliance of ethnic minorities in business on co-ethnic markets.[38; 39] While this may be a deliberate strategy,[24] Light has argued that, in the case of black Americans, their concentration in ethnic enclaves traps them in a potentially disadvantaged cycle from which it is difficult to break into the mainstream of officially registered businesses.[19] UK studies have stressed the importance of the need for successful break-out into mainstream white-dominated markets,[40; 41] an issue that we would expect to be more important where markets are limited and peripheral. The related issue of location and the geographical characteristic of concentration of ethnic businesses in inner-city areas has further highlighted problems of break-out.

In the UK, the success of ethnic-minority entrepreneurs has been officially recognised in the past – for example, with reports from the Ethnic Minority Business Initiative (EMBI)[42] – but the constraints that such entrepreneurs have overcome have not always received the same recognition. Their success has been achieved in marginal economic environments of the inner city and with limited access to either resources or mainstream markets. Debate on developing the need for break-out, following the EMBI report, led to the view that the success of ethnic-minority businesses can only be secured through the development of more diversification into different sectors with discussion about the best way to secure strategies to move away from dependence on ethnic market niches.[30; 41] The ability of ethnic firms to achieve successful break-out has been shown to depend on successful integration of a holistic strategy involving marketing, finance, human resources and 'key' contacts with mainstream markets.[43]

Motivation

Attempts in the literature to explain the importance of ethnic-minority entrepreneurs concentrate on the relative primacy of 'negative' or 'positive' factors in the motivations and development of ethnic-minority small firm owners – for example, Ward and Jenkins.[25] The debate surrounds whether or not the discrimination faced by ethnic minorities in the labour market was the predominant motivating factor in business ownership and entrepreneurship; or whether positive factors, such as a group's background experience of business ownership, were more important in the motivation decision. Although Curran and Blackburn[30] have indicated that motivational factors such as 'independence' were significant in entry to entrepreneurship, there is little doubt that a history of disadvantage and discrimination has led to the concentration of ethnic-minority firms and entrepreneurs in marginal areas of economic activity. At the time of writing, a study nearing completion by the author with colleagues, in Scotland, has found contrasting experience of ethnic-minority business owners, with some in growth businesses in global markets, but some were still trading in marginal economic environments, which were subject to particular problems associated with high crime rates, incidences of racism and high levels of insurance premiums.[44]

Curran and Blackburn[30] found, in their study, perhaps surprisingly, that positive factors associated with the desire to be independent were higher than expected, and they claim that this was on similar levels to white-owned businesses. To some extent, the strong motivational factors were confirmed by our research with African and Caribbean entrepreneurs in UK cities, and with Asian entrepreneurs in Scotland.[32; 45] Over 80 per cent of African-Caribbean and Asian entrepreneurs agreed with positive statements concerning ambition and control of their environment. Yet, for a significant minority, negative factors associated with the lack of opportunity elsewhere were also important. Over 40 per cent (for both groups) agreed that they had faced discrimination in previous employment. In such circumstances, discrimination and the lack of opportunities in the labour market are significant 'push' factors. Evidence from these studies showed that such entrepreneurs were often more highly qualified than equivalent white entrepreneurs, a result confirmed by the more recent UK study for the British Bankers' Association (BBA).[34] Analysis of motivation factors with African and Caribbean entrepreneurs showed that a 'mix' of positive and negative factors were important in start-up and motivation. Negative factors included the lack of employment opportunities (although this may also be a significant factor for white entrepreneurs) and the lack of career opportunities when in employment. It may be that African and Caribbean entrepreneurs have the characteristics we would expect of white entrepreneurs. However, evidence of discrimination and frustrated career ambitions was found to be a factor with some African and Caribbean entrepreneurs.

Although a number of issues remain unresolved in motivation, such as the low participation rate of African and Caribbeans in entrepreneurship, attention has shifted from start-up to enterprise development issues. For example, ethnic-minority entrepreneurs are perceived to be located in ethnic niche markets, such as Asian clothing firms supplying the needs of the Asian community or Caribbean hairdressers supplying a service that meets the needs of their community. The issue of 'break-out' from this reliance upon ethnic niche markets has come to the fore and has been recognised as a policy issue for ethnic-minority entrepreneurs.

■ ■ ■ ■ Diversity in Entrepreneurship: Policy

In this section we return to the issue of policy and support, given the diversity discussed in the previous sections, and the varying participation rates in entrepreneurship. Policy and support for ethnic minorities and for women entrepreneurs are issues that have risen up the policy agenda as attention has focused on the potential of Asian and ethnic-minority entrepreneurs for high levels of entrepreneurial activity and the need to ensure that women are well represented in entrepreneurial activity, a factor found to be significant by GEM reports in nations with high levels of entrepreneurial activity.[46]

Women and Entrepreneurship: Policy

The importance of women's enterprise in the development of national economies and national economic growth has been highlighted by recent research from the Global Entrepreneurship Monitor (GEM) findings. For example, the 2001 GEM report[46] urged governments to take action on women's enterprise: 'There is perhaps no greater initiative a country can take to accelerate its pace of entrepreneurial activity than to encourage more of its women to participate' (p. 5).

This has provided the background for national enterprise support agencies, such as the Small Business Service (SBS) in England and the Enterprise Networks in Scotland, to intervene to strengthen the role of women in entrepreneurial activity. In England, a consultation exercise by the SBS[47] led to the launch of the Strategic Framework for Women's Enterprise in collaboration with Prowess (a national UK network to promote women's enterprise) in May 2003.[48] In Scotland, the author was involved in research that provided some of the context for the development of national policy. The research, for the Scottish Executive, examined the feasibility of a National Centre for Women's Enterprise (NCWE) for Scotland.[49] The study drew on a comprehensive mapping exercise of existing support and provision for women's enterprise in Scotland. The study recommended the establishment of a dedicated National Unit for Women's Enterprise (NUWE) (to be operated between Scottish Enterprise and Highlands and Islands Enterprise) rather than a separate NCWE. This recommendation was accepted by the Scottish Executive, leading to the launch of the NUWE in March 2003.[50]

In our report for the Scottish Executive, we identified a number of key policy themes for the development of enterprise support for women.[49] These were categorised as: explicit support vs mainstreaming; direct vs indirect provision; diversity management and other issues.

Explicit Support vs Mainstreaming

This issue concerns whether enterprise support for women should be explicitly provided, for example as a separate programme, or 'mainstreamed' and provided as part of standard business programmes. Separate provision could be made in a number of support programme areas, including start-up, business development, innovation and funding; assuming a specific case could be made that support programmes for funding need to be separate and distinctive. Theoretically, however, there is an argument that it is better to ensure that mainstream programmes are sufficiently sensitive to women's needs, only making explicit women's support provision where there are specific needs (perhaps with separate funding requirements). The 'mainstreaming' approach has the advantage of avoiding duplication and ensuring that all enterprise support is sensitive to issues concerning women in business.

Direct vs Indirect Provision

It is arguable that an initiative for women's enterprise, such as a national unit or strategy, could take a number of different roles including advocacy, advice, support and training. In principle, these roles may be direct or indirect. A direct role would involve a unit engaged in providing direct support, advice and training. This may include a direct funding role and specialist assistance. In theory, the case for direct support provision of this nature relies upon the identification of deficiencies and gaps in the present provision of support that would allow such a role for a national unit/centre or for other forms of direct support provision. However, it also raises issues of proper integration with the existing delivery mechanisms.

The indirect role would require a national agency or initiative working alongside existing support providers such as Business Link Operators (BLOs) and other organisations such as Chambers of Commerce and banks to provide indirect advice and support, taking an advocacy and 'championing' role for women's enterprise. A national unit in this role is recognised as a centre of expertise, of information, and possibly takes a direct research role. The national launch (in the UK) of the Prowess initiative, a previously local model, in October 2002, reflects this model.[51]

Diversity Management

In undertaking our research for the Scottish Executive, it became apparent that there was a strong business case for the adoption of equal opportunities approaches to enterprise support, although it is also the case that there are obligations, legally to ensure that minority groups have access to enterprise support. It is clear that national policies should incorporate approaches that do not discriminate on the grounds of gender, race, sexual orientation, disability or age. Diversity management recognises individuals as 'different'.[52] A positive approach to managing diversity incorporates an approach that recognises and incorporates such diversity.

Other Policy Issues

Views of women's enterprise support can be affected by stereotypical perceptions of the nature of their business ownership and their associated needs. For example, as is the case with access to formal sources of finance, there is little research support for the view that women lack confidence, yet this can still be a feature of some stylised perceptions. For example, women do under-report or give a low estimation of their skill levels in surveys on entrepreneurship, which policy and programme designers can confuse with a general lack of confidence.[53] Issues discussed earlier, regarding the possible lack of engagement (to the same extent as men), with the support networks, the longer lead times in start-up and business development, and the access to resources, especially finance, do have enterprise support implications. Papers that focus on policy have recommended measures that could alleviate some of these issues, including improved access to micro-credit, a central women's business unit/centre to develop policy, regional business women's centres, improved access to networks and the co-ordination of support through a national unit for women's enterprise.[8]

The consultation, development and launch, in May 2003, of the SBS's Strategic Framework for Women's Enterprise,[48] could be seen as a welcome and significant step forward in the development of a cohesive, long-term and integrated policy on support for women's enterprise, in England. It could also be viewed as a significant attempt to draw together previously diverse, limited and local initiatives, focused on women's enterprise, into a strategic policy framework and guidelines for delivery by BLOs and RDAs. However, in a review paper, we concluded that the priorities and actions of the Strategic Framework were relatively low-key, localised and highly targeted initiatives that were more about accessing micro-finance, start-up grants and social inclusion than they were about introducing significant changes to women's enterprise support.[54] Yet the main, primary objective of the Strategic Framework was to encourage more women to start businesses:[48] 'The overall objective is to increase significantly the numbers of women starting and growing businesses in the UK, to proportionately match or exceed the level achieved in the USA' (p. 4).

The initiatives outlined in the Framework, however, were relatively small and piecemeal. We concluded that such measures will never meet such an ambitious stated objective; instead it would probably require a complete structural overhaul of the education system and economy.[54]

Ethnic-minority Entrepreneurship: Policy

It is arguable that similar principles to those of support for women's enterprise apply to support for ethnic-minority enterprise owners. For example, Ram and Smallbone, in their review,[55] considered good practice to include instruments or initiatives that are focused on the distinctive support needs of ethnic-minority businesses, or specific subgroups; delivery approaches that are based on engagement and interaction with ethnic-minority communities; culturally sensitive delivery methods; and approaches that include strategies for drawing ethnic-minority business owners into mainstream support. In a review of support for five cities, arising from the UK study for the British Bankers' Association,[56] it was found that each of the localities had a different pattern and mix of mainstream agencies, specialised ethnic business-focused enterprise agencies, intervention by local authorities and ethnic-minority business associations. In both England and Scotland, mainstream agencies have inclusivity as an important objective, yet the main issue has been a lack of engagement by ethnic-minority entrepreneurs with support agencies.[56]

A Lack of Engagement

It is now well established, from previous research, that ethnic-minority entrepreneurs are reluctant to access mainstream enterprise support provision.[57] For example, in a survey for Humberside TEC of 292 EMBs, of which 45 per cent were Chinese-owned, only 4 per cent had used business support previously, compared with 66 per cent of all businesses. Moreover, nearly three-quarters of EMBs had never used any form of business support, compared with 32 per cent of all firms.[58] In London, one study suggested that the low level of use of mainstream support provision was related to the ethnic-minority business owner's general perception of the support environment, misgivings about the support that is offered, confusion caused by the continued fragmentation of the support infrastructure and a failure of agencies to deliver 'one-stop' support in practice.[59]

The relative failure of mainstream support provision to reach ethnic-minority enterprise owners has contributed to the development of specialised enterprise support agencies, based on funding from a variety of sources and initiatives, which have tended to change over time, thereby contributing to changing fortunes for individual agencies. However, instead of being complementary and well co-ordinated with mainstream provision, many of these specialist agencies have operated alongside BLOs rather than working closely with them, although there are exceptions. For example, Ram reported a lack of integration between specialised and mainstream provision in his study of enterprise support for African-Caribbeans in different city locations in the UK.[60] In practice, the pattern of enterprise support for EMBs varies between cities, depending on the mix of mainstream and specialised agencies.

Another issue concerns the language and forms of communication used by mainstream business support providers to communicate with potential EMB clients, which could be improved through a greater use of ethnic-based media, such as radio and newsletters, to disseminate information on business support issues. In one study involving the author, we found that one of the gaps in enterprise support strategy in Glasgow, at the time, was limited use of ethnic-based media. Such factors help to explain the low level of use of formal sources of external advice and assistance by EMBs, particularly at start-up.[61]

It could be that the low take-up of business support from formal agencies reflects a low level of perceived need, or a lack of interest, by ethnic-minority entrepreneurs in receiving external assistance, which is a more extreme form of the apathy shown by many small business owners (regardless of their ethnicity) towards business support providers. However, there is evidence to suggest that the low level of use of mainstream business support agencies cannot be put down to the lack of interest on the part of the business owners[62; 63] since both studies found their South Asian samples receptive to appropriate business support. The reliance on social networks, which are embedded in ethnic communities, may provide strong social capital but it may also militate against accessing mainstream sources of support and advice.[64]

The principal obstacles for support agencies, therefore, can be associated with identifying and reaching ethnic-minority entrepreneurs. Ram and Smallbone suggest that when this is linked to often inadequate databases, together with the inappropriateness of the 'product-oriented' approaches used by support agencies, it may not be surprising that formal support is bypassed by ethnic-minority business owners.[55]

Finally it has been suggested that ethnic-minority entrepreneurs' needs are different from those of other small businesses, which Ram and Jones have indicated are associated with their sector, size and geographic distributions.[57] In terms of sector, South Asians are strongly represented in the catering, clothing and food retailing sectors,[65] Chinese in catering,[66] and African and Caribbeans in construction.[67] Although our research has shown that new-generation EMB owners are favouring emergent sectors,[61] traditional sectoral concentrations remain important and, therefore, have to be taken into consideration when formulating support policies for ethnic-minority entrepreneurs.

■ ■ ■ ■ Conclusions

This chapter has celebrated the diversity of enterpreneurship through a focus on women and ethnic-minority entrepreneurs. Even within these categories, however, diversity is a key theme. Diversity in entrepreneurship will always provide an issue for policy because it is not possible to treat any group of entrepreneurs as being homogeneous; the needs of business owners will vary and their needs will depend as much on the characteristics of their businesses (on their size, on their sector and on their location) as on whether they are owned by women, men or ethnic minorities. However, from the evidence that has been reviewed in this chapter, it is possible to identify the distinctive experiences of ethnic-minority and women entrepreneurs. It is noticeable that the evidence does suggest that some ethnic-minority enterpreneurs – especially, for example, African and Caribbeans – do have very different experiences when accessing bank finance than do other entrepreneurs.

Ethnic-minority enterprise development has succeeded largely outside mainstream support and largely without access to special support. For example, in some areas, success has been achieved through entrepreneurs and other community leaders taking individual action and setting up their own initiatives, using ethnic literature to ensure that firms and entrepreneurs are engaged.

The diversity of ethnic-minority enterprise is increasing. Generational issues have not been explored in this chapter, yet new young Asian and other ethnic-minority entrepreneurs are entering entrepreneurship from very different backgrounds than those of their parents and grandparents. While the family experience and tradition is still important in the Asian community, many of these new young ethnic-minority entrepreneurs may have a family background that does not have the tradition of business ownership. It is these new entrepreneurs that are forging the future of ethnic-minority enterprise development in the UK. They have different expectations, are often highly educated, and enter entrepreneurship against a background of high family expectations not to follow a career in self-employment.

Women are also increasing their participation in entrepreneurship, yet policies, such as the recently launched Strategic Framework,[48] still take a piecemeal approach to support and assume that women entrepreneurs have homogeneous needs, when, in practice, diversity characterises their experience. In the case of both women and ethnic-minority entrepreneurs policies continue to defy the variety of their experience, participation and activity.

Below, we provide a case study (Alternative Publishing Ltd, part A only) of an ethnic-minority business that has been tracked for some time. Started by two young Asian entrepreneurs, it represents an example of the emergence of a new generation of ethnic-minority entrepreneurs with very different backgrounds and start-up aspirations from those that might have been associated with earlier generations. The business has, subsequently, changed significantly and further material can be obtained through the online resource centre's learning and teaching material.

Alternative Publishing Ltd (Part A)

Background

Alternative Publishing Ltd (AP Ltd) was started by two young entrepreneurs, Majid Anwar and Suhail Rehman. The firm focused on business services in desktop publishing and associated computer services such as software development. It was established in a UK city centre.

Both entrepreneurs were in their early twenties when the idea of starting in business was first conceived. They were British born, but of Asian background. Apart from this characteristic they both have very different histories. Majid was from a medical family and had himself followed this career after leaving school. Suhail was the same age, but had studied avionics at university and his position differed in that his family had a predominantly business background.

They met through one of their extra-curricular activities – community work – to which they both allotted significant amounts of time. This afforded an opportunity to put something of human value back into the community that they had been brought up in and so help young people from an inner-city environment. Both had a desire to help their ethnic community.

After leaving university they found professional jobs with strong career structures. Majid started work as a junior doctor working in various hospitals, while Suhail started work as a software engineer with GEC Ferranti.

Motivating Factors Leading to Business Start-up

Putting Profits into Community Projects

The entrepreneurs' main motivating factor was the desire to put something back into their ethnic community. They had also devoted a lot of time to voluntary work. The plan was to skim off, in the future, some of the profits and put them into a charitable fund that would benefit others within the ethnic community to realise their aims (and also enter business).

The Desire to Empower Themselves

Majid had a strong desire to be able to empower himself. Starting a business was one way in which he could take his own decisions about every aspect of his life. This wish to empower himself was not an easy option. He wanted to be able to influence the decisions regarding the course of his life and had to justify them to himself, his family and the members of his ethnic community that had supported his career.

Family Background

For Suhail, the reasons for going into business were broadly similar, though his family involvement in business gave him an additional motivation to take this course. He had always had an inclination to go into business from an early age, though he felt that due to a lack of work experience it would have been unwise to do so straight from university. Thus he had followed the plan that he had set himself of going to work for a few years for a large company.

Barriers to Entry

The Influence of the Ethnic Community

The two men experienced much cumulative pressure to continue with a professional career. In the Asian community a great deal of emphasis is placed upon the younger generation achieving a professional career, in contrast to their parents, who may not have had the same educational and career opportunities. Therefore they faced much opposition from members of the ethnic community, who were not able to appreciate why they were motivated to start a business. Also, because of the value placed upon a professional career, to leave their jobs meant a consequent loss in status, which in addition resulted in a narrowing of their marriage prospects.

Loss of Professional Status

The other factor that might be seen to mitigate against a business start-up was that their professional careers offered them relative security with the prospect of high salaries in the future.

Planning and Implementing the Business Start-up

The Choice of Business

Both the founders possessed a strong interest in publishing and printing from their days of voluntary work, where knowledge of publishing had been acquired. They were both interested in computing as a result of their extra-curricular activities and, in Suhail's case, his previous job as a software engineer.

Finally, both partners recognised that future technological changes were going to make computing skills and knowledge even more crucial for a publishing career and their interests, as mentioned, already fitted this trend. From the outset both of them knew there was a gap in the market that had yet to be satisfied, and initial market research had established the feasibility of business entry.

Planning and Initial Phase

Even though they had identified publishing as a route to take, both founders were in only the early stages of planning. They realised that market research had to be done before any business could be started. In the initial phase they had to do a lot of the marketing themselves. They discovered that the building they were located in was actually the hub of the printing industry in the city centre. This was a feature that had not been known, but it proved fortuitous since it provided plenty of opportunities for networking. As a result, both Majid and Suhail were able to use the location as the basis for forging contacts and creating a network of links within the sector.

The marketing skills required for desktop publishing are different from those needed for more traditional printing. The importance of networking soon become apparent, as did the need to forge contacts. Therefore, they decided to bring in another partner and recruited Imran as a third director. Imran was older than the other two founders. They reckoned that his greater experience relative to them would be useful in making contacts.

In terms of director responsibilities, it was decided that Majid should be responsible for the design and artwork, while Suhail would deal with sales, marketing and administrative duties.

Customers and Competition

They had to make various decisions about how to deal with customers and elicit business. The path taken was to listen to the requirements and specifications of the customer for the job. From this the directors would then go back to them with a price for the job and a sample.

Majid and Suhail estimated that the public sector was the chief market they wanted to develop. They recognised that there were many projects emanating from these authorities that would require new skills and expertise. In the initial phase they encountered two features of this sector: first, that the culture was generally less competitive and demanding; second, that the sector was generally difficult to break into or, as Majid put it, 'business tends to go round in circles'.

By contrast, the competitive market was variable. For example, in some areas, such as traditional printing, trading patterns were vertical with some competition, whereas in new areas there was little or no competition. In these new areas of desktop publishing and 'printing with technology' it was possible to set their price. This was where they were offering specialised services and in these cases it was possible to dictate price. In areas where there was a lot of competition, there was little customer loyalty and they were compelled to negotiate prices each time. As a result, both directors felt that to get themselves established in such a market took a lot longer than for some of their more specialised niche markets.

Included with this part of the case are financial extracts and forecasts from the business plan for the first year (see Tables 1 and 2, below).

Table 1: *Financial Projections for AP Ltd Year 1*

Expenditure

Insurance, electricity, rent & rates	£ 6,000
Wages	£ 4,800
Telephone	£ 1,500
Subscriptions (journals, etc.)	£ 100
Consumables	£ 1,500
Legal & professional fees	£ 500
Advertising/publicity	£ 2,000
Equipment	£ 5,500
TOTAL	£21,900

Income

TOTAL from directors/investors	£15,600

Sales

Turnover for first year	£25,000

Assets

As equipment less 20% depreciation

Liabilities

VAT

Directors loans

TOTAL EXPENDITURE	£21,900
TOTAL income	£40,600
NET profit before Tax	£18,700
NET profit margin	43%

Table 2: *AP Ltd Cash Flow Forecast*

	Oct M1	Nov M2	Dec M3	Jan M4	Feb M5	Mar M6	Apr M7	May M8	Jun M9	Jul M10	Aug M11	Sep M12	TOTAL
Expenditure													
Insurance, electricity, rent & rates	1500	0	0	500	500	500	500	500	500	500	500	500	£ 6000
Wages	400	400	400	400	400	400	400	400	400	400	400	400	£ 4800
Telephone/Postage			375			375			375			375	£ 1500
Subscriptions (journals etc.)	75			25									£ 100
Consumables	100	20	20	50	150	160	160	160	160	170	170	180	£ 1500
Legal & professional fees		500											£ 500
Advertising/publicity	400	150	150	300	125	125	125	125	125	125	125	125	£ 2000
Equipment	700	200	200	4000			400						£ 5500
TOTAL expenditure	3175	1270	1145	5275	1175	1560	1585	1185	1560	1195	1195	1580	**£21900**
Income													
Directors/investors	12300	300	300	300	300	300	300	300	300	300	300	300	£15600
Sales		500	1000	1000	1500	2000	2000	3000	3000	3000	4000	4000	£25000
TOTAL income	12300	800	1300	1300	1800	2300	2300	3300	3300	3300	4300	4300	**£40600**
Cash flow	9125	–470	155	–3975	625	740	715	2115	1740	2105	3105	2720	**£18700**
Opening Balance	12300	9125	8655	8810	4835	5640	6200	6915	9030	10770	12875	15980	
Closing Balance	9125	8655	8810	4835	5640	6200	6915	9030	10770	12875	15980	18700	

Review Questions 3.1 ■ ■ ■ ■ ■ ■ ■ ■ ■ ■ ■ ■

1. Why do official participation rates for women in business tend to underestimate their importance?

2. Why might women face higher start-up barriers than do men?

3. How does the pattern of self-employment in women and ethnic minorities, in the UK, illustrate diversity?

4. How might this diversity be changing?

Review Questions 3.2 ■ ■ ■ ■ ■ ■ ■ ■ ■ ■ ■ ■

1. Commercial banks and mainstream support agencies may be seen by ethnic-minority entrepreneurs as 'white' institutions. This can be overlain with perceptions of prejudice in such institutions against them. What could the banks do to reduce such perceptions in order to improve access to formal bank finance? Similarly, what could support agencies do?

2. Why are ethnic-minority entrepreneurs important to Britain's future prosperity in the twenty-first century?

3. What are the five main ethnic-minority groups in the UK?

4. Which group appears to be the most under-represented in entrepreneurship? What factors might account for this?

Review Questions 3.3 ■ ■ ■ ■ ■ ■ ■ ■ ■ ■ ■ ■

1. Give examples of factors that would be regarded as positive and negative motivations for ethnic-minority entrepreneurs?

2. How would you expect motivations to differ between new-start business owners in different ethnic-minority groups?

3. In the past, problems of accessing resources may have caused some ethnic-minority entrepreneurs to enter sectors that have low barriers to entry – for example, clothing manufacture, retailing and wholesaling. How is increased competition in these sectors likely to affect such ethnic-minority businesses today?

Review Questions 3.4 ■ ■ ■ ■ ■ ■ ■ ■ ■ ■ ■ ■

1. Why has policy on support for women in enterprise become important?

2. One policy support initiative for women's enterprise in the UK was the launch of the Strategic Framework by the SBS. What was its main objective?

3. Why is the issue of mainstream vs specialised support relevant to both ethnic-minority and women's enterprise support policies?

4. What factors may explain the lack of engagement and the low take-up of support by ethnic-minority entrepreneurs?

Suggested Assignments ■ ■ ■ ■ ■ ■ ■ ■ ■ ■ ■ ■

1. Consider the case of Alternative Publishing Ltd. Should Majid and Suhail start the business? In your answer, consider the advantages and disadvantages of entrepreneurship for these two ethnic-minority entrepreneurs.

2. There has been considerable research effort into understanding characteristics of ethnic-minority entrepreneurs, the issues that they face, and their potential in economic regeneration and recovery. Using material from this chapter, discuss the potential reasons for this attention, focusing on Asian ethnic-minority entrepreneurs.

3. Why should black African and Caribbean entrepreneurs have been neglected as a focus of research on ethnic minorities?

4. Critically discuss the nature of recent support initiatives for women's enterprise in the UK.

5. You are a business adviser to a new women's enterprise, seeking to start in the UK:

(a) explain the relevance of recent policy initiatives, and recommend networks that they may consider joining as form of advice and information

(b) review and evaluate the following websites

- www.prowess.org.uk
- www.scottishbusinesswomen.com.

Recommended Reading ■ ■ ■ ■ ■ ■ ■ ■ ■ ■ ■ ■

Carter, S., Anderson, S. and Shaw, E. (2001) *Women's Business Ownership: A Review of the Academic, Popular and Internet Literature,* Small Business Service, London.

Ram, M. and Jones, T. (1998) *Ethnic Minorities in Business*, Small Business Research Trust, Milton Keynes.

Ram, M., Smallbone, D. and Deakins, D. (2002) *Ethnic Minority Businesses in the UK: Access to Finance and Business Support*, British Bankers' Association, London.

SBS (2003) *A Strategic Framework for Women's Enterprise: Sharing the Vision – A Collaborative Approach to Increasing Female Entrepreneurship*, SBS, London.

Internet resources

www.scottishbusinesswomen.com

www.prowess.org.uk

References

1 Small Business Service (2004) *A Government Action Plan for Small Businesses: The Evidence Base*, SBS/DTI, London.

2 ONS (2004) 2001 Census, Office for National Statistics, London.

3 Galloway, L., Brown, W. and Arenius, P. (2004) 'Gender-based Differences in Entrepreneurial Behaviour: A Comparative Examination of Scotland and Finland', *International Journal of Enterprise and Innovation Management*, Vol. 3, no. 2, pp. 109–19.

4 FSB (2004) *Lifting the Barriers to Growth in UK Small Businesses,* FSB, London.

5 FSB (2002) *Lifting the Barriers to Growth in UK Small Businesses,* FSB, London.

6 Carter, S., Anderson, S. and Shaw, E. (2001) *Women's Business Ownership: A Review of the Academic, Popular and Internet Literature*, Small Business Service, London.

7 Prowess (2003) Membership document, Prowess, Norwich.

8 Carter, S., Shaw, E. and Wilson, F. (2003) 'Securing a Business Loan: How Women Entrepreneurs View Banks and How Banks Them', paper presented to the 2003 Babson Entrepreneurship Research Conference, Boston, MA.

9 Shaw, E., Carter, S. and Brierton, J. (2001) *Unequal Entrepreneurs: Why Female Enterprise is an Uphill Business*, The Industrial Society, Policy Paper, London.

10 McGregor, J. and Tweed, D. (2002) 'Profiling a New Generation of Female Small Business Owners in New Zealand: Networking, Mentoring and Growth', *Gender, Work and Organization*, vol. 9, no. 4, pp. 420–38.

11 Marshall, J. (1994) 'Revising Organisations by Developing Female Values', in R. Boot *et al*. (eds), *Managing the Unknown*, McGraw-Hill, Maidenhead.

12 Ahuja, M. (2002) 'Women in the Information Technology Profession: A Literature Review, Synthesis and Research Agenda', *European Journal of Information Systems*, vol. 11, no. 1, pp. 20–34.

13 Grampian Enterprise Trust (1997) *Women in Business: Encouraging Growth*, Grampian Enterprise Trust, Aberdeen.

14 Read, L. (1995) *Raising Bank Finance: A Comparative Study of the Experiences of Male and Female Business Owners*, Routledge, London.

15 SBS (2003) *Women's Enterprise Strategic Framework: Consultative Document*, Ethnic Minority and Women's Enterprise Unit, SBS, London.

16 ONS (2003) Report on Ethnicity in the UK, ONS, London.

17 Scottish Executive (2004) *Analysis of Ethnicity in the 2001 Census – Summary Report*, Office of the Chief Statistician, Scottish Executive, Edinburgh.

18 SBS (2004) *A Government Action Plan for Small Business: The Evidence Base*, Small Business Service, London.

19 Light, I. (1984) 'Immigrants and Ethnic Enterprise in North America', *Immigrants and Ethnic Enterprise in North America,* vol. 7, no. 2.

20 Bonacich, E., Light, I. and Wong, C. (1977) 'Koreans in Business', *Society*, vol. 14, pp. 54–9.

21 Light, I. (1980) 'Asian Enterprise in America', in Cummings, S. (ed.), *Self-help in Urban America*, Kennikat Press, New York, pp. 33–57.

22 Glasgow, D. (1980) *The Black Underclass*, Jossey-Bass, San Francisco.

23 Waldinger, R. (1988) 'The Ethnic Division of Labour Transformed: Native Minorities and New Immigrants in Post-industrial New York', *New Community*, vol. 14, no. 3.

24 Waldinger, R., Aldrich, H., Ward, R. and associates (eds) (1990) *Ethnic Entrepreneurs,* Sage, London.

25 Ward, R. and Jenkins, R. (eds) (1984) *Ethnic Communities in Business*, Cambridge University Press, Cambridge.

26 Waldinger, R., Aldrich, H., Ward, R. and associates (1989) *Ethnic Entrepreneurs*, Sage, London.

27 Light, I. and Bonacich, E. (1988) *Immigrant Entrepreneurs*, California University Press, Berkeley.

28 Werbner, P. (1990) 'Renewing an Industrial Past: British Pakistani Entrepreneurship in Manchester', *Migration*, vol. 8, pp. 7–41.

29 Ward, R. (1991) 'Economic Development and Ethnic Business', in J. Curran and R. Blackburn (eds), *Paths of Enterprise*, Routledge, London.

30 Curran, J. and Blackburn, R. (1993) *Ethnic Enterprise and the High Street Bank*, Kingston Small Business Research Centre, Kingston University.

31 Ram, M. and Deakins, D. (1995) *African-Caribbean Entrepreneurship in Britain*, University of Central England, Birmingham.

32 Deakins, D., Hussain, G. and Ram, M. (1993) *The Finance of Ethnic Minority Entrepreneurs*, University of Central England, Birmingham.

33 Bank of England (1999*) The Financing of Ethnic Minority Firms in the UK: A Special Report*, Bank of England, London.

34 Ram, M., Smallbone, D. and Deakins, D. (2002) *Ethnic Minority Businesses in the UK: Access to Finance and Business Support*, British Bankers' Association, London.

35 Smallbone, D., Ram, M., Deakins, D. and Baldock, R. (2003) 'Access to Finance by Ethnic Minority Businesses in the UK', *International Small Business Journal*, vol. 21, no. 3, pp. 291–314.

36 Deakins, D., Ram. M., Smallbone, D. and Fletcher, M. (2003) 'Ethnic Minority Enterpreneurs and the Commercial Banks in the UK: Access to Formal Sources of Finance and Decision-making by their Bankers', in C.H. Stiles and C. Galbraith (eds), *Ethnic Entrepreneurship: Structure and Process*, Elsevier, Oxford, pp. 293–314.

37 Wilson, K.L. and Portes, A. (1980) 'Immigrant Enclaves: An Analysis of the Labour Market Experiences of Cubans in Miami', *American Journal of Sociology*, vol. 86, pp. 295–319.

38 Reeves F. and Ward, R. (1984) 'West Indian Business in Britain', in R. Ward and R. Jenkins (eds), *Ethnic Communities in Business*, Cambridge University Press, Cambridge.

39 Jones, T. and McEvoy, D. and Barrett, J. (1992) 'Raising Capital for the Ethnic Minority Small Business', paper presented for the ESRC Small Business Research Initiative, University of Warwick, September.

40 Ram, M. (1993) *Managing to Survive: Working Lives in Small Firms*, Routledge, London.

41 Ram, M. and Hillin, G. (1994) 'Achieving Break-out: Developing a Strategy for the Ethnic Minority Firm in the Inner City', paper presented to the Ethnic Minority Small Firms Seminar, UCE, Birmingham, March.

42 Ethnic Minority Business Development Initiative (EMBI) (1991) *Final Report*, Home Office, London.

43 Ram, M. and Hillin, G. (1994) 'Achieving Break-out: Developing Mainstream Ethnic Minority Businesses', *Small Business and Enterprise Development*, vol. 1, no. 2, pp. 15–21.

44 Deakins, D., Ishaq, M., Smallbone, D., Whittam, G. and Wyper, J. (2005) *Minority Ethnic Enterprise in Scotland: A National Scoping Study, Final Research Report*, Scottish Executive, Edinburgh.

45 GEM (2003) *Global Entrepreneurship Monitor Executive Report*, Babson College/London Business School, London.

46 GEM (2001) *Executive Report*, Kauffman Center for Entrepreneurial Leadership, Babson College, Boston, USA.

47 SBS (2003) *Women's Enterprise Strategic Framework: Consultative Document*, Ethnic Minority and Women's Enterprise Unit, SBS, London.

48 SBS (2003) *A Strategic Framework for Women's Enterprise: Sharing the Vision: a Collaborative Approach to Increasing Female Entrepreneurship*, SBS, London.

49 Deakins, D., Wilson, L. and Whittam, G. (2002) *National Centre for Women's Enterprise: Feasibility Study, Final Research Report*, Scottish Executive, Glasgow.

50 Scottish Executive (2003) *National Unit for Women's Enterprise*, press release, March.

51 Prowess (2003) Prowess Profile: Newsletter, no. 1, Spring/Summer, Prowess, Norwich.

52 Kirton, G. and Greene, A.-M. (2000) *The Dynamics of Managing Diversity: A Critical Approach*, Butterworth-Heinemann, Oxford.

53 Birley, S. (1989) 'Female Entrepreneurs: Are They Really any Different?', *Journal of Small Business Management,* vol. 27, no. 1, pp. 7–31.

54 Wilson, L., Whittam, G. and Deakins, D. (2004) 'Women's Enterprise: A Critical Examination of National Policies', *Environment and Planning C: Government and Policy*, vol. 22, no. 5, pp. 799–815.

55 Ram, M. and Smallbone, D. (2004) 'Policies to Support Ethnic Minority Enterprise: The English Experience', *Entrepreneurship and Regional Development,* vol. 15 no. 2, pp.151–66.

56 Deakins, D., Ram, M. and Smallbone, D. (2003) 'Addressing the Business Support Needs of Ethnic Minority Firms in the UK', *Environment and Planning C; Government and Policy*, vol. 21, no. 4, pp. 843–59.

57 Ram, M. and Jones, T. (1998) *Ethnic Minorities in Business*, Small Business Research Trust, Milton Keynes.

58 Humberside TEC (1999) *Other Ethnic Businesses in Humberside,* Research Briefing no.14, Humberside TEC.

59 GLE/CEEDR (2000) *Review of Business Support for Ethnic Minority Owned Businesses (EMBs) in London, Final Report,* Greater London Enterprise, May.

60 Ram, M. (1998) 'Enterprise Support and Ethnic Minority Firms', *Journal of Ethnic and Migration Studies*, vol. 24, no. 1, pp. 143–58.

61 Deakins, D., Majmudar, M. and Paddison, A. (1997) 'Developing Success Strategies for Ethnic Minorities in Business: Evidence from Scotland', *New Community*, vol. 23, no. 3, pp. 325–42.

62 Marlow, S. (1992) 'Take-up of Business Growth Training Schemes by Ethnic Minority Owned Firms', *International Small Business Journal,* vol. 10, no. 4, pp. 34–46.

63 Ram, M. and Sparrow, J. (1993) *Supporting Asian Businesses,* University of Central England Business School, UCE, Birmingham.

64 Flap, H., Kumcu, A. and Bulder, B. (1999) 'The Social Capital of Ethnic Entrepreneurs and their Business Success', in J. Rath (ed.), *Immigrant Businesses: The Economic, Political and Social Capital*, London, Macmillan.

65 Curran, J. and Burrows, R. (1988) *Enterprise in Britain: A National Profile of Small Business and the Self-employed*, Small Business Research Trust, Milton Keynes.

66 Song, M. (1997) 'Children's Labour in Ethnic Family Business: The Case of Chinese Take-away Business in Britain', *Ethnic and Racial Studies*, vol. 20. no. 1, pp. 690–716.

67 Curran, J. and Blackburn, R. (1993) *Ethnic Enterprise and the High Street Bank,* Kingston Business School, Kingston University.

Sources of Finance:
Overview of Issues and Debt Finance

Learning Outcomes

At the end of this chapter you should be able to:

1 discuss the importance of alternative sources of finance for entrepreneurs, small and medium-sized enterprises

2 describe why entrepreneurs and SMEs are at a disadvantage compared with large firms in financial markets

3 appreciate some of the problems that face the providers of finance to the SME sector

4 compare survey results and known national characteristics on the importance of sources of finance for start-up entrepreneurs and existing ventures

5 describe research findings comparing risk assessment practices of English and Scottish bank managers and be able to indicate the main differences in these practices

6 appreciate and account for the importance of bank finance as a source of external finance for entrepreneurs and small firm owners.

■ ■ ■ ■ ■ Introduction

This chapter is concerned predominantly with sources of finance for entrepreneurs and small and medium-sized enterprises (SMEs), taking the definition of SMEs as that given in Chapter 2. Thus for many small firms certain sources of finance are not available due to entry barriers. For example, many entrepreneurs and SMEs are automatically excluded from some financial sources, such as the Stock Exchange, and face difficulties raising some types of finance, such as long-term loans, because of the automatically higher risk associated with firms that have little equity in the form of share capital. In the majority of cases the only equity is that of the proprietors. This chapter will give an overview of the sources of finance, but its focus is on debt finance. Chapter 5 will examine sources of venture finance. However, some time will be spent here on the theoretical issues that provide the foundation for an examination of this important area.

It is worth making a distinction between the theoretical basis of entrepreneurs' and SMEs' finance and what we know about the sources of finance they actually use. It is easy to hypothesise, from what has been said above, about the difficulties facing entrepreneurs and small firms; that they are likely to rely heavily on personal savings and equity for long-term finance and perhaps trade credit for short-term finance. However, these hypotheses need to be balanced with what entrepreneurs and small firm owners actually do (i.e. the empirical evidence). We will consider each in turn.

There is a variety of sources of finance available to the entrepreneur and small and medium-sized firm. A simple way of classifying these sources is shown in Figure 4.1. This figure shows sources of finance classified as internal and external.

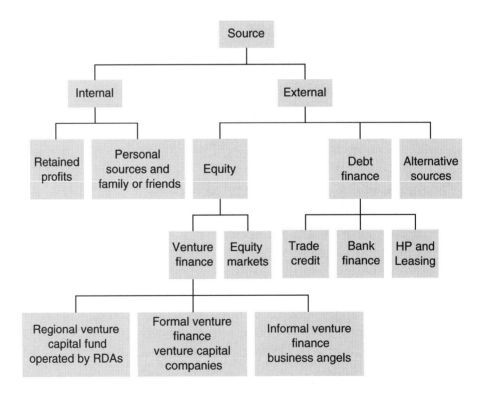

Figure 4.1: *Sources of Finance*

Internal sources of finance include the personal equity of the entrepreneur, usually in the form of savings, remortgage, or perhaps money raised from family and friends. This is sometimes referred to as the '3Fs' of small firm start-up finance – that is, family, friends and founder. After the initial start-up of the firm, retained profits and earnings provide internal capital. Usually, within a small firm, it is normal for internal sources to provide the major proportion of the firm's capital and financial structure. External finance can be drawn from a number of sources. As shown by Figure 4.1, the principal sources for the entrepreneur are advances from banks, equity from venture capitalists and informal investors and short-term trade credit. Other external sources may include leasing, hire purchase and factoring. In the UK the small firm entrepreneur may qualify for grants or 'soft loans' from government bodies such as the DTI (e.g. Regional Selective Assistance, RSA) or qualify for other schemes such as the Small Firms' Loan Guarantee Scheme (SFLGS). Local government may also provide loans and grants and there are a number of agencies that have attempted to set up their own financing schemes for small firms. These may include venture capital and loans from enterprise agencies, Business Links, Regional Development Agencies (RDAs) or in Scotland the Local Enterprise Companies (LECs) and other development agencies.

Whether entrepreneurs face real difficulties in raising external finance can be disputed; but the concern with this area on the part of policy-makers has given rise to the range of assistance that is now available to small firms and entrepreneurs. In particular, small-scale, community-based funds have been the subject of recent initiatives through funds established via the Small Business Service (SBS), such as funds and schemes supported from the Phoenix Fund.[1] Small-scale loan schemes or micro-credit schemes have been established in deprived areas where it can be difficult for potential entrepreneurs to raise external finance because of limited wealth and personal savings. Start-up firms in such localities may also be seen as having greater risk than those in other localities by potential funders and may pay higher interest rates as a result. For example the Bank of England commented in its most recent report[2] that evidence suggests 'that businesses in deprived areas represented on average a somewhat greater credit risk than those elsewhere in the country' (p. 14). In a recent review of the need for schemes to provide additional sources of external finance for small firms, the SBS concluded that some start-up firms and small businesses faced difficulties in accessing the debt finance they required.[3]

Whether schemes, such as those supported through the Phoenix Fund, are effective is an issue we touch upon later, but they have arisen at least in part because of theoretical concerns that small firm entrepreneurs will be at a disadvantage in raising finance compared to large firms. In particular, concern has centred on whether entrepreneurs face finance gaps because the supply of relatively small amounts of finance that small firms require, less than £200,000, can be uneconomic to provide and subsequently monitor by financial institutions (especially when considering sources of equity capital). We now turn to consider these issues in more detail.

■ ■ ■ ■ Issues for Entrepreneurs and Small Firms

Finance Gaps

If gaps arise they do so because of mismatches between supply and demand. The existence of a finance gap will arise because demand from small firms is greater than the willingness of financial institutions to supply the finance at current market conditions. For finance such as bank loans, these gaps may be termed credit rationing.

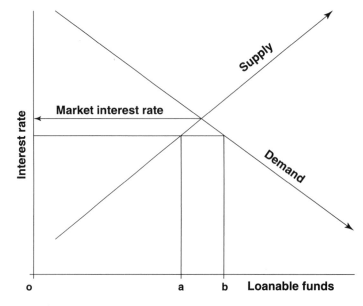

Notes: (i) The market interest rate is likely to be established below the equilibrium level due to state and Bank of England regulation.
(ii) The demand for loanable funds is assumed to consist of homogeneous and 'good' propositions seeking bank finance implying a 'gap' which could be met by rationing.

Figure 4.2: *Demand and Supply for Bank Credit*

A gap may exist such as that illustrated by Figure 4.2, where demand exceeds the available supply at current market rates of interest.

In Figure 4.2, the total advances that small firms would like to take up are given by *ob*. However, the amount that banks are willing to supply is given by *oa*. Hence the existence of a debt gap given by the distance *ab*. Governments can attempt to close this gap by shifting the supply curve of (debt) finance to the right by the introduction of schemes such as the Small Firms Loan Guarantee Scheme (SFLGS).

The discussion so far is an oversimplification of the market for small firm entrepreneurs' finance. For example, we are assuming that all propositions from small firms that banks receive are homogeneous. This will patently not be the case and we would expect some propositions to be treated more favourably than others. An equally important point arises about whether the 'good' propositions receive finance and the 'poor' propositions do not. This is the problem of adverse selection that is discussed in more detail below.

Finance gaps, however, have been recognised for over 60 years. They were first highlighted by the Macmillan Report of 1931[4] and subsequently termed the 'Macmillan gap'. Macmillan found, at the time, that small businesses and entrepreneurs would find it difficult to raise amounts of less than £200,000, equivalent to £4 million today. The Stock Exchange required a minimum figure of this amount to allow the trading of equity capital in a firm. There is little doubt that this gap has been substantially narrowed with the development of the venture capital industry in the UK. However, various official reports and other researchers have pointed to the continued existence of an equity gap in the UK[5] and the recent SBS review of evidence[2] suggested that 'Small businesses find it difficult to obtain modest amounts of private equity finance' (p. 51). There is general consensus that there is still a gap for raising equity of amounts below £250,000, although, as discussed in the next chapter, there have been important recent developments in the promotion of sources of informal venture capital, and the recent announcement by the Bank of England that it was no longer concerned with the production of its annual report on the finance of small firms would suggest that the official view is that there are no longer significant issues for small firms in raising finance and hence finance gaps.[6] However, it is arguable that an equity gap for entrepreneurs and small firms still exists because of the factors discussed below.

Reasons for the Continued Existence of Equity Gaps

1. It is not economic to issues shares for relatively small amounts of equity on the Stock Exchange (e.g. commission costs are high for small issues of less than £1 million).

2. Difficulties can exist in getting a listing on the Stock Exchange. This did become easier with the development of the Unlisted Securities Market (USM) and the Third and Over the Counter (OTC) markets, but the need for a trading record of at least three years is a barrier to many small firms. The demise of the USM in 1993 was a testimony both to the problems of entrepreneurs and small firms in the raising of equity and to the problems of providers in the administration of markets for relatively small amounts of equity capital. The development of the Alternative Investment Market (AiM) has been more successful, however, and has provided a successful alternative stock market to the London Stock Exchange, particularly for smaller and medium-sized firms to gain a listing.

3. It is not economic for venture capitalists to provide relatively small amounts of equity capital. The reasons for this are that venture capital companies will want to monitor the performance of the company closely, because they supply equity – not debt – capital and are consequently not guaranteed a return. Furthermore, the costs of arranging the finance and the appraisal of propositions are generally fixed costs.[7] A full discussion of venture capital is given in the next chapter.

4. Venture capitalists require high rates of return because they are assuming higher risks than the banks. Only certain high-performing entrepreneurs and firms, the high-growth firms, will be able to achieve the high rates of return required by venture capitalists who have in turn to satisfy the requirements of the shareholders in the venture capital fund. As a consequence of this, venture capitalists tend to concentrate on certain sectors of the economy only, or on certain types of finance, such as management buy-outs (MBOs) (see Chapter 5). Recent figures on the formal venture capital industry show that the majority of the sector's funds are invested in MBOs and management buy-ins (MBIs),[8] so that the importance of this sector for the finance of entrepreneurs and small firms is limited.

5. Venture capitalists will apply a 'due diligence' procedure to any proposition that is being considered for investment. This will take a considerable period of time and only a small proportion of applications for formal venture capital eventually receive funding after the due diligence procedure. Less than 5 per cent of applications for such formal venture capital will receive funding from this sector. It is worth noting that, for a time, due diligence was short-circuited during the Internet 'bubble' of 1999–2000, with the need to secure

venture finance in 'days' rather than 'months'. Well-publicised Internet companies' problems since then have seen such short-circuit mechanisms largely decline – for example, the relative demise of First Tuesday, a networking market mechanism for Internet entrepreneurs and venture capitalists that was popular in terms of attendance during the Internet company (dotcom) boom.[9]

6. Venture capitalists will also require an exit route for the sale of their shareholding after a period of time with their investment in the entrepreneurial concern. The normal method of seeking an exit route for such a holding will be to seek an initial public offering (IPO) on the Stock Exchange or AiM. Thus, venture capitalists will seek high-growth entrepreneurial concerns that can be turned within a short period (say five years) into public companies and provide an IPO as an exit route for their holding and their funds.

7. Venture capitalists will also seek to take an active part in the management of the company in order to safeguard their investment. They will seek to add value to their investment through an active role in the management and use their networking capabilities to open up additional opportunities for the growth of the entrepreneurial concern. The extent to which venture capitalists can add value to the management of investee companies has been one of the concerns in the venture capital sector.

Informal venture capital, which has seen important developments in recent years, has considerable potential to reduce equity gaps for small firms and is discussed in more detail, together with a full discussion of the formal venture capital industry, in the next chapter. For the rest of this chapter we focus on the banks as a source of entrepreneurial finance.

Finance and the Banks

For the entrepreneur, banks are easily accessible (through high-street branches) and provide short-term debt finance that in theory is attractive; the entrepreneur does not give up control and debt may be provided at times to suit the entrepreneur. However, banks, theoretically, face issues in assessing propositions from entrepreneurs. These issues arise in any investment situation where providers and borrowers have different sets of information. However, for banks we get two problems: adverse selection and moral hazard.

Adverse Selection

Adverse selection occurs when either the bank provides finance for a venture that subsequently fails or the bank refuses finance for a venture that would have been successful. It may occur because the bank does not have all the available information or the information is imperfect. The difficulty here is that the information required by the bank to assess perfectly the risk of the proposition is not costless to obtain. However, it can be argued that banks should reduce the mistakes they make, since they should have the skills and resources necessary to increase the frequency of correct decisions.

Moral Hazard

Moral hazard is more difficult for the bank to control. Once an entrepreneur has raised the bank loan, there is no guarantee that he or she will act in the best interests of the bank. Therefore, moral hazard is a monitoring problem for the bank and, for relatively small amounts of finance, it is not economic for banks to monitor performance closely. For this reason banks will usually require security, yet this contributes to the problems facing entrepreneurs. Those entrepreneurs without substantial equity and with insufficient security will fall into the debt gap.

Bank assessments of small firm applications for loan finance are examples of decision-making under uncertainty incorporating asymmetric information for the provider and the client. The foundations of analysis of possible mismatches between supply and demand that can occur under these conditions have been laid down by Akerlof's seminal 1970 paper.[10] Writers have developed the significance of these conditions for finance theory using a principal-agent framework.[11; 12; 13] The relevance of these insights is limited when considering the finance of entrepreneurs and small firms who have restricted access to financial markets. Concepts of moral hazard and adverse selection, however, are still important and have been further refined by later writers.[14; 15; 16]

Stiglitz and Weiss have shown that the problems of moral hazard and adverse selection are likely to produce credit rationing, insufficient credit available for all sound propositions.[17] It is possible to argue that these problems can lead to a credit glut[18] and at least one report has suggested that growing firms who wished to expand with sound propositions were able to raise finance when they needed to.[19] However, surveys for the Forum of Private Businesses and the Federation of Small Businesses[20; 21] still suggest that there are mismatches between providers (the commercial banks) and entrepreneurial business owners suggested by the theoretical papers. The review by the SBS on the evidence for access to debt finance by small firms supports the view that some entrepreneurs and small firms face difficulties in accessing debt finance.[3] In recent years, however, there is evidence that such difficulties have eased and that the number of small firms and entrepreneurs reporting difficulties has declined.[2] At the time of writing we have enjoyed a period of remarkably low interest rates (by historical standards), a period in which interest rates have been declining. It is not just mortgage lending that has grown in recent years, but official statistics show that total bank lending to small businesses (defined by the Bank of England as those with less than £1 million turnover) rose by £2900 million in 2003.[2] At the time of writing, this relatively benign financial climate has recently come to an end, with increases in interest rates at the end of 2003 and during 2004, but there seems to be evidence that conditions for accessing and acquiring debt finance have improved along with methods of risk assessment by the main commercial banks, which could explain the withdrawal of concern of the Bank of England with this area.[6] However, the importance of such issues is still debatable and is dealt with in more detail below.

Previous research by the author[22; 23] on the risk-assessment practices of banks in the UK has revealed that adverse selection certainly has occurred in the UK. Although this research was conducted some time ago, and it is recognised that bank manager practices have changed and are now supported by techniques of credit-scoring,[2] nevertheless the research revealed some issues in the way that bank managers assess propositions, which will still apply today; these are due to the nature of relatively short-term lending and the nature of risk assessment for debt finance. Using a real business plan, the author has previously taken the role of entrepreneurs seeking a funding proposition from 30 bank officers in the UK for a new venture. At the time, it was expected that bank officers would place more importance on the abilities and experience of the entrepreneur, since financial information that might appear as financial projections of income and costs in the cash flow forecast will be subject to uncertainty and treated with caution. Of course, with new propositions there is no financial track record of profitability and other criteria that may be used to assess existing propositions, such as liquidity, sales growth, debtors and other measures of financial performance. However, we found at the time that greater weight was placed upon uncertain financial information than the abilities, experience and qualifications of the potential entrepreneur. There was a bias in approach to financial criteria whereas important management criteria were discounted. Table 4.1 illustrates the importance of different information sought by bank managers on the proposition.

Table 4.1: *Criteria Used or Sought on the Proposition*

Information	Percentage of managers
Gearing	83%
Entrepreneurs' personal financial position	73%
Forecasted balance sheet and P & L account	66%
Entrepreneurs' drawings	63%
Entrepreneurs' contacts in industry	60%
Timing of income payments	60%
Contingency plans	57%
Entrepreneurs' personal collateral	50%
Market research	50%
Entrepreneurs' qualifications and careers	43%
Cash flow assumptions	40%
Entrepreneurs' starting separately (iii)	37%
Role of IT consultant	33%
IT development costs	27%
Business/managerial strategy	13%
Enterprise and small business experience	10%

Notes: (i) n = 30.

(ii) These are selective criteria.

(iii) Applied in this case because results are based on a team-start proposition.

We found that, of the 30 bank officers, 50 per cent would have backed the proposition and 50 per cent would not, but that there was also considerable variation in the approach of different officers. We can see from this table that only 10 per cent of managers considered small business experience and enterprise ability important. Further research by the author[23] with German bank officers revealed much greater importance in Germany placed on managerial information.

More recently, evidence still suggests for banks that financial credit history and financial projections in the business plan are more important factors in risk assessment than 'human capital' factors such as management experience and training.[3]

For information, Table 4.2, gives the bank managers' decisions according to an arbitrary scale on the proposition. At the time 50 per cent of managers were prepared to lend with security and 50 per cent were not – a remarkable variation. Whether this result would be repeated today is open to conjecture. It is likely that the advent of credit-scoring has reduced the degree of variability in decision-making by bank managers when faced with such propositions. This has been confirmed by a recent study by Mason and Stark, who compared the investment practices of bank managers, business angels and venture capitalists[24] and found that bankers place greater weight on financial information when faced with the same proposition. They also claimed[24] that their results were contrary to our previous findings of variability in decision-making, with their results showing bank managers 'exhibiting consistency, not only in

Table 4.2: *Bank Managers' Decisions*

Score out of 10 (i)	Number of officers
0	1
1	4
2	4
3	3
4	3
5	1
6	3
7	10
8	1
9	0
10	0
Total	30

Notes: (i) The score (out of 10) was applied arbitrarily by the authors to the 'favourability' of bank managers' decisions on the case example proposition. A score of '5' and above was positive; below '5', the proposition was rejected by the bank manager.

their approach, but also in their decision' (p. 241). These results from this more recent study are not surprising, given the advent of centralisation and credit-scoring in the commercial banks. In addition, since Mason and Stark conducted their research with only three bankers, we should reserve judgement on whether there have been significant improvements in the consistency of bankers' decision-making. Even very recently the author has continued to encounter entrepreneurs recounting their experiences of approaching a number of banks with different accept or reject decisions on their propositions.[25] It is likely that some variability in decision-making by bank managers remains, although this may well have been reduced over the past decade.

The Role of Security

Bank officers will stipulate requirements on the entrepreneur that may involve frequent monitoring of information to reduce moral hazard. However, a cost-minimisation approach will also include using methods that ensure commitment on the part of the entrepreneur. We would expect collateral (assets that may be pledged as security) to have an important role because it can ensure commitment and also provides a fail-safe method for the bank to recover losses in the case of the form of adverse selection that involves selecting a business failure. In conditions of uncertainty, signalling is obviously important and, following Spence,[26] a number of writers have developed theoretical implications of the importance of signalling.[27; 28; 29] The importance of signalling commitment has also been recognised.[30] Thus liquidity constraints and uncertainty combine to encourage the provider of finance to require security when this is available. Also Chan and Kannatas have pointed out that the type of security provided by the entrepreneur can offer information to the provider.[31]

Collateral, however, is not without costs and its own problems; for example, there are valuation problems, there might be depreciation to consider and it might be necessary to revalue collateral at intervals. The taking of collateral, then, needs to be balanced against the costs of management for the bank. Also the taking of collateral does nothing to reduce adverse selection. It merely provides a method for the bank to recover (some) potential losses where it considers risks to be high. However, if we assume that bank managers are risk averse, we can expect that collateral will be required where risks are perceived to be high – for example, with new technology entrepreneurs or with propositions that have high gearing. Security is still commonly required by bank managers, even though there has been an improvement in assessment methods and information discussed earlier.[25] Security, in practice, will often be a critical requirement where risk is perceived to be high, such as the proposition that was involved in our research. For example, of those that would have backed the proposition all required security.

Theoretically, adverse selection should not occur if the bank has perfect information and can rely with certainty on cash-flow predictions. Following Altman,[32] we have argued that it is necessary to define two different categories of adverse selection. First, the bank could approve a proposition that turns out to be a business failure. Second, the bank could refuse to accept a proposition that turns out to be a business success. As illustrated in Table 4.3, we define these categories as Type II and Type I errors respectively.

As can be seen in Table 4.3, it is more likely that bank officers would be concerned with avoiding Type II errors (partly because Type I errors will not be discovered) and, in our earlier study, we concluded that this contributed to adverse selection.[33]

Systems that control for Type II errors may minimise risk, but they also miss profitable opportunities associated with business propositions that might contain higher risk but provide profitable opportunities for growth in the business of the bank. These

Table 4.3: *Potential Outcomes from Decision-making on a Proposition*

Outcome	Funded	Not funded
Proposition successful	Correct decision	Type I error
Proposition fails	Type II error	Correct decision

Note: The reader may like to note that this classification of potential errors reverses the original Altman classification.

hypotheses provide theoretical explanations of why bank officers may turn away small firm propositions that have high potential for growth and profitability.

> ### Raising Entrepreneurial Finance: The Role of Security and the Small Firms' Loan Guarantee Scheme
>
> Most modern economies have a state-sponsored loan guarantee scheme with the main objective being to assist those entrepreneurs with little security to raise bank finance. The state accepts that bankers will require security, although the importance of this is changing for bankers (see the section on credit-scoring, below).
>
> In the UK, the Small Firms' Loan Guarantee Scheme (SFLGS) provides a vehicle for those entrepreneurs with little security with the government guaranteeing up to 75 per cent of the loan. In the UK, take-up rates have improved on this scheme but the evidence seems to suggest that the use and promotion of the SFLGS by bankers has been variable.[34] To qualify for the scheme, propositions have to be put forward to the Small Business Service (SBS) by bankers, and it requires additional paperwork to be undertaken by bankers. Under the early operation of the scheme, in the 1990s, default rates were high but in more recent years these have improved, as have take-up rates.[5]
>
> The scheme is intended to be self-financing, and the entrepreneurs who qualify pay a premium interest rate of 0.5 to 1.5 per cent. The amount borrowed under the scheme can be up to a maximum of £250,000 over a period of seven years.
>
> The SFLGS in previous years has excluded some sectors. From a study involving the author, on access to finance by ethnic-minority businesses (EMBs),[35] it was suggested that the SFLGS may disadvantage EMBs due to concentrations of EMBs in retailing, a sector that was excluded under the SFLGS. It was recommended that the SBS should review the operation of the SFLGS in the light of difficulties faced by EMBs. Following a separate review by the DTI, the SFLGS was changed in 2003 to include additional sectors and is now operated by the SBS.[36]

Credit-scoring

The advent of computerised credit-scoring for personal customer loan applications has been mirrored with the recent introduction by some banks of credit-analysis systems of applications for credit by business customers, or a form of credit-scoring. The most recent Bank of England report suggests that the trend towards credit-scoring techniques for business loan applications has become increasingly prominent.[2] Credit-scoring relies upon the application of predictable variables for an individual's credit rating, such as occupation, postcode of home address, family commitments and previous payment record. Scores are attached to each of the criteria, which will lead to an automatic acceptance/rejection decision issued by computer, effectively disenfranchising the bank officer of any responsibility to make subjective judgements about individual applications. When such systems are applied to business applications, in theory, the potential for variation in bank manager decisions (as discussed above) should be reduced to a minimum. However, this also means that individual bank manager discretion to use local knowledge and local information about the entrepreneur is removed, perhaps leading to automatic rejections that, before the advent of quantitative analytical credit-scoring, would have been carefully considered by the banks. The Bank of England reports[2] that, 'Qualitative techniques [of decision-making] based around a manager's judgement are increasingly being supported or even supplemented by computer-based quantitative analysis'.

At the time of writing, in the UK, each of the main commercial banks – HBOS, Barclays, HSBC, Lloyds/TSB, NatWest/RBS – operates different systems for credit applications from entrepreneurs. Three of the banks have adopted a centralised system where the role of the bank manager has become a purely relationship role, with credit applications referred to a central credit risk unit.[37] The manager still has a role in preparing the application, but has no discretionary powers in decision-making on the application, which is credit-scored by the central risk unit. The other three commercial banks have adopted a form of credit-scoring for business applications, but have retained local discretion in decision-making.

Credit-scoring has brought costs and benefits for banks and entrepreneurs. It may automatically rule out some applications (which would otherwise be successful) because of the credit history of the entrepreneur or because of previous credit judgements (for example, a county court judgement, which will automatically result in a reject decision) but it has also meant that bank manager discretion can be increased and it has reduced the extent of security levels required.[37]

Credit-scoring, however, at the time of writing, cannot be used with start-up applications, which implies that there will still be considerable variety in banks' decision-making for start-up applications as indicated by our previous research.

It can be argued that some entrepreneurs are disadvantaged by bank managers' formal methods of risk assessment, whether operating qualitative and heuristic-based decision-making or more quantitative, credit-scoring techniques. For example, the SBS has argued in the recent Strategic Framework for Women's Enterprise, reviewed in the previous chapter, that 'Traditional credit-scoring systems discriminate against women, who tend to have a less detailed and more fragmented financial track record' and claims outright that female entrepreneurs suffer 'prejudice on the part of lenders'.[38] The author's involvement in research studies with ethnic-minority entrepreneurs (the EMB study) and their access to finance has produced studies that suggest some entrepreneurs from different ethnic groups may also be disadvantaged.[35] However, rather than outright prejudice, as suggested by the SBS's Strategic Framework document, in reality it is different and highly variable practices by bank managers that account for differences in treatment by different groups of entrepreneurs. For example, the EMB study suggested that good practice by bank managers, where they were involved in local ethnic-minority communities, led to a greater understanding of business practices and familiarity with propositions from the ethnic-minority community, allowing them to influence decision-making practices favourably even where these were centralised.[35]

Are the Commercial Banks a Complex Monopoly?

It can be claimed that the UK banking system could be classed as a complex monopoly (particularly since the RBS has taken over NatWest and the Bank of Scotland has taken over the Halifax). In addition, 80 per cent of the small business banking market is controlled by only two of the main commercial banks. In the UK a complex monopoly is not automatically a violation of anti-trust laws, as it might be in the USA, for example; however, such a complex monopoly is grounds for investigation by the Competition Commission. The investigation reported to the DTI in 2001 and the recommendations were announced in 2002.[39] The report ruled that some commercial banks were making excessive profits from the small business sector and the UK government has subsequently announced new requirements for the trading practices of the main commercial banks with their small business customers.[39] These measures, however, were not targeted at the processes of decision-making.

As a result of its investigation, the Competition Commission recommended a number of 'behavioural remedies' to be introduced by the commercial banks in their practices with small business customers. However, the effect of these remedies could be seen to be largely focused on improving transparency of operations and of charges, something that small firm organisations, such as the Federation of Small Businesses, had been pressing for for a number of years. In addition the main commercial banks were asked to introduce additional choices in the nature of current accounts held by business owners, so that they were more in line with charges imposed on personal customer current accounts.

To some extent the jury is still out on whether the complex monopoly enjoyed by the commercial banks is against the public interest. The Director General of Fair Trading will review the operations of the commercial banks with small business customers and decide whether there should be further investigation by the Competition Commission and also review whether the small business banking market is sufficiently competitive.[36] This will be after a 'probationary period' to allow the commercial banks to improve their services to small business customers.

Some Empirical Evidence

In terms of empirical research, it is known from various sources that entrepreneurs and small firms are highly dependent on internal sources of finance, as might be expected to follow from our earlier discussion in this chapter. Research by Cambridge University's Centre for Business Research (CBR) 1992–2002[40] has indicated that bank finance is by far the most important source of external finance for entrepreneurs and small firms, although its relative importance has declined over the past decade. Figure 4.3 gives its figures for the importance of external sources of finance received by small firms in the period 2000–02.

From research undertaken as part of a project on the financing needs of ethnic-minority entrepreneurs, published data on the percentage accessing finance is shown in Table 4.4.[37] This shows that 39 per cent had attempted to raise finance in the previous year.

It is likely that internal sources and the entrepreneur's equity will be very important for start-up finance. For comparative purposes, using our study of start-up small firms,[42] we report the results in terms of importance for sources of finance in Table 4.5. Although, it shows that a high proportion of start-ups do use bank finance, a more

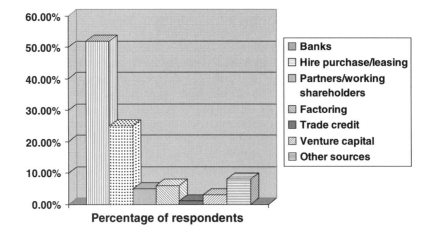

Figure 4.3: *External Sources of Finance for Small Firms 2000–02*

Source: ESRC Centre for Business Research (1992–2002) *The State of British Enterprise Reports,* Department of Applied Economics, University of Cambridge, Cambridge

significant feature is the comparative importance of personal savings, which are rated significantly higher than bank finance in importance as a source of finance.

Relationships Between Entrepreneurs/ Small Firms and the Banks

Work on the relationship between entrepreneurs and small business owners and their banks has been carried out in the comprehensive surveys by Binks *et al.*[20] for the Forum of Private Business. Bank charges, although frequently cited in the press, may not be the most important concern for small business owners and entrepreneurs; but Binks *et al.* did find that only 26 per cent of respondents thought that bank charges

Table 4.4: *External Finance Sought by Ethnic-minority Business Owners at Start-up*

Ethnic Group	Proportion of business owners seeking source of finance
African-Caribbean	31%
Pakistani	35%
Indian	41%
Bangladeshi	34%
Chinese	51%
All ethnic businesses	39%

Source: Smallbone *et al.* (2001)[41]

Table 4.5: *Start-up Finance for a Sample of 60 Start-up Entrepreneurs in Scotland*

Source	Percentage of Respondents	Importance (mean score)
Personal sources	80%	4.2
Enterprise Allowance Scheme*	66%	2.9
Local govt grant	50%	2.1
Trade credit	44%	1.7
Bank overdraft	37%	1.5
Other public sector	29%	1.2
Family and friends	20%	1.1
Bank loan	22%	0.9
Venture capital	7%	0.2
PSYBT**	12%	4.86
Other source	7%	0.2

Note:* The importance of the EAS is accounted for by the large majority of respondents which were trading for less than one year.
** Prince's Scottish Youth Business Trust (applies to young entrepreneurs only, less than 26 years old).

were good value for money. We have noted earlier that small business owners have now been given more choice and transparency in the operation of their bank accounts as a result of the recommendations of the Competition Commission. In addition, there have been improvements by the banks, particularly in staff training and developing specialised corporate and enterprise manager positions, but entrepreneurs do have genuine grievances if charges are not itemised and the bank operates a hands-off policy. This is something that the banks have tried to correct with their Small Business Charters. However, Binks *et al.* considered that: 'Bank charges, interest rates and the banks' demand for collateral remain important constraints on small firms'.[20]

Over time, relationships between entrepreneurs and the banks seem to have improved, although the surveys carried out for the FPB indicate that the extent of this improvement varies between the different commercial banks.[43] For example, there has been an overall improvement in the relationships, but individual commercial banks have also made efforts to improve their relationships with small business customers. The authors comment, 'The overall improvement in bank performance may reflect more positive trading conditions for businesses and banks but also genuine substantive improvements in bank service quality' (p. 1152). The SBS review of evidence suggested that, in general, conditions for accessing bank finance had improved in the UK, together with improved relationships between small firm owners and their banks.[3]

Banks and Entrepreneurs: Mutual Guarantee Schemes – Untapped Potential?

Mutual Guarantee Schemes (MGSs) are popular in European countries, notably Spain, France and Germany, but, at the time of writing, exist only as small pilot schemes in the UK.[44] Figure 4.4 illustrates the principles of an MGS. It operates through a 'club' of member firms who establish an MGS fund with a commercial bank. They are able to borrow at below normal market rates from the bank. In return, members provide mutual guarantees. Banks have the attraction or reduced risk of lending as a result of the guarantee and, hence, should have no need for additional security.

It is claimed that MGSs have additional advantages for member small firms through the improvement of management competencies and encouragement of members to participate in training schemes.[44]

In the UK, MGSs have not been part of policy promotion and have only recently been established. Establishing an MGS presents considerable legal barriers as well as achieving co-operation and networking of member small firms. However, pilot schemes have been established with the assistance of the National Association of Mutual Guarantee Schemes (NAMGS), which all differ in their practice and membership.

In theory the co-operative principles of MGSs should heighten awareness of members to support and advice, and provide self-help. Evidence in Europe, however, suggests that problems can arise with the administration of individual societies and with ensuring the agreement of members.[45]

Despite the potential of MGSs to encourage beneficial networking between small firm entrepreneurs, in the UK they will remain of only minor importance while they are not part of a policy promotion.

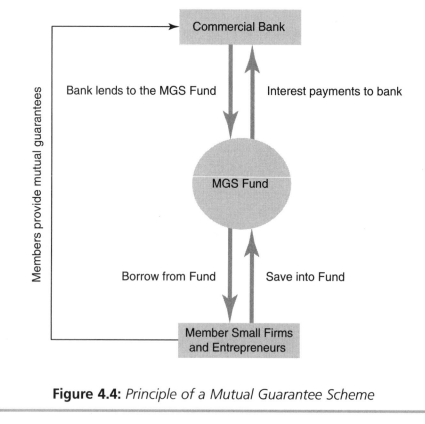

Figure 4.4: *Principle of a Mutual Guarantee Scheme*

■ ■ ■ ■ Conclusions

In this chapter, we have taken an overview of the important issues in the finance of entrepreneurs and small firms. Much of this discussion has centred on finance gaps and their implications for entrepreneurs and small firms. We have tried to show, theoretically, why these gaps might emerge, given problems of uncertainty and asymmetric information.

We have shown that entrepreneurs and small firms continue to be dependent on banks for external finance, despite schemes that attempt to improve the availability of equity capital. We have shown that some entrepreneurs also face problems in raising bank finance, that UK bank practices of risk assessment can be variable and that adverse selection (where potentially viable projects are not receiving finance) can exist through variability in bank manager practice.

By now you should be able to discuss the advantages and disadvantages of the most important of these sources. You should also have an understanding of why small firms and entrepreneurs are at a disadvantage compared to larger firms in financial markets, as well as an appreciation of the problems that face providers of finance.

This chapter has focused on debt finance; the following chapter will examine in more detail sources of equity finance (including formal and informal venture finance) and some of the issues in raising equity.

Before the next chapter, however, a mini case study is provided of bank manager questions that were asked in our case study of Peters & Co; we also discuss the case of technology-based entrepreneurial start-ups that can be seen as a special case. The full version of the Peters & Co case study is available in the students' online resource material and further discussion is also available in the lecturer's online resources.

Raising Bank Finance

The case study of Peters & Co involved a business plan for team start but with limited equity investment by the three co-directors. Each of the three committed £10,000 equity and required a bank loan of £60,000 to cover the forecast deficit on the cash flow. This meant a debt to equity ratio or gearing ratio of 2:1, whereas bankers' preferred gearing ratios are 1:1. Typical bankers' comments on this proposition were as follows.

We like to see the entrepreneurs match the bank to show commitment.
You will be using the bank's money without matching it yourself.

A typical interview by a bank manager focused on the following issues.

1. What are your assumptions behind the income shown in the cash-flow statement?

2. How many orders do you expect to achieve per month?

3. When will your income be paid?

4. What customers have indicated that they will deal with you?

5. Why do you need an office premises with high rents in a town centre?

6. What role will each of the entrepreneurs take in the business?

7. What can you do that is better than your competitors?

Being prepared for such questions meant that the interview could be handled confidently. Among the answers given at the time were the following.

1. The cash flow is based on extensive experience of the three co-directors and represents a conservative estimate of income with a small number of orders in the first months rising to 12–15 at the end of the first year.

2. We will be building to achieving 20 per month after the first year.

3. It is fee-based income paid in instalments for each job.

4. We had guaranteed orders from exclusive clients we had known for 15 years or more.

5. Prestigious offices necessary for the type of clientele.

6. Roles were clearly defined with tasks such as marketing/finance split between different directors.

7. Our competitive edge is based upon the application of the latest CAD techniques to quantity surveying. This gave us a technology-related advantage over our competitors, allowing a full cost-based service from design to build.

Raising Entrepreneurial Finance: Technology-based start-ups a special case?

Technology-based start-ups can be seen as a special case[40] with distinct financing needs due to the following factors.

1. Extensive R&D periods for product development. This necessitates raising finance for R&D and prototypes, known as *seed capital*.

2. Although patents can be used to protect new products/processes, they are intangible assets and banks are unwilling to accept them as security.

3. Developing cash-flow forecasts for the business plan can be problematic since, with new products, existing markets do not exist. Consequently banks are unwilling to lend against forecasts.

4. The new technology will need a technology appraisal to determine its viability and banks are not equipped to undertake such approaches.

The financing of technology-based start-ups is seen as a special case by the government with recognised potential market failure to provide debt and equity finance.[44] The government scheme to assist technology-based start-ups in the UK is the Small Firms Merit Award for Research and Technology (SMART). SMART provides grants to help new-start technology-based entrepreneurs research and develop new innovative products. Grants vary from £2500 to £150,000; they are awarded on a competitive basis and assist with developing prototypes and market testing.

The problem with SMART for many entrepreneurs[43] is that grant funding is only for the research and development of prototypes, it does not provide funding for the often lengthy time required to achieve full commercialisation.

Review Questions 4.1

1. What difficulties do entrepreneurs face in raising equity finance? How do you expect this to differ with start-ups and with established firms?

2. List the main sources of debt and equity finance for entrepreneurs.

3. Taking the bank manager–entrepreneur relationship:

   (a) what flows of information might exist between the bank manager–entrepreneur?

   (b) why might adverse selection and moral hazard exist for bankers as a result of the nature of such flows of information?

Review Questions 4.2

1. What factors might account for the variation of decisions by bank managers in our research using a real business plan for a start-up proposition? (Hint: consider the earlier discussion on the role of information and adverse selection, and your answers to Review Questions 4.1.)

2. Taking this further, why should some bank managers ask for security and others not?

3. What is the role of security in bank lending? Why might some entrepreneurs be disadvantaged by the security requirements of the banks?

4. You are a senior strategy manager with a commercial bank. You are given the results from our study reported in Tables 4.1 and 4.2. What action might you take to improve the consistency of decision-making in the bank?

Review Questions 4.3

1. The empirical evidence in this chapter suggests that entrepreneurs have a preference for finance in a distinct order: personal sources, debt from banks and then venture capital sources. This result has been called the Pecking Order Hypothesis and it is thought that entrepreneurs will seek finance in this order of preference. What factors would account for such a 'pecking order' of preference by entrepreneurs? (Hint: consider the obligations of entrepreneurs to debt and equity funders.)

2. What is the main purpose of the government-sponsored Small Firms' Loan Guarantee Scheme? Do you consider that there is still a need for such a scheme?

3. What do you understand by credit-scoring?

4. What implications for entrepreneurs might exist from the advent of credit-scoring applied by the commercial banks to business applications?

5. What benefits might a Mutual Guarantee Scheme provide to its member small firms and entrepreneurs?

Suggested Assignments ■ ■ ■ ■ ■ ■ ■ ■ ■ ■ ■

1. Using the Peters & Co case study available in the student's online learning resource material, you are required to:

■ familiarise yourself with information on the venture

■ prepare for a role-play exercise by taking the role of one of the entrepreneurs

■ research additional information on sources of finance and risk assessment

■ carry out a role-play exercise by arranging an interview with your bank manager (tutor).

2. Complete a report on the issues in the finance of start-up entrepreneurs.

3. Collect material on lending and services to small firms and entrepreneurs from the local high-street banks, including charges.

(a) Compare the services and discuss whether there are any differences in services or charges.

(b) Do you agree with the Competition Commission Report[37] that the UK commercial banks are a complex monopoly (uncompetitive), and would you agree that they overcharge their small business customers?

Recommended Reading ■ ■ ■ ■ ■ ■ ■ ■ ■ ■ ■

Bank of England Annual Reports (1994–2004) *Finance for Small Firms,* nos. 1 to 11, Bank of England, London.

Bank of England (2001) *Financing of Technology-based Small Firms*, Bank of England, London.

Deakins, D. and Hussain, G. (1994) Financial Information, the Banker and Small Business: A Comment, *The British Accounting Review*, vol. 26, pp. 323–35.

Fletcher, M. (1994) 'Decision Making by Scottish Bank Managers', *International Journal of Entrepreneurship Behaviour and Research*, vol. 1, no. 2, pp. 37–53.

References

1 Small Business Service (2001) *Phoenix Fund and Early Growth Fund*, Small Business Service, DTI, London.

2 Bank of England (2004) *Finance for Small Firms: An Eleventh Report*, Bank of England, London.

3 Small Business Service (2004) *A Government Action Plan for Small Business: The Evidence Base*, Small Business Service, DTI, London.

4 HM Government (1931) *Report of the Committee on Finance and Industry* (Macmillan Report), CMND 3897, HMSO.

5 For example, Bank of England (1994–2001) *Finance for Small Firms Annual Reports*, Bank of England, London.

6 Bank of England (2004) Statement, Bank of England, London.

7 Harrison, R. and Mason, C. (1991) 'Informal Investment Networks: A Case Study from the UK', *Entrepreneurship and Regional Development*, vol. 3, no. 2, pp. 269–79.

8 BVCA (2003) *Venture Capital in the UK: Annual Report*, British Venture Capital Association, London.

9 Bank of England (2001) *Finance for Small Firms – An Eighth Report*, Bank of England, London.

10 Akerlof, G. (1970) 'The Market for Lemons: Qualitative Uncertainty and the Market Mechanism', *Quarterly Journal of Economics*, vol. 89, pp. 488–500.

11 Mirrlees, J.A. (1974) 'Notes on Welfare Economics, Information and Uncertainty', in M. Balch, D.

McFadden and S. Wu (eds), *Essays in Economic Behaviour Under Uncertainty*, North Holland.

12 Mirrlees, J.A. (1975) *The Theory of Moral Hazard and Unobservable Behaviour*, Nuffield College, Oxford.

13 Jensen, M.C. and Meckling, W.H. (1976) 'Theory of the Firm: Managerial Behaviour, Agency Costs and Ownership Structure', *Journal of Financial Economics*, vol. 3, pp. 305–60.

14 Harris, M. and Townsend, R.M. (1981) 'Resource Allocation Under Asymmetric Information', *Econometrica*, vol. 49, pp. 33–64.

15 Hellwig, M. (1987) 'Some Recent Developments in the Theory of Competition in Markets with Adverse Selection', *European Economic Review*, vol. 31, pp. 319–25.

16 Magill, M. and Shafer, W. (1991) 'Incomplete Markets', in W. Hildenbrand and H. Sonneschein, (eds), *The Handbook of Mathematical Economics*, vol. IV, North Holland.

17 Stiglitz, J. and Weiss, A. (1981) 'Credit Rationing in Markets with Imperfect Information', *American Economic Review*, vol. 71, pp. 393–410.

18 De Meza, D. and Webb, D. (1987) 'Too Much Investment: A Problem of Asymmetric Information', *Quarterly Journal of Economics,* vol. 102, pp. 281–92.

19 Aston Business School (1991) *Constraints on the Growth of Small Firms*, DTI, HMSO.

20 Forum of Private Business (2000; 2002) *Small Businesses and their Banks*, FPB, Knutsford.

21 Federation of Small Business (2000) *Barriers to Survival and Growth in UK Small Firms*, FSB, London.

22 Deakins, D. and Hussain, G. (1991) *Risk Assessment by Bank Managers*, University of Central England Business School, Birmingham.

23 Deakins, D. and Philpott, T. (1993) *Comparative European Practices in the Finance of Small Firms: UK, Germany and Holland*, University of Central England Business School, Birmingham.

24 Mason, C. and Stark, M. (2004) 'What do Investors Look for in a Business Plan? A Comparison of the Investment Criteria of Bankers, Venture Capitalists and Business Angels', *International Small Business Journal*, vol. 22, no. 3, pp. 227–48.

25 Deakins, D., Ishaq, M., Smallbone, D. and Whittam, G. (2004) *Minority Ethnic Enterprise in Scotland: A Scoping Study*, Interim Research Report for the Scottish Executive, Edinburgh.

26 Spence, A.M. (1974) *Market Signalling*, Harvard University Press.

27 Crawford, V. and Sobell, J. (1982) 'Strategic Information Transmission', *Econometrica*, vol. 50, pp. 1431–51.

28 Quinzii, M. and Rochet, J.C. (1985) 'Multidimensional Signalling', *Journal of Mathematical Economics*, vol. 14, pp. 261–84.

29 Cho, I.-K. and Kreps, D. (1987) 'Signalling Games and Stable Equilibria', *Quarterly Journal of Economics*, vol. 102, pp. 179–221.

30 Milgrom, P. and Roberts, J. (1982) 'Limit Pricing and Entry Under Incomplete Information: an Equilibrium Analysis', *Econometrica*, vol. 50, pp. 443–59.

31 Chan, Y. and Kannatas, G. (1985) 'Asymmetric Valuations and the Role of Collateral in Loan Agreements', *Journal of Money, Credit and Banking*, vol. 17, no. 1, pp. 84–95.

32 Altman, E.I. (1971) *Corporate Bankruptcy in America*, Heath Lexington.

33 Deakins, D. and Hussain, G. (1994) 'Financial Information, the Banker and Small Business: A Comment', *The British Accounting Review*, vol. 26, pp. 323–35.

34 Deakins, D. Ram, M., Smallbone, D. and, Fletcher' M. (2002) 'Decision-making and the Development of Relationships with Ethnic Minority Entrepreneurs by UK Bankers', paper presented to the 2002 Babson Entrepreneurship Research Conference, Boulder, Colorado, June.

35 Ram, M., Smallbone, D. and Deakins, D. (2002) *Ethnic Minority Businesses in the UK: Access to Finance and Business Support,* British Bankers Association, London.

36 Bank of England (2003) *Finance for Small Firms – A Tenth Report*, Bank of England, London.

37 Deakins, D., Ram, M., Smallbone, D. and Fletcher, M. (2004) 'Ethnic Minority Entrepreneurs in the Commercial Banks in the UK: Access to Formal Sources of Finance and Decision-making by their Bank Managers', in C.H. Stiles and C.S. Galbraith (eds), *Ethnic Entrepreneurship: Structure and Process*, Elsevier, Oxford.

38 Small Business Service (2003) *A Strategic Framework for Women's Enterprise*, Small Business Service, DTI, London.

39 Competition Commission (2002) *A Report on the Supply of Banking Services by Clearing Banks to Small and Medium-sized Enterprises within the UK*, Competition Commission Report, DTI, London (Cm 5319).

40 ESRC Centre for Business Research (1992–2002) *The State of British Enterprise, Reports*, Department of Applied Economics, University of Cambridge, Cambridge.

41 Smallbone, D., Ram, M., Deakins, D. and Baldock, R. (2001) 'Access to Finance by Ethnic Minority

Businesses in the UK', *International Small Business Journal*, vol. 21, no. 3, pp. 291–314.

42 Deakins, D., Graham, L., Sullivan, R. and Whittam, G. (1997) *New Venture Support: An Analysis of Mentoring Provision for New Entrepreneurs*, Paisley Enterprise Research Centre, University of Paisley.

43 DTI (1994) *An Evaluation of the Small Firms Merit Award for Research and Technology (SMART)*, DTI, London.

44 National Association of Mutual Guarantee Schemes (1997) *Mutual Guarantee Schemes: An Overview*, NAMGS paper, Altrincham.

45 Hughes, A. and Leube, B. (1997) 'The Extent and Nature of Mutual Guarantee Schemes in Europe', paper presented to the ESRC Seminar Group on Finance of Small 7:55 PM 5/17/2005l Firms, Durham.

Sources of Venture Finance

Learning Outcomes

At the end of this chapter you should be able to:

1 discuss the nature of the equity gap for small firms' finance

2 describe the differences between formal and informal venture capital

3 discuss the nature of the formal venture capital industry

4 discuss the potential of business angels for closing the equity gap for small firms' finance

5 describe the process of a venture finance investment

6 advise an entrepreneur on requirements of venture capital companies, if seeking venture finance.

■ ■ ■ ■ Introduction

As the previous chapter makes clear, the bulk of academic and policy discussions regarding small firm finance have tended to concentrate on the firm's ability to access bank debt; or, to rephrase, the extent to which small firms are 'debt rationed'.[1] This is as it should be. Studies invariably conclude that, where such funding is sought, banks are significantly the most important source of external finance for the SME sector.[2] The most recent Cambridge University survey,[3] for instance, reported that around 79 per cent of sample firms approached banks for finance during the period 1997–99 (of which, 89 per cent were successful in accessing at least some funds), while, in contrast, less than 7.2 per cent of firms sought access to venture capital over the same period (of which a remarkable 59 per cent were, at least partially, successful).

However, notwithstanding the dominance of banks as a potential source of finance – indeed, in many respects, as a result of it – there has been growing concern over the shortage of long-term risk capital, or equity, within the financial structure of many small firms.[4] Reliance upon bank debt to fund start-up or growth and development, may give rise to a number of problems. Among the most obvious of these is the imposed short-termism. Debt capital is not patient capital and term loans rarely exceed three to five years. However, perhaps more importantly, debt capital is seldom committed capital. As discussed in the previous chapter, debt may be secured (against either the business's or the owner's assets) and requires periodic repayment of interest and ultimate payment of the principal. This places the firm in an extremely exposed position in the event of a slump in sales or other pressures on profitability and, crucially, cash flow. In situations where firms default on debt repayments, and as a last resort, banks may either repossess assets or force the company into receivership (after government, banks have 'first call' on the assets of insolvent firms). Accordingly, and at least for those firms with significant growth potential, commentators argue that patient and committed risk capital, the returns to which will be contingent upon the success of the business, is more appropriately required.

The idea that there exists an 'equity gap', or deficiency in the provision of smaller amounts of risk capital, is not new. The inability of UK small firms to access small-scale risk capital for either start-up or business development has been widely accepted since at least the 1931 Macmillan report,[5] and thereafter, in government terms, the 1971 Bolton report,[6] the 1979 Wilson report[7] and the 1989 Williams report.[8] This gap has traditionally been thought to fall somewhere between the resources that may realistically be provided by private individuals (such as the entrepreneur, family, friends and associates) and the capital required for stock market flotation (though this is clearly very wide, and a 'new equity gap' of between £50,000 and £500,000 is now more commonly recognised). Accordingly, it is with reference to the amelioration of equity gaps, that the current chapter seeks to outline the potential and actual role played by venture capital.

■ ■ ■ ■ The Nature of Venture Capital

So, what is venture capital? As the name suggests, it is capital that clearly involves a degree of risk. However, more specifically, venture capital may be defined, generically, as financial investment in *unquoted* companies, which have significant growth potential, with a view to yielding substantial capital gains in line with the additional risk and illiquidity of an investment, which cannot be freely traded during the lifetime of the investor's commitment to the business. Moreover, venture capital is thought to

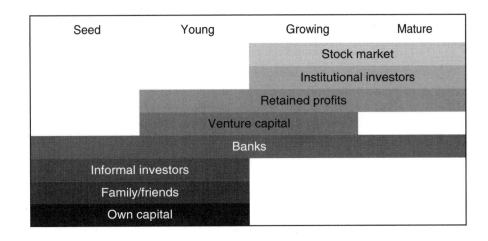

Seed	Young	Growing	Mature

Stock market

Institutional investors

Retained profits

Venture capital

Banks

Informal investors

Family/friends

Own capital

Figure 5.1: *Stage Model of Finance*
Source: Adapted from Netherlands, Ministry of Economic Affairs 1999

provide the bridge between the levels of capital that may be provided by the founder, their family and friends, and private investors – which is often exhausted at the prototype or 'proof-of-concept' and start-up stages (if a technology-based entrepreneur) – and the significant amounts required for a stock market listing and to attract large-scale institutional investments (Figure 5.1).

Classic venture capital assists young and growing firms with the potential for significant future growth, and is frequently a complement to debt finance. However, venture capital is fundamentally equity orientated. As Mason and Harrison[9] note:

The objective [of venture capital] is to achieve a high return on the investment in the form of capital gain through an exit, achieved by the sale of the equity stake rather than through [interest or] dividend income. Exit is normally achieved either through an initial public offering (IPO), involving the flotation of the company on a stock market where its shares are traded freely, or through a trade sale in which the venture capital fund, normally along with all the other shareholders in the company, sell out to another company. (p. 15)

Within this broad framework, a number of 'types' of venture capital are commonly identified, as described below.

■ Institutional venture capital (or formal venture capital) – investments in entrepreneurial ventures by firms of full-time professionals who raise finance from pension funds, banks, insurance companies and other financial institutions.

■ Informal venture capital (or business angel finance) – investments by wealthy private individuals who are prepared to use their financial resources to make risk investments based upon their experience and interests. Business angels are often retired senior executives of large companies, or entrepreneurs who have sold their companies and now wish to use the money.

■ Corporate venture capital (or corporate venturing) – minority investments made by large companies in smaller enterprises for a principally strategic (such as gaining a window on new technologies) rather than an exclusively financial motive. As McNally[10] notes, '[t]he combination of a small firm's know-how, inventive efficiency and flexibility and a larger firm's financial, production, marketing and distribution resources can provide opportunities for synergies that can contribute to both firms' competitive advantage' (p. 16).

■ Public-sector venture capital – while government plays a role in encouraging private-sector venture capital – through policy instruments such as the Enterprise Investment Scheme or offering (primarily, capital gains) tax incentives – it may, more occasionally, act more directly as a provider of venture finance. The most visible examples of such direct public-sector activities, during the 1970s and 1980s, included the investment arms of the Scottish and Welsh Development Agencies.[11] However, the trend is emphatically towards hybrid, public–private partnerships.[12] In such cases (e.g. the new Regional Venture Capital Funds, to which the English Regional Development Associations contribute), private- and public-sector capital is pooled, though fund management is undertaken along private sector (institutional) lines and follows a largely commercial imperative, rather than being bound by exclusively social or welfare considerations. Nonetheless, such funds aim at filling 'gaps', or alleviating deficiencies, in mainstream venture capital provision, by ensuring a more even spatial distribution of activity, or by directing a larger proportion of the fund towards higher-risk, early-stage and high-technology investments.

However, despite the growth in public-sector and corporate venturing, these 'types' of venture capital still account for a relatively small proportion of private-sector equity investments. The bulk of investment activity remains the province of institutional venture capitalists and business angels. Accordingly, these latter two form the basis of the current chapter.

Clearly, to the extent that it involves equity investment in smaller firms with a view to capital gain, venture capital is not a new phenomenon. Throughout history, wealthy private individuals have frequently invested in smaller enterprises or ventures, sharing part of the risk, in return for a share in the outcome. However, in its formal, institutional guise, venture capital is largely a contemporary phenomenon, dating from the post-Second War period.[13; 14] In the United States, the genesis of the institutional venture capital industry is typically traced to the founding of American Research and Development Corporation (ARD) in 1946 and, in the UK, the founding of the Industrial and Commercial Finance Corporation (ICFC, now renamed 3i plc) by the Bank of England and the major clearing banks, in 1945. In both instances, these were probably the first firms, as opposed to individuals, dedicated to providing risk capital to new and potentially super-growth firms, principally in manufacturing or technology-based sectors. However, contrary to popular mythology, neither US industry nor, as is generally accepted, UK industry experienced much growth until considerably later. As Timmons[15] observes, 'the [US] venture capital industry did not experience a growth spurt until the 1980s, when the industry "went ballistic" – rising from approximately $0.5 billion, in 1977, to just over $4 billion in 1987' (pp. 441–3). Similarly, in the UK, venture capital investments rose from £66 million, in 163 companies, to £1.65 billion, in 1569 companies, over the period 1981–89.[16] However, notwithstanding the lag in activity, these early progenitors effectively established the 'rules of the game', which have served to determine the 'shape' of independent venture capital firms on both sides of the Atlantic. That is, in common with many of the more successful early venture capital firms, the dominant contemporary legal form is of a limited partnership.[a] Specifically, venture capital funds usually comprise a management

---

[a] Though, as a matter of historical interest, ARD, as a result of institutional investor reluctance, was structured as a publicly traded, closed-end fund and marketed mostly to individuals.

company (whose directors are the general partners), which raises risk capital from financial institutions (the limited partners). The key issue here, however, is that venture capital firms are essentially intermediaries in the venture capital process (Figure 5.2).

As Figure 5.2 makes clear, the use and economic impact of venture capital is likely to be a function of a number of underlying supply- and demand-side framework conditions. On the demand side, it is clear that the flow of good entrepreneurial projects, allied to a willingness to share equity, is a necessary element of a successful venture capital system. This in turn is likely to be a function of the education and innovation systems, and of the prevailing culture in society, and will be facilitated, or hindered, by institutional framework conditions, such as the nature and level of taxation, legislation and regulation. On the supply side, the flow of venture capital funds will be determined by, among other things, the efficiency of financial markets and the availability of alternative investment opportunities, investor attitudes towards risk and return, the taxation system and the growth prospects of the economy as a whole. It is worth noting, however, that the relative efficacy of demand and supply mechanisms is not independent. It is surely no coincidence that those economies with comparatively low institutional barriers to entrepreneurship tend also to have relatively

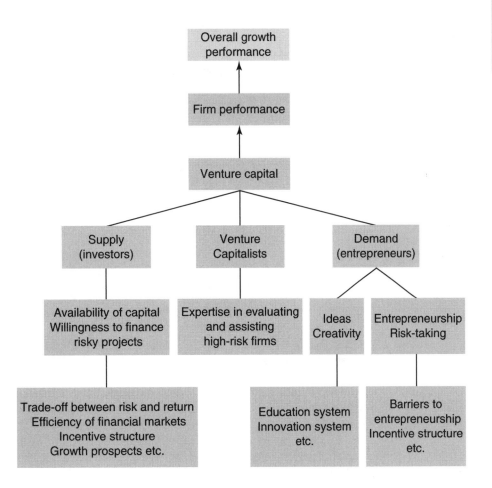

Figure 5.2: *The Nature of Venture Capital*
Source: Adapted from Baygan and Freudenberg[17]

more active venture capital industries and vice versa.[17] Countries with high-level venture capital activity and low barriers to entrepreneurship include the USA, the UK, Canada and Sweden. By contrast, countries such as France, Italy, Austria and Switzerland tend to have lower levels of venture capital activity and relatively higher barriers to entrepreneurship.

Notwithstanding the potential negative association between venture capital activity and barriers to entrepreneurship, the role of venture capitalists per se remains the same – that is, as intermediaries. In this model of the system, venture capitalists bring expertise in evaluating, assisting and monitoring high-risk firms. Entrepreneurs are in want of capital and investors are in want of expertise and knowledge. Venture capital firms encourage the former and provide the latter. In particular, their *raison d'être* concerns the ability to reduce the costs of information asymmetries (see below). As Amit *et al*.[18] note:

Venture capitalists operate in environments where their relative efficiency in selecting and monitoring investments gives them a comparative advantage over other investors . . . [accordingly] . . . Venture capitalists should be prominent in industries where informational concerns are important, such as biotechnology, computer software, etc., rather than in 'routine' start-ups such as restaurants, retail outlets, etc. The latter are risky, in that returns show high variance, but they are relatively easy to monitor by conventional financial intermediaries. (p. 441)

So venture capital firms attenuate information asymmetries (i.e. reduce the costs of incomplete information), providing, as a minimum, finance and assistance to firms and expertise to investors. But, to what end? As Figure 5.2 intimates, the general supposition holds that the involvement of venture capitalists will lead to the superior performance of investee firms and, ultimately, to growth in the economy as a whole. Indeed, studies undertaken on behalf of the venture capital associations in the USA and Europe have noted that VC-backed companies outperform *Fortune* 500/FT-Excel 500 companies in terms of employment growth, exports and investment.[16; 17] It should be noted, however, that since only firms with demonstrable growth potential are likely to received VC backing, this finding is perhaps less remarkable than it appars at first glance. Nevertheless, the European Venture Capital Association[9] describes venture capital-supported companies as 'engines for our economies' (p. 2).

■ ■ ■ ■ The Scale and Scope of Venture Capital

Now that we understand a little about the nature of venture capital, the next questions one might ask are: 'How much is there?', 'Where does it come from?' and 'Where does it go?' That is, what is the scale and scope of venture capital activity?

Table 5.1 provides a partial answer to the first of these questions for a number of European economies. After growing substantially in the closing years of the last century (with a particular surge from 1998–2000) the amounts invested peaked in 2000 and have declined rapidly since (though they are still above mid-1990 levels). Moreover, as the table makes clear, in absolute terms, the United Kingdom dominates European venture capital activity, followed, at some distance, by Germany and France. Venture capital activity in Europe, however, lags some considerable distance behind that in the United States. In 2000, for instance, funds invested in the USA were over five times total European investments.[19] Given the historical make-up of the financial systems within these countries, this is not surprising. Tylecote,[20] for instance, distinguishes between different capital market regimes. In historically 'stock exchange-based'

Table 5.1: *Total Private Equity/Venture Capital Investment (EUR million)*

	2000	2001	2002	2003
Denmark	€ 285.05	€ 282.25	€ 219.19	€ 169.24
France	€ 2,592.09	€ 1,592.65	€ 722.89	€ 465.28
Germany	€ 3,312.71	€ 2,008.62	€ 676.89	€ 539.02
Ireland	€ 716.30	€ 403.27	€ 214.29	€ 118.60
Sweden	€ 1,831.47	€ 1,180.07	€ 496.46	€ 325.30
Switzerland	€ 639.19	€ 400.28	€ 260.51	€ 171.00
UK	€ 7,368.78	€ 3,186.12	€ 1,602.47	€ 1,091.53
Other European	€ 5,289.39	€ 1,890.17	€ 765.92	€ 524.63

Source: Dow Jones, VentureOne and Ernest & Young

economies (such as the USA and the UK), larger firms look to the stock market as a major source of equity and investment. Accordingly, banks play only a limited role in providing risk capital 'since their lending is *transactional* rather than relational' (p. 262). Each loan is considered a one-off, secured against collateral or against the scrap value of the firm's assets. In these economies, venture capital is viewed as an alternative source of risk for those firms that cannot bear the transaction costs associated with a market listing. By contrast, in 'bank-based' economies (e.g. Germany and Japan), comparatively few firms are 'listed' on the stock exchange and the market is not considered a major source of funds. Rather, firms rely on private (or occasionally state) banks as the principal source of external finance. Loans are no longer of a one-off nature and lending is relational rather than transactional:[20] 'seen as part of a long-term relationship in which the firm is bound to inform the bank fully as to its position and prospects and the bank is committed to support the firm through bad times, in return for influence over its policy and personnel' (p. 262).[b] In such instances, banks become adept at managing or alleviating information asymmetries and the opportunities for venture capitalists are limited.

However, this historical distinction between stock exchange and bank-based financial systems has become somewhat blurred. For instance, many economies, formerly classed as 'bank-based' (such as Germany), have begun a drift towards occupying some middle ground between bank- and stock exchange-based systems (as evidenced by the prospective takeover of the London Stock Exchange by either the Deutsche Börse or Euronext – itself a merger of the Dutch, Belgian and French exchanges – and the growth in venture capital activity throughout Continental Europe;[9] while UK banks, for instance, would undoubtedly argue that they have made a shift towards relationship-based, rather than transaction-based lending. However, the figures still point to more vigorous venture capital activity in the UK and the USA. However, if one controls for the size of the respective economies (see Figure 5.3), the

---

[b] This argument is given *in extremis*.

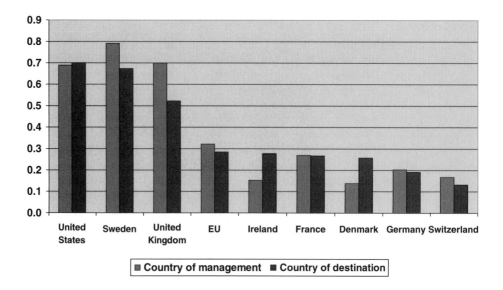

Figure 5.3: *Private Equity and Venture Capital Investment as a % of GDP (1999–2001)*
Source: OECD

gap between the USA and the UK is considerably reduced and these 'top' performers are joined by Sweden. Indeed, the data in Figure 5.3 point to higher funds under management in Sweden than in either the UK or the USA. Moreover, though not shown in Figure 5.3, other northern European economies (notably Iceland and the Netherlands) also record higher than average venture capital activity as a proportion of GDP. Disappointingly, however, aggregate VC investment in Europe is less than half that in the USA. Recognition of this deficiency led the Committee of Wise Men to:

urge governments and the European institutions to pay particular attention to ensuring that there is an appropriate environment for the development of the supply of risk capital for growing small and medium sized companies, given the crucial importance of this sector for job creation.[21]

Yet, notwithstanding international comparisons, the figures paint a picture of a fairly buoyant venture capital market in the UK, if less so in Europe as a whole. But where does the capital come from? As Figure 5.4 indicates, the bulk of 'tracked' private equity, or formal venture capital, is raised from large institutional investors – primarily pension funds, banks and insurance companies. Typically, venture capital represents only a small proportion of the portfolio of investments held by these funds and is, in this sense, a peripheral activity. Provided that these investors are holding diversified portfolios they will not be worried about the idiosyncratic risks of a single project, but only how the risk of the project contributes to the risk of their overall portfolio. Accordingly, the promise of very high returns offered by VC-backed companies may prove to be an attractive investment opportunity, for a limited proportion of the total fund, set against the risk-return profile of their other investments. Murray[4] notes that, even during the boom years of the late 1980s, the amount invested in venture capital was consistently less than 1 per cent of annual institutional investment in the UK. Moreover, he argues, '[t]his plausibly explains why most institutional investors are prepared to allow independent venture capital companies to manage their limited

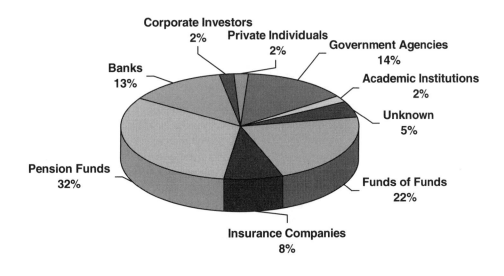

Figure 5.4: *UK Private Equity by Source in 2003*
Source: BVCA Report on Investment Activity 2003 (2004)

exposure to this specialist activity rather than bringing the investment responsibility in-house' (p. 139).

In contrast to institutional investors, academic institutions, government, private individuals and corporate investors make a limited contribution to 'visible', or formal, venture capital activity. Though, in the case of corporate investors and private individuals, the data in Figure 5.4 undoubtedly under-represents their contribution. Corporate investors, for instance, often invest directly, while the greater proportion of investments by private individuals is 'informal', and indeed invisible, and so not covered by the methodology of the EVCA.

Finally, in this section, we turn to the destination of venture capital finance or, more specifically, the types of investment that are made. Typically, five broad types, or stages, of investment are distinguished,[22] as follows.

1. Seed financing – Aims to facilitate pre-market development of a business concept. It is an investment made very early in the business development cycle and is frequently concerned with research and development, the manufacture of prototypes, or business planning and market research activities prior to bringing a product to the market and commencing large-scale production. This is often called 'proof-of-concept' funding.

2. Start-up financing – Investment in those firms that have made few, if any, commercial sales. However, product development and market research activities are complete and funding is required to support initial production and marketing activities.

3. Expansion finance – Capital provided to support the growth and development of an established company. Occasionally commentators discern a further three substages within the broad heading of expansion finance: *first stage* (when a firm has begun trading but requires further capital to materially increase production); *second stage* (when additional finance is required to increase production capacity and expand into new markets);

mezzanine finance (which seeks to provide further expansion or working capital with a view to an initial public offering).

4. Replacement capital – The provision of finance[22] 'to allow existing non-venture capital investors to buy back or redeem part, or all, of another investor's shareholding' (p. 18).

5. Buy-in/buy-out finance – Management buy-out (MBO) finance is provided to enable the current operating management to acquire a significant shareholding in the firm they manage. By contrast, management buy-in (MBI) finance enables managers from outside the company to buy into it. A less frequent occurrence, in this category, is the curiously named buy-in management buy-out (BIMBO), which allows the incumbent management to purchase the business they manage with the assistance of some incoming management.

Figure 5.5 illustrates the distribution of investment funds and investments among these stages for the UK. As the graph makes clear, the vast majority of venture capital is directed towards later-stage financing. Indeed, recent European figures suggest that the trend is increasingly towards fewer, larger and later-stage (principally buy-out) investments (see www.evca.com). Given that information asymmetries, associated costs and risks are likely to be reduced in situations where firms have an established track record this is unsurprising. Moreover, and notwithstanding our belief in the ability of venture capitalists to more efficiently manage information asymmetries, one would anticipate that,[18]

they will still prefer projects where monitoring and selection costs are relatively low or where the costs of information asymmetries are less severe. Thus, within a given industry where venture capitalists would be expected to focus, we would expect [them] to favour firms with some track records over pure start-ups. (p. 441)

Furthermore, it is known that the transaction costs of venture investments are proportionately higher for smaller projects.[23] Thus, we would expect a higher

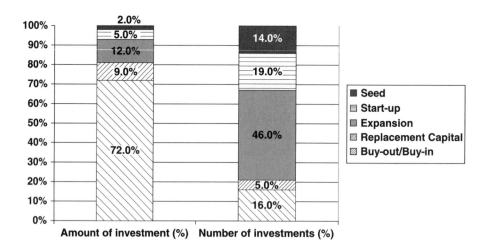

Figure 5.5: *Stage Distribution of UK Investments in 2003*
Source: BVCA Report on Investment Activity 2003 (2004)

proportion of funds and of deals to be directed to larger-scale expansion or buy-out projects. Yet, despite the logic of these trends, a number of concerns are rightly raised. In particular, a number of recent publications[24; 25; 26] have highlighted the special problems faced by small high- and new-technology-based firms in accessing appropriate venture finance. The general consensus holds that,[25]

The distinctive requirement of technology-based firms at seed, start-up and early stage is for genuine risk capital. Amounts required may be relatively small, but investment horizons may be long . . . Classic venture capital *should provide part of the answer, but the industry in the United Kingdom has tended to focus less on early stage investments (especially in technology) and more on development capital and MBOs/MBIs. (p. 6)*

Another concern, hinted at in the second line of the above quote, relates to the typical size of VC investments. In general, due to the disproportionate burden of transaction costs, very few venture capitalists are willing to invest less than £500,000, while the average investment is often in excess of £1 million.[27] Indeed, in 2003 the average amount invested in the UK was £3.198 million. Undoubtedly, this bald figure is skewed by a few extremely large later-stage investments. Nonetheless, the average early-stage investment was still over £600,000. Clearly, a predilection for investments of this scale necessarily excludes many promising small and early-stage entrepreneurial firms. From a supply-side perspective, this is believed to be the basis of the new equity gap discussed earlier.

One proffered solution to these observed deficiencies in institutional venture capital provision saw the launch, in the Finance Act 1995, of Venture Capital Trusts (VCTs). VCTs are quoted companies that aim to encourage investment in smaller, unlisted (unquoted and AiM-quoted companies) UK companies by offering private investors tax incentives on funds up to £100,000 in return for a five-year investment commitment. Certain types of activity, or 'qualifying firms', are ineligible for investment under the scheme. Generally, these activities are similar to those excluded under the Enterprise Investment Scheme (EIS) and, most notably, include land and property development. However, it is not yet clear to what extent VCTs may address the bias towards expansion and buy-in/buy-out finance. One other potential solution may be provided by the informal venture capital market. That is, as commentators have increasingly suggested, business angels may, in this context, be effective 'gap funders'.[28] Accordingly, we return to the role of informal investors later in this chapter.

Asymmetric Information, Adverse Selection, Moral Hazard and Venture Capital

Although we have already discussed the nature and implications of asymmetric information, adverse selection and moral hazard in relation to bank finance (and for a discussion in relation to debt finance see Chapter 4), there are additional implications for venture finance. We have already noted a general belief in the function of venture capitalists as managers or attenuators of information asymmetries. Indeed, this viewpoint is fairly well established in the academic literature.[18; 29; 30] Accordingly, it is worth briefly outlining what we mean by information asymmetry and its implications for the venture capital investment process. This can be compared with our discussion on the implications for bankers in the previous chapter.

In the economics literature, the classic exposition of the effects of information asymmetry on market efficiencies probably dates from Akerlof's[31] example of the market for used cars. In this illustration, sellers of used cars have private information about the quality of the cars they are selling, which is not available, *ex ante*, to potential buyers. Accordingly, as a result of the opportunistic behaviour of some sellers, poor-quality cars (or lemons, as Akerlof terms them) dominate, and the market selects 'adversely'. In other words, buyers demonstrate a preference for potentially not buying a good car rather than potentially buying a lemon. In this situation, the market collapses and few deals are done.

Adverse selection problems of this kind are likely to arise in most real-world contracting situations and, in the current context, it is generally held that, 'without such financial intermediaries [i.e. specialist venture capital firms], the market would tend to fail. This is because relatively poorly informed investors who were drawn into bad projects ("lemons") would subsequently cease to provide venture capital finance'.[30] In venture capital contracting relations, the investee firm is liable to have information not readily available to the potential investors. Moreover, firms have a clear incentive to 'talk up' or provide an optimistic view of their business history, current position or project potential.[32] On the other hand, investors may find it prohibitively costly to determine the true nature of these. This is often characterised as a problem of 'hidden information' and, it is suggested, venture capital firms are sufficiently experienced and specialised in such high-risk investments to be able to cope with, or reduce, information asymmetries of this type. However, this is by no means to suggest that venture capitalists eliminate the potential for adverse selection. Indeed, since the proportionate costs of 'due diligence' (i.e. gathering the requisite information about a potential investee firm) are generally believed to be inversely related to firm size and age, adverse selection may still persist in the market for seed, start-up and early-stage investments. This, in turn, may partly explain the observed preference for later-stage, and larger-scale, expansion and buy-out/buy-in financing. Nonetheless, the key issue is that venture capitalists serve to reduce the *ex ante* information asymmetries that lead to adverse selection and ameliorate the problems of 'hidden information', which may deter institutional investors from direct involvement in venture capital activity.

As also discussed in Chapter 4, information asymmetries commonly occur *ex post*. Here, the general idea is that the (partial) separation of ownership and control creates scope for moral hazard. A firm that is insured, in part, against the risk of failure, through the sale of equity, may alter its behaviour in such a way as to act to the detriment of investors. To use the jargon of economics, the firm (agent) will seek to maximise its own utility irrespective of whether or not this coincides with the maximisation of the investor's (principal's) utility. This, in turn, leads to higher agency costs, as the investor firm is required to supervise and monitor the activities of the investee firm. At this point, agency problems (and the requisite agency costs) are thought to be highest when the level of *ex ante* information asymmetry is high (as noted above), when the agent has the incentive and ability to affect the distribution of income streams and when partial ownership permits agents to consume firm resources/assets at a lower cost than their value to the firm and/or the investor.[33] Such a situation commonly marks the small firm–investor relationship. While the notion of adverse selection is fairly unproblematic (associated with problems of 'hidden information'), we may more clearly term moral hazard an 'asymmetry of interests' associating them with problems of 'hidden actions'.[34; 35] Moreover, high agency costs inevitably lead to higher direct and indirect funding costs for the innovative small firm. That is, institutional investors are likely to require a greater equity holding from small firms than from large, for a proportionately similar investment. One commonly suggested means to mitigate moral hazard, or minimise agency costs, is through staged investment, which creates the option to abandon the project and provides an incentive for the entrepreneurial firm to act 'appropriately'. In addition, syndication (i.e. co-ordinated investment by two or more venture capitalists) may be a further means to reducing the problems caused by information asymmetries.[36] Nonetheless, the most common means of reducing moral hazard is through tightly specified contracts, though clearly these are costly to enforce. Again, however, the key issue is that venture capitalists are better placed to manage *ex post* information asymmetries than the institutional investors they represent.

■ ■ ■ ■ ■ The Investment Process

Before outlining a 'typical' investment process, to the extent that such a thing exists, it is worth reiterating the low levels of venture capital use in the small firm sector generally (studies invariably put the figure at between 2 and 4 per cent of firms). This, in itself, is hardly remarkable. Since we know that very few firms enjoy significant growth,[2] only a small number of firms will, in turn, represent sufficiently attractive investment opportunities to venture capitalists. Moreover, research suggests that venture capital firms[9] 'are seeking companies that can provide an internal rate of return of at least 30% in the case of established companies, rising to 60% or more for seed and start-up investments' (p. 15). Accordingly, it is likely that many of the best projects will eschew venture capital as too costly, choosing instead to leverage longer-term debt. For instance, it is suggested that, in addition to allowing individual entrepreneurs to maintain control, the acceptance of debt may act as a positive market signal[34; 37; 38; 39] – that is,[34] 'high-quality managers [of high-quality projects] will signal their quality by choosing a capital structure involving a large percentage of debt, that will not be copied by the low-quality manager' (p. 321). This debt cannot be assumed without a high degree of confidence in the profitability of the project and the ability of the firm to make periodic repayments. Further, acceptance of debt may also signal the entrepreneur's unwillingness to share in the expected gains from any investment. In part, the extent to which the requirement for returns in excess of 30 per cent acts as a disincentive to seek venture capital may point to an additional asymmetry to those discussed above: an 'asymmetry of expectations'. Indeed, this asymmetry of expectations may go to the heart of the debate regarding the extent to which 'equity gaps' are demand- or supply-side phenomena. As Moore and Garnsey[35] note, there exists a clearly established 'expectations gap between the owners of firms and venture capitalists, in terms of the scale of returns required and the size of the equity stake demanded' (p. 509).

However, notwithstanding the relative peripherality of venture capital, a growing number of (high growth potential) firms are thought to be seeking it. Yet, of these firms, a very small proportion of applications that are assessed ever gain access to capital; and this does not include the great many applications that are not given more than the most cursory screening. For instance, a recent study of the Midlands Enterprise Fund[40] noted that, of 206 applications assessed, only three investments were made – i.e. an investment ratio of 1.46 per cent. While this fund was particularly specialised, in having both economic development and commercial imperatives, investment ratios of this magnitude are fairly standard. Accordingly, it is important that we have an appreciation of the process by which venture capitalists decide which projects to fund and which to discard.

To this end, a number of studies have sought to delineate the investment cycle, invariably describing it as a sequential process of between five and ten steps.[41; 42; 43] However, at the risk of oversimplifying things, these have largely served to extend Tybejee and Bruno's[44] early work, and have been broadly faithful to its essence. Tybejee and Bruno outline an ordered process, comprising five key steps: deal

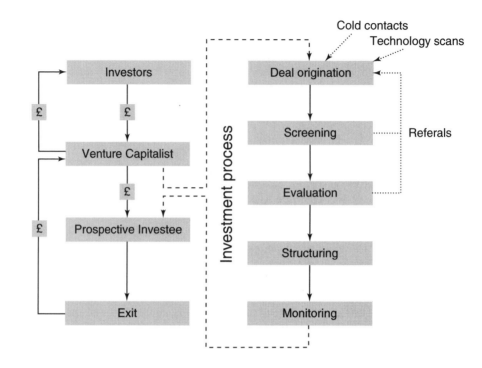

Figure 5.6: *The Venture Capital Process*

origination; screening; evaluation; deal structuring; and monitoring or post-investment activities,[44] as illustrated in Figure 5.6.

We will now look at each of these five steps in detail.

1. Deal origination – Prospective investments may come from a number of sources, including unsolicited applications and technology scans. However, the most common means are either through an intermediary or by referral from another financial institution.

2. Screening – It is common to further subdivide this step – for example, into venture capital specific and generic screening.[43] However, the essence is much the same. Screening consists of an examination of the business plan in an attempt to identify features that warrant further investigation. Rather worryingly, UK studies[45] have suggested that the average first reading time for an application is between 10 and 15 minutes.

3. Evaluation – In the first instance, this stage is likely to comprise a series of meetings between the venture capitalist and the managers/directors of the applicant firm. Thereafter, and crucially, due diligence is undertaken. As a minimum, this is likely to include: a thorough analysis of the financial viability of the proposition and the accuracy, or appropriateness, of financial projections; credit searches on the company and its owners; an appraisal of the firm's operating history.

4. Structuring – Having decided, in principle, to invest, this stage involves negotiations over the nature of the investment. At its simplest, the issue may be thought of as 'How much equity for how much money?' However, the

provision of third-party equity is usually only one element in the final deal. Additional sources of finance may also include secured and unsecured debt from banks, loan notes, and various convertible instruments. Clearly, this is liable to be the most sensitive stage in the investment process, as entrepreneurs become anxious over perceived inequities.

5. Monitoring – According to Boocock and Wood[40] 'One of the characteristics of venture finance is an *active* interest in the performance of investee companies . . . a combination of capital and consulting' (pp. 40–2, emphasis added). In general, as an agency problem, the emphasis is on effective communication and the flow of information. In this circumstance, the venture capitalist normally takes a non-executive seat on the board. However, more occasionally, the VC may assume a more 'hands-on' approach, where this course of action is deemed necessary.

The above process lays out, in simple terms, the role of venture capitalists in identifying, appraising, investing in, and subsequently monitoring and advising on business projects. It also makes clear the various points at which investment decisions are made. For instance, Murray[4] notes that approximately 80 per cent of applications are rejected at the initial screening stage, often for tangible reasons associated with the size of investment, or the industry or activity; although in the Boocock and Wood study,[40] 31 per cent of rejections were as a result of an 'incomplete plan'. Further rejections are likely to occur as a result of due diligence – finding 'skeletons in the closet' – or the inability to settle upon an agreed deal structure. For obvious reasons, though, rejections become less common as the investment process progresses. Notwithstanding this, the general objective of the process is to pare down the many applications to a few attractive investment opportunities.

Yet something is clearly missing from the preceding description. Though not part of the 'investment process' as outlined in Figure 5.6, *exit* is plainly an integral part of the venture capital process as a whole. As earlier discussions have made clear, the objective of the venture capitalist is to realise a capital gain through the sale of equity, rather than through interest or dividend income. The ultimate necessity of exit shapes every aspect of the venture capital decision-making process, from the sorts of investments made[46] to the amounts and timing of capital committed. Accordingly, some brief comments seem appropriate. To this end, it is common practice to identify five principal exit routes,[47] as follows.

1. *Initial Public Offering (IPO)* – In an IPO, the firm offers shares for sale to public investors. While the venture capitalist will ordinarily not offer all (or even part) of its equity stake immediately, common convention still holds an IPO as a form of exit, since it inevitably presages a full exit at some future date.

2. *Trade sale* – Sometimes known as an 'acquisition exit', in a trade sale the *entire* firm is sold to a third party. The purchaser is typically a business entity that is in the same, or similar, business to the selling firm (e.g. a competitor, supplier or customer). Following acquisition, the purchasing firm may choose to integrate the purchased firm into its own business, or allow continued operational independence in order to preserve the factors responsible for past successes. In either case, strategic access to products, markets or technologies is the primary motivation for the transaction.

3. *Secondary sale* – A secondary sale differs from a trade sale in that only the venture capitalist sells to a third party. The entrepreneur(s) and other investors retain their stakes in the venture. Frequently, this involves selling to

another venture capitalist, where the purchaser exhibits greater confidence in the prospects of the venture, or believes that it can bring greater technological familiarity or a more relevant set of skills to bear. Alternatively, the purchaser may be a strategic acquirer (as above), seeking a window on the firm's technology, often with a view to 100 per cent acquisition at some later date.

4. *Buyback/MBO* – In a buyback, the entrepreneur(s) or management team will repurchase the shares held by the venture capitalist. In some instances, this will be prompted by the exercise of contractual rights ceded to the venture capitalist at the time of the initial investment. Such rights may include the power to 'put' its shares to the entrepreneur(s) after a stated period of time, or if certain performance targets are not met (e.g. the failure to go public).

5. *Write-off* – A write-off takes place when the venture capitalist walks away from its investment. Usually this will involve the failure of the investee company, and is sometimes equated with insolvency or bankruptcy. However, occasionally the venture capitalist may continue to hold shares in a barely profitable enterprise.

Figure 5.7 outlines recent patterns of venture capital divestments (i.e. exits) for the UK. Given the headlines devoted to it in the late 1990s, it is perhaps surprising that IPOs account for as little as one-quarter of divestment activity (including sales of quoted equity), by amount, and considerably less as a proportion of the number of exits (1 per cent if only 'true' IPOs are considered). Importantly, write-offs constitute around one-sixth of divestments by both amount and number of exits. Indeed, European data (www.evca.com) would seem to suggest that the recent trend is away from IPOs and trade sales and towards secondary sales and write-offs (though this may be a partial function of the economic downturn and poor capital market conditions that marked 2001 and 2002 in particular).

Beyond these external factors, the choice of exit strategy is influenced by a variety of other concerns, including the company's financial performance and stage of

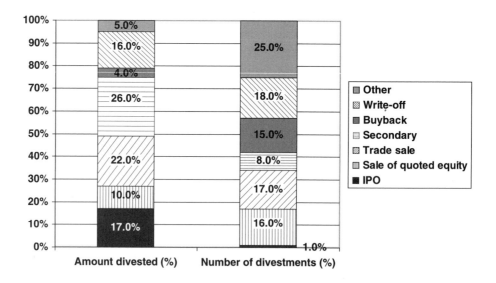

Figure 5.7: *UK Divestments in 2003*

development, industry and capital market condition, the venture capitalist's reputation, and the profile of partners in the venture capital syndicate.[48] However, just as the venture capitalist brings expertise to bear on the investment decision, and upon subsequent monitoring and assistance, so the venture capitalist exercises judgement in relation to the exit decision:[47] 'determining *when* and by *what means* and for *what consideration* the investment will be exited' (p. 8) – subject to prevailing constraints.

While the foregoing gives an idea of *when* the investment decision occurs, given low investment rates, it is important to also understand *why* the decision to invest is made, or not. To this end, a myriad of criteria are invariably identified by academic studies, many of which correspond with those employed by banks to assess lending proposals (see Chapter 4). On the whole, the approach tends to emphasise the balance between negative risk factors and positive return factors.[44] Specifically, these may include the attractiveness of the proposed market, the intended company strategy (e.g. level of product differentiation, existence of proprietary product), the size and stage of investment, the investors' technological or product market familiarity, the entrepreneur's own commitment, and the geographic location of the venture. However, as Murray[4] notes, there has been a surprising degree of convergence among the many academic studies in this area. To illustrate, he quotes MacMillan *et al.*,[49] such that:

There is no question that irrespective of the horse (product), horse race (market), or odds (financial criteria), it is the jockey (entrepreneur) who fundamentally determines whether the venture capitalist will place the bet at all.

Clearly, certain baseline criteria must be established in respect of the 'horse', 'horse race' and 'odds'. However, the key point is that 'shortcomings of senior management' are the most commonly cited reason for failure in investment applications.

■ ■ ■ ■ Informal Venture Capital and Business Angels

Earlier in the chapter we hinted at the potential role business angels may play as 'gap funders'. That is, there is a generally held belief that,[50]

Business Angels fill the financing gap between founder, family and friends . . . and the stage at which institutional venture capital funds might become interested. Because of their high transaction costs, venture capital funds typically have a high minimum investment size, a minimum efficient overall fund size and a correspondingly restricted number of portfolio companies which can be evaluated, invested in and monitored . . . In the UK there are very few funds that are willing to invest less than £500,000, and the average investment by a venture capital fund in an early stage investment is over £1 million. (p. 137)

Business angels are private, high-net-worth individuals who make direct investments in unquoted companies with which they have no family connection. It has been assumed that the bulk of angels are 'cashed-out' entrepreneurs who seek to act as value-added investors, contributing commercial acumen, contacts and entrepreneurial skills. In this sense, informal venture capital may be thought of as 'smart money'.[51] However, a study of 144 business angels in Scotland found that the majority were not previous entrepreneurs but had careers in large firms and financial institutions.[52] Far more than institutional venture capitalists, business angels adopt a hands-on role providing an array of strategic, monitoring and supporting inputs. Research indicates that entrepreneurs who have raised finance from angels report their most valuable contribution is as a sounding board for management. Moreover, angels invest predominantly at seed and start-up stages and provide relatively small amounts of capital. For instance, while the average investment by a venture capital fund in an early-stage investment is over £1 million, business angels typically invest less than £100,000 (although larger amounts are possible in situations where deals are syndicated). However, given their hands-on involvement, business angels are fairly infrequent investors, managing only a few investments at a time.

Furthermore, it is important to understand that business angels are not philanthropists or altruists. They are motivated, first and foremost, by capital gain – typically in the region of 20 per cent per annum, over the life of the investment, though they may derive some 'psychological income' from being involved with a new business and helping to develop the next generation of entrepreneurs. Given that the primary reason for investing is pecuniary, it is hardly surprising to find that business angels are at least as selective as formal venture capitalists. For instance, one study of Canadian private investors[53] noted that 72.6 per cent of deals were rejected on the basis of 'first impressions', while a further 15.9 per cent were rejected after a detailed reading of the business plan. In other words, a cumulative 88.5 per cent were rejected without ever meeting the principals of the business. Moreover, given similarities in objectives and context, one should anticipate that the investment process would be broadly similar to that utilised in the case of formal venture capital, though perhaps with less attendant bureaucracy in the form of professional advisers and, crucially, over a shorter time frame. Mason and Harrison[51] have suggested that business angels, in deciding whether to invest, are primarily concerned to answer four key questions.

1. Is there a market for the product or service, is it growing and how competitive is it?

2. Will the product or service be competitive? Does it merely represent a 'me-too' product or service?

3. Is the entrepreneurial team credible? What is the experience and expertise of the management team?

4. What is the upside potential of the venture? Relatedly, why is the money being sought and to what use will it be put?

Again, the essence of these questions is not remarkable and simply paraphrases the criteria employed by other investors or providers of external finance. The key issue, however, is the private investor's ability to adequately assess these concerns. That is, since business angels frequently invest in areas where they have prior experience or a declared interest, one may anticipate that they will often be uniquely placed, in the sense of having a comparative advantage, to accurately gauge the potential of a given opportunity.

However, irrespective of process, the consensus holds that private, or informal, investors are the primary source of external equity for new firms (i.e. for those seeking seed or start-up capital). Yet, this axiom relies heavily upon anecdotal evidence and upon speculation or estimation. As noted earlier, the bulk of informal venture capital is invisible and there is simply no way to accurately measure the scale of business angel activity. That is,[51]

Most business angels strive to preserve their anonymity, although some have a high profile. There are no directories which list business angels and there are no public records of their investments. It is therefore impossible to say how many business angels there are, or how much they invest in aggregate. (p. 110)

However, despite these difficulties, attempts have been made to estimate the size of the informal venture capital market. One recent effort[50] extrapolated from the visible proportion of the UK market ('the tip of the iceberg'). This visible proportion is represented by Business Angel Networks (BANs). BANs are essentially intermediary organisations, of which there are currently 48, that seek to reduce inefficiencies in the market by acting as an information conduit, or 'dating agency', bringing investors and entrepreneurs together. Accordingly, and taking BANs as a starting point, these authors estimate that, in 1999, private investors made at least 1800 *early-stage* investments involving a total investment of £220 million. When one contrasts this with the 241 investments, involving a total investment of £228 million, made by venture capital funds in the same period, then the considerable contribution, especially in the provision of smaller amounts of capital, made by business angels becomes clear. Moreover, while the authors admit that the evidence upon which this estimate is based is somewhat 'flimsy', they maintain that, at worst, it is likely to significantly understate the level of business angel activity.

The general implication is that, in situations where entrepreneurs are seeking less than £250,000, they may more appropriately direct their efforts towards the informal venture capital market rather than institutional venture capital funds.

Conclusions

This chapter has sought to outline the role of venture capital, as genuine risk capital, in supporting the start-up and development of high-risk, but high growth potential, new and small firms. Given the higher-levels of information asymmetries, which are invariably associated with higher-risk projects, and the necessarily longer-term investment horizon, it is suggested that the sale of equity, through venture capital intermediaries, may be a more appropriate source of funding than bank debt. This is likely to be particularly true for firms in high- and new-technology-based industries.

However, the chapter also noted the formal venture capitalist's preference for later-stage and larger-scale investments, most especially MBOs/MBIs. In light of the disproportionately high transaction costs associated with investments in smaller and younger firms, this is not in itself remarkable. Yet it has led to the identification, by many, of a 'new equity gap', impacting upon firms seeking relatively small amounts of 'classic' venture capital. In other words, formal venture capitalists are unlikely to be attracted by investments of less than £250,000 in firms with little or no track record, or in emerging but untested technologies. Clearly there is a role for public/private partnerships in ameliorating these concerns, and some positive signals are being sent, most notably by the development of regional venture capital funds in England. However, the 'gap' may more usefully, or more significantly, be met by independent or syndicated private investors, or business angels. Notwithstanding the foregoing, it is important that we recognise that this is not merely a supply-side issue. Many venture capital funds and business angels bemoan the quality of proposals that come their way. Moreover, many entrepreneurs eschew equity funding, viewing it as dissolution of their control. If autonomy was central to the start-up decision this is understandable. However, it is important to educate entrepreneurs that it may be better to own part of an orchard rather than the whole of an apple.

Finally, with respect to the investment decision-making process, we detailed some of the myriad, and logical, factors that influence the investor's judgement. However, we noted the common finding that both venture capital funds and business angels invest, first and foremost, in people.

Review Questions 5.1

1. Review your understanding of the difference between venture finance and debt finance. What is classic venture capital?

2. Why are venture capitalists seen as financial intermediaries?

3. What factors might account for the explosive growth in the venture capital industry in the 1980s and 1990s?

4. How do venture capitalists reduce the costs of information asymmetries?

Review Questions 5.2

1. What amounts of finance can be considered within the size of the equity gap for entrepreneurial small firms seeking to raise venture finance?

2. From the discussion given in this chapter, why do you think that this equity gap arises?

3. What are the main sources of venture finance funds in the UK?

4. Why is the apparent gap between the UK and the USA for venture finance funds not as large as it might appear?

Review Questions 5.3

1. 'There are only ever going to be a small number of firms suitable as venture finance investments.' Give reasons for this statement from demand and supply perspectives.

2. What are the main stages in the venture capital cycle? And why is it a cycle?

3. What are the major differences between business angel investors and venture capital companies?

4. What are the advantages of business angels (over VC companies) for an entrepreneur seeking to raise entrepreneurial finance?

5. How would you advise such an entrepreneur, seeking to raise venture finance, on the best ways to find a business angel investors?

Suggested Assignments

1. Identify and interview an entrepreneur about his or her attitude towards sharing equity.

2. List the pros and cons associated with investing in the different investment stages.

3. As an entrepreneur, list the pros and cons associated with both formal and informal venture capital.

4. Visit the following websites and compile a report on the level of venture capital activity in the UK, the USA and Europe:

- www.bvca.co.uk
- www.evca.com
- www.nvca.com.

Recommended Reading ■ ■ ■ ■ ■ ■ ■ ■ ■ ■ ■

Amit, R., Brander, J. and Zott, C. (1998) 'Why do Venture Capital Firms Exist? Theory and Canadian Evidence', *Journal of Business Venturing*, vol. 13, pp. 441–66.

BVCA (1998) *A Guide to Venture Capital*, BVCA, London.

Mason, C. and Harrison, R. (1999) 'Venture Capital: Rationale, Aims and Scope', Editorial, *Venture Capital*, vol. 1, no. 1, pp. 1–46.

Murray, G. (1996) 'Venture Capital', in P. Burns and J. Dewhurst (eds), *Small Business and Entrepreneurship*, Macmillan, London.

Tybejee, T. and Bruno, A. (1984) 'A Model of Venture Capital Investment Activity', *Management Science*, vol. 30, pp. 1051–66.

Wright, M. and Robbie, K. (1998) 'Venture Capital and Private Equity: A Review and Synthesis', *Journal of Business Finance Accounting*, vol. 25, pp. 521–70.

References

1 Cressy, R. (1996) 'Are Business Start-ups Debt-rationed?', *Economic Journal*, vol. 106, pp. 1253–70.

2 Storey, D. (1994) *Understanding the Small Business Sector*, Routledge, London.

3 Cosh, A. and Hughes, A. (2003) *Enterprise Challenged*, Centre for Business Research, University of Cambridge.

4 Murray, G. (1996) 'Venture Capital', in P. Burns and J. Dewhurst (eds), *Small Business and Entrepreneurship*, Macmillan, London.

5 Macmillan (1931) *Report of the Committee on Finance and Industry*, Cmnd 3897, HMSO, London.

6 Bolton (1971) *Report of the Committee of Inquiry on Small Firms*, Cmnd 4811, HMSO, London.

7 Wilson (1979) *The Financing of Small Firms*, Interim Report of the Committee to Review the Functioning of the Financial Institutions, Cmnd 7503, HMSO, London.

8 Williams, P. (1989) *Financing of High-technology Businesses: A Report to the Paymaster General*, HMSO, London.

9 Mason, C. and Harrison, R. (1999) 'Venture Capital: Rationale, Aims and Scope', Editorial, *Venture Capital*, vol. 1, no. 1, pp. 1–46.

10 McNally, K. (1995) 'Corporate Venture Capital: The Financing of Technology Businesses', *International Journal of Entrepreneurial Behaviour and Research*, vol. 1, no. 3, pp. 9–43.

11 Doran, A. and Bannock, G. (2000) 'Publicly Sponsored Regional Venture Capital: What can the UK Learn from the US Experience?', *Venture Capital*, vol. 2, pp. 255–86.

12 Harrison, R. and Mason, C. (2000) Editorial: 'The Role of the Public Sector in the Development of a Regional Venture Capital Industry', *Venture Capital*, vol. 2, pp. 243–54.

13 Bygrave, W. and Timmons, J. (1992) *Venture Capital at the Crossroads*, Harvard Business School Press, Boston, MA.

14 Wright, M. and Robbie, K. (1998) 'Venture Capital and Private Equity: A Review and Synthesis', *Journal of Business Finance Accounting*, vol. 25, pp. 521–70.

15 Timmons, J. (1999) *New Venture Creation: Entrepreneurship for the 21st Century*, McGraw-Hill, Boston.

16 Murray, G. (1992) 'A Challenging Market Place for Venture Capital', *Long Range Planning*, vol. 25, pp. 79–86.

17 Baygan, G. and Freudenberg, M. (2000) *The Internationalisation of Venture Capital Activity in OECD Countries: Implications for Measurement and Policy*, STI WP 2000/7, OECD, Paris.

18 Amit, R., Brander, J. and Zott, C. (1998) 'Why do Venture Capital Firms Exist? Theory and Canadian Evidence', *Journal of Business Venturing*, vol. 13, pp. 441–66.

19 Bottazzi, L. and Da Rin, M. (2002) 'Venture Capital in Europe and the Financing of Innovative Companies', *Economic Policy*, April, pp. 231–69.

20 Tylecote, A. (1994) 'Financial Systems and Innovation', in M. Dodgson and R. Rothwell, *The Handbook of Industrial Innovation*, pp. 259–67, Edward Elgar, Cheltenham.

21 Committee of Wise Men (2001) final report of the Committee of Wise Men on the regulation of European Security Markets, Brussels, http:/europa.eu.int/comm/internalmarket/en.

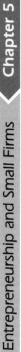

22 BVCA (1998) *A Guide to Venture Capital*, BVCA, London.

23 Brouwer, M. and Hendrix, B. (1998) 'Two Worlds of Venture Capital: What Happened to US and Dutch Early Stage Investment', *Small Business Economics*, vol. 10, pp. 333–48.

24 CBI (1996) *Tech Stars: Breaking the Growth Barriers for Technology-based SMEs*, London.

25 Bank of England (1996) *The Financing of Technology-based Small Firms*, London, October.

26 HM Treasury (1998) *Financing of High Technology Businesses: A Report to the Paymaster General*, London, November.

27 BVCA (2000) *Report on Investment Activity 1999*, BVCA, London.

28 Mason, C. and Harrison, R. (1995) 'Closing the Regional Equity Gap: The Role of Informal Venture Capital', *Small Business Economics*, vol. 7, pp. 153–72.

29 Admati, A. and Pfleiderer, P. (1994) 'Robust Financial Contracting and the Role of Venture Capitalists', *The Journal of Finance*, vol. 49, pp. 371–402.

30 Reid, G. (1999) 'The Application of Principal-agent Methods to Investor–Investee Relations in the UK Venture Capital Industry', *Venture Capital*, vol. 1, pp. 285–302.

31 Akerlof, G. (1970) 'The Market for Lemons: Quality Uncertainty and the Market Mechanism', *Quarterly Journal of Economics*, vol. 84, pp. 488–500.

32 Seaton, J. and Walker, I. (1997) 'The Pattern of R&D Finance for Small UK Companies', in R. Oakey, and S.-M. Mukhtar (eds), *New Technology-based Firms in the 1990s, Volume III*, London, Paul Chapman, pp. 71–91.

33 Jensen, M. and Meckling, W. (1976) 'Theory of the Firm: Managerial Behaviour, Agency Costs and Ownership Structure', *Journal of Financial Economics*, vol. 3, pp. 305–60.

34 Goodacre, A. and Tonks, I. (1995) 'Finance and Technological Change', in P. Stoneman, *Handbook of the Economics of Innovation and Technological Change*, Blackwell, Oxford, pp. 298–341.

35 Moore, I. and Garnsey, E. (1993) 'Funding for Innovation in Small Firms: The Role of Government', *Research Policy*, vol. 22, pp. 507–19.

36 Lerner, J. (1994) 'The Syndication of Venture Capital Investments', *The Financier*, vol. 23, pp. 16–27.

37 Ross, S. (1977) 'The Determination of Financial Structure: The Incentive-signalling Approach', *Bell Journal of Economics*, vol. 8, pp. 23–40.

38 Myers, S. and Majluf, N. (1984) 'Corporate Financing and Investment Decisions When Firms Have Information that Investors Do Not', *Journal of Financial Economics*, vol. 13, pp. 187–221.

39 Giudici, G. and Paleari, S. (2000) 'The Provision of Finance to Innovation: A Survey Conducted Among Italian Technology-based Small Firms', *Small Business Economics*, vol. 14, pp. 37–53.

40 Boocock, G. and Wood, M. (1997) 'The Evaluation Criteria Used by Venture Capitalists: Evidence From a UK Venture Fund', *International Small Business Journal*, vol. 16, pp. 36–57.

41 Silver, A. (1985) *Venture Capital: The Complete Guide for Investors*, John Wiley & Sons, New York.

42 Hall, G. (1989) 'Lack of Finance as a Constraint on the Expansion of Innovatory Small Firms', in J. Barber, J. Metcalfe and M. Porteous (eds), *Barriers to Growth in Small Firms*, London, Routledge.

43 Fried, V. and Hisrich, R. (1994) 'Toward a Model of Venture Capital Investment Decision Making', *Financial Management*, vol. 23, pp. 28–37.

44 Tybejee, T. and Bruno, A. (1984) 'A Model of Venture Capital Investment Activity', *Management Science*, vol. 30, pp. 1051–66.

45 Sweeting, R. (1991) 'UK Venture Capital Funds and the Funding of New Technology-based Businesses: Process and Relationships', *Journal of Management Studies*, vol. 28, pp. 601–22.

46 Gompers, P. and Lerner, J. (2001) 'The Venture Capital Revolution', *Journal of Economic Perspectives*, 15, pp. 145–68.

47 Cumming, D.J. and Macintosh, J.G. (2000) *The Extent of Venture Capital Exits: Evidence from Canada and the United States*, University of Toronto Law and Economics Research Paper No. 01–03.

48 Nahata, R. (2003) *The Determinants of Venture Capital Exits: An Empirical Analysis of Venture Backed Companies*, Vanderbilt University Working Paper, 900128.

49 MacMillan, I., Siegal, R. and Subba Narishima, P. (1985) 'Criteria Used by Venture Capitalists to Evaluate New Venture Proposals', *Journal of Business Venturing*, vol. 1, pp. 126–41.

50 Mason, C. and Harrison, R. (2000) 'The Size of the Informal Venture Capital Market in the United Kingdom', *Small Business Economics*, vol. 15, pp. 137–48.

51 Mason, C. and Harrison, R. (1997) 'Business Angels are the Answer to The Entrepreneur's Prayer', in S. Birley and D. Muzyka (eds), *Master Entrepreneurship*, FT/Prentice Hall, London, pp. 110–14.

52 Paul, S., Johnston, J., Whittam, G. and Wilson, L. (2002) 'Are Business Angels Entrepreneurs', paper presented to the Small Business and Enterprise Development Conference, Nottingham, April.

53 Feeney, L., Haines, G. and Riding, A. (1999) 'Private Investors' Investment Criteria: Insights from Qualitative Data', *Venture Capital*, vol. 2, pp. 121–45.

Innovation and Entrepreneurship

He that will not apply new remedies must expect new evils; for time is the greatest innovator. *(Francis Bacon)*

The factory of the future will have only two employees, a man and a dog. The man will be there to feed the dog. The dog will be there to keep the man from touching the equipment. *(Warren Bennis)*

Learning Outcomes

At the end of this chapter you should be able to:

1 define innovation in the context of the entrepreneurship process

2 describe the advantages and disadvantages for small firms in the innovation process

3 describe factors affecting the nature of dynamics in the innovation process

4 discuss the importance for small firms of external linkages with the innovation process

5 describe the factors that affect innovative performance in different industrial sectors

6 discuss concepts that determine how designs are adopted and become dominant.

■ ■ ■ ■ Introduction

Academics and policy-makers rarely understate the importance of industrial innovation. In a world where such consensuses are rare, the common view[1] holds that, '[i]n all highly-industrialised nations the long-term growth of business and (thus) of regions [and, one may safely assume, nations] stems from their ability to continually develop and produce innovative products' (p. 391). Indeed, Chris Freeman, the doyen of innovation theorists, goes further,[2] suggesting that 'not to innovate is to die' (p. 266). While one may quibble about the appropriateness of such imperatives, it is nonetheless clear that innovations, of varying scale and scope, positively impact upon the performance of firms in aggregate and, by implication, economies.[3; 4; 5] Moreover, in contrast to earlier convictions, it has gradually become clear that there is no firm size uniquely suited to innovation. That is, both large and small firms have significant, and often complementary, roles to perform in the process of technological development and innovation broadly defined.[6] With this in mind, this chapter seeks to outline the distinct contribution made by smaller firms to industrial innovation, and identifies some key enabling and constraining factors.

■ ■ ■ ■ What Do We Mean by Innovation?

The most obvious link between innovation and entrepreneurship, or innovation and small firms, may arguably be traced to the early work of Joseph Schumpeter.[7] With respect to the nature of innovation, Schumpeter identified five principal sources of 'creative destruction' (see box).

Schumpeter's Forces of Creative Destruction

1. The introduction of a new good (or a significant improvement in the quality of an existing good)

2. The introduction of a new method of production (i.e. an innovation in processes)

3. The opening of a new market (in particular an export market in a new territory)

4. The 'conquest of a new source of supply of raw materials or half-manufactured goods'

5. The creation of a new type of industrial organisation (i.e. an administrative innovation)

Clearly, then, this conception is far broader than technical advance, narrowly defined; though Schumpeter was unambiguous in excluding merely marginal or aesthetic changes. Moreover, this more eclectic view is certainly attractive. As an OECD[8] workshop on 'SMEs: Employment, Innovation and Growth' concluded, 'Most high growth firms are not innovative in a technical sense, but may include marketing innovations or cross-national alliances. Most high-tech firms are not high growth. . . . Most new jobs are created by low innovation, low growth traditional firms' (pp. 57–8). In other words, the best-performing firms are those occupying mature industries and engaged in marketing or administrative innovations, and *not* the high-technology or new-technology-based firms that dominate policy deliberations. However, notwithstanding this observation, a narrow technological view of innovation dominates the academic and popular debate. A prime example is the influential pan-European Community Innovation Surveys (CIS), which have been exclusively concerned with product and process innovations and with substantive changes in the technology underlying these. Undoubtedly, this is a little disappointing and will afford only a partial understanding of innovations and innovators – most especially in large sections of the small firms sector. Indeed, perhaps the most worrying consequence of this approach is the almost inevitable conclusion that service firms are not innovative. While this is a long-held view in the economics literature, there is an emerging body of work that points to considerable innovation within services (particularly organisational innovation)[9] and the inadequacy of the narrow technical view.[10]

Unfortunately the current chapter compounds these weaknesses. In part this is an issue of space; in part a function of how much we know. A great deal of work remains to be done to elaborate these broader patterns of innovation, most especially within services. In contrast, our understanding of product and process innovation is reasonably well developed. Moreover, while there may be some ambivalence with regard to the performance of individual firms (and one may argue that firms engaged in technical innovation will exhibit greater variety of performance), innovations of this type undoubtedly impact upon economic performance in aggregate. To that extent, a narrow technical focus is not without merits. While the picture painted will be incomplete, it is nonetheless valuable. Indeed, one should note that Schumpeter's five forms of innovation are not mutually exclusive. Process innovations, for instance, are often accompanied by changes in workforce organisation. Similarly, product innovations often serve new markets or require new methods of engaging with existing markets. Indeed, it is increasingly difficult to simply categorise innovations in accordance with Schumpeter's taxonomy. By way of illustration, is the firm that introduces an online stock-listing and order-processing service engaging in product, process or market innovation?

Irrespective of the answer to this question, what is clear is that all kinds of innovation involve 'newness'. That is, innovation is fundamentally concerned with novelty. However, this is not to say that innovation is simply invention. Invention is only part of the process – and, indeed, may not be part of the process at all. The concept of innovation is more involved and embraces the *commercial* application of inventions (often for the first time). Thus, innovation incorporates both creation or discovery aspects, and diffusion or utilisation aspects. The difficulty, however, is that novelty is ultimately a relative concept. When we say that something is 'new', to whom do we mean it is new, and in what respect (e.g. new technologies or new combinations of existing technologies) do we measure this 'newness'? For example, was the first online travel agency innovative even though the medium and technology had previously been used successfully to sell books? Was the IBM 5150 PC, which revolutionised the personal computer market, an innovation, even though it was essentially an amalgam of existing technologies (e.g. television monitor, QWERTY keyboard, printed circuit boards, memory chips, semiconductors, and so on)?

To this end, a number of simple models have been developed to better understand the 'domain of innovation'. Figure 6.1 outlines perhaps the most popular of these.[11] This model is commonly used in studies of small firm innovation to distinguish levels of 'innovativeness' and has been central to the measurement of innovation in successive Community Innovation Surveys (CIS). These surveys have explicitly asked firms whether they had introduced new products or processes in a given time period and whether these were new to the industry or new to the firm only. Implicit in the distinction is the existence of a hierarchy of innovation. Products or processes that are new to the firm, but not to the industry or market, are essentially imitations (though the term 'imitation'

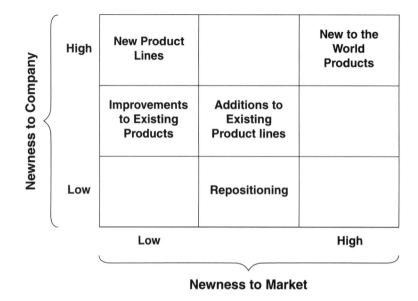

Figure 6.1: *Classification of Innovations*
Source: Cooper (1993)

should not be understood pejoratively). In contrast, products or processes that are new to both the firm and the market fit more closely with Schmookler's[12] classic, if contended, definition of innovation:

When an enterprise produces a good or service or uses a method or input that is new to it, it makes a technical change. The first company to make a given technical change is an innovator. Its action is innovation.

The empirical literature often labels these levels of innovation 'incremental' and 'novel', respectively. While the jargon is simply a matter of convenience, there is some evidence that firms introducing relatively 'novel' innovations (i.e. those that are new to the industry or market) differ from their less- and non-innovative peers along a number of dimensions, including the propensity to cooperate,[13] access to finance,[14] training[15] and performance.[16] Without doubt, the distinctions implied in Figure 6.1 are helpful in understanding and categorising innovations, and have contributed to both academic debate and policy formation. However, models of this type are concerned with innovation outputs and inevitably have less to say about the innovation processes.

To the extent that innovation is concerned with discovery through to diffusion, it is clear that understanding innovation involves understanding process as well measuring output. One easy inference to draw from this is that innovation, as a commercial phenomenon, is somehow a linear process – beginning with basic science and ending in sales; or beginning with an articulated customer need, which is subsequently developed into a saleable product. Indeed, just such a conception dominated academic and industrial thinking from the 1950s up until the early 1970s; conceived of as either 'science-push' innovation (in which the emergence of new opportunities based upon new technologies drives the process; see Figure 6.2) or 'demand-pull' innovation (reflecting more stationary technology, an increase in the importance of marketing to firm growth and a 'needs'-driven innovation agenda; see Figure 6.3). Rothwell[17] terms these linear approaches the 'First-generation Innovation Process' and the

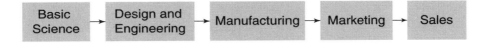

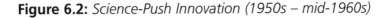

Figure 6.2: *Science-Push Innovation (1950s – mid-1960s)*

'Second-generation Innovation Process' respectively, and notes that systematic empirical evidence, available for the first time in the mid-1970s, had suggested that, 'the technology-push or need-pull models of innovation were extreme and atypical examples of a more general process of *interaction* between, on the one hand, technological capabilities and, on the other, market needs' (p. 9, emphasis added). It is this idea of interaction that underpins current thinking.

This view of innovation, as a process of complex links and feedback mechanisms, is most notably represented by Kline and Rosenberg's[18] 'chain-linked' model and by Rothwell and Zegveld's[19] 'coupling' model (Figure 6.4). In both these models innovation is conceived of as a network of inter-organisational and extra-organisational communication paths, linking the various in-house functions and allowing the firm to articulate with both the marketplace and the wider scientific and technological community. At each stage of the development process, innovation endeavours may be informed by internal and external user constituencies and by the external technological state of the art. The principal difference between the models relates to the source of innovative ideas. In Kline and Rosenberg's model the process is seen as starting with the identification of a market need. Rothwell and Zegveld, however, are less prescriptive and allow for the interplay of markets and technology during the idea-generation process. Irrespective of these differences, the basic premise of bilateral interaction and feedback underpins both models. With a view to conceptualising innovation, this is certainly a more satisfactory representation of the intricacy one would anticipate, given the degree of market and technological uncertainties involved. Moreover, persistent internal and external feedback mechanisms and reference points are likely to reduce waste and increase the speed of acceptance of the final product or process, thus contributing, ultimately, to innovation success.

Rothwell[17] designated this the 'third generation' and proceeded to describe a further two generations: the fourth-generation 'parallel/integration' model (inspired by innovation practices at Nissan); and the fifth-generation 'systems integration and networking' model (with the emphasis on time/cost trade-offs). However, to the extent that the third generation represents innovation as a process of 'interactive learning and collective entrepreneurship'[20] it is broadly in line with accepted wisdom (providing conceptual underpinning for the CIS). Central to the third generation is the pervasive idea[21] that 'innovation by firms cannot be understood purely in terms of independent decision making at the level of the firm' (p. 73). Nor, realistically, is it likely to be confined to a series of simple phased, bilateral or dyadic interactions, as Figure 6.4 suggests. Rather, many commentators now hold that innovation is increasingly a matter of collective action. In other words, innovation may, more appropriately, be considered

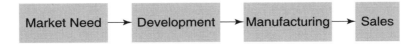

Figure 6.3: *Demand Pull Innovation (mid-1960s – early 1970s)*

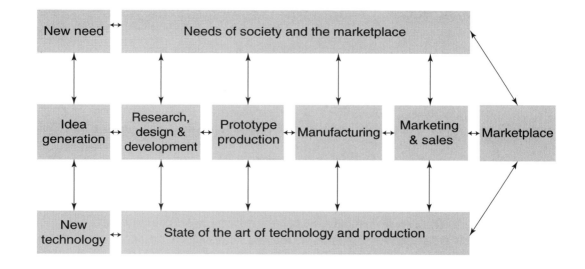

Figure 6.4: *The 'Coupling' Model*
Source: Adapted from Rothwell[38]

the product of networks of related actors, operating within systems of innovation. Tether[22] argues that, in consequence, 'the old debates about firm-size, market structure and innovation are becoming outmoded, as the boundaries of the firm are becoming increasingly "fuzzy"' (p. 947). While one may feel that this overstates the case, there is little doubt that the idea of 'innovation networks' enjoys considerable favour in both policy and academic circles. Indeed, the benefits of innovation networking may be of particular relevance to small firms and we return to this issue towards the end of the chapter. In the meantime, our concern is, more directly, with the relationship between innovation and firm size.

■ ■ ■ ■ Innovation and Firm Size

However, before outlining some of the more popular approaches to the issue of firm size and innovation, it is worth revisiting Schumpeter's contribution to the debate and the influence it has had upon prevailing thought. In his initial deliberations, what one may term 'Schumpeter Mark I', Schumpeter[7] proposed that it was the exceptional creative drive of independent entrepreneurs that led to the introduction of radical new products and the creation of new industries, undermining the status quo and driving changes in market structures (see also Chapter 1). This is the Schumpeter who takes pride of place in many undergraduate entrepreneurship courses. However, in *Capitalism, Socialism and Democracy*, Schumpeter[23] adopts what appears to be a diametrically opposite position, arguing that:

The monopolist firm will generate a larger supply of innovations because there are advantages which, though not strictly unattainable on the competitive level of enterprise, are as a matter of fact secured only on the monopoly level.[24]

Essentially, this later Schumpeter ('Schumpeter Mark II') suggests that, since the process, or task, of innovation has become increasingly routinised (over the first half of the twentieth century), admitting increasing returns to scale, large firms are likely to possess advantages over smaller rivals. For instance, large firms may be able to spread the risk of innovation over a number of projects, adopting a portfolio approach, whereas smaller firms are often constrained to put 'all their eggs in one basket'. Moreover, if firms are liable to innovate only where positive post-innovation returns, accounting for development costs, are anticipated, one may plausibly assume that a high degree of market power (i.e. the ability to set prices above marginal cost), frequently associated with larger size, would be the first best condition for innovation. Indeed, a belief in the importance of monopoly power in stimulating innovation underpins the international system of patents. At the risk of oversimplifying, successful patents, conferring exclusive rights to make and sell a given product, create fixed-term monopolies, preventing imitation and allowing firms to recoup research and development expenses. Importantly, Schumpeter was primarily concerned with how these market structure effects, rather than firm size per se, would impact upon the propensity to innovate. Yet, while a high degree of market power often implies larger size, the two are not inevitably associated. In contrast, J.K. Galbraith was more direct in his assessment of the relationship between innovation and firm size, noting that:

There is no more pleasant fiction than that technical change is the product of the matchless ingenuity of the small man forced by competition to employ his wits to better his neighbour. . . . Because development is costly, it follows that it can be carried on only by a firm that has the resources which are associated with considerable size.[25]

This view, that 'big is best', or that large firms are at the heart of the process of innovation and wealth and welfare creation has, until relatively recently, prevailed. However, over the last 25 years, a 'new learning' has emerged.[24] Empirical studies in both the USA and the UK[26; 27; 28; 29] noted that,[30] subject to certain sectoral variations, 'small firms can keep up with large firms in the field of innovation' (p. 335) and, indeed, may more efficiently use R&D inputs to generate innovation outputs. In other words, rather than searching for some firm size uniquely and unequivocally optimal for innovation, it is vital that we recognise that small and large firms may fulfil different and often complementary roles – what Rothwell terms 'dynamic complementarity'.[6]

Dynamic Complementarity

In a much-cited paper, Rothwell[6] suggests that the relative importance of firms of different sizes to innovation in a particular industry is likely to depend upon the *age* of that industry. In a related paper, Rothwell[28] draws upon Kaplinsky's[31] studies of the computer-aided design (CAD) industry to illustrate the point (see Figure 6.5). In this industry, the early running was made by large, technologically advanced, mechanical engineering firms in the defence, aerospace and automotive industries (involving collaborations with mainframe computer manufacturers such as IBM). Importantly, development of the technology was primarily for 'own use', with little or no 'market' for CAD beyond this. The second phase of the industry's evolution is characterised by a rapid diffusion of the technology to other sectors, principally electronics. The emergence of new, independent firms provided, in large part, the impetus for this diffusion. Many of these firms were established by software writers spinning off from firms with experience of CAD software in the aerospace and automotive industries. Others, from the electronics sector itself, were attracted by the obvious future potential of the CAD sector. As Kaplinsky[31] notes, 'The consequence was a variety of new firms, initially making digitising equipment and subsequently moving to the supply of complete turnkey systems' (p. 44), that is, systems supplied, installed, built and ready for immediate use.

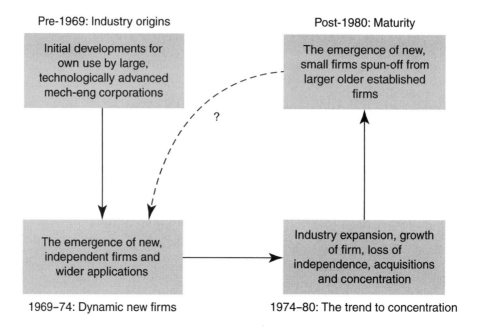

Figure 6.5: *The Evolution of the CAD Industry*
Source: Kaplinsky, [31], *The Journal of Industrial Economics* Blackwell Publishing

In the third phase of the industry, CAD equipment began to penetrate manufacturing. The rate of diffusion proved so rapid that industry growth rates increased from 55 per cent per annum to 80 per cent per annum. All firms adopted a strategy of expanding their range of applications to comprehensively cover all industries. This diversification and expansion required financial resources beyond the scope of internal revenues, and firms took recourse to debt, venture capital and the stock markets – in this way diluting ownership and independence. As firms grew in size, some came to hold more dominant positions. At the same time, large firms from other, CAD-using, sectors began acquiring specialist CAD firms, sparking a period of horizontal and vertical integration. In this way, and in addition to growing firm size, the third phase in the industry's evolution was marked by growing organic trends towards concentration and a tendency for formerly independent CAD firms to be swallowed up by existing multinationals. The final stage of the industry's evolution, termed 'maturity' by Kaplinsky, witnessed the emergence, once again, of small firms spun off from larger, older and established firms. These firms evolved to serve the lower ends of the market. That is, market segments characterised by demand for cheaper, lower-capability systems than those offered by established firms and demanded by established customers. Thus, while the trend towards concentration continued in the existing industry, new entrants began to offer dedicated systems to new users, whose engineering data-processing requirements were less extensive and whose budgets were limited.

From the evolution of the CAD industry and his own work on the US semiconductor industry,[32] Rothwell[28] sketches some general patterns, as follows.

■ In both industries, established large corporations played a crucial role in early invention and innovation. Importantly, however, initial development activity was geared to 'own use'.

- In both cases, much of the rapid diffusion and market growth resulted from the formation and expansion of new-technology-based firm (NTBFs).

- In both CAD and semiconductors, the technological entrepreneurs behind the NTBFs often emerged from established firms, bringing both technology and applications know-how with them.

- In both instances, large corporations and venture capital played a significant role in funding the start-up and growth of NTBFs.

- In both cases, the industries rapidly became highly concentrated and the focus of external takeover activity.

- As both industries matured, scale economies became increasingly important and stable oligopolies formed, leaving only specialist market niches for new and small firms.

The Dynamics of Innovation

Rothwell's specific observations fit reasonably well with more general models of the 'dynamics of innovation', perhaps the most compelling of which was initially developed by William Abernathy and James Utterback.[33] This model, subsequently elaborated in detail by Utterback,[34] holds that the rates of product and process innovation are related and vary over the course of the industry life cycle. The early stage of the industry is characterised by considerable radical product innovation. Firms are said by Utterback[34] to be 'unencumbered by universal technical standards or by uniform products expectations in the marketplace [and] experiment freely with new forms and materials' (p. 81). In other words, firms are not sure what is technically possible and customers are unable to clearly articulate their wants. The consequence is considerable variety in the fundamentals of the various products producers bring to the market, and high rates of product innovation within individual producers as their products are refined through further R&D and exposure to customers and competition. At this stage, processes must be flexible enough to accommodate the flurry of product changes. As such, they tend to be crude and inefficient, relying upon general-purpose machinery and highly skilled labour. There are no specialised tools or machines and products are assembled in a series of, often skill-intensive, discrete steps.

However, this period of radical product innovation eventually ends with the emergence of a dominant design (see box). Producers become better informed about what is technically possible and customers are better able to judge how well the various alternatives satisfy their more settled expectations. Accordingly, the scope for radical product innovation diminishes and the emphasis shifts to manufacturing greater quantities of the dominant design at lower costs, to meet the demands of an expanding market. In other words, the emphasis shifts to cost-reducing process innovation and to exploiting emerging scale economies. Firms dedicate their research efforts to improving production techniques and developing specialised machinery (which often requires lower-skill, lower-cost labour), which serve, in turn, to further open up the market. By way of illustration, Utterback points to studies of the US automotive industry, which suggested that improvements in processes had reduced the time taken to manufacture a car from a pre-Model-A (i.e. the original Ford) 4600 man hours ('roughly the time required to build an average house') to approximately 20 man hours in 1990.

Dominant Design

A dominant design in a product class is, by definition, the one that captures the allegiance of the marketplace, the one that competitors and innovators must adhere to if they are to command significant market following. The dominant design usually takes the form of a new product (or set of features) synthesized from individual technological innovations introduced independently in prior product variants . . .

. . . a dominant design embodies the requirement of many classes of users of a particular product, even though it may not meet the needs of a particular class to quite the same extent as would a customized design. Nor is a dominant design the one that embodies the most extreme technical performance. It is a so-called satisficer of many in terms of the interplay of technical possibilities and market choices, instead of an optimizer for a few . . .

A dominant design drastically reduces the number of performance requirements to be met by a product by making many of those requirements implicit in the design itself. Thus, few today would ask if a car had an electric starter and electric windshield wipers, or whether a typewriter could produce upper- and lower-case letters, or whether a computer had a built-in disk drive, though these were unique features in models that preceded the dominant design . . .

Source: Utterback, pp. 24–6[34]

More importantly, for our current purposes, what are the implications of this model for the relationship between firm size and innovation? To this end, the model suggests initially few producers serving a small market of 'gadgeteers' or 'lead users' with highly differentiated and unsettled products. As a result of the smallness of the market and the effective customisation of products, these initial producers are almost invariably small. As the market expands, and both producers and consumers become better informed, there is an explosion of competition. A rash of new firms enters the industry to exploit the commercial potential offered by the new technology, and the rate of product innovation begins to slow. Crucially, in these early days producers compete not so much with each other as against customer scepticism towards the new technology (embodied, as it is, in unrefined products). However, the appearance of a dominant design, says Utterback,[34] shifts the bases of competition:

. . . as product capabilities and features are crystallized through the emergence of a dominant design, competition between firms stabilizes. The number of competitors drops off quickly after this landmark event for the industry, and the bases of competition shift to refinements in product features, reliability and cost. From the crystallization, a set of efficient producers usually emerges. (p. 87)

Following the emergence of a dominant design the product begins to take on many of the characteristics of a commodity. In the growing market, firms become focused upon producing higher volumes at lower costs, with scale economies assuming greater importance. This, in turn, tends to favour those firms with greater facility in process innovation and integration and with more highly developed engineering and technical expertise. The explosion of competition witnessed prior to dominant design is mirrored in an implosion of competition, post-dominant design, and a move to stable oligopoly.

Number of Firms

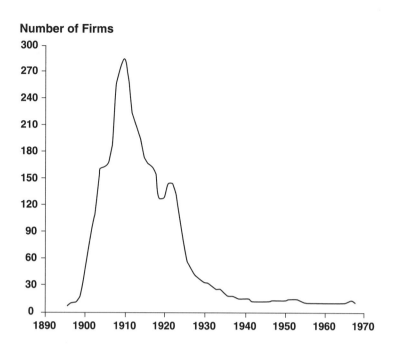

Figure 6.6: *Population of US Automobile Manufacturers*
Source: Simon (1995)

This 'shifting ecology of firms' is nicely illustrated by the evolution of the US automobile industry (see Figure 6.6). The early days of this industry were marked by considerable variation in the fundamentals of the product. Early pioneers experimented with steam and electric engines, as well as with the enduring, petrol-driven internal combustion engine. An astonishing variety of unique styles emerged from hundreds of workshops, many based on the open-body 'horseless carriage'. Concurrently, many new firms entered, often formed to exploit 'innovations' – new body designs, transmission systems, steering mechanisms, and so on. As the data in Figure 6.6 suggest, the number of manufacturers rose from four in 1895 to a peak of 274 by 1909. However, after this point, the number drops away rapidly, with a slight reversal of the trend in the early 1920s. By 1929 there were only 30 firms in the industry and by 1960 the figure had fallen to a low of seven. Importantly, that this 'shakeout' began after 1909 is probably not coincidental; nor is the second peak witnessed in the early 1920s. In the first instance, late 1908 saw the introduction of Ford's Model-T. Following the introduction of the Model-T, company policy was to keep up with demand by developing more specialised machine tools and innovations in the production process. Although the 'Tin Lizzie' was a technically advanced automobile, it was by no means technically revolutionary. Rather, it was Ford's emphasis on manufacturability and on process innovation that revolutionised the industry. The second wave of exits appears to coincide with the introduction, by Dodge, of the all-steel, closed-body automobile. As well as dramatically improving the strength and rigidity of the chassis, this innovation allowed manufacturers to shift from hand forming of exterior body panels to the highly capitalised, but highly efficient process of machine stamping.[34] Both cases ushered in eras of larger-scale production or more standardised products at lower cost, with the attendant economies of scale leading to fewer firms of larger size.

One of the more reassuring implications of dynamics theories of the sort presented by Utterback[34] is their ability to reconcile the apparently contradictory Schumpeter

'Mark I' and 'Mark II'. According to Freeman and Soete[2] there are essentially two types of Schumpeterian models of innovation: 'entrepreneurial innovation' and 'managed innovation'. In the former, new basic technologies emerge, drawn from new scientific developments, largely outside existing large firms. Risk-taking, fast-reacting entrepreneurs take advantage of the technological opportunities offered and through radical innovation develop and grow new industries and new product groups. During this stage of the industry cycle small, fast-growing firms play the major innovative role. Over time the initial technology and markets mature, average firm size and industry concentration increases and inventive activity becomes increasingly undertaken in the large-scale, in-house R&D laboratories of large firms (which may have previously been the small entrepreneurial firms of the initial cycle stages). Little scope exists for major product innovation. Consumers become more informed and market requirements are increasingly well specified, resulting in minimal differentiation between competing products. As a result, price competition moves to the fore and the focus of development efforts rests primarily with process improvement aimed at cost reduction. Thus, small firms are involved in radical new product innovation and major improvements, while large firms are concerned with process innovation and minor product improvement.

A Less Dynamic View

If the models described above are taken to be universally applicable, then one must inevitably conclude that the role of small firms in innovation is likely to be transitory or confined, in the long run, to small specialist niches that are unattractive to large firms. However, this is not the case. Compelling though the models are, their applicability is restricted to mass-production industries where customer preferences are (or become) relatively uniform. In industries where customers value variety, a different pattern is likely to prevail. This is likely to apply to many service sectors and, within manufacturing, to industries such as scientific instruments and textiles. Indeed, the success enjoyed by small Italian textile and leather manufacturers (in what has been termed the 'Third Italy'), during the 1970s and 1980s, provided much of the impetus for the development of the 'Flexible Specialisation' thesis by Piore and Sabel,[36] as a counterpoint to the prevailing, large-firm-orientated 'Fordist' mass-production views that dominated (see also Chapter 2). The flexible specialisation thesis sees mass production giving way to networks of specialist small firms, employing skilled workers to produce a variety of customised goods. According to this view, mass production progressively dominated the period 1900–1970, but has been in crisis since. The breakdown of international regulatory mechanisms, more diverse markets, and new manufacturing techniques combined with flexible work practices, have served to lessen the impact and importance of scale economies. Relatedly, a common refrain in the management literature has been concerned with the value of concentrating on 'core competencies' as a means of accessing 'economies of specialisation'.

Unfortunately, however, the debate is traditionally couched in bi-polar terms. Flexible specialisation is replacing Fordism; it is 'post-Fordist'. Presenting the theories in this 'either/or' way has made it easy for critics of flexible specialisation to question its validity by simply pointing to the many industries and locations where Fordist practices continue. The 'Third Italy', then, is merely representative of a special case rather than a general trend. Though the debate is ongoing, and considerably more involved than this discussion permits, allowing for the coexistence of both mass production and flexible specialisation seems a more reasonable position. In this way one may conceive of the two models as occupying extremes in some continuum of industrial organisation. The point taken on the continuum, by any given firm or industry, is likely to be a function of a number of factors, which may include: the maturity of the technology, the uniformity of demand, the level of skilled labour required, the availability of finance, the culture of the industry or locale, and so on. The issue, however, is that some industries continue to value product variety and producer flexibility, irrespective of their age, and show no signs of shifting to models of mass production. In these industries smaller firms dominate and dominate innovation activity. This view is not 'less dynamic' in the sense that time or history doesn't matter, but in the sense that innovative advantage does not inevitably pass from small to large firms.

Empirical studies tend to confirm these sectoral variations in the relationship between innovation and firm size. Freeman and Soete,[2] for instance, note that smaller firms are apt to make a larger contribution to innovation activity in fields characterised by radical, but relatively inexpensive, innovation and where both development costs and entry barriers are low. Similarly, Acs and Audretsch[26; 27] found that small firms enjoy relative innovation advantages in industries where the total rate of innovation is high, R&D intensity is low, and where there is a large component of skilled labour. In contrast, large firms dominate industries that are capital-intensive, concentrated and advertising intensive, and where development costs are generally high. For example:[2]

In the chemical industry, where both research and development work are often very expensive, large firms predominate in both invention and innovation. In the mechanical engineering industry, inexpensive ingenuity can play a greater part and small firms or private inventors make a larger contribution. (p. 234)

Small Firm Advantages and Disadvantages

Consideration of the sectors in which small firms appear to hold a comparative innovation advantage might lead one to conclude that smaller firms do well in industries that place a premium on flexibility and resourcefulness, while they do less well in industries where resources and resource management are critical. This is also true of the dynamic theories. At the genesis of the industry, firms' structures are organic, there is limited task definition and few formal procedures. Such structures facilitate rapid communication both within the organisation and with the marketplace, and are necessary to accommodate the frequent major changes in products and, to a lesser extent and latterly, processes. However, as the innovation focus shifts from product to processes and from radical to incremental, informal control gives way to an emphasis on structure, goals and rules. The organisational becomes hierarchical and rigid and individuals' tasks are more clearly defined. In essence, we are witnessing a shift from an *organic* to a *mechanistic* organisational form. The former rewards entrepreneurship, while the latter rewards superintendence and administration.

Regardless of whether one is interested in the innovative advantages and disadvantages of small firms at a particular stage in a given industry's evolution or, more generally, *ex tempus* in a given sector of the economy, it is tempting to describe small firms as behaviourally advantaged but materially constrained. This is a common and well-established view, and Table 6.1 (again, adapted from Rothwell's work) gives more detail to the general statement. Whether in fulfilling the role of rapid product developer and diffuser, or in more mature markets, small firms are thought to enjoy unique advantages associated with: lack of bureaucracy; flat management structures; efficient, often informal, internal communications systems; resourcefulness; flexibility and adaptability through nearness to markets. By contrast, small firms face constraints associated with: lack of technically qualified labour; poor use of external information and expertise; difficulty in attracting/securing finance, and related inability to spread

Table 6.1: *Advantages and Disadvantages of Small Firms in Innovation*

Advantages	Disadvantages
Management: Lack of bureaucracy; greater risk acceptance; entrepreneurial management; rapid decision-making	Lack of formal management skills
Marketing: Nearness to markets ensures fast reaction to changing market requirements; may dominate niche markets	Little or no market power; poor distribution and servicing facilities; geographic market expansion may prove prohibitively costly
Technical manpower: Considerable scope for cross-functionality; technologists often 'plugged-in' to other departments	Often lack suitably qualified specialists (which may also constrain external networking); often unable to support formal R&D efforts
Communications: Efficient and informal internal communication facilitates rapid internal problem-solving	Lack of time and resources to forge external technological linkages
Finance: SMEs often considered more 'R&D efficient' (i.e. innovation can be relatively less costly); 'bootstrapping' possible	Difficulties accessing external finance; cost of capital relatively high; reliance upon short-term debt; inability to spread risk
Growth: Potential for growth through 'niche' or differentiation strategies	Difficulties accessing finance for growth; entrepreneurs often unable to manage growth
Government schemes: Government schemes established to facilitate small firm innovation (e.g. SMART1, SMART2)	High transaction costs involved in accessing schemes; few resources available to manage collaborative schemes; lack of awareness
Regulation: Some regulations are applied less rigorously to small firms	In general, however, the relative unit cost of regulatory compliance is higher for small firms; patent system prohibitively complex and costly
Collaboration: Flexibility and rapid decision-making may make firms attractive partners	Firms suffer from power asymmetries in collaboration with larger partners; little, or no, supply chain influence
Organisation: Suffer less from routinisation and inertia	Suffer more from uncertainties and associated costs
Human resources: Flat management structures and local project ownership are likely	High staff turnover; little formal training

Source: Adapted from Rothwell [28]

risk; unsuitability of original management beyond initial prescription; high cost of regulatory compliance. To reiterate, in the process of industrial innovation small firms appear to be behaviourally advantaged and resource constrained. The challenge, then, for both small business managers and policy-makers, is to find ways to preserve these behavioural advantages While simultaneously mitigating the resource constraints.

The resolution of this dilemma is not as simple as one might initially suppose. For instance, as stage models of firm growth indicate (see Chapter 8) increasing firm size is invariably accompanied by problems of control. That is, as the firm gets larger, it becomes more difficult for the entrepreneur to effectively monitor and supervise all facets of the firm's activities. Moreover, the measures employed to affect control, reduce waste or prevent unilateralism by subordinates, commonly reduce flexibility. Layers (or hierarchies) of management are introduced, ways of doing things become proceduralised and routinised, and paper systems evolve. In essence, the organisation becomes less an entrepreneurial firm and more a bureaucratic firm. There seems to be implicit trade-off between the alleviation of resource constraints and the preservation of behavioural advantages. This is simply a rephrasing of the 'innovator's dilemma'.[37] However, as noted earlier, one fashionable solution involves encouraging small firms to engage in innovation networks, thereby accessing the necessary resources for innovation through external linkages (with supplier, customers, etc.), while maintaining the flexibility and adaptability associated with smaller size.

▪ ▪ ▪ ▪ ▪ Innovation Networking

There is a growing body of both conceptual and empirical literature on the promise of innovation networks for small firms, which has had, in its turn, considerable influence on industrial policy.[38, 39, 40, 41, 42] Frequently, advocates of network approaches to innovation highlight an increasing division of labour among organisations as a first principle compelling collaboration or interaction.[41] That is, increasing uncertainty, associated with changing technology and global competition, has encouraged many firms (and, indeed, many nations) to concentrate on fewer and fewer core competencies, relying upon trade, or co-operation, for others.[43] This effective disintegration of the vertical value chain has been taken as evidence of a move from hierarchical governance structures (based upon threat and coercion) to network governance structures (based upon reciprocity and trust).[44] In contrast to the pre-eminence of Fordist and Taylorist practices during the immediate post-war period, in many industries the efficient organisation of production is increasingly associated with vertical disintegration and flexibility.[45; 46] The conclusion one is generally asked to reach is that 'co-operation is good, more co-operation is better' – at least where innovation activities are concerned. The implied collaboration imperatives, which inevitably draw from such a proposition, have been directed at the small firm sector with particular vigour. MacPherson,[47] for instance, suggests that 'there is little doubt that few SMFs [small and medium-sized firms] can successfully introduce new products without resorting to some form of external collaboration' (p. 127). While, one may conceive of large firms undertaking most innovation activities internally, small firms, with limited internal resources, are likely to require co-operation with others to complete many research projects.[48]

In this regard, the instrumental benefits of inter-firm or inter-organisational collaboration are thought to revolve around the amelioration of internal resource constraints or competency gaps. More specifically, a recent review of the literature[49] suggests that the innovation benefits of networking include those listed in the accompanying box.

Benefits of Networking

- Cost and risk sharing
- Obtaining access to new technologies and markets
- Speeding products to markets
- Pooling complementary skills
- Safeguarding property rights when complete or contingent contracts are not possible
- Acting as a vehicle for obtaining access to external knowledge

By and large, empirical evidence tends to support the hypothesised link between networking and innovation. Figure 6.7, for instance, is taken from a recent study of 'Northern British' SMEs.[50] As the figure clearly suggests, there is an increasing propensity to co-operate, with all potential partners, as firms become more innovative. Indeed, while Figure 6.7 only relates to product innovation within manufacturing firms, broadly similar patterns were recorded for process innovation and within services. However, the danger is that one interprets these findings to indicate that innovation networks are inevitably good, and that more networking activity is inevitably better. What is also clear from the data in Figure 6.7 is that a great many of even the most innovative firms were not involved in formal innovation networks. That is, networking is neither a necessary nor sufficient condition for innovation.

In this vein, recent empirical work by Oerlemans *et al.*[39] suggests an important caveat: that the network view of innovation 'overemphasises an inter-organisational approach to organisational processes' (p. 300). When one controls for a variety of internal resources, networking imperatives are more appropriately couched in conditional terms: co-operation in *certain types* of innovation activity, with *particular organisations*, is associated with higher levels of innovation in *some firms* – conversely, many sources of innovation-related collaboration are not correlated with higher levels of firm-level innovativeness. The relative merits of innovation networks and the form they take is likely to be contingent upon a variety of, more or less related, factors

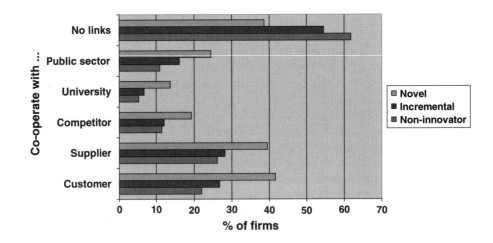

Figure 6.7: *Product Innovation and Co-operation (Manufacturing)*
Source: Freel and Harrison (2005)

(e.g. appropriability concerns; technological maturity; knowledge codifiability; the relative power of partners, and so on). Moreover, indeed crucially, the empirical evidence points to the importance of extensive internal resource. As Angel[51] notes, 'it is likely that the impact of technological partnering on innovation and economic performance is mediated by a variety of other variables, including the internal resources of the firm involved' (p. 335). Indeed, from their work on the Product Development Survey (PDS), Love and Roper[40; 52] go further, suggesting that in-house R&D and networking are substitutes rather than complementary inputs to the innovation process. As such,[52] 'measures that promote networking may have the perverse effect of reducing the extent and sales success of plants innovation activity' (p. 657). While one may feel that this overstates the case, it is clear that[53] 'there is a great discrepancy between, on the one hand, a general agreement that innovation should be understood as an interactive process and, on the other, very limited knowledge about the purpose and nature of this interaction and why it matters so much' (p. 20). In other words, the interactivity of the innovation process may also refer to collaborations and iterations involving departments and individuals within the firm as well as, perhaps less frequently, external co-operation and networking; though the issue is by no means clear-cut.[54]

Finally, a further feature of the data in Figure 6.7 warrants some comment. Where innovation-related links are observed, these occur predominantly along the value chain, with relatively few firms engaged in networks involving universities, competitors or public-sector organisations. This is consistent with observations from similar studies. Yet one should not consider this surprising, providing as it does empirical confirmation of Nooteboom's conceptual framework. Nooteboom[55] suggests that, when internal knowledge, competency or resource limitations are appreciated, the rational entrepreneur will conclude that there is a need to delegate or share responsibility for those decisions, or processes, upon which the limitations impact. Successful delegation (or, in this case co-operation)[55] 'requires trust in a dual sense: the other party (to whom judgement is delegated) has no interest in giving wrong advice (disinterestedness), and is capable of giving good advice (competence)' (p. 342). The requirement for both disinterestedness and competence is likely to lead small firms to interact, first, with those agencies with which they have daily contact, such as customers and suppliers, and thereafter with frequent local contacts (e.g. banks and accountants – considered subcontractors/suppliers in Figure 6.6). Interaction with competitors, universities and public-sector agencies is likely to be lower. While competitors are likely to be highly competent (incorporating an appreciation of the relevant priorities), there exist question marks over their disinterestedness. With regard to public-sector support agencies and universities, the reverse may be true – that is, high levels of disinterestedness but low levels of competency. In the absence of prior evidence of trustworthiness, the individual firm is unlikely to commit to joint ventures in which it has limited control over final appropriability (other than through costly legal means – either *ex ante* contracts or *ex post* legislation). Trust is an iterative process, based on the social programming of values and routinisation of co-operative conduct. And routinisation, in its turn, 'is based on proven past performance and reliability of a co-operative relationship'.[56] A recent study of small manufacturing firms,[57] for instance, suggested that small firms consistently (irrespective of whether they are classed as innovators or non-innovators) rank 'established long-term relationships' and 'frequency of contact' as the key factors stimulating collaboration. The likely absence of such trust-creating mechanisms militates against collaboration with competitors, while their likely presence favours value chain linkages.

Clearly, if the network model of innovation is to be seen as the panacea for small firm resource constraints, much remains to be done to elaborate the conditions under

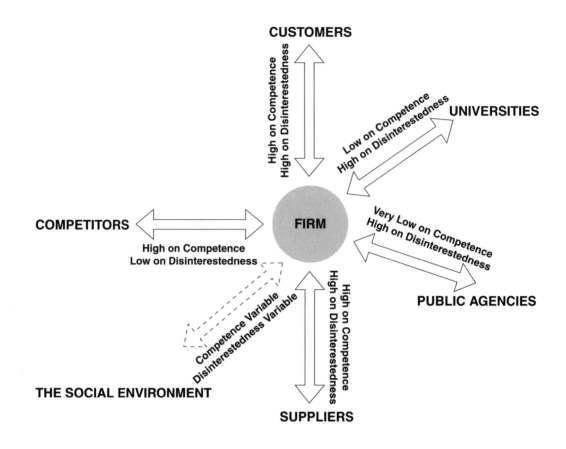

Figure 6.8: *The Effect of Perceptions of Disinterestedness and Competence on Firms' External Linkages*

which innovation networks generate economic benefits and the processes through which these are captured.

■ ■ ■ ■ Conclusions

Innovation, or the presence of novelty, is often taken as a prerequisite for entrepreneurship. Moreover, the rhetoric of policy-makers and small firm academics frequently implies that small firms enjoy a comparative advantage with respect to certain types of industrial innovation. In this chapter we have argued that the innovative contributions of small firms vary across industry sectors and through the industry life cycle, at least with respect to technical innovations. In new industries, where technology is still evolving, small firms have a more significant role to play than in mature mass-production industries, where the innovation focus has switched to cost-reducing process innovation and minor product enhancements. However, in these industries, small firms may benefit from innovations in structure, supply or markets, as producers of complementary products or in serving specialist niches. In addition, small firms may enjoy comparative advantage in industries that serve smaller, fragmented markets, where consumers value variety and where manufacturing flexibility carries a premium – irrespective of the *age* of the industry.

As innovators, small firms enjoy a number of advantages relative to their larger counterparts. These advantages are fundamentally behavioural and relate to the internal organisation of activities, and the manner in which small firms articulate with customers and markets. Flexibility, resourcefulness and speed are at the root of the small firm's innovation advantage. However, small firms also face a number of constraints. These are manifest in the high proportion of small firms failing to innovate. Studies of small firms regularly report in excess of 40 per cent of firms introducing no new products or processes in a given time period[58] – irrespective of whether these are new to the industry or new to the firm only. Such constraints, or barriers, to innovation seem largely to relate to resources: to skills, finance, information, and so on. Consequently, increasing levels of small firm innovation, as an objective of policy, is likely to involve measures aimed at improving access to resources, but that also go some way to preserving organisational flexibility. At the time of writing, innovation networks have quickly established themselves as a popular policy response, though there remain significant gaps in our knowledge of when and how they work.

As a final comment in this chapter, it is worth reiterating one important, but often overlooked, 'fact' about innovation. That is, there is substantial evidence that the majority of commercially significant innovations are technologically incremental, rather than radical.[59] In other words,[20] '[t]he first step in recognizing innovation as a ubiquitous phenomenon is to focus upon its gradual and cumulative aspects . . . Almost all innovations reflect already existing knowledge, combined in new ways' (p. 8). Accordingly, we must be wary of the presumption that innovation is something only high- or new-technology-based firms do and that innovation is somehow inevitably bound up with invention. The scope for small firms to add value through innovation is not limited to a narrow range of industries.

Review Questions 6.1

1. Why does Schumpeter have two diametrically opposed views on the role of the entrepreneur in innovation (Schumpeter Mark I and Mark II)?

2. What are Schumpeter's forces of creative destruction?

3. To what extent is the Internet revolution an example of 'creative destruction'? (Hint: see also Chapter 1.)

4. How would you advise a local development agency wishing to encourage innovative entrepreneurship, particularly in relation to the creation of conducive environments?

Review Questions 6.2

1. What are the advantages of small firms over large firms in the entrepreneurship and innovation process?

2. Why has technological change encouraged innovative activity associated with entrepreneurial, small firms? (Hint: see also Chapter 2.)

3. Why are large firms suited to innovative activity in certain sectors? What are these sectors?

4. Is innovative activity linked to a firm's life cycle? (Hint: see also Chapter 8.)

Review Questions 6.3

1. What are the external interactions that can exist for innovative entrepreneurs that will influence the process of innovation?

2. How does your answer relate to the question of networking by firms and innovative activity? (See Review Questions 6.2.)

3. What are the principal ways that customers can be used to advantage by innovative entrepreneurs?

4. What role could support agencies take with innovative entrepreneurs?

Suggested Assignments ■ ■ ■ ■ ■ ■ ■ ■ ■ ■ ■ ■ ■

These questions refer to the Aquamotive case study, which is available from the student online learning resources centre.

As a basis for discussion:

1. With hindsight, was the strategy to use MBS to gain time and finance, as well as business experience, correct?

2. What are the difficulties faced by entrepreneurs in the innovation process as demonstrated by Aquamotive?

3. How can these be overcome?

4. What are the risks for a potential investor in Aquamotive?

As a role play:

Students are allocated roles through a briefing sheet that asks them to adopt one of the following roles.

■ Two students play the role of Alex and Marion.

■ One student plays the role of a business angel who has £100,000 to invest and is searching for an engineering opportunity.

Students who take on the roles of Marion and Alex must sell their idea to the business angel, who then has to justify his/her decision as to whether or not to invest in Aquamotive.

Additional assignments:

1. Identify a significant innovation introduced by a small firm or solo entrepreneur. What factors may have contributed to the success of this innovation? What barriers might the firm or entrepreneur have faced? (This is likely to be a web-based exercise.)

2. Identify a local small firm that has recently (in the last three years) introduced a new product and/or process. Interview the lead entrepreneur with respect to the motivation driving their innovation, the difficulties encountered and the success achieved.

3. Hold a class discussion around the theme of e-commerce generally and dotcom enterprises specifically. What opportunities are available to small firms? What factors are likely to determine the success of dotcoms?

Recommended Reading ■ ■ ■ ■ ■ ■ ■ ■ ■ ■ ■ ■

Hoffman, K., Milady, P., Bessant, J. and Perren, L. (1998) 'Small Firms, R&D, Technology and Innovation in the UK: A Literature Review', *Technovation*, vol. 18, no. 1, pp. 39–55.

Moore, I. and Garnsey, E. (1993) 'Funding for Innovation in Small Firms: The Role of Government', *Research Policy*, vol. 22, pp. 507–19.

Nooteboom, B. (1994) 'Innovation and Diffusion in Small Firms: Theory and Evidence', *Small Business Economics*, vol. 6, pp. 327–47.

Rothwell, R. (1983) 'Innovation and Firm Size: A Case for Dynamic Complementarity; Or is Small Really Beautiful?', *Journal of General Management*, vol. 8, no. 3, pp. 5–25.

Rothwell, R. (1984) 'The Role of Small Firms in the Emergence of New Technologies', *Omega*, vol. 12, no. 1, pp. 19–29.

Rothwell, R. (1994) 'Towards the Fifth-generation Innovation Process', *International Marketing Review*, vol. 11, pp. 7–31.

References

1 Sternberg, R. (2000) 'Innovation Networks and Regional Development – Evidence from the European Regional Innovation Survey (ERIS): Theoretical Concepts, Methodological Approach, Empirical Basis and Introduction to the Theme Issue', *European Planning Studies* 8, pp. 389–407.

2 Freeman, C. and Soete, L. (1997) *The Economics of Industrial Innovation*, 3rd edn, Pinter, London.

3 Geroski, P. and Machin, S. (1992) 'Do Innovating Firms Outperform Non-innovators?', *Business Strategy Review*, Summer, pp. 79–90.

4 Geroski, P. and Machin, S. (1993) 'Innovation, Profitability and Growth Over the Business Cycle', *Empirica*, 20, pp. 35–50.

5 Freel, M. (2001) 'Do Small Innovating Firms Outperform Non-innovators?', *Small Business Economics*, vol. 14, pp. 195–210.

6 Rothwell, R. (1983), 'Innovation and Firm Size: A Case for Dynamic Complementarity; Or is Small Really Beautiful?, *Journal of General Management*, vol. 8, no. 3, pp. 5–25.

7 Schumpeter, J. (1934) *The Theory of Economic Development*, Harvard University Press, Cambridge, MA.

8 OECD (1996) *SMEs: Employment, Innovation and Growth – The Washington Workshop*.

9 Tether, B. and C. Hipp (2002) 'Knowledge Intensive, Technical and Other Services: Patterns of Competitiveness and Innovation', *Technology Analysis and Strategic Management* 14, pp. 163–82.

10 Drejer, I. (2004) 'Identifying Innovation in Surveys of Services: A Schumpeterian Perspective', *Research Policy* 33, pp. 551–62.

11 Cooper, R. G. (1993) *Winning at New Products: Accelerating the Process From Idea to Launch*, 2nd edn, Perseus Books Publishing, USA.

12 Schmookler, J. (1966) *Invention and Economic Growth*. Harvard University Press, Cambridge, MA.

13 Tether, B. (2002) 'Who Cooperates for Innovation, and Why? An Empirical Analysis', *Research Policy* 31, pp. 947–68.

14 Freel, M. (1999) 'The Financing of Small Firm Product Innovation in the UK', *Technovation*, vol. 19, no. 12, pp. 707–19.

15 Johnson, J., Baldwin, J. and Diverty, B. (1996) 'The Implications of Innovation for Human Resource Strategies', *Futures* 28, pp. 103–19.

16 Freel, M. and Robson, P. (2004) 'Small Firm Innovation, Growth and Performance: Evidence from Scotland and Northern England', *International Small Business Journal*, vol. 22, no. 6, pp. 559–71.

17 Rothwell, R. (1994) 'Towards the Fifth-generation Innovation Process', *International Marketing Review*, vol. 11, pp. 7–31.

18 Kline, S. and Rosenberg, N. (1986) 'An Overview of Innovation', in R. Landua and N. Rosenberg (eds), *The Positive Sum Strategy: Harnessing Technology for Economic Growth*, National Academic Press, Washington, DC.

19 Rothwell, R. and Zegveld, W. (1985) *Reindustrialization and Technology*, Longman, Harlow.

20 Lundvall, B. (1995) *National Systems of Innovation: Towards a Theory of Innovation and Interactive Learning*, London, Pinter (first published 1992).

21 Smith, K. (2000) 'Innovation as a Systemic Phenomenon: Rethinking the Role of Policy', *Enterprise and Innovation Management Studies*, vol. 1, pp. 73–102.

22 Tether, B. (2002) 'Who Cooperates for Innovation, and Why? An Empirical Analysis', *Research Policy* 31, pp. 947–68.

23 Schumpeter, J. (1950) *Capitalism, Socialism and Democracy*, 3rd edn, Harper & Row, New York.

24 Acs, Z. and Audretsch, D. (1993) 'Innovation and Firm Size: The New Learning', *International Journal of Technology Management*, vol. 8, no. 5/6, pp. 23–35.

25 Galbraith, J. K. (1952) *American Capitalism*, Houghton Mifflin, Cambridge, MA.

26 Acs, Z. and Audretsch, D. (1987) 'Innovation, Market Structure and Firm Size', *The Review of Economics and Statistics*, vol. 69, no. 4, pp. 567–74.

27 Acs, Z. and Audretsch, D. (1988) 'Innovation in Large and Small Firms: An Empirical Analysis', *The American Economic Review*, vol. 78, no. 4, pp. 678–90.

28 Rothwell, R. (1989) 'Small Firms, Innovation and Industrial Change', *Small Business Economics*, vol. 1, no. 1, pp. 51–64.

29 Pavitt, K., Robson, M. and Townsend, J. (1987) 'The Size Distribution of Innovating Firms in the UK: 1945–1983', *Journal of Industrial Economics*, vol. 35, pp. 297–316.

30 Van Dijk, B., Den Hertog, R., Menkveld, B. and Thurik, R. (1997) 'Some New Evidence on the Determinants of Large and Small Firm Innovation', *Small Business Economics*, vol. 9, pp. 335–43.

31 Kaplinsky, R. (1983) 'Firm Size and Technical Change in a Dynamic Context', *The Journal of Industrial Economics*, vol. 32, no. 1, pp. 39–59.

32 Rothwell, R. and Zegveld, W. (1982) *Industrial Innovation and Public Policy*, Francis Pinter, London.

33 Abernathy, W. and Utterback, J. (1978) 'Patterns of Industrial Innovation', *Technology Review*, vol. 80, no. 7 pp. 41–7.

34 Utterback, J. (1996) *Mastering the Dynamics of Innovation*, HBS Press, Cambridge, MA.

35 Simon, K. (1995) *Shakeouts: Firm Survival and Technological Change in New Manufacturing Industries*, unpublished dissertation, Carnegie Mellon University, http://www.rpi.edu/~simonk/pdf/ksimonsphd.pdf.

36 Piore, M. and Sabel, C. (1984) *The Second Industrial Divide: Possibilities for Prosperity*, Basic Books, New York.

37 Miller, D. and Friesen, P. (1982) 'Innovation in Conservative and Entrepreneurial Firms: Two Models of Strategic Momentum', *Strategic Management Journal*, vol. 3, pp. 1–25.

38 Rothwell, R. (1991) 'External Networking and Innovation in Small and Medium-sized Manufacturing Firms', *Technovation* 11, pp. 93–112.

39 Oerlemans, L., Meeus, M. and Boekema, F. (1998) 'Do Networks Matter for Innovation? The Usefulness of the Economic Network Approach in Analysing Innovation', *Tijdschrift voor Economische en Sociale Geografie* 89, pp. 298–309.

40 Love, B. and Roper, S. (1999) 'The Determinants of Innovation: R&D, Technology Transfer and Networking Effects', *Review of Industrial Organisation* 15, pp. 43–64.

41 Sternberg, R. (2000) 'Innovation Networks and Regional Development – Evidence from the European Regional Innovation Survey (ERIS): Theoretical Concepts, Methodological Approach, Empirical Basis and Introduction to the Theme Issue', *European Planning Studies* 8, pp. 389–407.

42 Freel, M. (2003) 'Sectoral Patterns of Small Firm Innovation, Networking and Proximity', *Research Policy* 32, pp. 751–70.

43 Archibugi, D., Howells, J. and Michie, J. (1999), 'Innovation Systems and Policy in a Global Economy', in D. Archibugi, J. Howells and J. Michie (eds), *Innovation Policy in a Global Economy*, Cambridge University Press, Cambridge pp. 1–18.

44 Nelson, R. (2000) 'National Innovation Systems', in Z. Acs (ed.), *Regional Innovation, Knowledge and Global Change*, Pinter, London, pp. 11–26.

45 Hansen, N. (1990) 'Innovative Regional Milieux, Small Firms and Regional Development: Evidence from Mediterranean France', *Annals of Regional Science*, 24, pp. 107–23.

46 Lawson, C. (1999) 'Towards a Competence Theory of the Region', *Cambridge Journal of Economics* 23, pp. 151–66.

47 MacPherson, A. (1997) 'The Contribution of External Service Inputs to the Product Development Efforts of Small Manufacturing Firms', *R&D Management* 27, pp. 127–45.

48 Bayona, C., Garcia-Marco, T. and Huerta, E. (2001) 'Firms' Motivations for Cooperative R&D: An Empirical Analysis of Spanish Firms', *Research Policy* 30, pp. 1289–308.

49 Pittaway, L., Robertson, M., Munir, K., Denyer, D. and Neely, A. (2004) 'Networking and Innovation: A Systematic Review of the Evidence', *International Journal of Management Reviews* 5/6, pp. 137–68.

50 Freel, M. and Harrison, R. (2005) 'Innovation and Cooperation in the Small Firms Sector', *Regional Studies*, forthcoming.

51 Angel, D. (2002) 'Inter-firm Collaboration and Technological Development Partnerships within US Manufacturing Industries', *Regional Studies* 36, pp. 333–44.

52 Love, J. and Roper S. (2001) 'Location and Network Effects on Innovation Success: Evidence for UK, German and Irish Manufacturing Plants', *Research Policy* 30, pp. 643–62.

53 Maskell, P. and Malmberg, A. (1999) 'The Competitiveness of Firms and Regions', *European Urban and Regional Studies* 6, pp. 9–25.

54 Freel, M. (2002) 'On Regional Innovation Systems: Illustrations from the West Midlands', *Environment and Planning C: Government and Policy* 20, pp. 633–54.

55 Nooteboom, B. (1994) 'Innovation and Diffusion in Small Firms: Theory and Evidence', *Small Business Economics*, vol. 6, pp. 327–47.

56 Nooteboom, B. (1999) 'Innovation, Learning and Industrial Organisation', *Cambridge Journal of Economics* 23, pp. 127–50.

57 Freel, M. (2000) 'External Linkages and Product Innovation in Small Manufacturing Firms, *Entrepreneurship and Regional Development*, vol. 12, pp. 245–66.

58 CBR (2000) *British Enterprise in Transition*, Department of Applied Economics, University of Cambridge.

59 Audretsch, D. (1995) 'Innovation, Growth and Survival', *International Journal of Industrial Organisation* 13, pp. 441–57.

Information and Communications Technologies and E-business

By Dr Laura Galloway[a]

Learning Outcomes

At the end of this chapter you should be able to:

1 describe factors that affect the adoption of ICT by entrepreneurs and small firms

2 discuss the ways that entrepreneurs can strategically use ICT

3 explain how different environments and policies can affect the adoption of ICT by entrepreneurs and small firms

4 describe the different ways that entrepreneurs can utilise e-business and trading on the Internet

5 discuss the potential business benefits of ICT and Internet use

6 describe some drawbacks of Internet business strategies that must be taken into account by firms

7 discuss the strategic benefits of collective/collaborative online presence for firms

8 describe entrepreneurial e-business strategies

9 describe examples of e-business and Internet start-up businesses.

[a]Much of the research for this chapter has come from studies conducted along with Professor David Deakins at the University of Paisley and, particularly, collaboration with Dr R. Mochrie at Heriot-Watt University.

■ ■ ■ ■ Introduction

Innovation in the use of information and communications technology (ICT) has been very rapid in the last 30 years. ICT now impacts on most aspects of modern life, not least on business and entrepreneurial business start-up. This chapter will describe and discuss the ways in which ICT has impacted on business practice and how it has affected competitiveness, particularly for entrepreneurs and the small firms sector.

Several commentators have noted that there is a lack of cohesion in understanding of issues relating to and affecting ICT use for business.[1] This is, in part, due to the inclusive nature of ICT – access is afforded to all – all may realise some benefits (social and business) and also because the proliferation of ICT has been rapid.[2] Currently, therefore, studies of business use of ICT are often specific to common subgroups such as industry, firm type, geographical location and business orientation. Without much in the way of holistic understanding of business use of ICT, commentators such as Ramsay, et al.[3] have contended that our knowledge 'is at present under researched, conceptually confused and widely generalised' (p. 253). This has implications for those with an interest in understanding and supporting ICT use, such as policy-makers. Similarly, for entrepreneurs and small firms themselves, confusion prevails in terms of what ICTs to use; how they might benefit business and internal practice; and to what extent they might become increasingly necessary for firm survival. While researchers and industry are currently[4] 'engaged in an intensive period of e-commerce exploration and experimentation' (p. 2) in order to improve our understanding of the impact of ICT on business, there is still much evidence to suggest that, while barriers to use for small firms prevail, there can be considerable advantages for entrepreneurs and small firms from ICT use. Before examining entrepreneurial strategies with ICT that might exploit such advantages, we will examine what is meant by ICT (see box).

What is ICT?

Modern ICT use can be split into two distinct subgroups for small firms:

1. the use of technology to streamline, analyse or use information for business purposes

2. the use of technology to communicate information, via research or dialogue.

The first of these groups may include the use of technology for financial record-keeping, database collation and use, and software-assisted design – that is, standalone computer technologies.

The latter may include business use of communications technology for financial transacting, ordering, researching or developing relationships with customers and suppliers – that is, telephone- or Internet-facilitated technologies.

■ ■ ■ ■ ICT Use and Small Firms

Several researches have found that small firms are less likely to use ICT, compared with large firms.[5; 6] These studies show that small firm owners appear to be less aware of the varieties of technology available to them for business use and less inclined to facilitate the changes necessary within the firm in order to make appropriate use of technology.[4] In terms of Internet use, it is claimed that small firms lag even further behind. Ramsay et al.[3] cite statistics from the European Observatory for SMEs, which show that 'SMEs are not using . . . the Internet . . . for commercial transactions' (p. 251) to any great extent, and Anderson and Lee[7] note that Internet use for business among small firms is highly variable as 'progressive SMEs engage in e-commerce, but many [others] are stuck at the web presence point'. However, contrary to findings that firms in rural areas have even lower rates of ICT take-up than those elsewhere,[8; 9] a study involving the author found that the rate of ICT use in firms in rural Scotland was actually higher than expected.[10] However, the extent to which ICT was used by respondent firms in the sample firms from this study was limited. It may be the case that awareness of ICT is growing among small firms, but that increased information as to how they can impact on business practice at the firm level is required.

There have been, and continue to be, various reasons why ICT take-up among small businesses is relatively low. Suggested reasons for low take-up of ICT in small firms are given in the accompanying box.

Reasons for Low Take-up and Use of ICT by Small Firms

- The limitations of the technology available, such as cost, and availability and speed of Internet access,[11; 12] most of which will be resolved in time as costs reduce and higher speeds of Internet access, such as broadband, evolve
- Cost and availability of ICT expertise[1]
- Time and effort required for acquiring new ICT skills[13]
- Real or perceived lack of need, as many small firms trade locally and as such are often well served by conventional business methods, while others who might well benefit from ICT use may not be aware of the potential benefits for their firms[3; 14]
- An adversity to innovative business practices, or 'organisational inertia'[4; 5]

Despite the various identified barriers to adoption of ICT in small firms, many are reaping the significant advantages they can afford.

The Use of Standalone Technology

The use of technology includes the use of non-Internet-based tools and there is evidence that these offline technology solutions are used to a larger extent, and have been used for longer, in firms than are Internet-based technologies.[15] For example, Daniel[14] cites research by Mitev and Marsh, which found that business use of ICT 'tended to be confined to tools to automate standard administrative functions such as accounting, budgeting, inventory control and word processing packages' rather than extended to communications technologies (p. 234). The use of standalone technology for business purposes has had a highly significant effect on business operations, in that their use is now almost universal.[14] There is no doubt that, for small firms, the adoption of standalone ICT applications to meet specific business needs can provide benefit and, indeed, can often be a fundamental aspect of competitive advantage.[16]

Previous studies have found that the three most commonly used ICT applications in small firms are:[13; 15]

1. word processing
2. financial management
3. producing accounts.

These are all examples of standalone ICT use, rather than Internet-based communications technology. The technological revolutionising of business has not, therefore, come from the Internet, but rather has come from the standalone software made available for purposes specific to acknowledged need.

The Internet, as a global and inclusive communications network, has taken the technological revolution to a new level, however, as its reach and complexity has the potential to change the nature of business practice irrevocably and globally.

■ ■ ■ ■ The Use of the Internet

Throughout the late 1990s the dotcom industry boomed. Entirely Internet-based businesses were created and grown, usually at massive expense, often 'burning out' before a profit was ever made.[17] What has emerged since is that the most common form of Internet business is not, in fact, 'pure Internet', but rather is a traditional business that uses the Internet to best advantage. Subsequently, there are three types of firm in the modern business world:

1. those that exist in traditional, physical form

2. those that exist entirely on the Internet (for example, lastminute.com)

3. those that exist in both states; this latter type of firm is usually referred to as a 'hybrid' business.

The importance for small firms of having an Internet presence has been illustrated by Chaston, who observes that 62 per cent of US online trade is through traditional companies with an Internet presence rather than 'pure' dotcoms.[18] Most firms found on the Internet nowadays are, in fact, hybrid to some extent (i.e. most have an alternative, offline form, from traditional, physical presence, to catalogue or telephone facility). A good example of a well-known, traditional company that has become hybrid is Tesco, which exists now as the traditional Tesco supermarket, as well as Tesco.com, which uses the Internet for marketing and trading through its online shopping facility. Most large traditional firms are now hybrid, as some form of web presence becomes commonplace and, indeed, expected by consumers.

Research has found that offline, traditional sales can be enhanced by an online presence. Fasiq reports on a National Retail Federation survey in the USA, which found that consumers who visit a retailer's website spend 33 per cent more annually at the same retailer's stores as brand identity is reinforced by online presence.[19] For small firms, these benefits of the Internet are as applicable as they are to large firms and, in particular, can improve their competitiveness within the context of global markets dominated traditionally by large companies. (The various aspects of improved competitiveness are detailed later in this chapter). Further, entrepreneurial small firms pursuing growth via diversification, innovation or increased market share often find an online presence, when accompanied by appropriate strategy, highly effective. For example, the case of Hullachan (see the Entrepreneurship in Action box on p. 18 of Chapter 1), a shoe design and manufacture business, shows that the company found online presence and the facilitation of online trade so effective as a growth mechanism that, in order to meet demand, some manufacture had to be outsourced, thus increasing value for both Hullachan and its new partners.

The Internet Advantage for Entrepreneurs and Small Firms

In this section the potential and advantages of having an Internet presence, for entrepreneurs and small firms, are examined in greater detail.

An Internet presence can give advantages in terms of:

- improved business functions
- improved markets.

These are now examined in turn.

Improved Business Functions

Internal Efficiency: The potential benefits of business use of the Internet include affording greater internal efficiency. To illustrate, Leatherman[20] identifies that 'the internal functions of business operations, such as order placement, inventory control, technical specification procurement and product distribution, from paper-based to electronic transactions can dramatically reduce business costs and increase productivity' (p. 4).

Suppliers: Baourakis *et al.*[21] identify that by making use of Internet channels 'firms have the ability to find a greater number of suppliers, to communicate and interact internationally with a larger number of companies involved in the supply chain' (p. 582), and that this can be advantageous in terms of cost reduction for firms as well as improved efficiency. Correspondingly, despite the spectacular success of some business-to-consumer firms, such as Amazon and easyJet, the most common online trade sector is not business-to-consumer retail, but rather is business to business (up to 80 per cent of online trade). This implies that the business-to-business infrastructure (i.e. those throughout the supply chain) is benefiting from the ease, speed and lower cost of ordering and purchasing materials and services the Internet can allow, compared with the traditional supply chain infrastructure.[7; 22] The implications for small firms (entrepreneurial or lifestyle) that often operate with tight margins are thus obvious.

Networking: Networking activity,[23] as a 'social communication process which encourages the sharing of knowledge' (p. 263), has been shown by several commentators to have a positive influence on business.[24; 25] However, some experts question the applicability of the Internet to the creation of networks for business purposes. It is contended[23] that while the Internet can provide channels for network communication, it is only effective 'where it is used alongside relevant people management and organisational practices' (p. 263). This is because face-to-face interactivity facilitates trust, rapport and tacit knowledge and these are essential for effective networking. Virtual networking, in isolation, is therefore a poor substitute. However, there is increasing discussion about the use of the Internet for specific networking purposes. For example, Reynolds notes that online networks have been shown to be effective for collaborative purchasing by larger firms.[2] Additionally, Tse and Soufani[26] refer to networks of different firms offering common or complementary products/services becoming 'an essential form of organisation' (p. 310). This 'product bundling' is not a new idea. Reynolds refers to conventional specialist 'bundling' (e.g. by mail order), but notes that with the increased proliferation of the Internet it has become a more efficient way of marketing products and services because 'they are rendered more visible . . . by making use of electronic channels' (p. 420).

Small businesses – such as those trading in niches or rural areas, for example – have an opportunity to exploit this. Indeed, Sparkes and Thomas[27] and Baourakis *et al.*[21] have identified collective online presentation of niche products, from Wales and Crete respectively; and the author has identified similar collective activity among rural businesses that use the rural locality as the common brand.[10; 28] These collaborations promote trade with customers who are attracted not by the products being offered, specifically, but by the 'brand'. Again, this use of collaborative manipulation of perceptions of what is being offered is not new, and successful Internet operators have consistently exploited the distinctions between goods and services offered; for example, Reynolds cites Amazon.com, which acts as a service provider of reviews, suggestion services, and so on, to complement, support and enhance its core business of selling books.[2] What is new is that the Internet can afford similar collaborative opportunities to any group of firms, including small firms that might previously have been prohibited from such activity by barriers such as costs and the organisational complexity required for such endeavours. While organisation and strategy are still fundamental to the success of collaborative activity, the Internet comprises a medium where the barriers to realising collaborative opportunities are greatly reduced in terms of providing a communications network for collaborators and for customers, as well as a low-cost means of bundling products/services effectively.

Improved Markets

Improved Access to Markets: Baker[29] notes that 'Internet users in the home rose by 76 per cent to six million in the UK during 1998, with the use at the office up 54 per cent to 5.3 million in the same period' (p. 26). Even if a firm does not have online trade facilities, therefore, the Internet can give firms the advantage of increased profile in that it can allow them to present information to a vastly increased number of potential customers, and provide another channel for the purposes of brand building, advertising and marketing.[26; 30; 31]

The most obvious advantage of the Internet for small businesses, however, is its facilitation of direct trade with global markets. Grant reports the International Data Group estimates that 'e-commerce grew to $600 billion in 2001, a 68 per cent increase over 2000'.[32] In the USA, Zinkhan[33] estimates that 'approximately 50 million Americans are currently on-line' (p. 412), and cites Granic (2001) by stating that 'more than half of those . . . also shop there'.[34] The potential benefits to business are thus obvious and, indeed, Cardinali[35] observes, 'e-commerce is growing at a meteoric rate of greater than 150 per cent per year' (p. 347). With access to increasing markets throughout the world, entrepreneurs and small firms have a unique opportunity to expand either business-to-business or business-to-consumer operations from the traditional and local, to the global.[2; 13; 36]

A More Level Playing Field: Because of the 'virtual' nature of Internet presence, entrepreneurs and small firms can compete on a more level playing field. For example, the location and size of a company are less limiting than they once were, as with an effective website and sound online transaction facilities a young, small company can appear to be more established than it is and as such can be in a position to compete with older, larger and more experienced firms.

24-hour Trading: As the sun sets in one part of the world, it rises in another. Additionally, with the constraints of work, home and family, the pace of modern life today, for many people, has resulted in a move away from the nine-to-five trading tradition. Many people find 'out of hours' purchasing more convenient. The Internet has the capacity to facilitate this, in that as Buhalis and Main[8] note, 'the internet is gaining commercial viability . . . and enables [firms] to keep doors open 24 hours a day, at minimal cost to customers all over the world' (p. 201).

Increased Interaction with Customers: Personalised customer service is another appealing advantage of the Internet for businesses, in that it has the potential to increase customer loyalty.[7] Firms can develop and keep a profile of customers relatively easily, either by monitoring their purchases, or by asking customers directly to divulge information about themselves.[21][b] For example, if an online travel agent knows that a customer usually purchases weekend city breaks it can target its advertising to that customer appropriately. It can further refine this tailored service if it has information about customers' personal details (e.g. posting or e-mailing offers of reduced-price children's facilities to those with no children would not only be an unnecessary expense, but would also be a waste of both the firm's and the customer's time).

Relationships with customers also permit customer preferences to be communicated and this can inform modifications to products, the availability of complementary or supplementary products, and even new products to add to the range.[21] These can provide further entrepreneurial opportunities, not previously easily obtained, particularly by small firms.

The Downside

Access to large global markets and increased internal efficiency may sound appealing, but in fact they have to be very carefully managed. Customer loyalty is of utmost importance on the Internet as competitors are only a click away and customers will defect to them if the quality of experience is poor. Because of this, trade facilitated by the Internet must be both attractive to customers and reliable. Advertised costs, product descriptions, special online offers, delivery times, prices (including taxes and, if appropriate, postage costs) must be clearly stated, unambiguous and fulfilled as promised, if the small firm is to realise the benefits of an online presence fully. Hawkins and Prencipe[4] and Tse and Soufani[26] also note that benefits may be highly industry- or firm-specific. For example, trading online with remote markets is inappropriate for firms that provide customers with perishable or low-value products as time for transport and profitability, respectively, make this unfeasible. And, as Hawkins and Prencipe note, where 'the physical movement of material goods' is involved, global trade is only as reliable as the physical transport infrastructure, as reliance on this to get goods to customers continues to be an issue for firms.[4] In the absence of a substantial organisational distribution infrastructure, as is the case for many small firms, these can be significant obstacles to success. Equally, a small firm can find itself in trouble if it has underestimated the marketing potential of the Internet or has overestimated its ability to provide goods or services to other businesses or consumers as, in either case, the firm will be unable to fulfil customer orders on time.

Planning, management and strategic implementation is vital if a firm is to best exploit the Internet for business purposes. As is the case with all aspects of business, use of the Internet is not risk-free. It requires careful consideration in order that maximum advantage to a firm is achieved, and appropriate direction and administration in order to manage and control its use. A small firm must, therefore, consider carefully what it aims to achieve by web presence and the form of web presence most appropriate and most suited to its overall strategy.

Summary

Overall an Internet presence can provide powerful benefits for entrepreneurs and small firms, but like any other area of business strategy it needs to be planned carefully and

---

[b] If the latter method is used, it is prudent to give customers the choice as to whether or not they divulge personal details, and to make explicit the company's policy on the use of customer data. It is counter-productive for a company's customer service methods to alienate customers or to contravene data protection regulations.

Table 7.1: *The Internet: Summary of Advantages and Risks for Entrepreneurs and Small Firms*

Potential Advantages	Potential Risks
Greater markets, both locally and globally	Meeting increased customer expectations both locally and globally
Greater networking through increased contacts	Maintaining and managing relationships of increased networks
Increased contact with suppliers	Managing relationships with suppliers, with loss of personal contact
24/7 trading	Maintaining reasonable response times, potential lost opportunities
Increased advertising	Ensuring quality and security
Potential for e-business trading	Maintaining security
More equal playing field with large firms	Increased competition and increased knowledge to competitors
Access to resources	Need for search and monitoring facilities
Enhancements from advances in e-technologies	Need to maintain investment in ICT

managed with an appropriate *e-business strategy*. There are potential risks associated with the downside of the Internet, and a summary of advantages and risks is given in Table 7.1.

Degrees of Web Presence

There are varying degrees to which a small firm may have an Internet presence. Thelwall identifies five types of business website:[37]

1. company information and contact details
2. company information and contact details, and information about specific products or services
3. an online catalogue comprising details about the company's range of products
4. an online mail-order catalogue providing the opportunity to order online or by fax, phone, etc.
5. a cyberstore – the ability to accept payment online through an automated process.

Research has shown that web presence, managed appropriately, can have a positive impact on offline sales even where a firm's presence is low level (i.e. where a website comprising contact details and a basic advert for the firm is the extent of inclusion). For example, one survey of retailers found that up to a quarter of offline sales were influenced by the firm's website.[38]

Websites

In order to have an Internet presence, a website is an obvious necessity. Firms can create their own sites, or contract this task out to one of the many companies that specialise in this area (for example, the firm Virtual Scotland, profiled in the case study at the end of this chapter, provides, among its various other services, website design and construction at www.itcdesign.com). A domain name is also necessary, and there are several facilities for domain name registration available, including 123Domain Names (www.123domainnames.co.uk), Nominet (www.nic.uk) and Verio (www.verio.com). A company can either launch a site on its own server or buy space from an Internet service provider (ISP). ISPs provide connection to the Internet and charges range from a one-off fee to a monthly/yearly/bi-yearly, and so on, charge.

Regardless of the type or capability of the website, a company must ensure that its site is aesthetically appealing, easy to understand and easy to use. For example, customers will be quickly turned off by a site that is difficult to navigate or that has inconsistencies. It is also important to remember how your customers access the Internet. If your customers are home Internet users or small businesses, where access to the Internet is via a relatively slow telephone line/modem connection, they will not be prepared to wait long for graphics, sound, movement and the like to load, no matter how spectacular they are. One estimate is that Internet users will wait an average of 10 seconds before giving up on a site and moving on. As more and more consumers have access to broadband technology, however, connection, access and download speeds are increasing generically, thus reducing the need to limit the size of files required for website aesthetics and function. However, it is important to note that most consumer-based broadband provision is still based on telephone lines and as such is still relatively slow.[39] If a firm trades direct with consumers, therefore, attention must still be given to how and what is presented on the Internet in terms of size and corresponding speed of download for potential customers.

Getting Found on the Internet

Whatever type of Internet presence a company has, it is worthless if nobody knows it is there, particularly potential customers. Attracting visitors and customers to a site is a very important part of business Internet use, and has to be consistently maintained.

Search Engines and Directories

Search engines and directories are different things. Search engines – e.g. Lycos (www.lycos.co.uk) and Northern Light (www.northernlight.com) – tend to use software called spiders or crawlers to search the Internet for key words (for example, a brand, product or service). When changes are made to a website, crawlers/spiders will find the changes and a company's listing can be affected. Although a search engine can locate a site without that site being registered, registration is important as it maintains a company's presence even when changes to the site are made. It used to be the case that the greater amount of key words embedded into the text of a website, the more likely a search engine was to locate that site. This meant that websites that had nothing to do with the key word, but that belonged to companies or individuals who wanted traffic to their site in the hope of 'capturing' it, could embed many lexical items in their site – often invisibly – and could be included in the search results. This exploitation has been counteracted to a large extent by greater sophistication of search engine software. Some search engines – e.g. Alta-Vista (www.altavista.co.uk) and Google (www.google.co.uk) – include a supplementary directory service.

Directories – e.g. Yahoo (www.yahoo.co.uk) – use human assessment of a website. A company (or individual) has to apply for inclusion in a directory and a person assesses the application and the website before accepting it.

Meta-search facilities, such as Ask Jeeves (www.ask.co.uk), are also available. These use a variety of engines and directories to perform a search. A good guide to search facility inclusion is Search Engine Watch (www.searchenginewatch.com).

Whatever the type of search facility, the idea is that a company will want its website to be one of the first results of a search. In order to do this a business must maintain its registration with search engines and directories. There are online companies that, for a price, will do this so that the client firm does not have to spend time regularly maintaining its inclusion.

Links

Other methods of online advertising include banners (small advertisements that appear on another website, usually at a cost), affiliate programmes and associates, where a firm pays for a link from a related site to its own or has a mutually beneficial link agreement on an associated website (i.e. links to each other appear on each site). Again, there are online companies that will source and contact potential associates and affiliates for a firm – e.g. Link Share (www.linkshareuk.com) and Response Republic (www.responserepublic.net).

Low-tech Methods

There are a number of effective methods and techniques that allow entrepreneurs and small firms to maintain their presence and market their name on the Internet (see box).

Effective Ways for Entrepreneurs and Small Firms to Advertise a Website

- Adding the web address to all e-mails using a signature file (included in e-mail programs)
- Mentioning the web address on an answerphone message
- Including the web address in all traditional advertising
- Adding the web address to stationary, business cards, etc.
- Maintaining the site and product/service details regularly.[39]

Security

With customer service an optimal part of a firm's online trade, security is critical. Reasons for this include to:

- limit the amount of damage to your site by Internet vandals
- ensure that employees do not waste company time and money on Internet activities other than those associated with their jobs
- ensure that sensitive customer and company data – especially financial data – are not available
- prevent e-mails of a defamatory or derogatory nature becoming public (it can take only a matter of minutes for e-mail to reach the public domain due to its speed and copy functions).

There are means of protecting a website. For instance, various technology methods such as firewalls can be used to stop hackers, and software that disallows the use of websites containing 'barred' lexical items can stop employees abusing company time on the Internet. It is also a good idea for a firm to have disclaimers attached to all employees' e-mails clearly stating that the company is not responsible for the text contained therein. A small firm may not have the resources for all these measures, but they can be outsourced to companies such as Click Sure (www.clicksure.com) and Zeuros Network Solutions (www.zeuros.co.uk), who specialise in these areas.

In addition to electronic security, there are several low-tech means of adding security.[40] These include:

■ restricting Internet access to employees who work directly with the Internet trade side of the firm or require access for some other work-related reason

■ having computers clearly visible within an office to restrict those with Internet access to relevant use

■ storing all financial data – including company data, as well as customer's credit card details – offline, preferably on a separate offline computer

■ requiring employees to sign a non-disclosure agreement as part of their contract, to ensure that they do not abuse access to customer data such as e-mail addresses, home addresses, telephone numbers etc., as well as company information.

Doing Business on the Internet

For entrepreneurs and small firms, Internet trading, as with other forms of marketing and trading, needs to be part of an overall business and growth strategy to be of optimum benefit.[3; 41] It is not enough to create a website and post it on the Internet. Even if the website is merely an online advertisement with no e-commerce capability, it is important to update product/service details regularly. A site with more sophisticated facilities, such as online ordering and payment, requires close monitoring and maintenance. For some small firms this is best served by having expertise and responsibility for Internet trading in-house and, for others, it will be more cost-effective to receive support from external sources. There are many independent web-hosting and maintenance, and ICT and online solutions companies, including MHz (www.mhzscotland.com) and Wheel (www.wheel.co.uk).

Many statistics exist that show real and projected figures for increases in online spending – for example, E-Insight (www.e-insight.com), Commerzbank (www.commerzbank.com), BT (www.bt.com) – all of which show that both online business-to-business and online business-to-consumer trade is constantly increasing. The benefits to businesses with an Internet presence over those without are, therefore, obvious; more important, it is the entrepreneurial firms that have exploited e-business opportunities to ensure continued growth that have really benefited. For example, entrepreneurial firms such as Ryanair and easyJet have exploited the Internet to maintain their strategy of low-cost fares to gain market share. Similarly, in the case of Hullachan, mentioned earlier (see also the case study in Chapter 1), the company experienced substantial and rapid growth as a direct result of the implementation of an e-business strategy. Most important, and what firms that successfully exploit the Internet have in common, is that online business and trade are an integral part of strategic direction and fit with overall business strategy. While it is undeniable that e-business has opened up new opportunities, currently it is traditional firms that have exploited and are benefiting most from these opportunities.

The Future of Business on the Internet

For entrepreneurs the Internet, as part of the technological revolution, presents immeasurable new possibilities, many of which we can't yet imagine. While firms can no longer ignore the impact of an online presence, new ways in which the Internet can proffer profitability are inevitable. The initial 'goldrush' of the dotcom era proved rash, and sustainability has been achieved by strategic planning on the part of those that survived as entirely online entities, as well as those that have become hybrid. With improved trust and use, as a transaction medium,[33] increasingly 'the internet is uniquely poised to promote and deliver services, both to individual and business customers' (p. 423).

Certainly, the Internet and ICT are already established as mainstays of modern culture, and from the business point of view,[21] 'the internet is now considered as an established channel for commercial transactions' (p. 580). The way is now clear for true innovation and entrepreneurial acumen to exploit this evolving medium. As Small[42] claims, 'it is at the crest of such a wave . . . that fortunes can be made, new careers forged, new businesses created, fresh and imaginative techniques and strategies formulated' (p. 1).

■ ■ ■ ■ Conclusions

This chapter has described the various extents to which small firms can use information and communications technologies for efficiency and commercial advantage. There are, essentially, three degrees of implementation of ICTs for firms, comprising:

1. use of specific applications (often in the standalone context) to improve efficiency of specific aspects of firm activity
2. use of networks (internal and Internet-based) to ease communications
3. use of the Internet for business purposes, ranging from low-level participation (e.g. increased profile) to high-level participation (e.g. fully e-commerce-enabled trading).

The competitive advantages of Internet activity cannot be underestimated and as a medium for increasing business activity, including trade, it has already proved effective in both the business-to-business and business-to-consumer contexts. For all firms, e-business participation is worthy of serious consideration, and if advantages are to be realised effectively, participation must be appropriately planned and in line with the strategic direction and aims of the firm. Conversely, however, it appears that the future of Internet-based business also includes opportunities for those who are able to operate flexibly and able to judge and respond quickly to the changing environment. The future of e-business, therefore, is likely to comprise two types of business activity. The first, and most appropriate for traditional firms with additional Internet participation, is that activity is planned and is an appropriate strategic 'fit'. Conversely, and most appropriate to new Internet-only firms, is that while the idea must be well thought out, and appropriate preparation for entry and ongoing participation conducted, maintaining a dynamic, reactive strategy is equally important for survival within the context of the continually evolving medium. The case study that follows, on Virtual Scotland, illustrates how this new way of looking at and conducting business can be effective on the Internet and, further, how it can present new and exciting opportunities for those entrepreneurial, flexible and creative enough to take them.

Starting an E-business – Forbes Manson and Virtual Scotland

Background

At the age of 27, Forbes Manson already had experience of IT and the Internet having worked for a small company in the games and entertainment sector, and having completed a degree in Business Information Technology at his local university. Forbes believed that the Internet held many opportunities, and as a student he elected to study entrepreneurship and enterprise alongside his core subjects, and look for gaps in the online market. He identified that, at that time, there were no detailed guides to facilities, attractions and information about his native city, Glasgow.

Development of the Idea

Forbes' entrepreneurship elective at university provided him the opportunity to research and develop a business idea and complete a feasibility study. It also required him to prepare a working business plan. Forbes used his idea of an online information service and guide to Glasgow as his focus for these assignments, and through this was able to develop and refine the idea.

Competition

Forbes identified that information sites about Glasgow tended to be specific to one particular aspect of the city (e.g. history or pubs), but there was no site that constituted a comprehensive information service about the city, including history, culture, places to go, and so on. Forbes also noted that information sites about Glasgow do not offer visitors much in the way of linked information. So, while competition did exist, Forbes concluded that he could provide a service with a broader range and at a lower cost than his competitors. This more holistic service links up information in such a way that if customers access his site for information about, for example, movies being shown in the city, they will not only receive a list of appropriate cinemas with links to route maps, film titles, times and dates, and so on, but will also receive information about other related facilities within a one-mile radius (e.g. pubs, restaurants, nightclubs), again including links to maps and other appropriate information (e.g. restaurant menus, prices). Additionally, unlike his competitors, an availability and booking service is offered at no extra charge to business.

Realisation

Forbes' vision of a comprehensive online guide to Glasgow first started to become a reality when he registered the domain names www.virtualscotland.net and www.inyourcity.com. Virtual Scotland is registered as a limited company and originally offered web hosting, design, maintenance, advice and advertising via local directories. The first of these local directories is inyourcity for Glasgow (inyourcity.co.uk/glasgow/), which generates revenue from advertising the services included, providing links to their sites and, where there is no site, creating one. Services and information available through inyourcity include local information, news, weather, events (e.g. concerts, exhibitions), cinema, shopping, area guides, virtual tours (e.g. of museums) and a business search facility.

As a means of attracting and maintaining interest in the site Forbes was also keen to establish a community 'feel' to the service. Chat rooms and noticeboards are key features of inyourcity and are mainly responsible for the fact that inyourcity.com attracted between 7000 and 8000 visitors per month *before* any businesses had bought into the service and before any target advertising had taken place.

Organisation

Forbes and his mother Isobel own Virtual Scotland, each with a 50 per cent interest. As the operational partner, Forbes is the managing director of the company, while Isobel is the company's secretary. There are two other employees who work on an ad hoc basis to assist Forbes with website content, design and creation.

Web hosting is rented from a third party, which deals with all back-up and security issues.

Virtual Scotland is based within Glasgow city centre, at the heart of the city's business and entertainment communities.

Start-up Costs

Virtual Scotland operates from office space owned by Forbes' family. There is, therefore, no office rental to pay. Equipment and fees for start-up were estimated at £20,000. While banks and other external types of funding were considered, both directors' savings were sufficient to cover the cost of start-up, so debt finance was not necessary.

Sales

It took almost a year to complete the infrastructure necessary for inyourcity.com to start to generate revenue. With the site finished, Forbes and his team had to sell the idea to businesses. Initially restaurants, sports venues, nightclubs and bars were targeted. While focusing on sales to businesses, the inyourcity team consistently advertise throughout Glasgow to those who comprise a market for these businesses. As Forbes puts it,

Unlike our competitors, we intend to avoid a massive advertising campaign at the start which will increase visitors in numbers not matched by the amount and variety of businesses we are facilitating online. Instead, what we intend doing is to slowly, but consistently, increase the profile of the company. By taking this bit-by-bit long-term approach we plan to avoid being missed by the target market, and to gradually establish our name within people's consciousness.

Internet Strategies

A year into trading, Forbes was concerned that the Virtual Scotland side of the business – the web hosting, design and maintenance services – were not selling well in the face of increasing competition. On the other hand, he found that his strategy in terms of forming online communities was highly successful, particularly with young people participating in online forums based on various nightclubs throughout the city. The original plan for the creation of these forums and communities was to have a strong consumer base with which to encourage firms to become customers of inyourcity in order to access them. Forbes found that while this did work throughout the inyourcity range, most lucrative were the very highly populated nightclub forums. As a result, not only could he attract advertisers keen to market to these niche groups, but he could also negotiate strategic partnerships with the various organisations that own nightclubs in Glasgow. In response to changing priorities and customer demand, the structure of the organisation has changed too. Virtual Scotland remains the central company within which all activities are based, while iycdesign.com is the point of access for website design and construction services, and the original inyourcity/glasgow facility is still operational and valuable to the business. Additionally, Forbes has subsequently created a further product, alternativenation.net, which acts as a portal to nightclub websites (most often created and maintained by Forbes), hosts nightclub-based forums and provides other related services, such as events promotion. The success of this part of the business is such that, in partnership with nightclub owners, Forbes has become involved in activities such as record production and other spin-off selling. This is a far cry from the original Virtual Scotland and inyourcity idea, and is testament to Forbes' flexible approach and exploitation of strategies of emergence, highly appropriate for trading in the complex and unpredictable environment of the Internet. As Forbes puts it, 'We go with what works and wind up what doesn't.'[c]

[c] For information about the incidence and use of strategies of emergence and their appropriateness to Internet entrepreneurship, see Small, P. (2000) *The Entrepreneurial Web*, ft.com/Pearson Education, London.

Review Questions 7.1

1. Give examples of ICT applications useful for increasing internal business efficiency.

2. What are the reasons that some firms do not use ICT as much as they could?

3. How would you advise firms with regard to the implementation of ICT use for business purposes?

Review Questions 7.2

1. How can small entrepreneurial firms use the Internet to compete with large firms?

2. What are the different ways that firms may use the Internet?

3. How would you advise an entrepreneur looking to start a new firm on developing an Internet strategy?

Review Questions 7.3

1. What differentiates firms that have survived as pure dotcoms from those that have failed since the dotcom boom?

2. To what extent is planning an integral part of pure Internet-based business?

3. What skills and characteristics are most likely to produce success for pure Internet traders?

Suggested Assignments

The following questions are based on the Virtual Scotland case study on pp. 151–2 of this chapter.

Discussion questions

1. As the initial targets for inyourcity sales are nightclubs, sports venues, restaurants and bars, what is the target market inyourcity should be aiming its advertising at in order to generate sales to these types of business?

2. As a young company with limited cash, how would you advertise to this market?

3. Once revenue is established, would you change your advertising strategy and, if so, how?

4. A major problem inyourcity has faced is that its bank refuses to allow it to set up a direct debit arrangement with companies, claiming that it is more cost-effective for it if payments are made by standing order. A direct debit facility would allow inyourcity to draw money owed monthly from a company's bank account, whereas a standing order would have to be set up by the purchasing company to transfer the money into inyourcity's account. From the point of view of both the business customers and inyourcity, a direct debit arrangement is best because it means that transaction occurs with the least hassle for the business customer. Inyourcity's bank is refusing to allow a direct debit arrangement because it considers it too costly to set up when currently there are few sales. How would you deal with this 'catch 22' situation of being unable to generate sales fully because you don't have a direct debit facility to transact them?

5. How would you attract participants to alternativenation.net?

6. Give examples of some ways in which Forbes can generate revenue from alternativenation.net forums.

Written assignment

7. What should Forbes' short-, medium- and long-term strategy be? What would you do if you were Forbes?

Recommended Reading ■ ■ ■ ■ ■ ■ ■ ■ ■ ■ ■

Foresight Information, Communications and Media Panel (2000). *Let's Get Digital*, DTI, London.

Foresight (2001) *Electronic Commerce Task Force Report*, DTI.

Sweeney, S. (2002) *101 Ways to Promote Your Web Site*, 4th edn, Maximum Press.

Turban, E., Rainer, R.K. and Potter, R.E. (2005) *Introduction to Information Technology*, 3rd edn, John Wiley & Sons.

Internet Sources ■ ■ ■ ■ ■ ■ ■ ■ ■ ■ ■

Statistics

www.e-insight.com

www.bt.com

www.shop.org

Search engines

www.altavista.co.uk

www.google.co.uk

www.ask.co.uk

Directories

www.yahoo.co.uk

Useful links

www.linkshare.com

www.iycdesign.com

http://searchenginewatch.com

www.UK-business.net

References

1 Matlay, H. and Addis, M. (2003) 'Adoption of ICT and E-commerce in Small Businesses: An HEI-based Consultancy Perspective', *Journal of Small Business and Enterprise Development,* vol. 10, no. 3, pp. 321–65.

2 Reynolds, J. (2000) 'E-commerce: A Critical Review', *International Journal of Retail and Distribution Management*, vol. 28, no. 10, pp. 417–44.

3 Ramsay, E., Ibbotson, P., Bell, J. and Gray, B. (2003) 'E-opportunities of Service Sector SMEs: An Irish Cross-border Study', *Journal of Small Business and Enterprise Development*, vol. 10, no. 3, pp. 250–64.

4 Hawkins, R. and Prencipe, A. (2000) *Business to Business E-commerce in the UK: A Synthesis of Sector Reports*, commissioned by the Department of Trade and Industry (DTI), London.

5 Fillis, I., Johansson, U. and Wagner, B. (2003) 'A Conceptualisation of the Opportunities and Barriers to E-business Development in the Smaller Firm', *Journal of Small Business and Enterprise Development*, vol. 10, no. 3, pp. 336–44.

6 Jones, C., Hecker, R. and Holland, P. (2003) 'Small Firm Internet Adoption: Opportunities Forgone, a Journey not Begun', *Journal of Small Business and Enterprise Development*, vol. 10, no. 3, pp. 287–97.

7 Anderson, M. and Lee, G. (2003) 'Clicks and Mortar: The E-commerce Experience for Scottish SMEs', presented at the 26th ISBA Small Firms Policy and Research Conference: SMEs in the Knowledge Economy, Guildford.

8 Buhalis, D. and Main, H. (1998) 'Information Technology in Peripheral Small and Medium Hospitality Enterprises: Strategic Analysis and Critical Factors', *International Journal of Contemporary Hospitality Management*, vol. 10, no. 5, pp. 198–202.

9 Smallbone, D., North, D., Baldock, R. and Ekanem, I. (2002) *Encouraging and Supporting Enterprises*

in Rural Areas, Report to the Small Business Service, DTI, London.

10 Deakins, D., Galloway, L. and Mochrie, R. (2003) *The Use and Effect of ICT on Scotland's Rural Business Community*, Research Report for Scottish Economists' Network, University of Stirling, Stirling.

11 Farmer, C. (1996) 'Nothing but Net', *Success*, vol. 43, no. 3, p. 58.

12 Friedlander, A. (2002) 'Networked Technologies and the Internet: A Brief Historical Perspective', Benton Foundation online publication.

13 Lawson, R., Alcock, C., Cooper, J. and Burgess, L. (2003) 'Factors Affecting Adoption of Electronic Commerce Technologies by SMEs: An Australian Study', *Journal of Small Business and Enterprise Development*, vol. 10, no. 3, pp. 265–76.

14 Daniel, E. (2003) 'An Exploration of the Inside-out Model: E-commerce Integration in UK SMEs', *Journal of Small Business and Enterprise Development*, vol. 10, no. 3, pp. 233–49; and Mitev, N.N. and Marsh, A.E. (1998) 'Small Business and Information Technology: Risk, Planning and Change', *Journal of Small Business and Enterprise Development*, vol. 5, no. 3, pp. 228–45.

15 Mitchell, S. and Clark, D. (1999) 'Business Adoption of Information and Communications Technologies in the Two-tier Rural Economy: Some Evidence from the South Midlands', *Journal of Rural Studies*, vol. 15, pp. 447–55.

16 Pollard, C.E. and Hayne, S.C. (1998) 'The Changing Face of Information Systems Issues in Small Firms', *International Small Business Journal*, vol. 16, no. 3, pp. 70–87.

17 Wolff, M. (1999) *Burn Rate*, Orion Books, London.

18 Chaston, I. (2000) 'Small Firms and the Impact of the Internet', paper presented to the ISBA Conference, Business Link, Lincolnshire, July.

19 Fasig, G. (2000) 'Firms Find Internet can Reinforce Brand Identity', *Cincinnati Enquirer*, September.

20 Leatherman, J.C. (2000) 'Internet-based Commerce: Implications for Rural Communities', *Reviews of Economic Development Literature and Practice*, no. 5, US Economic Development Administration, Washington, USA.

21 Baourakis, G., Kourgiantakis, M. and Migdalas, A. (2002) 'The Impact of E-commerce on Agro-food Marketing: The Case of Agricultural Co-operatives, Firms and Consumers in Crete', *British Food Journal*, vol. 104, no. 8, pp. 580–90.

22 Kaplan, S. and Sawheny, M. (2000) 'E-hubs: The New B2B Marketplaces', *Harvard Business Review*, vol. 78, no. 3, pp. 97–103.

23 Swan, J., Newell, S., Scarbrough, H. and Hislop, D. (1999) 'Knowledge Management and Innovation:

Networks and Networking', *Journal of Knowledge Management*, vol. 3, no. 4, pp. 262–75.

24 Chell, E. and Baines, S. (2000) 'Networking, Entrepreneurship and Microbusiness Behaviour', *Entrepreneurship and Regional Development*, vol. 12, no. 3, pp. 195–215.

25 Lechner, C. and Dowling, M. (2003) 'Firm Networks: External Relationships as Sources for the Growth and Competitiveness of Entrepreneurial Firms', *Entrepreneurship and Regional Development*, vol. 15, no. 1, pp. 1–16.

26 Tse, T. and Soufani, K. (2003) 'Business Strategies for Small Firms in the New Economy', *Journal of Small Business and Enterprise Development*, vol. 10, no. 3, pp. 306–20.

27 Sparkes, A. and Thomas, B. (2001) 'The Use of the Internet as a Critical Success Factor for the Marketing of Welsh Agri-food SMEs in the Twenty-first Century', *British Food Journal*, vol. 103, no. 5, pp. 331–47.

28 Galloway, L., Mochrie, R. and Deakins, D. (2004) 'ICT-enabled Collectivity as a Positive Rural Business Strategy', *International Journal of Entrepreneurial Behaviour and Research*, vol. 10, no. 4, pp. 247–59.

29 Baker, P. (1999) 'Islands Urged to Cash in on E-commerce Revolution', *FOCUS*, Summer/Autumn, pp. 26–7.

30 Jacobs, G. and Dowsland, W. (2000) 'The Dot-com Economy in Wales: The Long Road Ahead', paper presented at the 7th Conference of UKAIS, Swansea.

31 Turban, E., Lee, J., King, D. and Chung, M.H. (2000) *Electronic Commerce: A Managerial Perspective*, Prentice-Hall, London.

32 Grant, E.X. (2002) 'E-commerce to Top $1 Trillion in 2002', *E-commerce Times*, 13 February, www.ecommercetimes.com.

33 Zinkhan, G.M. (2002) 'Promoting Services via the Internet: New Opportunities and Challenges', *Journal of Services Marketing*, vol. 16, no. 5, pp. 412–23.

34 Granic, M. (2001) 'Opportunities and Challenges of Interactive Market Research', paper presented at the 4th AMA School for Advanced Marketing Research, Futures, LLC, Athens.

35 Cardinali, R. (2001) 'Taxing the Internet: Leveling the Playing Field or Milking the Cash Cow?', *European Business Review*, vol. 13, no. 6, pp. 346–52.

36 Amit, R. and Zott, C. (2001) 'Value Creation in E-business', *Strategic Management Journal*, vol. 22, no. 3, pp. 493–520.

37 Thelwall, M. (2000) 'Effective Websites for Small and Medium Sized Enterprises', *Journal of Small*

Business & Enterprise Development, vol. 10, no. 2, pp. 149–59.

38 Shop.org (2004) *The State of Retailing On-line 7*, Forrester, exec. summary available at www.shop.org.

39 Galloway, L. (2004) 'Is Broadband the Answer for Rural Business?', paper presented at RENT Conference, Copenhagen, October.

40 Coussins, C. (1999) *11 Point Plan for Business on the Internet*, Hullachan, Glasgow.

41 Rodgers, J.A., Yen, D.C. and Chou, D.C. (2002) 'Developing E-business: A Strategic Approach', *Information Management and Computer Security*, vol. 10, no. 4, pp. 184–92.

42 Small, P. (2000) *The Entrepreneurial Web*, ft.com/Pearson Education, London.

Entrepreneurial and Growth Firms

Learning Outcomes

At the end of this chapter you should be able to:

1 discuss the strengths and weaknesses of the main entrepreneurial growth theories

2 identify and describe some of the important factors that may affect growth in small firms

3 explain the importance of an understanding of the process of growth to the development of small firms' policy

4 describe and discuss the complexity of growth

5 evaluate the current developments in growth theory with reference to empirical evidence and existing knowledge.

■ ▩ ▩ ▩ Introduction

There is a basic distinction between the person or entrepreneur that wishes to go into self-employment to pursue their own interests (and perhaps enters self-employment because there is no or little alternative) and the person or entrepreneur that enters small business ownership because they have a desire to develop their business, to achieve growth, expand employment and grow into a medium-sized or a large firm. The former type of small business owner has very different managerial objectives from the latter. The objectives of the first will be concerned with survival and maintenance of lifestyle, whereas those of the second type will be concerned with growth and expansion, with the entrepreneur perhaps eventually owning several companies.

Many people who were made redundant due to 'downsizing' of traditional manufacturing firms in the past entered self-employment as small business owners. They were normally sole traders, employed few or no people, and their major objectives were likely to be concerned with survival and maintaining sufficient income to ensure that the business provided them and their family with, in their turn, sufficient income. These small businesses, which are the overwhelming majority of small firms in the UK, are sometimes called 'lifestyle' businesses. In other words, the owner-manager is only concerned with maintaining a lifestyle that he or she may have been accustomed to in a previous form of employment. A minority of small firms may be called 'entrepreneurial firms'; their owners will be concerned mainly with the strategic objective of achieving growth, and will often go on to own more than one firm.

There has been much speculation about whether such 'entrepreneurial firms' can be identified *ex ante*, that is, before they achieve growth, rather than *ex post*, after they have demonstrated growth. This presents a problem for researchers and policy-makers, and for investors such as venture capitalists who will want to identify high-growth and high-performing firms. It is a classical adverse selection problem created by uncertainty and limited (if not asymmetric) information. Despite the inherent built-in difficulties of identifying such growth firms, this has not stopped policy-makers from establishing support agencies such as the Business Links to support growth firms. This problem has also not stopped researchers from attempting to identify the characteristics and features of such growth firms and their entrepreneurs.

There is no agreement on exactly what measure to use to distinguish a high-performing firm. Should performance be measured on the basis of employment created or by some other criterion, such as profits, turnover or financial assets? Attention has, nonetheless, focused on identifying growth firms rather than identifying the constraints that may block the growth potential of many entrepreneurs and small firms. The inherent problem for policy-makers, however, is that environments that favour the expansion of some firms may not remain stable. There are only certain windows of marketing opportunity that can lead to the success of entrepreneurs and to growth firms. The right timing has proved to be crucial in many circumstances, even if other equally crucial factors might be in place. We saw with the Aquamotive case (available in the student online resources for Chapter 6) that the right product may not lead to growth and success if the timing is wrong and the environment has not been supportive. Even very successful entrepreneurs may not be able to recreate their success. There may be a unique combination of circumstances and perhaps the right combination of people that produce the high-growth firm. The rest of this chapter reviews theory, evidence and approaches to growth firms. It also provides basic concepts that will be referred to in some of the subsequent chapters, especially Chapters 9 and 10.

Almost 40 years ago Edith Penrose[1] classically noted that:

The differences in the administrative structures of the very small and the very large firms are so great that in many ways it is hard to see that the two species are of the same genus . . . we cannot define a caterpillar and use the same definition for a butterfly. (p. 19)

Yet, logically, there must exist a process through which small becomes large – one need only look at such visible exemplars as Microsoft, Apple or Dell. This process of growth, and growth firms themselves, have been and remain one of the main foci of research into entrepreneurship and small firms. The focus is further heightened by the contention that only a small number of small firms enjoy the bulk of growth in any given period. That is to say,[2] 'job creation amongst small firms is heavily concentrated within very few such firms' (p. 35).

This view, drawing impetus and support from the work of Colin Gallagher and others, [3; 4; 5] has, in effect, become accepted wisdom in the small firms literature. As a rule of thumb; 'out of every 100 small firms four will be responsible for 50 per cent of the employment created in a given time period'. Further, this body of research has had considerable influence upon small firms policy. Accordingly, blanket and early-stage support schemes, such as EAS and BSUS, have been all but abandoned in England, left to the discretion of Business Links, while in Scotland many of the LECs, though persisting with versions of these schemes, have begun to shift a proportion of their resources towards targeted support. In essence, the aim now is to 'pick winners' or, in Scottish Enterprise parlance, 'create winners'.[6]

Given limited resources and the desire to maximise returns or minimise losses, the attraction of a satisfactory predictive model, or growth theory, to policy-makers, financial institutions, support services and potential investors is clear. As a result, a commendable amount of research has attempted to articulate the process of growth or identify those characteristics that distinguish growth firms from their stable or declining counterparts. The purpose of this chapter is to review the major contributions to date and to make some comment on the future direction of work in this area.

■ ■ ■ ■ The (Neo-classical) Economics Approach

From the perspective of standard (or neo-classical) economics *all* firms within an industry are compelled, by the existence of a U-shaped average cost curve (Figure 8.1) and by universal profit-maximising behaviour, to expand their size until they reach (but do not exceed) the scale corresponding, given available technology, to the minimum feasible cost. In other words, all firms must grow until such time as the minimum efficient scale (MES) is reached. That is, the process of growth is at an end in so far as this process of optimisation is ended.

The minimum efficient scale is the point at which all scale economies are exhausted. Thereafter, the balance of diseconomies of scale serves to increase the average cost of each unit of production, leading to the U-shaped short-run average cost (SRAC) curve depicted in Figure 8.1. Moreover, as Figure 8.1 suggests, for very low levels of output, costs are lowest with plant size $SRAC_1$. Costs for plant size $SRAC_2$ are relatively high for these lower levels of output because of the higher fixed costs associated with this plant size. However, as output expands, plant size $SRAC_1$ would be required to operate beyond designed capacity, incurring high variable costs and accruing scale diseconomies. At these higher levels of output, $SRAC_2$ becomes the 'optimum' plant size. This argument can be progressed for the total number of feasible plant sizes, with

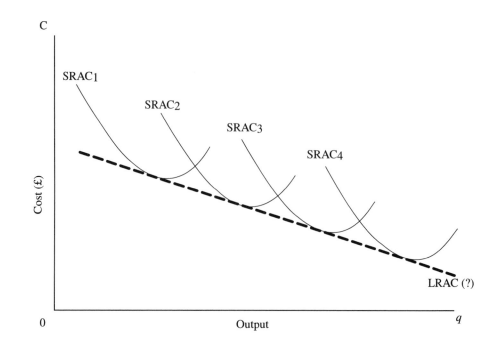

Figure 8.1: *Costs in the Short and Long Run*

the long-run average cost (LRAC) curve represented by the minimum point on each successive SRAC curve.

Following this logic, it becomes clear that, in the short run, growth is constrained by the fixity of capital – by each firm's ability to expand plant and machinery or, most simplistically, to expand factory capacity or build new factories. In the long run, growth will be limited only by market demand, or the willingness of consumers to purchase expanding output. As Marshall[7] noted, in this view, the long-run size of the firm will only be increased 'other things being equal, by the general expansion of the industry' (p. 460). However, Penrose[1] points out that, 'To say that the expansion of a firm which can produce unspecified new products is limited by 'demand', is to say that there are no products that the firm could produce profitably' (p. 13). In a world of conglomerates this is clearly an erroneous position. While there may be some 'optimum' output for each of the firm's product lines, there is unlikely to be an 'optimum' output for the firm as a whole. As such, under neo-classical theory, there can be no limits to the size of firms as long as there exist product markets that may profitably be exploited.

Problems arise when one confronts this elegant theory with empirical evidence. In this event, as Ijiri and Simon[8] note, 'the theory either predicts the facts incorrectly or makes no predictions at all' (p. 10). Clearly, firms, in the 'real world', within any given industry, are not of a uniform size (subject to some 'frictional' disequilibria), as the theory would suggest. In fact, firm size distributions within modern industrial economies tend to be highly skewed – with a small number of large firms dominating. Moreover, the theory fails to explain the changes in business concentration witnessed over the last 60 years (namely, the rise in concentration post-Second World War up to the end of the 1960s, and the reversal of this pattern from the mid-1970s).

There are a number of fairly obvious reasons, which explain why the theory fails to converge with real-world observations. Perhaps the most important involves recognising that competition is never perfect and is rarely pure. In other words, according to O'Farrell and Hitchens,[9] 'Many small firms, even if they are not efficient, may reach the minimum efficient size for their industry by selling to relatively uncompetitive and partially protected local and regional markets' (p. 1366).

The essential corollary to this is to note that business firms are not faced with the same cost curves. Without doubt, firms are marked by differences in their ability to access, *inter alia*, managerial resources, skills, technology and finance – and by the relative efficacy of these resources. In other words, firm competencies vary and, relatedly, relative costs vary. Moreover, firm strategies vary. A great many firms do not grow, at least in part, because they do not wish to grow. To talk in terms of an 'average' or 'representative' firm, as this theory implies, is clearly inappropriate and unhelpful when trying to comprehend the underlying factors that influence the occasional growth of individual firms. An appreciation that firms differ is an essential starting point for understanding why they differ (i.e. why some firms grow and others do not).

■ ■ ■ ■ Chance Models

As noted above, observation of real-world data on firm size suggests a highly skewed size distribution, with a few large firms and a larger tail of smaller firms. Such skewed distributions, of which the lognormal is perhaps the most familiar, may be generated by a stochastic process in which the variate (i.e. the size of firms) is subjected to cumulative random shocks over time. That is, with a sufficient number of observations, a mechanical chance model can be used to infer the size distribution of a *population* of firms that resembles actual empirical distributions. In other words, viewed in aggregate, firm size follows a 'random walk'. This 'fact' is the almost universal conclusion of econometric studies of both large and small firm growth.

The first, and most famous, exposition of this theory is Robert Gibrat's[10] 'Law of Proportionate Effect'. Leaving aside the associated mathematics, Gibrat suggested that:

- the causes of size change are numerous
- no single cause exerts a major influence on the phenomenon
- any influence is independent of firm size.

The final premise (that growth is independent of size), which gives the law its name, may be rephrased as[11] 'the probability of a given proportionate change in size during a specified period is the same for all firms in a given industry – regardless of their size at the beginning of the period' (p. 1031). It is this element of Gibrat's Law that has been subjected to the most rigorous testing, with generally negative conclusions. All in all, empirical results show a general tendency for growth rates to be negatively correlated with size, While their variance appears to decrease as size increases. In other words, taken in aggregate, small firms exhibit higher, but more erratic, growth rates. However, notwithstanding the falsifiability of Gibrat's proportionality hypothesis, it is the first two premises that, conceptually, present the most compelling logic. To illustrate, consider a study by Westhead and Birley;[12] having identified *88* variables hypothesised to influence firm growth, and subsequently conducted a large-scale postal survey, they found two (in the case of manufacturing) or three (in the case of services) factors exerted a statistically significant influence on growth rates. However, the authors acknowledged that these factors '. . . "explain[ed]" a relatively small proportion of the variance [in sample firm growth]' (p. 28). Many factors may be thought to influence firm growth, but their influence is seldom significant or consistent.

Obviously, to suggest that all successful businesses or entrepreneurs were merely lucky is to considerably overstate the case. However, Reid and Jacobsen,[13] while acknowledging that eliminating all factors but chance from the equation is to put the case too strongly, suggest that 'it is a necessary caution to those who would ignore the role of chance in determining the fortunes of a small entrepreneurial firm' (p. 81). These authors go on to offer anecdotal evidence, from their experiences with entrepreneurs and business owners, in support of attributing significance to the role of chance – of 'lucky breaks' and grateful perplexion, as well as the predictable 'hard-luck stories'. Such evidence, though lacking in academic or scientific rigour, is likely to be echoed in the experiences of most small firm researchers. It is surely undeniable that, in the presence of uncertainty and bounded rationality, fortune will play a significant, if variable, role in determining which firms will succeed. As Nelson and Winter[14] note, 'luck is the principal factor that finally distinguishes winners from near-winners – although vast differentials of skills and competence may separate contenders from non-contenders'.

Yet, in spite of a general belief in the influence of serendipity, it is clear that abstract stochastic models, of the type developed by econometricians, have little predictive or explanatory power at the level of the individual firm. Crucially, a better understanding of the growth processes of individual firms is central to the agenda of small firm academics and the business and public policy communities.

■ ■ ■ ■ Stage Models of Growth

With respect to the development of firm-level models of growth, much of the early theoretical and empirical work, during the 1970s and 1980s, attempted to conceptualise the metamorphosis of Penrose's caterpillar in terms of stage, or life-cycle, models of firm growth. These models, normally incorporating five stages, envisage an inevitable and gradual movement along a known growth trajectory – the classic 'S-curve' (Figure 8.2). At each stage the organisation undergoes changes in management practices and style, organisational structure, degree of internal formality of systems and strategy, in such a way that the stage-five firm is truly distinct from the stage-one firm from which it derived.

In this section we briefly outline two of the most commonly cited stage models of growth: those of Greiner[15] and Churchill and Lewis.[16] Taking them chronologically, the Greiner model posits a linear, continuous relationship between time and growth, postulating periods of incremental, trouble-free growth (evolution) punctuated by explicitly defined crises (revolution). Each period of evolution has a clear set of attributes that characterise it, and each stage, which ultimately degenerates into crisis, is a solution to the crisis of the previous stage (Table 8.1).

The crises outlined by Greiner form the bottom row of Table 8.1. In more detail these are as follows.

■ Crisis of leadership – the shift from a phase 1 firm to a phase 2 firm is triggered by a crisis of leadership. More sophisticated knowledge and competencies are required to operate larger production runs and manage an expanding workforce. Capital must be secured to underpin further growth, and financial controls must be put in place. The company must hire additional executive resource, and restructure to meet these challenges.

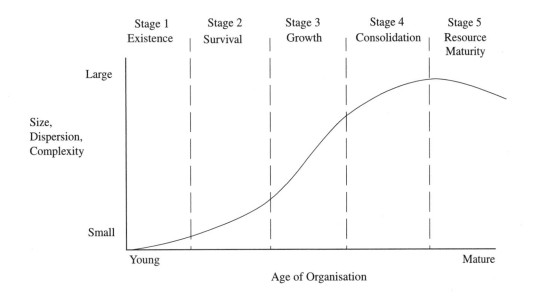

Stage 1   Stage 2   Stage 3   Stage 4   Stage 5
Existence   Survival   Growth   Consolidation   Resource Maturity

Figure 8.2: *Life-cycle Growth Model of the Entrepreneurial Firm*

Table 8.1: *Greiner's Model of Firm Growth*

Attribute	Phase 1 Creativity	Phase 2 Direction	Phase 3 Delegation	Phase 4 Co-ordination	Phase 5 Collaboration
Management Focus	Make & Sell	Efficiency of Operations	Expansion of Market	Consolidation of Organisation	Problem-solving and Innovation
Organisation Structure	Informal	Centralised and Functional	Decentralised and Geographical	Line Staff and Product Groups	Matrix of Teams
Top Management Style	Individualistic and Entrepreneurial	Directive	Delegative	Watchdog	Participative
Control System	Market Results	Standards and Cost Centres	Reports and Profit Centres	Plans and Investment Centres	Mutual Goal Setting
Management Reward Emphasis	Ownership	Salary and Merit Increases	Individual Bonus	Profit Sharing and Stock Options	Team Bonus
Crises	**Crisis of Leadership**	**Crisis of Autonomy**	**Crisis of Control**	**Crisis of Red Tape**	**Crisis of ?**

■ Crisis of autonomy – the control mechanisms implemented as a result of the first crisis become less appropriate as the physical size of the company increases. Line employees and line managers become frustrated with the bureaucracy attendant upon a centralised hierarchy. Line staff are more familiar with markets and machinery than executives, and become[15] 'torn between following procedures and taking initiative' (p. 42). It has become necessary for the company to delegate to allow sufficient discretion in operating decision-making.

■ Crisis of control – top executives begin to perceive a loss of control as a consequence of excessive discretion resting with middle and lower managers. There exists little co-ordination across divisions, plants or functions:[15] 'Freedom breeds a parochial attitude' (p. 43). Top management must seek to regain control, not through recentralisation, but through the use of (undefined) 'special co-ordination techniques'.

■ Crisis of red tape – the 'watchdog' approach adopted by senior management, in phase 4, and the proliferation of systems and programmes leads to a crisis of confidence and red tape. Line managers object to excessive direction, and senior managers view line managers as unco-operative and disruptive. Both groups are unhappy with the cumbersome paper system that has evolved to meet the challenges of the previous period. The company has become too large and complex to be managed through an extensive framework of formal procedures and controls. Movement to phase 5 requires a shift to 'interpersonal collaboration'.

■ Crisis of? – the crisis into which phase 5 degenerates remains undefined in Greiner's model. He can find no 'consistent' empirical evidence that points to the nature of this crisis and the subsequent phase 6. However, he hypothesises that this crisis will revolve around the 'psychological saturation' of employees, which will occur as a logical result of the information age. Consequently organisations will evolve with dual structures of 'habit' and 'reflection', allowing employees to move periodically between the two for periods of rest – or some alternative format whereby 'spent' staff can refuel their energies.

The revolutionary components of Greiner's paradigm are perhaps atypical of the broader set of stage models (although Scott and Bruce[17] imply a similar set of crisis triggers). By contrast, Churchill and Lewis,[16] although commenting upon Greiner, present a more general depiction of growth models where transition from stage to stage has no explicit trigger (Table 8.2). Further, Churchill and Lewis include a sixth stage by dividing the standard 'Success', or 'Growth', stage into growth firms and what may be described as 'comfort' or 'lifestyle' firms; comfort firms (stage 3-D) are those that, having achieved economic viability and chosen not to proactively seek further growth, can be assured of average or above-average profits in the long run, provided that managerial incompetence is avoided and the environment does not change to destroy their market niche.

In addition to those represented in Table 8.2, Churchill and Lewis include a further two factors in their paradigm that do not allow for easy tabulation: 'Organisation' and 'Business and Owner'. Addressing 'Organisation', in the first instance, the authors[16] posit an internal organisational structure of progressively increasing horizontal and vertical complexity, thus allowing for greater managerial sophistication and delegation. In the first instance 'the organization is a simple one – the owner does everything and directly supervises subordinates' (p. 33). Ultimately, however, as resources allow and complex operations require, 'the management is decentralized, adequately staffed, and experienced'; extended hierarchies have evolved with detailed reporting relationships.

Table 8.2: *The Churchill and Lewis Model of Firm Growth*

	Stage 1 Existence	Stage 2 Survival	Stage 3-D Success-Disengage	Stage 3-G Success-Growth	Stage 4 Take-off	Stage 5 Maturity
Management Style	Direct Supervision	Supervised Supervision	Functional	Functional	Divisional	Line and Staff
Extent of Formal Systems	Minimal to Non-existent	Minimal	Basic	Developing	Maturing	Extensive
Major Strategy	Existence	Survival	Maintaining Profitable Status Quo	Get Resources for Growth	Growth	Return on Investment

With regard to the 'Business and Owner' factor, this tracks the importance of the original owner-manager from an initially increasing central role to an eventual peripheral capacity when the organisation has reached 'resource maturity' (Figure 8.3). In the early stages the owner *is* the business. He/she performs all the major tasks and is the principal supplier of energy, direction and capital. In contrast, by the resource maturity stage,[16] the 'owner and the business are quite separate both financially and operationally' (p. 40).

Following both Tables 8.1 and 8.2, along individual rows, from left to right, we see a logical progression in the sophistication of the individual factors. The implication appears to be that firms move from an informal and ill-defined birth, through a quasi-Taylorist state, culminating in the highest level of managerial and organisational refinement yet imagined. While there are obvious differences in the nuances of these models, they are sufficiently alike to permit consolidation. Thus, generalising, explicitly these models are intended to facilitate owner-managers and senior executives in recognising the stage at which their organisation stands and consequently identifying the skills required for further progression or, in the case of Greiner, the likely impending crises. Yet, while these models have the advantage of highlighting the notion that managerial skill requirements are not of a 'once and for all time' nature, there are fundamental flaws associated with their rigidity. From the literature,[18; 19] the standard critique is fourfold.

1. First, most firms experience little or no growth and therefore are unlikely ever to reach stages 3, 4 or 5. While Greiner allows for the conscious decision to remain in a particular stage, and Churchill and Lewis provide numerous

Figure 8.3: *Business and Owner**

*Smaller circle represents owner. Larger circle represents business. Adapted from [8].

'break-off' paths for disengagement or failure, it nonetheless remains implicit that the 'norm' for firms is to follow and complete the process.

2. Second, the models do not allow for a backward movement along the continuum or for the 'skipping' of stages. It is surely conceivable that many firms will reach 'take-off' only to find themselves plunged back into a struggle for survival due to unexpected changes in markets, technology or consumer preferences. In addition, the requirement for the firm to complete each individual stage, before moving forwards, seems excessively limiting. In the case of the Churchill and Lewis model, we can envisage some firms moving from 'existence' to 'growth' with such speed that 'survival' is either negligible or non-existent. We can also conceive of a start-up that is sufficiently large as to fulfil the criteria for Churchill and Lewis's stage 3-G.

3. Third, and perhaps most significantly, the models do not permit firms to exhibit characteristics from one or more stage, to become hybrids. As brief illustrations: from Greiner we can conjecture a situation whereby top management style is participative (phase 5) while the organisation structure is informal (phase 1); from Churchill and Lewis, a situation such that formal systems are either maturing (stage 4) or extensive (stage 5) and yet the major strategy is survival (a new franchisee may be one such example).

4. Fourth, the idea that firms are occasionally able to learn and adjust with greater effect in response to crises than in periods of relative stability seems entirely plausible. Yet, that crises occur in the non-random manner suggested, given the inherent uncertainty within which firms operate, is far less credible. It is conceivable that some firms will lurch from crisis to crisis and that these crises will not be of leadership, autonomy, control and red tape, but of market stagnation, market saturation, technology, finance or skills (i.e. a mixture of internal and external crises, rather than the purely internal crises Greiner conjectures). It is also conceivable that other firms will enjoy smooth growth over a relatively uninterrupted horizon.

Stage models do place a welcome emphasis on the role of history in defining the future shape and success of an organisation. Greiner explicitly notes the importance of 'historical actions . . . [as] . . . determinants of what happens to the company at a much later date' (pp. 45–6). Where difficulties arise is in the interpretation of this historicity, path dependency and crisis-stimulated growth. The frameworks suggested are overly rigid. The inevitability of each stage and each crisis is implausible. To assume that firms move from one stage to another along a narrow path, shaped only by periods of regularly recurring crises, ignores the variability and complexity of firm growth, the copious causes and the inconsistency of their influence.

■ ■ ■ ■ Predictive Modelling of Growth

In his final criticism of stage models, Storey[18] notes that the 'models describe, rather than predict' (p. 122). Accordingly, it is to the body of literature concerned with predictive modelling of firm growth that we turn in this section.

Financial Models

The early work undertaken by Storey et al.[20] concentrated on the role of standard financial variables in predicting successful small firms. This method, adapted from use with large corporations, adopted an inverted approach to predicting small firm success – predicting failure and identifying success by implication. After initial testing of 'univariate ratio analysis' (consideration of individual financial ratios in progression rather than as a composite) proved inappropriate, Storey and colleagues shifted their focus towards methods of multivariate inquiry (principally 'multiple discriminant analysis'). In short, while univariate analysis suggested, predictably, that low profitability and high gearing ratios were positive correlates of small firm failure, the researchers' 'optimum' multivariate model utilised cash flow and asset structure variables as their primary predictors. On the basis of this final model, Storey et al.[20] claimed a 75 per cent success rate in distinguishing between failed firms and survivors.

Several criticisms can be levelled at this technique, as listed in the accompanying box.[a]

Criticisms of Predictive Financial Models

1. The technique offers no historical insight. That is, there is little consistent evidence to suggest that the variables alter significantly as the companies approach failure, nor is there any indication of the underlying causes of failure.

2. As a predictive model for rapid-growth firms, the technique would appear inadequate. Since its purpose is to identify firms that will fail, the model is unable to distinguish between the small proportion of growth firms and the bulk of survivors.

3. The model takes little account of the human capital factors that assuredly play a considerable role in determining survival and growth.[21; 22]

Characteristics Approach

Subsequently, efforts to distinguish growth firms from their stable or declining contemporaries have tended to place a greater emphasis on non-financial characteristics of the owner-manager and the firm. In a comprehensive review and synthesis of the research literature,[b] Storey[18] postulates that small firm growth is driven by three integral component sets: characteristics of the entrepreneur (identifiable pre-start); characteristics of the firm (identifiable at start); characteristics of the corporate strategy (identifiable post-start). From the empirical studies reviewed, Storey isolates those factors where 'consistent' evidence of influence was available (Table 8.3).

Table 8.3: *Storey's Characteristics Approach*

The Entrepreneur	The Firm	Strategy
Motivation	Age	External Equity
Education	Legal Form	Market Positioning
Managerial Experience	Location	New Product Introduction
Teams	Size	Management Recruitment
Age	Market/Sector	
	Ownership	

---

[a] For a more detailed critique see pp. 78–83 in Reid and Jacobsen.[13]
[b] Summarised effectively in Chapter 2 of Barkham et al.[25]

The Entrepreneur

Motivation The conjectured influence of motivation has a tidy, intuitive and appealing logic. It is suggested that individuals who are 'pulled' into business ownership, and whose motivations are consequently positive, are more likely to develop growth firms than those who are 'pushed' and whose motivations are correspondingly negative. However, in common with other areas of entrepreneurship, motivation is likely to be a more complex process, often the result of an interplay of factors.[23] Simplifying motivation into an artificial dichotomy ('pull' versus 'push') is likely to be misleading.

Education There are two contrasting hypotheses presented for this factor. First, it may be argued that education provides a foundation from which the entrepreneur can undertake the personal and professional development necessary for successful entrepreneurship and that education will endow the entrepreneur with greater confidence in dealing with bankers, customers and suppliers. This, again, seems entirely plausible. Conversely, however, it may also be argued that 'business ownership is not an intellectual activity' (p. 129) and that the educated entrepreneur will quickly become wearied with the many tedious tasks that form the remit of most owner-managers. From the 18 studies that form Storey's review, evidence is found to support the former hypothesis in preference to the latter. More specifically, further research[24] has indicated that, while a first degree in a science or engineering subject may be most appropriate for high-technology entrepreneurs, it is likely that a trade qualification is more suited to success in many mainstream firms. It would appear that education, not to a level but of a type, influences the entrepreneur's ability in the given environment and, consequently, the firm's chances of growth. However, since little effort is made to explain the effect education has on firm processes we cannot explain why various types or levels of education *occasionally* influence growth. For instance Barkham *et al.*,[25] in their four-region study of the determinants of growth, note that 'Education matters ... but in an indirect way, and the disadvantage of poorer education can be overcome by those who adopt similar strategies to graduates' (p. 140); the authors suggest that education per se does not influence growth, but rather education influences strategic choice, which, in turn, influences growth. The underlying process issues remain hidden.

Managerial Experience Management is literally concerned with the management of people. In this vein, it is often suggested that, in all but the very smallest firms, the principal activity of the entrepreneur is the co-ordination of the work of other individuals. Hence prior managerial experience and, consequently, experience in the co-ordination role will allow the entrepreneur to more effectively attend to his remit and subsequently meet business objectives. There is also a parallel argument regarding the higher 'reservation wages' those with managerial experience are likely to have. Individuals with high reservation wages are unlikely to enter into self-employment without a corresponding high degree of confidence in a successful outcome. In either instance, prior managerial experience is thought to positively impact upon firm growth.

Teams Storey[18] notes that 'Since the management of a business requires a range of skills . . . businesses owned by more than a single individual are more likely to grow than businesses owned by a single person' (p. 130). This view is often taken to be axiomatic by both academics and policy-makers. However, from his research with high-technology firms (often viewed as the industrial sector representing the greatest growth potential) Oakey[26] noted that, 'rapid firm growth is strongly related to "single founder" businesses' (p. 16). On a different note, but perhaps as significantly, Vyakarnam *et al.*[27] argue that the core competency of successful entrepreneurs is the ability to build and manage effective teams – not the team itself. In this way, we may more appropriately conceive of the 'entrepreneurial team' as a dynamic and evolutionary phenomenon rather the static entity implied by characteristics or predictive models of firm growth. It is further argued by Vyakarnam *et al.* that the team-building process itself is 'non-linear, chaotic and unique', raising questions about the scope for policy to artificially contrive teams.

Age In line with the evidence viewed by Storey,[18] Cressy[24] argues that the critical characteristics of growth firms are associated with human capital variables – most significantly founder(s) age and team size. Much as with Gibb and Richie's 'social dynamic' model, age may be used as a proxy for accumulated capital (both human and material), though Gibb and Richie imply a degree of trade-off between accumulated capital, on the one hand, and energy and tolerance of risk, on the other. Notwithstanding this, it is interesting to note that research frequently points to a strongly increasing self-employment rate up to the 35–44 age group, declining thereafter, before rising dramatically again to peak in the post-65 age range.

The Firm

Legal Status In his review, Storey[18] finds overwhelming support for the contention that 'United Kingdom studies consistently point to more rapid growth being experienced by limited companies' (p. 140). Credibility with customers, suppliers and financial institutions is argued to be the principal benefit of incorporation. Although limited liability is often circumvented through the provision of personal guarantees to funding providers, it is difficult in the face of the evidence to dispute this hypothesis. However, from the perspective of predictive modelling it should be noted that legal form is by no means stationary. As Storey points out, 'we cannot reject the hypothesis that current legal status is a consequence rather than a cause of growth' (p. 141).

Age and Size The issues of firm size and age are often dealt with concurrently since it can be safely assumed that they are often related variables. While the relationship between size and age is by no means linear, we can plausibly suggest that in aggregate '[t]he more a firm grows (the bigger it is) the more likely it is to survive another period (the older it is)'.[28] With regards to growth, accepted wisdom states that small firms grow faster than large firms and that younger firms grow faster than older firms. From the point of view of policy, logic would superficially seem to endorse the support of small, new firms as a means to achieving employment policy objectives. On a cautionary note it should be understood that most studies deal with changing *rates* of growth and not with absolute growth. An additional caveat would be to note that since in practice all failures are omitted from empirical samples there is a tendency to overestimate small firm growth rates in relation to their larger counterparts.[29] Further, as recent research has noted, employment growth within the small firm sector is primarily a result of existing business expansion rather than new firm creation.[30; 31] Indirectly allied to this is the notion that[21] 'The probability of a firm failing falls as it increases in size and as it increases in age' (p. 17).

Location Since the bulk of small firms operate in localised markets, location (as a proxy for the buoyancy of these local markets) will presumably influence firm performance. In this vein, Storey suggests that, on balance, the empirical evidence indicates a higher propensity to grow more rapidly for firms located in accessible rural areas than for firms located both in urban areas and in remote rural areas – although no attempt is made to rationalise this finding. By contrast, more recent work by Westhead[32] found that 'the majority of firms suggested more than half their customers were located outside the county region of the businesses' main operating premises' (pp. 375–6) and that 'urban firms had recorded the largest absolute and standardised employment increases since business start-up' (p. 375). Fundamentally, the literature is decidedly equivocal on this point. Even the studies reviewed by Storey fail to reach consensus. Regardless, this factor does little to enhance our understanding of cause and effect. Location itself does not directly influence growth; rather a number of inconsistently related variables, such as physical and support infrastructure, resource munificence and availability of skilled labour, are the 'true' factors for which location acts as a fallible proxy variable.

Market/Industry Sector With regard to markets or industry sector, high-technology small firms have often been viewed as a potential panacea for the structural unemployment attendant upon the decline of traditional industries over the last 30 years. This view is reflected in the plethora of policy initiatives directed at this sector of the economy. However, as Oakey[26] stresses, what little evidence there is available to support this contention has been extrapolated from mainly American data. In contrast, and at the risk of repetition, recall the recent OECD[33] conclusion that:

Most high growth firms are not innovative in a technical sense, but may include marketing innovations or cross-national alliances. Most high-tech firms are not high growth. [and] Most new jobs are created by low innovation, low growth traditional firms. (pp. 57–8)

Concerned by policy-makers' excessively optimistic view of high- and new-technology small firms, Tether[34] notes that 'expectations of small firms as "atomistic" innovators and employment creators have become over-inflated' (p. 109).

Ownership Recently, a number of academic studies have indicated that a considerable amount of small firm growth is inorganic (i.e. growth through acquisition and through the development, by individual entrepreneurs, of other distinct businesses). The latter notion, often called 'portfolio entrepreneurship', has enjoyed a considerable surge in popularity.[35; 36; 37] Scott and Rosa[38] contend that the predilection of small firm researchers for firm-level analysis fails to recognise the contribution of the individual entrepreneur to wealth and capital accumulation. While this might be true, the survey-based methodologies employed have a tendency to overstate the case. For example, such remote, and often general, studies are unable to distinguish between those who have started another trading business and those who have merely registered another company for legal reasons. In addition, regardless of the merits of identifying portfolio entrepreneurs and shifting the focus of research from firm-level to individual-level analysis, the substance of the research findings to date has not advanced our ability to 'explain' the process through which wealth and capital are accumulated.

The Strategy

External Equity It is generally accepted that the sources of finance accessed and the corresponding financial structures of small firms will influence their propensity to grow. The relative reliance of firms on short-term, often overdraft, debt finance[39] is clearly far from ideal. To this end, Storey suggests that those firms that have either shared external equity or have been willing to allow an external holding in their company are more likely to grow than those who have, or are, not. This capital-for-equity exchange allows firms to circumvent the constraint imposed by short-term debt funding. Yet, we note two points that indicate the need for caution. First, as Storey himself points out, it may be the case that the only firms that attract external equity are those that have grown or exhibit obvious potential for growth. Consequently, there is no indication of the direction of causation. Second, irrespective of the inclination, or indeed disinclination, of small firms towards equity sharing, there undoubtedly exists some form of 'equity gap' (see Chapters 4 and 5).[40] In other words, many small firms, regardless of desire and strategic stance, are unable to obtain equity funding. It may be that this factor is, in part, not a true measure of strategy but is, instead, a measure of the beneficence of the external environment – an exogenous variable rather than an endogenous variable.

Market Positioning The temptation has always existed to characterise small firm competition as perfect in the economic sense,[41] with the implication that there are no consumer loyalties and products are largely commodities. In this way, firms are 'price takers', have no incentive to expand output, are unable to erect entry barriers and are overly vulnerable to market uncertainties. Clearly, if a little superficially, we can identify in many industries or markets a large number of small firms competing and this is undoubtedly part of the attraction of this view.

The argument for market positioning, then, is that growth firms overcome this lack of market power and pricing discretion by inhabiting niches or Penrosean interstices. Competition becomes monopolistic and the firm is able to set prices above marginal cost – making above normal profits, which help to finance growth and increase relative market share (thus reducing uncertainty). The general idea that competing on cost/price considerations is less attractive than a differentiation strategy is captured in Michael Porter's very popular generic strategies (Figure 8.4). Simply put, being the cheapest is, on its own, unlikely to be a winning strategy – particularly for small firms. Lower price has implications for margins and the ability to finance future growth. In addition, price frequently acts as a signal of quality and too low a price may suggest, rightly or wrongly, poor quality to many customers. This is not to suggest that having lower costs (or prices) is a bad thing. Simply, that if this is the sole basis of a firm's competitive advantage it is less likely to provide the platform for growth.

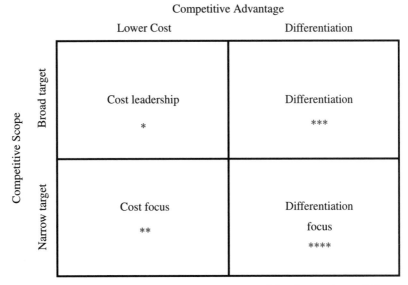

Figure 8.4: *Porter's Generic Strategies*

However, although a niche strategy may initially be advantageous, it is unlikely to provide the basis for long-term sustainable growth. Barber *et al.*,[42] for instance, suggest that,

[t]he challenge facing the growing firm can be stated in terms of a move from relatively narrow market niches in which it exploits a narrow range of distinctive assets into a situation in which it serves a larger number of market segments with a much broader skills and knowledge base. (pp. 15–16)

Another, and related, component of market position involves competitor characteristics. It may plausibly be argued that fast-growth firms, occupying market niches, see their primary competitors as other small firms occupying the same or adjacent niches.[41] Conversely, poorer-performing firms would be in direct competition with large firms where no niche exists. Accordingly, the large firms are able to take advantage of a relatively large market share (and associated market power) to the detriment of the small firm. While there is an internal logic to this argument the empirical evidence is, once again, inconclusive. For instance, Westhead and Birley[12] note that '[Growth] firms are associated with a strategic stance of competing with large employment sized firms rather than a decision to operate in markets saturated by fellow new and small firms' (p. 28).

New Product Introduction New product introduction is, as a means of differentiating one firm's products from another's, related to the above discussion of product differentiation and market niches. However, it is not clear whether the measure addresses products new to the market and industry, or simply those new to the firm (i.e. an extension of an individual firm's product range). Truly new products (i.e. those new to the market and/or industry) are often taken as a measure of innovative activity and it is suggested that innovative firms perform better than non-innovative firms.[43; 44] However, if we recall, from the discussion of market/industry sector above, Oakey[26] finds little evidence to support the contention that innovative firms enjoy super-growth. This is supported, in part, by Wynarczyk and Thwaites[45] who find that 'strong growth in employment is not a strong feature of the average innovative firm' (p. 186). Moreover, recent literature[46] suggests that firms whose efforts at innovation fail are more likely to perform poorly than those that make no attempt to innovate. To restate, it may be more appropriate to consider three innovation-derived subclassifications – i.e. 'tried and succeeded', 'tried and failed' and 'not tried' – rather than two. Dichotomising may serve to overstate the observed performance differential between innovative small firms and genuine non-innovators (i.e. those firms attempting no innovation), leading to the conclusion that firms not attempting to innovate are inevitably making an unwise choice. This is patently an erroneous position.

Turning to the second subfactor (i.e. products new to the firm only), one may logically suggest that the broadening of product or service portfolios would insulate the firm against localised market shocks, and consequently improve survival chances and increase likelihood of growth. Unfortunately, little or no work is available to support this final hypothesis.

Management Recruitment Recalling the stage models discussed in the earlier part of this chapter it can be seen that, as the firm grows, the managerial function becomes progressively more complex. This is likely to hold true, though perhaps not in the inevitable and incremental manner suggested by the stage models. As the firm grows the manager can no longer maintain effective control over the minutiae of day-to-day operations and is required to delegate certain tasks to wage employees within the firm. The owner-manager's task becomes the identification or recruitment and motivation of suitable individuals who can 'manage' in his/her stead – sometimes characterised as a move from 'doing' to 'managing' to 'managing managers'. In a very general way, this is linked to the Penrosean competency/resource theory of firm growth (the link may also extend to the earlier discussion of teams). Penrose[47] argued that the presence of sufficiently experienced executive resource was required for confident planning and subsequent growth. However, in the Penrosean model, executive resource would ideally be internally experienced, whereas Storey suggests that growth firms are more likely to recruit managers externally. Regardless, as Storey notes, there has been insufficient research in this area. Intuitively, it is likely that management recruitment is both a consequence and a cause of growth and any subsequent growth will be significantly influenced not by the presence of but by the efficacy of new management.

At this point some general comment on the issue of firm strategy seems in order. Not least because many similarly motivated texts devote considerably more space to the issue than we have allowed here. However, while there is undoubtedly a growing, if somewhat patchy, literature concerned with strategy in small firms, it is not clear to what extent this has improved our understanding of firm growth. Indeed, O'Farrell and Hitchens'[9] conclusion seems as pertinent now as it did almost 20 years ago:

Numerous studies testify to a strategy-performance relationship, although the findings are significant more for establishing the importance of a strategy than for telling what strategies to follow under particular circumstances.

Given the importance of context, attempts to be more specific often appear unreasonably prescriptive. The 'right' strategy is likely to be contingent upon a host of factors, both internal and external to the firm. On the other hand, simply making a value distinction between strategy and tactics, between long- and short-term planning, is not entirely helpful either. For the majority of small firms, the luxury of a three- or five-year planning horizon is one that they simply cannot afford amid the struggle for short-term survival.

However, to return to Storey's model: in addition to his triumvirate, Storey notes the importance of the 'wish to grow' in achieving growth (pp. 119–21). This conjecture is supported by Smallbone *et al.*,[48] who contend that 'One of the most important factors [in influencing growth] is the commitment of the leader of the company to achieving growth' (p. 59). While it can plausibly be argued that all small firms that grow do not do so willingly, occasionally being 'dragged' by a growing dominant customer, it would nonetheless seem prudent to include this factor in any predictive growth model.

The model described above clearly has a number of weaknesses – most of which are identified by Storey himself. Nonetheless, it represents the best available model, of its type. Moreover, the logic underlying the inclusion of individual variables is compelling and, in aggregate, they probably impact upon firms in much the way Storey envisages. Accordingly, it is emphatically not our intention to suggest that any of the factors discussed above do not influence firm growth – they undoubtedly do. Rather, there exists concern over the consistency of impact. And consistency is a prerequisite for prediction. Fundamentally, the influence of each variable is neither consistent nor, by consequence, predictable. Storey's model, and models of its ilk, neither describe, predict nor, more importantly, explain very well. To this end, we would echo Smallbone *et al.*[48] in suggesting that '[w]hile it may be possible to identify key success factors that affect the growth of SMEs, it is unlikely that a comprehensive model with predictive capability will emerge'.

It should be noted that Storey, in his turn, is chary of 'picking winners', most especially at start-up. Likening the process to a horse race, where the odds of backing a winner are unknown (though factors such as form or lineage may influence the outcome), Storey[49] suggested that, when 'gambling' with public money, it would be better to back horses after a significant number of hurdles had been cleared – that is, after the high number of failures, associated with the initial two- to three-year trading period, have occurred.

■ ■ ■ ■ ■ Barriers to Growth

At the same time as the predictive modelling literature has grown, other commentators have argued that the focus of research and policy should be towards relieving barriers to growth for small firms, rather than identifying generic characteristics or sets of characteristics.[23] Although such an approach does not concern itself directly with growth theories, it has merits that recommend its inclusion in a review chapter of this type. The suggestion that 'artificial' barriers to growth exist and that firms may grow more readily were these barriers to be removed may be viewed from a different perspective. Implicitly, this approach suggests that a particular external state or internal structure is more appropriate for growth than that which prevails in the absence of suggested interventions.

As part of an ACARD (Advisory Council for Applied Research and Development) and DTI-sponsored study designed to examine the barriers to growth faced by 'high flyers', Barber et al.,[42] summarising the literature, suggest that these constraints consist of three types: Management and Motivation; Resources; and Market Opportunities and Structure.[c] Specifically, these would include, *inter alia*: lack of management training, relatively low qualifications, reluctance to delegate and the need for new management skills and techniques as the organisation grows; access to finance, access to skilled labour and access to technology; market growth rates, size and frequency of purchases, degree of segmentation and opportunities for collaboration or merger. Many of the factors in this list are complements of, or related to, variables discussed in the previous sections. For example, lack of management training may equate with prior management experience, low qualifications with education, degree of segmentation with market positioning, and so on. However, the variable that sits least comfortably, although arguably loosely related to the earlier discussion of external equity, is that of access to finance. In addition, this is the most commonly cited and vigorously debated 'barrier' to growth.

Although the issue of finance was discussed in greater detail in Chapters 4 and 5, the following represents a brief recounting with a view to the current context. The argument generally focuses upon either the 'equity gap', discussed earlier, or access to bank finance – since most firms rely principally upon the latter method of funding. With regard to banks, it is often argued that some form of market failure or 'finance gap' in the provision of debt to small firms exists. In short, small firm demand for bank loans exceeds supply and the market fails to reach equilibrium at prevailing prices (interest rates set, by the Bank of England, below market equilibrium price). However, such an argument assumes homogeneous loan proposals, which is unlikely

---

[c] The work of the ACARD- and DTI-funded study was built upon by the later ACOST (Advisory Council on Science and Technology) study.[60] The findings of this second study served to support those of the first. In particular, it suggested that 'the ultimate barriers to growth relate to strategic management and lack of internal resources to make key business transitions' (p. v).

to be the case. Undoubtedly, some proposals will be of greater inherent worth than others. It is more likely that any difficulties relate to the relationship between small firms and their banks. Due to the nature of the banking relationship, in the presence of information asymmetries and moral hazard, adverse selection and credit rationing are liable to prevail, the risk-averse character of banks favouring potentially not selecting 'good' proposals in preference to potentially selecting 'bad' proposals.[50] As a 'remedy' it is suggested that, while perfect information is an unattainable ideal, there exists scope to improve information flows between small firms and their bankers.[51] There are further issues regarding the inconsistency of criteria used in, and the often subjective nature of, bank appraisal procedures.[52] Regardless of the plausibility of the above argument, and the laudability of the suggested response, there exists little empirical evidence that access to finance represents a significant barrier to growth.[24]

On a more general note, there exists a counter-argument to the suggested lifting of presumed barriers to growth. It is implied that entrepreneurs, or small business owner-managers, trading in hostile environments are more likely to develop the characteristics of self-reliance and determination required to succeed.[53] Consequently, policy should avoid lowering barriers or providing incentives that dull the development of these attributes. This is a generally untested hypothesis built upon principally anecdotal and ad hoc observations and it is doubtful whether such an extreme position would be of value in the generality of policy. While we might feel a policy of erecting or maintaining barriers is a step too far, Cressy's[24] suggestion that we should adopt a stricter German model that, by making start-up more difficult (or less easy), aims at raising the threshold quality of new ventures, has some merit.

■ ■ ■ ■ Conclusions

If this chapter were to provide a comprehensive review of all contributions to our understanding of small firm growth it would require a dedicated text in itself. Instead, we have contented ourselves with presenting key strands, which have had considerable influence on public policy and mainstream academic debate. Of these, less attention has been given to the somewhat abstract neo-classical economics and stochastic approaches. At the level of the firm, their ability to throw light upon the process of growth is limited and their inclusion serves merely to highlight the weaknesses incumbent upon theorising about averages or in aggregate.

The chapter also outlines two highly influential, though often criticised, stage models of growth. While implausibly rigid, stage models are truly process orientated and grant due attention to the role of history in determining the actions and structures of firms. However, we concur with Storey: the models describe rather than predict or, more significantly, explain (unless through equally implausible, non-random, defined crises).

On the other hand, the characteristics or predictive modelling approach to small firm growth has, itself, reached an impasse. The factors influencing growth are innumerable and are likely to defy classification in a simple, usable model. Attempting to isolate those where evidence of effect is 'consistent' appears fruitless. Perhaps more importantly, while many of the factors incorporated in such models *may* have considerable influence on the growth of small firms, any influence is likely to be contingent upon the given context.

More recently, emphasis has begun to shift from static analysis of, often categorical, proxy variables towards a more dynamic analysis of the processes of adaptation and learning.[54; 55; 56; 57] Simplistically, it may be suggested that, since growth necessitates change, those firms that have enjoyed sustainable growth are those that were most receptive to change and/or have managed change most effectively. This is in line with the view of growth as a process of adaptation and learning,[54] in which firms learn from their experiences of things going well and, perhaps more importantly, things going badly. Variations in how well firms learn and apply that learning may ultimately differentiate successful firms.[56] Within this context, learning is seen as a process of adaptation to changes in internal and external environments. This view owes much to Edith Penrose's[1] early work on competency- or resource-based theories of the firm. Penrose, for instance, noted that:

. . . *the growing experience of management, its knowledge of the other resources of the firm and of the potential for using them in different ways, create incentives for further expansion as the firm searches for ways of using the services of its own resources more profitably. (p. xii)*

Where limitations on growth exist, these relate to managerial competency and to the endowed resources (technology, skills, finance, etc.) of the firm. Moreover, in the sense that learning is cumulative, so the development of the firm is likely to be history or path-dependent:[58] 'Like the great men of whom Tolstoy wrote in *War and Peace*, "[e]very action of theirs, that seems to them an act of their own free will, is in bondage to the whole course of previous history" ' (p. 333).

The aim of such research is to discover and delineate the underlying processes of adaptive learning and growth, irrespective of context. Or, indeed, to determine whether such processes exist. Unfortunately, no coherent, testable model has been developed to date. The development of a suitable process theory of (small) firm growth remains one of the major challenges in entrepreneurship and the wider social sciences, though interested students are directed to a recent paper by Elizabeth Garnsey,[57] which serves as an excellent starting point.

Review Questions 8.1

1. How small is the proportion of new firms that may achieve significant growth?

2. Why are policies to select 'growth firms' attractive to policy-makers?

3. Is there any evidence to support Gibrat's Law that growth will be independent of firm size? Explain your answer.

4. Why do you think 'chance' plays a large part in successful (or unsuccessful) firm growth? Do any of the case studies discussed in this book support the role of chance in growth?

Review Questions 8.2

1. Compare Churchill and Lewis's and Greiner's models of firm growth. Why are they characterised as life-cycle models? How are they different?

2. What are the three broad categories of 'characteristics' in Storey's approach?

3. Can the characteristics approach explain firm growth?

4. Do any of the case studies in this book fit a life-cycle approach to entrepreneurial growth?

Review Questions 8.3

1. Why might finance be regarded as a barrier to entrepreneurial firm growth?

2. It was suggested that support agencies such as the Business Links might attempt to target their support at entrepreneurial growth firms. Why does evidence presented in this chapter suggest that this policy might be unproductive?

3. From the previous discussion in this chapter, and the illustration shown in Figure 8.3, why might the legal ownership of an entrepreneurial firm be a major barrier to growth?

Suggested Assignments

The following assignment is based on the Nichol McKay case study provided in the student online learning resources material. Further information on this case and teaching notes are also available in the lecturer's online resources.

Prepare a written report or plan for a classroom discussion to answer the following.

1. Consider the Nichol McKay case in light of Storey's tripartite model. How closely does Nichol McKay fit the criteria suggested in the model?

2. Where possible, can the direction/nature of cause and effect be determined?

3. At start-up would we have predicted Nichol McKay's subsequent growth and success?

Recommended Reading

ACOST (1990) *The Enterprise Challenge: Overcoming Barriers to Growth in Small Firms*, HMSO, London.

Barkham, R., Gudgin, G., Hanvey, E. and Hart, M. (1996) *The Determinants of Small Firm Growth*, Jessica Kingsley, London.

Churchill, N. and Lewis, V. (1983) 'The Five Stages of Small Business Growth', *Harvard Business Review*, vol. 61, May–June, pp. 30–50.

Freel, M. (1998) 'Policy, Prediction and Growth: Picking Start-up Winners?', *Journal of Small Business and Enterprise Development*, vol. 5, no. 1, pp. 19–32.

Greiner, L. (1972) 'Evolution and Revolution as Organisations Grow', *Harvard Business Review*, vol. 50, July–August, pp. 37–46.

Storey, D. (1994) *Understanding the Small Business Sector*, Routledge, London.

References

1 Penrose, E. (1995/1959) *The Theory of the Growth of the Firm*, Blackwell, London.
2 Storey, D. and Johnson, S. (1987) *Are Small Firms the Answer to Unemployment*, Employment Institute, London.
3 Gallagher, C. and Stewart, H. (1985) 'Business Death and Firms Size in the UK', *International Small Business Journal*, vol. 4, no. 1, pp. 42–57.
4 Doyle, J. and Gallagher, C. (1987) 'Size Distribution, Growth Potential and Job Generation Contributions of UK Firms', *International Small Business Journal*, vol. 6, no. 1, pp. 31–56.
5 Gallagher, C. and Miller, P. (1991) 'New Fast Growing Companies Create Jobs', *Long Range Planning*, vol. 24, no. 1, pp. 96–101.

6 Scottish Enterprise (1993) *Improving the Business Birth Rate: A Strategy for Scotland*, Scottish Enterprise, Glasgow.

7 Marshall, A. (1920) *Principles of Economics*, 8th edn, Macmillan, London.

8 Ijiri, Y. and Simon, H. (1977) *Skew Distributions and the Sizes of Business Firms*, North-Holland, Amsterdam.

9 O'Farrell, P. and Hitchens, D. (1988) 'Alternative Theories of Small-firm Growth: A Critical Review', *Environment and Planning A*, vol. 20, pp. 1365–83.

10 Gibrat, R. (1931) *Les Inégalités Economiques*, Sirey, Paris.

11 Mansfield, E. (1962) 'Entry, Gibrat's Law, Innovation and the Growth of Firms', *American Economic Review*, 52, pp. 1023–51.

12 Westhead, P. and Birley, S. (1995) 'Employment Growth in New Independent Owner-managed Firms in GB', *International Small Business Journal*, vol. 13, no. 3, pp. 11–34.

13 Reid, G. and Jacobsen, L. (1988) *The Small Entrepreneurial Firm*, Aberdeen University Press, Aberdeen.

14 Nelson, R. and Winter, S. (1978) 'Forces Generating and Limiting Concentration under Schumpeterian Competition', *Bell Journal of Economics*, vol. 9, pp. 524–48.

15 Greiner, L. (1972) 'Evolution and Revolution as Organisations Grow', *Harvard Business Review*, vol. 50, July–August, pp. 37–46.

16 Churchill, N. and Lewis, V. (1983) 'The Five Stages of Small Business Growth', *Harvard Business Review*, vol. 61, May–June, pp. 30–50.

17 Scott, M. and Bruce, R. (1987) 'Five Stages of Growth in Small Business', *Long Range Planning*, vol. 20, no. 3, pp. 45–52.

18 Storey, D. (1994) *Understanding the Small Business Sector*, Routledge, London.

19 Burns, P. and Harrison, J. (1996) 'Growth', in P. Burns and J. Dewhurst (eds), *Small Business and Entrepreneurship*, Macmillan, London.

20 Storey, D., Keasey, K., Watson, R. and Wynarczyk, P. (1987) *The Performance of Small Firms: Profits, Jobs and Failures*, Croom Helm, London.

21 Hall, G. (1995) *Surviving and Prospering in the Small Firm Sector*, Routledge, London.

22 Gallagher, C. and Robson, G. (1996) 'The Identification of High Growth SMEs', paper presented to the 19th National Small Firms Policy and Research Conference, Birmingham.

23 Freel, M. (1998) 'Policy, Prediction and Growth: Picking Start-up Winners?', *Journal of Small Business and Enterprise Development*, vol. 5, no. 1, pp. 19–32.

24 Cressy, R. (1996) 'Are Business Start-ups Debt Rationed', *The Economic Journal*, vol. 106, no. 438, pp. 1253–70.

25 Barkham, R., Gudgin, G., Hanvey, E. and Hart, M. (1996) *The Determinants of Small Firm Growth*, Jessica Kingsley, London.

26 Oakey, R. (1995) *High-technology Small Firms: Variable Barriers to Growth*, Paul Chapman, London.

27 Vyakarnam, S., Jacobs, R. and Handelberg, J. (1996) 'Building and Managing Relationships: The Core Competence of Rapid Growth Business', paper presented to the 19th National Small Firms Policy and Research Conference, Birmingham (unpublished, amended version).

28 Jensen, J.B. and McGuckin, R.H. (1997) 'Firm Performance and Evolution: Empirical Regularities in the US Microdata', *Industrial and Corporate Change*, vol. 6, no. 1, pp. 25–47.

29 Jovanovic, B. (1982) 'Selection and the Evolution of Industry', *Econometrica*, vol. 50, no. 3, pp. 649–70.

30 ENSR (1994) *The European Observatory for SMEs: 2nd Annual Report*, ENSR/EIM.

31 Smallbone, D. and North, D. (1995) 'Targeting Established SMEs: Does Their Age Matter?', *International Small Business Journal*, vol. 13, no. 3, pp. 47–64.

32 Westhead, P. (1995) 'New Owner-managed Business in Rural and Urban Areas in Great Britain: A Matched Pairs Comparison', *Regional Studies*, vol. 29, no. 4, pp. 367–80.

33 OECD (1996) *SMEs: Employment, Innovation and Growth – The Washington Workshop*.

34 Tether, B. (2000) 'Small Firms, Innovation and Employment Creation in Britain and Europe: A Question of Expectations', *Technovation*, vol. 20, pp. 109–13.

35 Birley, S. and Westhead, P. (1994) 'A Comparison of New Businesses Established by "Novice" and "Habitual" Founders in GB', *International Small Business Journal*, vol. 12, no. 1, pp. 38–60.

36 Scott, M. and Rosa, P. (1996) 'Existing Business as Sources of New Firms: A Missing Topic in Business Formation Research', paper presented to the Babson Entrepreneurship Research Conference, Seattle, USA.

37 Westhead, P. and Wright, M. (1997) 'Novice, Portfolio and Serial Founders: Are They Different?', paper presented to the Babson Entrepreneurship Research Conference, Boston, USA.

38 Scott, M. and Rosa, P. (1996) 'Has Firm Level Analysis Reached its Limits? Time for a Rethink', *International Small Business Journal*, vol. 14, no. 4, pp. 81–9.

39 Deakins, D. and Hussain, G. (1994) 'Financial Information, the Banker and Small Business: A Comment', *British Accounting Review*, vol. 26, pp. 323–35.

40 Murray, G. (1994) 'The Second 'Equity Gap': Exit Problems for Seed and Early Stage Venture Capitalists and their Investee Companies', *International Small Business Journal*, vol. 12, no. 4, pp. 58–76.

41 Storey, D. and Sykes, N. (1996) 'Uncertainty, Innovation and Management', in P. Burns and J. Dewhurst (eds), *Small Business and Entrepreneurship*, Macmillan, London.

42 Barber, J., Metcalfe, S. and Porteous, M. (1989) 'Barriers to Growth: the ACARD Study', in J. Barber, S. Metcalfe and M. Porteous (eds), *Barriers to Growth in Small Firms*, Routledge, London.

43 Rothwell, R. and Zegveld, W. (1982) *Innovation and the Small and Medium Sized Firm*, Francis Pinter, London.

44 Geroski, P. and Machin, S. (1992) 'Do Innovating Firms Outperform Non-innovators?', *Business Strategy Review*, Summer, pp. 79–90.

45 Wynarczyk, P. and Thwaites, A. (1997) 'The Economic Performance, Survival and Non-Survival of Innovative Small Firms', in R. Oakey and S. Muktar (eds), *New Technology-based Firms in the 1990s: Volume III*, Paul Chapman, London.

46 Audretsch, D. (1995) 'Innovation, Growth and Survival', *International Journal of Industrial Organisation* 13, pp. 441–57.

47 Penrose, E. (1971) 'Limits to the Size and Growth of Firms', in *The Growth of Firms, Middle East Oil and Other Essays* (first published in *American Economic Review*, vol. 45, no. 2).

48 Smallbone, D., Leigh, R. and North, D. (1995) 'The Characteristics and Strategies of High Growth SMEs', *International Journal of Entrepreneurial Behaviour and Research*, vol. 1, no. 3, pp. 44–62.

49 Storey, D. (1992) 'Should we Abandon the Support to Start Up Businesses', paper presented to the 15th National Small Firms Policy and Research Conference.

50 Deakins, D. and Hussain, G. (1991) *Risk Assessment by Bank Managers*, Birmingham Polytechnic Business School.

51 Binks, M. and Ennew, C. (1996) 'Financing Small Firms', in P. Burns and J. Dewhurst (eds), *Small Business and Entrepreneurship*, Macmillan, London.

52 Deakins, D., Hussain, G. and Ram, M. (1992) 'Overcoming the Adverse Selection Problem', paper presented to the 15th National Small Firms Policy and Research Conference, Southampton.

53 Dewhurst, J. (1996) 'The Entrepreneur', in P. Burns and J. Dewhurst (eds), *Small Business and Entrepreneurship*, Macmillan, London.

54 Wiklund, J. (1998) *Small Firm Growth and Performance: Entrepreneurship and Beyond*, dissertation series no. 3, Jönköping International Business School.

55 Costello, N. (1996) 'Learning and Routines in High-tech SMEs: Analysing Rich Case Study Material', *Journal of Economic Issues*, vol. 30, no. 2, pp. 591–7.

56 Freel, M. (1998) 'Evolution, Innovation and Learning: Evidence from Case Studies', *Entrepreneurship and Regional Development*, vol. 10, no. 2, pp. 137–49.

57 Garnsey, E. (1998) 'A Theory of the Early Growth of Firms', *Industrial and Corporate Change*, vol. 7, no. 3, pp. 523–56.

58 David, P. (1985) 'Clio and the Economics of QWERTY', *AEA Papers and Proceedings*, vol. 75, no. 2, pp. 332–7.

59 ACOST (1990) *The Enterprise Challenge: Overcoming Barriers to Growth in Small Firms*, HMSO, London.

International Entrepreneurship

CHAPTER

9

Learning outcomes

At the end of this chapter you should be able to:

1 describe how different cultures can affect entrepreneurial activity

2 apply criteria to describe different levels of entrepreneurship in different nations, such as high and low levels of entrepreneurial activity

3 discuss the factors that affect the level of entrepreneurial activity in different nations

4 describe the characteristics of the process of internationalisation

5 discuss competing theories of the process of internationalisation

6 discuss how all entrepreneurs are affected by the global economy

7 discuss opportunities and threats posed by the global economy

8 describe examples of the nature of entrepreneurship in advanced, transition and emergent economies.

■ ■ ■ ■ Introduction

Chapter 8 examined some of the factors in the growth process of entrepreneurial firms. One factor likely to be involved in the growth process is the ability to export or to internationalise through an overseas operation. For high-growth firms, establishing overseas markets is an essential part of the growth process. The ability to internationalise operations will be an important part of that process. Some start-up entrepreneurs may be able to start in global markets; such firms are sometimes referred to as 'born globals',[1] having markets overseas rather than in the UK; other firms may take longer to enter overseas markets and start from a domestic base. There are competing theories of this process of internationalisation, which will be examined in this chapter. Trading overseas requires some understanding of different cultures, different economies and different ways of 'doing business'. In this chapter we examine some of the characteristics of different cultures (which affect entrepreneurial behaviour), risk-taking and economic production methods in other nations – factors that need to be taken into account by entrepreneurs in the UK who are seeking to expand in overseas markets. We begin by noting the importance of the global economy, a trend, it is argued, that cannot be ignored by all small firm entrepreneurs, whether trading internationally or not.

■ ■ ■ ■ Global Markets

As we have stated a number of times before, the majority of small firm entrepreneurs do not wish to grow (and, by definition, do not wish to export or expand overseas). However, it is arguable that all entrepreneurs are affected by the globalisation of the economy. A number of forces have led to increased globalisation. All entrepreneurs have to trade in an economy that is affected by the trends or forces forming the global economy. Even if a firm's market is restricted to its local geographical area, it may face competitors that are based overseas and trading locally. Equally, the firm may be part of a supply chain whose end markets are global. For example, the West Midlands region of the UK is well known for the number of small firms based there that produce car components, supplying to local car manufacturers. All firms in the supply chain will be part of the global market and be unable to ignore trends in that market. A small firm producing car components in Coventry is probably affected more by events in Japan than by local events. While small firms can be embedded in local communities and dependent on the local infrastructure,[2] they are also dependent on global supply chains and markets.[3]

The Global Economy and 11 September 2001

Notwithstanding the tragic events of 11 September 2001, the immediacy of the effects of the terrorist acts unfortunately illustrated the dependency and interdependence of different sectors and economies that were felt by all sectors of the UK economy and by all entrepreneurial small firms.

The most publicised effects have concerned the major airlines and firms in the tourism sector, dependent on overseas visitors, yet it was unlikely that any firms were totally unaffected. Events organisers found that there were fewer people willing to travel to business conferences, insurance costs for business travel increased, time taken to travel to business meetings increased due to more thorough security checks, investment confidence in and prices on stock exchanges and financial markets were affected and there were changes in oil prices that further affected the costs of travel and moving goods.

Of course not all firms suffered adversely; there have been contrasting fortunes for large airlines and tour operators compared to those of low-cost operators such as easyJet (as will be discussed in the next chapter), but the event, if in a very dramatic way, illustrated the interdependency and immediacy that characterise trading relationships in the global economy.

Nowadays we are all affected by economic events in other economies whether they are taking place in Japan, Russia or closer to home. Ability to respond to these events, to manage with the increasing pace of change, will affect the sustainability and viability of all small firms; part of that increasing pace of change is the globalisation of the economy. A number of factors have contributed to the development of the global economy, factors that are increasing in importance. Some of them are listed in the accompanying box.

Factors Contributing to the Development of the Global Economy

- The development of e-business methods, as discussed in detail in Chapter 7
- Greater mobility of the labour force and labour skills
- Improved forms of communication (and information)
- New technological developments that favour smaller firms (e.g. biotechnology/micro-technologies)
- Reduction of barriers to trade, through agreements formed under the General Agreement on Tariffs and Trade (GATT), now subsumed under the World Trade Organization (WTO), and the increased importance of common trading areas such as the European Union
- Increased pace of change requiring flexible and speedy responses
- Privatisation and reduced barriers in emerging nations, with the development of economies in transition, the emergence of 'tiger economies' and the emergence of China as a major overseas market
- Increased mobility of labour force and other resources
- Growth of global capital markets
- Reduction of cultural barriers

The Process of Internationalisation

There are a large number of potential reasons why firms go global, which may be only partly explained by globalisation. It is also evident from observation that some firms go global immediately or quickly (born globals), while for others the process of internationalisation takes a longer period of time. The factors that might explain why firms go global include:

- entrepreneurial growth reasons, such as those examined in Chapter 8 (associated with growth of the firm)

- more market-based factors associated with internationalisation through participation in overseas markets; these factors may be associated with more effective use of ICT and e-business, as explained in Chapter 7.

From these 'sources' of internationalisation a number of theories have been postulated and, in the remaining part of this section, we explain and examine these competing theories of internationalisation in more detail.

Theoretical approaches to the process of internationalisation have been developed that offer competing perspectives. These have included the traditional stage model, a network model and a more recent model that can explain born globals as international new ventures. Each of these is briefly examined.

The Traditional Stage Model of Internationalisation

The first model, or stage model, is based on the hypothesis that a small firm entrepreneur will expand overseas only as more knowledge is gained about operating in overseas markets. Uncertainty and lack of knowledge act as a constraint, which means that a staged approach is taken to internationalisation.

The model assumes that the process of internationalisation is achieved through a series of stages and incremental decision-making by small firm owners and entrepreneurs. It is a gradual process that starts with an established small firm with an established domestic market.[4] Figure 9.1 illustrates the potential stages. Traditionally, the small firm owner/entrepreneur enters overseas markets through agents, having established a secure domestic base. Only when this stage is established, does the firm gain sufficient knowledge to open its own subsidiary as an overseas market is established, eliminating the need to operate through an agent and selling direct through its own employees working abroad. Finally, as knowledge of the market and practices increases, the final stage will involve overseas production.

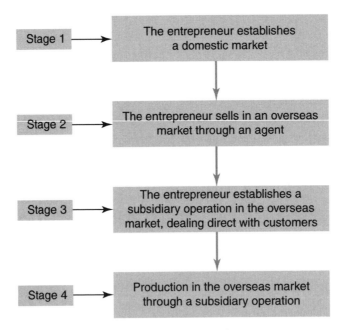

Figure 9.1: *The Process of Internationalisation: Stage Model*

It is worth noting that there is no connection between the stage models of internationalisation and the (stage) models of growth discussed in Chapter 8, such as those of Churchill, and Lewis and Greiner. The approaches have been developed totally separately.

The Network Model

The network model offers an alternative explanation to the internationalisation process of small firm entrepreneurs.[4] The principle on which the model is based is the importance of social capital for entrepreneurs. Entrepreneurs, through their networks (e.g. other entrepreneurs), receive enquiries from overseas; this leads to exporting and, with the development of trust the firm internationalises; unlike the stage model, however, there are no distinct and discrete stages, rather a smooth process. The network model suggests that business associations such as Chambers of Commerce will be natural channels for the development of enquiries and orders that will lead to internationalisation.

International New Ventures Model

The international new ventures (INVs) model recognises the importance of the development of globalisation, by identifying entrepreneurs that are in overseas markets from start-up. Such entrepreneurs are assumed to have global vision and seek to operate in international markets before domestic markets, and, in some cases, domestic sales only result from international sales. This was recognised in a study of software companies by Bell.[5] The characteristics of INVs have led to the term 'born global' to denote new entrepreneurial ventures that are established in global markets from inception. They are likely to be new-technology-based, with vested property interests in IPR that may be protected by the seeking of worldwide patents. An example of such a born global is provided by the Nallatech case (see the 'Entrepreneurship in Action' box on p. 187).

The characteristics of such companies are associated with:[6]

■ entrepreneurs who have global markets in mind

■ entry strategies that seek to establish a strong market presence overseas

■ the establishment of successor products early in their development.

The characteristics of INVs or born globals attract the attention of policy-makers since they represent the type of enterpreneurial activity that provides most benefit for local economies, and they are likely to be high-growth entrepreneurial firms, as discussed in Chapter 8.

Internationalisation: Implications for Entrepreneurs

High-growth entrepreneurial firms seeking to internationalise have to assess how to tackle globalisation and the penetration of overseas markets. Operating abroad usually involves one of four approaches:

1. production at home and *exporting* through partners or agents

2. production at home and *licensing* another firm to produce abroad

3. entering into a strategic joint venture agreement or partnership to exploit overseas markets (see below)

4. owning and controlling an overseas operation, through either a *de novo* operation or buying an existing operation.

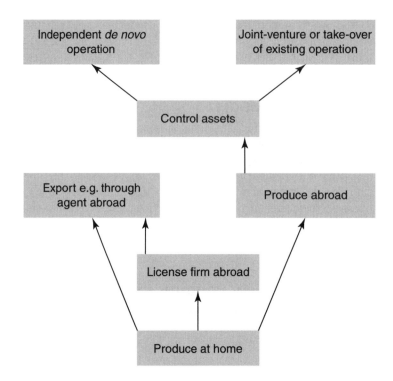

Figure 9.2: *Strategies for Internationalisation*

These alternative methods are illustrated in Figure 9.2. The strategy adopted will depend on the nature of the product or service, the requirements of the customer and the growth aspirations of the international entrepreneurial firm.

Figure 9.2 illustrates different strategic choices for the entrepreneurial growth firm. The strategy chosen will depend on a number of factors, such as cost, availability of finance, regulations in different countries, risk involved, availability of strategic partners and exchange rate risks, but not least the entrepreneurial culture of different areas and nations. We have insufficient space here for an adequate discussion of these factors; however, drawing on the example of the Aquamotive case study in Chapter 6 (available via the online learning resources for that chapter), we saw that the firm operated in global markets (supplying control feeding systems to fish farms). The strategy adopted to exploit such global markets was to seek strategic partnerships. Aquamotive was at an early stage of the development of the product, and was still operating on a small scale and with limited resources. Seeking strategic partners represented the best strategy for the firm, given its stage of development and given the resources it had available or could access. For a different firm, in a different technology, a different strategy might be preferable. For example, a high-growth information technology firm might quickly establish overseas operations through expansion abroad, by setting up overseas offices and production facilities, and operating subsidiaries as a multinational enterprise. Factors such as the need to be near to their customers (users of new software) and the lower cost of operating abroad would be important to such firms. This is further illustrated by the example of Nallatech (see the 'Entrepreneurship in Action' box).

ENTREPRENEURSHIP IN ACTION

Nallatech

By *Tom Farrell*

Technology-based companies that are international new ventures or born globals, as illustrated in the case of Aquamotive (Chapter 6), are often in global markets from their formation and their first day of trading, and even during their R&D and prototype development. This is illustrated further by the case of Nallatech.

Nallatech was founded in 1993 by Allan Cantle, who at the time was an electronics engineer with British Aerospace (BAe). He had been asked by a friend of the family to design a water pump controller, as there were no suitable products for the purpose on the market. He agreed to do this in return for help in setting up the business. In the event, the design was not immediately commercialised and the company stayed dormant for a couple of years. In August 1995, Allan's wife Sarah, a computer scientist who had been running the IT department for Pegasus Critical Illness Insurance, was relocated when Pegasus was taken over by Abbey National. This was the spur to incorporate the business, and Allan set up with a major design services contract from his previous employer BAe for a piece of design equipment used in training simulators. An entrepreneurship programme introduced him to Dr Malachy Devlin, whose PhD was in advanced computer algorithms and architectures. Dr Devlin's skills complemented those of the Cantles, and he was invited to join the company.

The breakthrough for the company occurred in December 1998 when Xilinx awarded Nallatech a contract to develop a board for its own design equipment, which is now in regular production, and Nallatech was the first company in Europe to be appointed an expert consultant in the Xilinx XPERT programme. By 2002, 75 per cent of the company's sales were supplied to blue-chip clients in 20 countries worldwide, including Sony, Philips, Texas Instruments, BAe, Xilinx and Motorola.

The demand for Nallatech's products had increased to such an extent that further organic growth could let competitors with deep pockets overtake the company's technological lead. In 2001, Nallatech appointed David Armour to facilitate a financing round. The result was a £2 million equity investment by a VC company. This covered Nallatech for the next five years of operation, allowing a marketing department to be created, an office set up in the USA, and the engineering department expanded.

Nallatech review questions

1. Why are technology-based entrepreneurs in global markets from an early stage?

2. Why is it strategically advantageous for technology-based entrepreneurs to internationalise with an overseas office rather than through an agent?

The examples of Nallatech and Aquamotive serve to illustrate the importance of internationalisation and global markets for technology-based firms. They can be quoted as examples of INVs or born globals. While noting the importance of such factors, for the rest of this chapter we focus on different cultures and how such cultures can affect entrepreneurial behaviour, a factor that will affect the strategy adopted by entrepreneurial firms to exploit the globalisation of local economies. As mentioned previously, support is provided by the government for entrepreneurs seeking to internationalise and export. However, before the present approach is discussed (see box), it may be noted that this approach is currently based on an assumption that exporting and internationalisation is achieved through a staged approach, and thus may not suit or 'fit' a much more rapid process of internationalisation.

Enterprise Support for Export and Trade Development

Small firm entrepreneurs face difficulties in exporting due to the greater financial requirements, longer credit terms and knowledge about overseas trade regulations needed. Historically, successive UK governments have attempted to provide support that met the perceived needs of small firms through finance (export credits) and access to information, and an 'export help' service provided through the DTI. However, there was still local variety in the form of advice provided and it is only recently that a national strategy has been developed that co-ordinates such support at a local level.

British Trade International has developed a national export development strategy that seeks to provide local assistance through locally based Local Export Partnerships. These represent a local partnership that combines the work of local agencies, which may include Chambers of Commerce, local authorities and Business Links/LECs. The role of each body varies, but generally Business Links work with small firms to develop capacity and awareness; Chambers of Commerce provide information, documentation and training; whereas local councils, where they are involved, may provide support for international trade missions.

Such support depends on linking entrepreneurs to such networks; specific support agencies may have, in addition, specific export mentoring programmes, such as that illustrated by the example of the Highlands and Islands Trade Export Partnership in the accompanying 'Entrepreneurship in Action' box.

ENTREPRENEURSHIP IN ACTION

Support for Exporters
The Highlands and Islands Trade and Export Partnership

The Highlands and Islands Trade and Export Partnership (HITEP) is funded by Highlands and Islands Enterprise (HIE) and Scottish Trade International. It operates as a partnership between the Highlands and Islands LEC Network, the five local councils in the Highlands and Islands, and Inverness and District Chamber of Commerce.

Integration is achieved through an export development manager based at HIE in Inverness, who acts as a facilitator and co-ordinator for HITEP. HITEP provides an extensive exporting advisory and information service for companies in the Highlands and Islands. More intensive training and mentoring help is provided through export mentors, and companies can also qualify for a range of assistance to help them break into new markets in Europe and overseas.

HITEP also operates an export club: the Highland Export Club, which provides a networking forum for local companies to exchange information, problems and experience, and raise awareness of events, training and overseas trade missions and exhibitions.

■ ■ ■ ■ ■ Different Entrepreneurial Cultures

In Chapter 1 we discussed how the entrepreneur is increasingly seen as a key actor in the economy and an *agent* of economic change. To perform this function the entrepreneur becomes a *problem-solver*, reconciling limited resources with the environment. The entrepreneur may be seen as having the same function in each economy yet the environment and resources will vary. In different economies, different cultures will affect the degree to which the entrepreneur is able to be the key actor and hence influence economic change. Some economies are perceived to contain environments that are more conducive to entrepreneurship than others. For example, the USA has an economy that is regarded as 'entrepreneurial' – that is, favouring the entrepreneur as the key agent of economic change. In the following sections we examine some of the factors that determine whether the nature of the environment and culture in different economies is entrepreneurial.

■ ■ ■ ■ Advanced Economies

Two contrasting attempts to assess the level of entrepreneurial culture and activity in different advanced nations are examined in this section. The first of these is the Global Entrepreneurship Monitor (GEM) approach[7; 8] this is contrasted with the approach of Casson.[9]

The GEM approach proposes that a causal relationship exists between the level of entrepreneurial activity in an economy and the level of economic growth. It should be noted that this assumption of such a one-way causal relationship has been criticised, as has the methodology applied by the GEM studies. An assessment and critique of this methodology has been given in Chapter 2 and the reader should also refer to that chapter; we are interested here in claims made about differences in entrepreneurial activity as a result of the GEM studies.

Economies will differ in their level of entrepreneurial activity, which will directly affect the growth of a nation's gross domestic product (GDP). GEM further proposes that factors affecting the level of entrepreneurial activity can by represented by means of a model. The GEM model consists of demand-side and supply-side factors that can be measured (represented in Figure 9.3). The demand side is represented by entrepreneurial opportunities and the supply side by entrepreneurial capacity.

The 1999 GEM report[7] examined 10 countries and classified them into three categories of entrepreneurial activity, as follows:

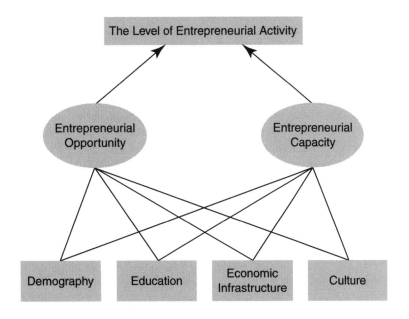

Figure 9.3: *The GEM Approach to Measuring Entrepreneurial Activity*
Sources: Global Entrepreneurship Monitor (2001) *Executive Report,* GEM Project, Babson College and London Business School, Boston, USA[7]

189

1. a group of countries with high rates of entrepreneurial activity, including the USA, Canada and Israel

2. a group of countries with medium rates of entrepreneurial activity, including the UK and Italy

3. a group of countries with low rates of entrepreneurial activity, including Denmark, Finland, France, Germany and Japan.

The 2001 GEM report expanded the number of countries to 29, including developing nations, which are surveyed annually to arrive at the measurement of entrepreneurial activity.[10] After an expansion to 37 countries surveyed in 2002, the 2003 GEM report reduced the number of surveyed countries to 27.[8] Comparisons across different cultures are obviously problematical. For example, GEM does not attempt to measure differences in culture. In addition, the use of a standard questionnaire survey across all 27 countries (in 2003), when infrastructures are very different, is also, of course, problematical; nevertheless, the GEM reports have received much attention as a benchmarking approach to the level of entrepreneurial activity. This approach owes something to that of Casson,[9] but is contrasted with it below.

Casson has attempted to analyse and classify the 'entrepreneurial' cultures of advanced, or developed, economies.[9] He made a distinction between 'high level' entrepreneurial behaviour, which he claimed is associated with the Schumpeterian concept of entrepreneurship, and 'low level' entrepreneurial behaviour, which he claimed is associated with the Kirznerian concept of entrepreneurship (as discussed in Chapter 1, where an explanation is given of these contrasting entrepreneurship concepts). Casson compared, at the time, seven advanced industrial economies (the USA, Japan, the UK, France, Canada, Sweden and Italy) and used a scoring system for certain characteristics of cultural attitudes and environment that are discussed below. Using this (weighted) scoring system he found that Japan and the USA had the highest and most conducive entrepreneurial cultures, whereas (of the seven nations), the UK and Italy had the lowest ratings.[9]

Casson claimed that there were two groups of characteristics of national cultures that determined these ratings. First, technical aspects of a culture, which included attitudes to the importance of scientific measurement, to taking a systems view and hence to the degree of sophistication in decision-making. Second, moral characteristics of a culture, which included the extent of voluntarism, types of commitment and attitudes to achievement. These groups of characteristics determined the extent to which a culture was conducive to 'high level' (Schumpeterian) entrepreneurship as opposed to 'low level' (Kirznerian) entrepreneurship. For example, Japan scored well on the national characteristic of a scientific approach to problems and a systems view to planning, which meant a willingness to accept logistical planning and awareness of interdependency. It scored lower with voluntarism – the extent of willingness to allow freedom for transactions – an area where the USA scored highly. For example, this was explained by Casson[9] as:

The philosophy of voluntarism . . . supports a political framework within which people are free to transact with whomever they like. Voluntarism opposes the concentration of coercive powers on institutions such as the state. (p. 92)

Casson's hierarchy of national entrepreneurial cultures was an attempt to provide objective measurements of subjective and intangible values of different national cultures. As such, the measurements could be subject to widely different interpretations. For example, Germany was a rather surprising omission from Casson's countries chosen for comparison and might score quite low on some of Casson's criteria, yet it would be accepted by many observers as a nation having, at the time, at least a medium level of entrepreneurial activity. Nonetheless, Casson's approach was an interesting attempt to analyse different levels of entrepreneurial cultures in different economies. In identifying factors that affect attitudes to scientific endeavour, to moral codes, to commitments, the approach provided a useful framework for discussion of features of different national cultures and different levels of entrepreneurial activity.

It would be a mistake, however, to view certain economies as 'model' or prototypical entrepreneurial economies. Quite different cultures with different systems, attitudes and infrastructures can result in high-level, advanced entrepreneurship. For example, in the early 1990s, the Scottish Enterprise *Business Birth Rate Enquiry* investigated two advanced regional economies to examine factors that accounted for their relatively high levels of entrepreneurial behaviour.[11] The two contrasting regions, Massachusetts in the USA and Baden-Württemberg in Germany, had quite different attitudes, characteristics and environments. Massachusetts was characterised by little state intervention and a dependence on private-sector venture capital to provide the risk capital to finance new ventures. Baden-Württemberg, however, was characterised by (regional) state-funded assistance and a reliance on bank loan finance to provide new venture capital. These two powerful regions demonstrated that, despite different characteristics in society and different infrastructures, both could produce advanced high-level entrepreneurship.

The Importance of Developed Networks

The common feature of advanced entrepreneurial economies is the extent of networking. As shown by the Scottish Enterprise study, Baden-Württemberg contained advanced networks focused through local Chambers of Commerce.[11] Massachusetts also had important networks, through venture capitalists and through integration with the Massachusetts Institute of Technology (MIT), which provided an important spin-out route for technology-based high-value start-ups. The importance of such support networks in Baden-Württemberg (B-W) has been highlighted by Kitching and Blackburn.[12] In a three-region study including B-W, Aarhus (Denmark) and London, they concluded that small engineering firms in London were disadvantaged by the lack of effective support networks. The level of networking and co-operative behaviour is not one of either the GEM or Casson's criteria; however, it is a recognised factor behind the success of areas such as the north-east of Italy, the 'Third Italy'.

Scottish Enterprise, following its enquiry, identified networking arrangements among new firms as a way to achieve growth and hence job creation:[13]

Networks are important: many of the solutions will be found in the actions of individual entrepreneurs, backed by their networks of family and friends. An important focus of action for the strategy is to improve the effectiveness of these networks and to make potential entrepreneurs more aware of what they can do themselves to achieve success. Part of this involves improving the support given by the formal support networks in the private and public sectors. (p. 4)

Similarly, in a more recent version of strategy, Scottish Enterprise claimed:[14]

To compete, companies will need to build strong partnerships through which information and ideas can flow quickly and to best mutual advantage. Spanning customers, suppliers, competitors and other supporting institutions such as the universities, colleges, research bodies and the utilities, these specialist networks or 'clusters' create more of the sparks that fuel innovation and generate synergies that power them to greater competitiveness. (p.1)

The benefits that can accrue to new firms operating in partnerships/ networks/clusters are the potential advantages of economies of scope. Services and inputs, such as advertising, training, access to loan finance at advantageous rates, consultancy advice, financial services – items that a single firm cannot easily afford or secure when operating independently – can be secured when operating as part of a larger group. It has also been demonstrated that external linkages with other firms encourage innovation (see Chapter 6). For example, Edquist et al. have illustrated, in the case of Gothia in Sweden, the importance of networking for product innovation in small manufacturing firms.[15]

While the organisational structure of firms operating in some kind of cohesive way may be given the title 'networking', firms producing in any economy take on some of the attributes of a networking structure. For example, by engaging in production and trade a firm deals with suppliers and customers, which necessitates a degree of co-operation and trust. These factors are regarded as essential attributes of the successful functioning of a network. There is also an element of risk and uncertainty within any business relationship. Trust arises in response to the threat of risk and uncertainty. When trust exists it minimises the potential risk and opportunism. Thompson underlines the importance of trust:[16] 'Co-operation is more secure and robust when agents have a trust because of the reputation of themselves and other agents in the network for honesty and consistency' (p. 58).

Risk and opportunism can also be reduced via contracting but, as Macaulay[17] notes, while detailed clauses are often written into contracts, they are seldom used:

. . . contract and contract law are often thought unnecessary because there are many non-legal sanctions. Two norms are widely accepted.

(1) Commitments are to be honoured in almost all situations;
(2) One ought to produce a good product and stand behind it. (p. 63)

In other words, an environment can develop where implicit contracting ensures a degree of trust and co-operation. Other, more established, relationships can develop beyond that of a purely contractual kind. Sako[18] identifies two other kinds of trust: competence trust, being a belief that a trading partner will fulfil a particular task; and goodwill trust, which occurs in situations where initiatives are undertaken beyond the specific remit of a contract:[19] 'The role of goodwill trust extends beyond existing relations and includes the transfer of new ideas and new technology' (p. 218).

While we have identified trust and co-operation as two attributes of an advanced economy, they can be strengthened to ensure the efficient operation of the network. This can be the key to the development of advanced entrepreneurial economies such as the Third Italy. For this to happen, contractual trust must be developed into goodwill trust. Economists using a game theoretical framework have demonstrated that, where firms attach sufficient weight to future interactions, punishment strategies can be employed to secure co-operation; when joining a formal organisation, such as a network, defectors and unco-operative players can be excluded. The problem with over-reliance on punishment strategies is that they could lead to distrust, which would threaten co-operation: 'If you trust me why are you monitoring my behaviour?' Axelrod suggests that co-operation can evolve over a period of time as firms gradually learn rules and norms of behaviour leading to co-operation.[20] In other words, through continual interaction and the belief of further interaction, the temptation to cheat diminishes. The participating firms build up reputations for co-operation and these reputations have to be protected.

We have indicated that, where established networks exist, these can involve policing by member firms in an attempt to prevent opportunistic behaviour on behalf of other member firms. Where no existing meaningful networking arrangements exist, policy bodies could attempt to facilitate such developments. In local economies where this has proven to be more successful, such as the industrial districts of the Third Italy, this has occurred in conjunction with the key agents in the region, such as the small firm entrepreneurs themselves, the equivalent of the local Chambers of Commerce, the relevant financial institutions and the local authorities. In other words, the key players in the local economy have been involved in the design and implementation of the strategy, which is a major factor in that these key players take on ownership of the organisation.

Thus it has been argued that the level of co-operation, trust and networking is a key factor determining the level (high/medium/low) of entrepreneurship in different cultures. This networking may be characterised by different forms, but it seems to be a necessary condition for high levels of entrepreneurship. This may also explain why Mutual Guarantee Schemes (MGSs), which depend on trust, networking and co-operation, have been established successfully in some European economies but not in others (see the discussion of MGSs in Chapter 4).

■ ■ ■ ■ ■ Economies in Transition

With the collapse of communism in eastern Europe and the former USSR, attention has focused on whether such nations can successfully transform into entrepreneurial economies (whether high or low level). Although it is well known, particularly with the high profile enjoyed by the Russian entrepreneur Roman Abramovich, that such economies do produce and provide opportunities for successful entrepreneurial activity, such nations are regarded as emergent economies, as potential new areas for entrepreneurs seeking new markets. Therefore, if they can achieve the features of advanced economies, as discussed in the previous section, new opportunities for firms seeking growth become available. Such economies have been grouped together with the rather optimistic term of 'economies in transition'. As in western Europe, this term obscures a great diversity of development: different nations are at different stages in the transition process. This partly reflects the situation before the break-up of the old Soviet bloc, where some states had semi-market economies (such as Poland) and others were completely government controlled (such as the Baltic states). It also partly reflects the different features and characteristics of such nations.

These transition economies have certain identifiable features, as listed in the accompanying box.

Features of Economies in Transition

- High levels of uncertainty and lack of information, implying opportunities for the Kirznerian entrepreneur
- A lack of formal financial infrastructure and sources of finance
- Limited markets and spending power within internal economies
- No formal regulation (e.g. for regulating new firms/companies)
- Varying degrees of former 'market economies' giving different attitudes and approaches to entrepreneurial activity
- Different levels of assistance, dependent on access to EU and western development aid

---

While there are obviously opportunities for entrepreneurship to flourish in such nations (Roman Abramovich being merely the most high-profile example), innovative or high-level entrepreneurship is difficult due to the lack of infrastructure that can provide the level of finance or risk capital required, the lack of networks, co-operative behaviour and trust (identified above as an important feature of advanced entrepreneurial regions) and the lack of infrastructure to support the small firm entrepreneur. In some nations, a tradition of co-operative ownership has led to problems with the establishment of individual entrepreneurship.[21]

Given the newness of 'economies in transition', there is still a limited literature on the characteristics of their culture and the way this affects entrepreneurial behaviour in such nations. However, a paper by Roberts and Tholen gives some insights into differences within these nations.[22] For example, their research showed considerable differences in Russia compared to other former Soviet bloc nations, with business development in Russia being more ad hoc and unplanned. Common characteristics across eastern European nations included:

■ unstable political regimes and hence the need for businesses to grow quickly

■ a lack of tradition of business ownership and comparatively few family firms

■ the absence of support services.

Differences were likely to be:

■ the source of new entrepreneurs (in Russia new entrepreneurs were former workers, whereas in other eastern European nations they were more likely to come from management levels)

■ higher growth ambitions in eastern Europe compared to Russia

■ fewer women entrepreneurs in Russia (in other nations women entrepreneurs accounted for around 30 per cent of new business ownership)

■ attitudes could vary to 'doing business' (entrepreneurs in Russia were likely to seek the 'big deal', whereas in other nations, such as Poland, a more realistic incremental development was adopted by entrepreneurs).

The transition economies of eastern Europe and Russia can be seen as containing a wide spectrum of different stages of progression to higher levels of entrepreneurship. Undoubtedly, much of it is low level, characterised by Casson[9] as Kirznerian, with some areas struggling to shake off attitudes that restrict creativity and innovative behaviour. In a comment that is probably representative of many such transition economies of eastern Europe, one native writer on Slovenia comments perceptively that,[23]

Traditionally, Slovenians have not been classified as exhibiting entrepreneurial traits. The collectivist culture, dependency upon the state, historical subordination by external powers and strong egalitarian values relative to the even distribution of social and material gains have combined with a conservative formal education system that rewarded obedience and diligence, and suppressed innovation and creativity. (p. 108)

A recent paper on entrepreneurship in Bulgaria[24] commented that the environment for entrepreneurial activity was 'hostile' and that entrepreneurial responses included the characteristics of 'short term orientation, informal networking, opportunism and surplus extraction' (p. 163).

The accession of some central and eastern European countries to the European Union on 1 May 2004, illustrates that some transition economies had developed sufficient features to be acceptable new members of the EU; these included Poland, Hungary, the Czech Republic, Slovakia, the Baltic states (such as Latvia, Estonia and Lithuania), and Slovenia (other states acceding were Cyprus and Malta). Yet others, notably Turkey and the Balkan states (such as Croatia, Montenegro and Bosnia-Hercegovina), have yet to satisfy conditions for EU entry, although some preparatory negotiations have been taking place with some states such as Croatia and Turkey.[25]

Western European nations have been involved in assisting the development of infrastructures in transition economies in eastern Europe, however, as one writer comments,[26]

It may well be that in the longer term, borrowing ideas which lead to a change in values and attitudes towards enterprise and small business and which change norms of behaviour, is a critical task in ensuring that a culture sympathetic to small business is created. (p. 26)

There can be considerable barriers to entrepreneurial and new firm development in the 'transition economies'. For example, adjustments have to be made by employees used to working for non-profit organisations to new cultures and working practices in small, privately owned firms. During periods of transition, recruitment of sufficiently motivated staff has been an issue.[27]

Smallbone and Welter, in a review paper, have summarised the key barriers to small and medium-sized firm development in countries in different stages of transition.[28] Those countries still at an early stage include the Ukraine and Belarus, and are characterised by a number of barriers to the development of higher levels of entrepreneurial activity. The main barriers are identified in the box entitled 'Economies in Transition 1'.

Economies in Transition 1: Early-stage Barriers

- High levels of bureaucratic regulation
- Inadequate legal frameworks
- Inadequate financial institutions
- High inflation
- Slow acceptance of private enterprise by government
- The existence of relatively high levels of corruption

By contrast, those countries at a later stage of transition, such as Poland, are characterised by the features given in the box entitled 'Economies in Transition 2'.

Economies in Transition 2: Later-stage Features

- Essential legislative framework in place
- Financial infrastructure adjusting to needs of private sector
- Limited supply of investment finance
- Developing business support infrastructure, but still not comprehensive
- Increasing competition from other indigenous entrepreneurs and small firms

Lynn has also indicated that opportunities for entrepreneurial small firm diversification vary across different economies in transition, providing greater entrepreneurial risk in those at earlier stages of transition.[29]

As illustrated above, transition economies are at very different individual stages of development, characterised by different levels of entrepreneurship. They face unique problems in transforming their society and cultures from former state dependency to ones where individual risk-taking is accepted and supported. The diversity of development, however, is such that to treat such economies collectively is probably mistaken. Each nation, and indeed each region, will evolve its own entrepreneurial characteristics and activity. It would also be mistaken to prescribe solutions from the West. Exporting support frameworks and practices may not be appropriate in different environments, even though lessons may be learned from practice elsewhere.[30] Lessons from emergent nations suggest that unique developments and infrastructures are required to overcome some of the barriers to entrepreneurial development. Some of these lessons are examined in the next section.

How important small firm entrepreneurs are in such transition economies has been the subject of some disagreement by writers. For example, one writer at least has claimed that small firms are still unimportant in such economies.[31] Others have claimed, in the case of Poland, that small firm entrepreneurs have become the engine of the Polish economy.[32] Such diametrically opposed opinions will take some time to reconcile as the transition economies continue to evolve and further evidence of the different levels of entrepreneurial activity emerges.

■ ■ ■ ■ Emerging Economies

In contrast to transition economies, the emerging economies contain examples of nations for which the entrepreneur and the small firm have always played a role in their economic development. In India the small firm sector has been a prominent part of the economy for the past 50 years.[33] Other emerging nations, of course, provide examples where entrepreneurial behaviour has been far longer in developing. For example, Kenya is still considered to have low levels of entrepreneurial activity.[34] Recent GEM reports put the emergent economies of Brazil, Mexico and Korea in their high band of entrepreneurial activity, India in their middle band, whereas some of the advanced industrial economies are in their low band.[10] The analysis given by the GEM reports also makes a distinction between 'opportunity' and 'necessity' entrepreneurship, claiming that opportunity entrepreneurship is characteristic of advanced nations and necessity entrepreneurship of emergent nations.[8] However, other writers have suggested that the distinction between opportunity and necessity entrepreneurship is too simplistic to be used to describe different entrepreneurial activities across different nations.[35]

There are obviously vast differences that exist in cultures, and concomitant entrepreneurial levels of activity in different emergent nations. We do not attempt to discuss such diversity here. However, it is worth noting examples of successful entrepreneurial behaviour, how certain groups have overcome barriers to entrepreneurial development, and the factors associated with such success. Such examples may have wider applications and lessons for advanced and transition economies.

In India a high need for co-operation to overcome substantial limitations on resources has been observed, and seems to be characteristic of entrepreneurial behaviour.[36] High levels of trust and co-operative behaviour have provided the basis for micro-credit unions,[37] examples of micro-business finance, which have provided the basis for models of investment trusts and alternative sources of micro-finance in cities in advanced nations.[38] They have also been the forerunners of micro-credit schemes established by policy-makers in transition economies.[39] Such attributes of entrepreneurial behaviour were discussed in an earlier section; India provides examples of flourishing networks and clusters.[40]

Other emergent nations often have complex factors that may have arisen from their history and inheritance as former colonial states, which affect cultural attitudes to entrepreneurship. For example, South Africa, according to one writer,[41] 'with its many cultures and dynamic and transforming socio-political environment, represents a particularly problematic case study with respect to the application of arguments' (p. 27). The legacy of apartheid in South Africa has caused some black entrepreneurs to respond entrepreneurially to adversity, whereas enterprise in other members of the black population has been stifled.[41]

The diversity of emergent economies is such that it is difficult to draw coherent patterns of factors that affect the level of entrepreneurship. For example, factors that may be important and conducive to entrepreneurial behaviour in one culture, such as co-operative behaviour and networks in India, may be restrictive in others. For instance, a study of small firm entrepreneurs in Turkey found that networks were dependent on traditional values, sectarian affiliations and the family environment.[42] The researcher claimed that such networks enforced their own inertia, preventing innovation in small firms in Turkey.

This complexity of factors reveals the infinite variety of entrepreneurial behaviour in emergent nations, variety to which we can only give the briefest of indications. In many cases we are only just beginning to learn about and appreciate this diversity. What is apparent is that we can't apply 'western' solutions to such diversity.

■ ■ ■ ■ Conclusions

In this chapter we have argued that individual entrepreneurs cannot isolate themselves from the globalisation of the economy. Every business trades in a global economy, which effectively means adopting strategies that enable the entrepreneur to optimise opportunities. These strategies will depend on resources available, key staff, type of product and the nature of technology. It may mean adopting joint venture strategies; it may mean adopting quality benchmarking techniques as part of a network of firms in a supply chain; it may mean forming networks to share resources, information and gain externalities. Entrepreneurs must think globally, even if they operate only in local markets.

Entrepreneurs who do 'internationalise' by operating in more than one country, must be aware of different entrepreneurial cultures in different nations. We have examined how, in advanced economies, different regions can have very different cultures yet still be successful. We have suggested that advanced networks may hold one key to successful entrepreneurial development in advanced economies. In transition economies the legacy of communism and state control has affected entrepreneurial development in different ways in different nations. Some have been more successful at overcoming this legacy; in others lack of a recent history of business ownership has been more of a hindrance. Similarly, in emergent nations entrepreneurs have reacted in different ways to historical legacies, whether this is apartheid in South Africa or colonialism in the Indian subcontinent.

Casson[9] has suggested that it is possible to identify characteristics in the cultures of different nations that will determine whether they have high or low levels of entrepreneurship. The GEM project has also attempted to identify factors affecting high- or low-level entrepreneurial activity. However, we have also seen that the infinite variety of international entrepreneurship defies classification and it can be claimed that inconsistent factors affect the level and success of entrepreneurial activity (such as networks). All entrepreneurs need to be aware of the global economy, but all entrepreneurs who wish to operate internationally must be aware of the infinite variety of cultures that still exists in the world economy.

Review Questions 9.1

1. What are the main forces of increased globalisation?

2. Why should no entrepreneur ignore these forces of globalisation?

3. What methods and approaches might enable a firm to become international in operation? Why might international entrepreneurial strategies vary?

4. Distinguish between high-level and low-level entrepreneurial activity. Give examples of countries that demonstrate such different levels of entrepreneurial activity.

5. What are the main components of an economy that might affect the level of entrepreneurial activity according to the Global Entrepreneurship Monitor (GEM) approach?

Review Questions 9.2

1. Give examples of nations that may be considered to be 'economies of transition' for the level of entrepreneurial activity.

2. Why are there likely to be large differences in the levels of entrepreneurial activity in such nations?

3. What features are likely to mark out the more advanced economies that are in this category?

4. Why should levels of networking, trust and co-operative behaviour affect the level of entrepreneurial activity in different economies whether advanced, in transition or emergent?

Review Questions 9.3

1. Give examples of nations that may be considered to be 'emergent economies' for the level of entrepreneurial activity?

2. Why are there likely to be large differences in the levels of entrepreneurial activity in such nations?

3. Using factors discussed in this chapter, why might they encourage high levels of entrepreneurial activity in such nations?

Suggested Assignments

1. Students are required to work in a small group with an identified small firm entrepreneur in their locality. They are required to assess how the firm could be affected by the global economy. A group report should cover the following points:

■ introduction with case material on the firm

■ analysis of strengths and weaknesses

■ analysis of opportunities and threats within the global economy

■ research with potential markets (the DTI provides publications on overseas markets)

■ conclusions.

2. Students are divided into small groups and each group is given a country to research, classified as a transition economy. Their tasks are to:

■ research information on the country, from sources such as the DTI's exporting publications

■ provide information from the GEM report on the level of entrepreneurial activity

■ present findings for full class discussion with students discussing differences between transition economies.

3. You are a consultant to a local firm wishing to obtain advice on exporting to eastern Europe. Write a report detailing national and local assistance, indicating differences in the nature of local and national support provided in your region or local area.

Recommended Reading ■ ■ ■ ■ ■ ■ ■ ■ ■ ■

Casson, M. (1990) *Enterprise and Competitiveness*, Clarendon Press, Oxford.

Ghauri, P. (2000) 'Internationalisation of the Firm', in T. Monir (ed.), *International Business, Theories, Policies and Practices*, Prentice Hall, London.

Global Entrepreneurship Monitor (2001) *GEM Executive Report*, GEM Project, Babson College and London Business School, Boston, USA.

Hisrich, R.D., McDougall, P.P. and Oviatt, B.M. (1997) *Cases in International Entrepreneurship*, Irwin, Chicago, USA.

Morrison, A. (ed.) (1998) *Entrepreneurship: An International Perspective*, Butterworth-Heinemann, Woburn, MA.

Scase, R. (1998) 'The Role of Small Businesses in the Economic Transformation in Eastern Europe', *International Small Business Journal*, vol. 16, no. 1, pp. 13–21.

References

1 Chell, E. (2001) *Entrepreneurship: Globalisation, Innovation and Development,* Thomson, London.

2 Atherton, A. and Sear, L. (2001) 'Are You One of Us? An Analysis of the Interactions and Linkages Between Small Businesses and their Local Communities', paper presented to the 24th National ISBA Small Firms Policy and Research Conference, Leicester, November.

3 Curran, J. and Blackburn, R. (1993) *Local Economic Networks: The Death of the Local Economy*, Routledge, London.

4 Ghauri, P. (2000) 'Internationalisation of the Firm', in T. Monir (ed.), *International Business, Theories, Policies and Practices*, Prentice Hall, London.

5 Bell, J. (1995) 'The Internationalisation of Small Computer Software Firms: A Further Challenge to Stage Theories', *European Journal of Marketing*, vol. 29, no. 8, pp. 60–75.

6 Jolly, V.K. Alahuta, M. and Jeannet, J.P. (1992) 'Challenging the Incumbents: How High Technology Start-ups Compete Globally', *Journal of Strategic Change*, vol. 1, no. 1, pp. 71–82.

7 Global Entrepreneurship Monitor (GEM) Report (1999) *Executive Report,* GEM Project, Babson College/London Business School, Boston USA.

8 Harding, R. (2003) Global Entrepreneurship Monitor (GEM) UK 2003, London Business School, London.

9 Casson, M. (1990) *Enterprise and Competitiveness*, Clarendon Press, Oxford.

10 Global Entrepreneurship Monitor (GEM) (2001) *Executive Report*, GEM Project, Babson College/London Business School, Boston USA.

11 Scottish Enterprise (1993) *The Business Birth Rate Enquiry,* Scottish Enterprise, Glasgow.

12 Kitching, J. and Blackburn, R. (1999) 'Management Training and Networking in SMEs in Three European Regions: Implications for Business

Support', *Government and Policy*, vol. 17, no. 5, pp. 621–36.

13 Scottish Enterprise (1993) *The Business Birth Rate Strategy*, Scottish Enterprise, Glasgow.

14 Scottish Enterprise (1998) *The Clusters Approach*, Scottish Enterprise, Glasgow.

15 Edquist, C., Eriksson, M.-L. and Sjögren, H. (2000) 'Collaboration in Product Innovation in the East Gothia Regional System of Innovation', *Enterprise and Innovation Management Studies*, vol. 1, no. 1, pp. 37–56.

16 Thompson, G. (1993) 'Network Coordination', in R. Maidment and G. Thompson (eds), *Managing the United Kingdom*, Sage, London.

17 Macaulay, S. (1963) Non-contractual Relations in Business: A Preliminary Study, *American Sociological Review*, vol. 45, pp. 55–69.

18 Sako, M. (1992) *Prices Quality and Trust: Inter-firm Relations in Britain and Japan*, Cambridge University Press, Cambridge.

19 Burchell, B. and Wilkinson, F. (1997) Trust, Business Relationships and the Contract Environment, *Cambridge Journal of Economics*, vol. 21, no. 2, pp. 217–37.

20 Axelrod, R. (1981) 'The Emergence of Cooperation Among Egoists', *American Review of Political Science*, 75, pp. 306–18.

21 Carlisle, B. and Gotlieb, A. (1995) 'Problems, Training and Consultancy Needs in SMEs in Russia – An Exploratory Study', paper presented to the 18th ISBA National Small Firms Policy and Research Conference, Paisley, November.

22 Roberts, K. and Tholen, J. (1997) 'Young Entrepreneurs in the New Market Economies', paper presented to a Conference on Enterprise in the Transition Economies, Wolverhampton, September.

23 Glas, M. (1998) 'Entrepreneurship in Slovenia', in A. Morrison (ed.), *Entrepreneurship: An International Perspective*, Butterworth-Heinemann, Woburn, MA, pp. 108–24.

24 Manolova, T.S. and Yan, A. (2002) 'Institutional Constraints and Entrepreneurial Responses in a Transforming Economy: The Case of Bulgaria', *International Small Business Journal*, vol. 20, no. 2, pp. 163–84.

25 Samardzija, V. and Cuculic, J. (2003) 'Regulatory Impact Assessment: Importance for the Process of Croatia's Integration into the European Union', paper presented at the 4th International Conference on the Enterprise in Transition, University of Split, Hvar, Croatia.

26 Batstone, S. (1998) 'SME Policy in Slovakia: The Role of Bi-lateral and Multi-lateral Aid', paper presented to a Conference on Enterprise in the Transition Economies, Wolverhampton, September.

27 A&O Research (1999) *Report on Entrepreneurial Activity in Görlitz: Regional Partnerships as a Means of Safeguarding Employment*, A&O Research, Berlin.

28 Smallbone, D. and Welter, F. (2001) 'The Role of Government in SME Development in the Transition Economies of Central and Eastern Europe and the Newly Independent States', paper presented at the 4th International Conference on the Enterprise in Transition, Hvar, Croatia.

29 Lynn, M. (1998) 'Patterns of Micro-enterprise Diversification in Transitional Eurasian Economies', *International Small Business Journal*, vol. 16, no. 2, pp. 34–49.

30 Danson, M., Helinska-Hughes, E. and Whittam, G. (2001) 'SMEs and Regeneration: A Comparison Between Scotland and Poland', paper presented to the Regional Studies Association Conference, Gdansk, Poland.

31 Scase, R. (1998) 'The Role of Small Businesses in the Economic Transformation in Eastern Europe', *International Small Business Journal*, vol. 16, no. 1, pp. 13–21.

32 Erutku, C. and Vallée, L. (1997) 'Business Start-ups in Today's Poland: Who and How?', *Entrepreneurship and Regional Development*, vol. 9, no. 2, pp. 113–26.

33 Das, K. (1998) 'Collective Dynamism and Firm Strategy: A Study of an Indian Industrial Cluster', *Entrepreneurship and Regional Development*, vol. 10, no. 1, pp. 33–50.

34 Dondo, A. and Ngumo, M. (1998) 'Entrepreneurship in Kenya', in A. Morrison (ed.), *Entrepreneurship: An International Perspective*, Butterworth-Heinemann, Woburn, MA, pp. 27–41.

35 Smallbone, D. and Welter, F. (2003) 'Entrepreneurship in Transition Economies: Necessity or Opportunity Driven', paper presented at the Babson Entrepreneurship Research Conference, Babson College, Boston, USA.

36 Schmitz, H. (1990) 'Small Firms and Flexible Specialisation in Developing Countries', *Labour and Society*, vol. 15, pp. 257–85.

37 Kashyap, S.P. (1988) 'Growth of Small-scale Enterprises in India: Its Nature and Content', *World Development*, vol. 16, pp. 667–81.

38 Nicholson, B. (1998) 'Aston Reinvestment Trust', paper presented to the ESRC Seminar Series, The Finance of Small Firms, University of Middlesex, January.

39 Cicic, M. and Sunje, A. (2003) 'Micro-credit Programmes in Bosnia-Herzegovina', paper presented at the 4th International Conference on the Enterprise in Transition, University of Split, Hvar, Croatia.

40 Das, K. (1996) 'Flexibility Together: Surviving and Growing in a Garment Cluster, Ahmedabad, India', *Journal of Entrepreneurship*, vol. 5, pp. 153–77.

41 Allie, F. and Human, L. (1998) 'Entrepreneurship in South Africa', in A. Morrison (ed.), *Entrepreneurship: An International Perspective*, Butterworth-Heinemann, Woburn, MA, pp. 27–41.

42 Özcan, G.B. (1995) 'Small Business Networks and Local Ties in Turkey', *Entrepreneurship and Regional Development*, vol. 7, no. 3, pp. 265–82.

Family Businesses

By Professor William Keogh,
Heriot-Watt University

Learning Outcomes

At the end of this chapter you should be able to:

1 describe and discuss the importance of family businesses in the business world

2 describe the range of family stakeholders in the family firm

3 discuss the advantages and disadvantages of starting and developing a family business

4 describe the problems of succession planning in the family business

5 describe the main elements involved in a succession plan.

■ ■ ■ ■ ■ *Introduction*

Entrepreneurial growth firms (discussed in Chapter 8) may be characterised by family ownership over a number of generations. Naturally, an entrepreneurial growth firm at some point in time will transfer ownership; in some cases this will be generational transfer of ownership to keep the business family owned. Long-established and growth businesses (see the box on the Fiat legacy) can be family-owned and it is this phenomenon that is examined in this chapter.

When most people think of a family business they might imagine it to be a relatively small organisation such as a local business passed on through a generation or more, such as a carpentry business or even the ownership of a farm. They may also be very old businesses such as the Zildjian Cymbal Company, now American, but founded in Constantinople (now Istanbul) in 1623, or Waterford Wedgwood of Dublin, founded in 1759. Family businesses play an important role in the economies of all countries. In the UK it is estimated that family-owned businesses account for three out of four businesses, and for the employment of nearly half the UK workforce.[1] In Australia it is estimated that the proportion of family businesses accounts for two-thirds of total firms.[2]

The Fiat Legacy

Fiat is one of Europe's largest companies, with interests in many different industries including transportation, bio-engineering and financial services. As well as manufacturing automobiles, the company is also involved in commercial vehicles, engine components and tractors. It was founded in 1899 by Giovanni Agnelli and other businessmen from Turin in Italy. The company began manufacturing automobiles and engine parts in the early part of the twentieth century, and an early aim was to control the manufacturing process and cut dependence on other suppliers.

With the help of Vittorio Valletta from 1921, the company began to grow and diversify. Agnelli set up a holding company in 1927 – Industrial Fiduciary Institute (IFI, Istituto Finanziario Industriale SPA) – which is owned and operated by Agnelli's heirs. In 1945, with the death of Giovanni Agnelli, Vittorio Valletta took over as president and managing director. In 1966 he was succeeded by Giovanni Agnelli III, the founder's grandson. A merger was struck with Ferrari in 1969 and Fiat also took control of Lancia. By 1999 it owned 90 per cent of Ferrari. Umberto, Giovanni's brother returned to Italy in 1972 as second-in-command after a successful sales career.

The company has endured turbulent years at home and abroad through competition and economic impacts on the Italian economy. It has thrived in developing markets such as eastern Europe and South America. In the late 1970s the company reorganised and modernised its manufacturing processes including the use of assembly robots. Output per worker increased by over 60 per cent.

Source: Derdak, T. (ed.) (1988) *International Directory of Company Histories*, St James Press, Chicago and London (vol. I; other references in vols II, III, IV, 11, 36); see www.fiatgroup.com.

The proportion of family firms surviving through to the third generation and beyond is small; figures from Leach and Bogod[3] show that only 24 per cent of family businesses survive to the second generation and that only 14 per cent survive to the next generation. However, although the large majority may not survive to the third generation, some of the survivors go on to become major international players. In fact, many of the big businesses emerging from families are household names such as Levi-Strauss, Mars, Wal-Mart and Michelin. In Italy, Gianni Agnelli has become renowned because of the vast power and influence acquired that spans industry, politics, finance, the press, culture and society. The Agnelli family owns the Fiat industrial complex, which not only makes cars, but a wide range of other products, such as defence equipment[4] (see the box on the Fiat legacy). Another family business to make it on the international scene (also Italian) is Benetton. This family business has developed a brand that has been extremely adept at inventing and reinventing itself. Essentially, the business is a rags-to-riches story of how the family came from humble origins to develop a global business phenomenon.[5]

Despite the importance of family-owned entrepreneurial businesses in modern economies, they have been the subject of comparatively little research and attention. However, this chapter will discuss issues associated with entrepreneurial family businesses that have received some attention and research. These issues include leadership, succession, sustainability and relationships within the family. The interested reader is encouraged to examine the texts listed in the recommended reading section at the end of the chapter for additional issues and insights into the areas of research in family-owned businesses. It is a potentially rich area that deserves further investigation by researchers in the entrepreneurial field.

The role of the family changes as the organisation develops and grows. Ownership and control may change over time as shareholders and professional management are brought in, and difficulties can be experienced – for example, in investment, direction and expansion. Family ownership may begin to move from total control to a diluted holding through the introduction of private or public shareholders. The life cycle of these development phases generally begins from the entrepreneurial owner-managed firm and this is passed through to the new generation after training and the development of the individuals. The next phase of the development generally coincides with a change in direction for the business that involves the inflow of new partners or shareholders. Overall, if handled successfully, this results in a power transfer from the family through to professional management. However, it is commonly the case that, although the large shareholding is no longer with the family, the names of the family and/or key individuals are retained because of their importance to shareholders and the market. For example,[6] Sir Adrian Cadbury was still chairman of the Cadbury board while his family held only 2 per cent of the shares (p. 107). In fact, from 1962 the Cadbury-Fry family held 50 per cent of Cadbury following the flotation of the company and this has been diluted over the years, including trustees of the family trusts diversifying portfolios into other areas following the change away from family ownership.

■ ■ ■ ■ ■ Defining the Family Business

Peter Drucker[7] stated that, 'The majority of businesses everywhere – including the United States and all other developed countries – are family-controlled and family-managed' (p. 45). Such family-owned businesses are started by entrepreneurs who initially have an idea for a business that is then launched and developed, either by them or their heirs.

Family businesses are all around us and also influence our lives in many ways. Taking part in a family business can perhaps be summed up by this statement from Carol Kennedy:[6] *'Being part of a family is a universal human experience, at once suffocating, infuriating, comforting and supportive'* (p. 1).

What Do We Actually Mean by a Family Business?

Defining the family business causes difficulties and generally people may perceive it as a firm where the ownership is controlled by the family unit. Alternatively, it may also be thought of as where a family member owns and manages the business, similar to a start-up small business. Other definitions may indicate that two or more members of the family are involved in owning and managing the business (e.g. a husband and wife team).

Therefore, at one end of the scale we have family businesses with turnover of $1 billion plus and, at the other end of the scale, we may have the one-person micro-business that the owner hopes, one day, to pass on to their heirs (or a family member involved in some capacity).

A recent publication by Family Business[8] was a compilation of the world's largest family businesses (i.e. those with annual revenue of $1 billion or more) and included data from 22 countries. A family business was broadly defined as a business that had a significant family presence such as ownership and management, but not necessarily both. Analysis of the top 200 companies shows that the USA had 99 companies in this group and the runner-up was France with 17 (Germany had 16). Korea had three companies in the top 200 but these were all in the top 25 with two in the top 10 (LG Group and Samsung Group). It was made clear that data had been missed from the compilation of the list because many companies operate through complex holding companies (particularly in Asia and Europe). The 200 listed companies had at least $1.7 billion annual turnover, and they came from a wide range of different industries and backgrounds.

In Britain, the ACCA estimates that three out of four businesses are family owned and that they tend to be longer-lived than those in the non-family category.[1] In comparing family businesses, as well as ownership, we have to consider size, turnover and the market(s) they serve. Even among the group of small to medium-sized enterprises – fewer than 250 employees (European definition) and fewer than 450 employees (OECD/US definition) – the idea that a two-person business comprising two brothers dealing in a service environment (such as web design), can be compared to a medium-sized family retail business is impractical and difficult to accept. The retail business will have pressures and problems that are similar to those that exist in growing firms in their particular sector, but with the added complication of the family.

It is difficult enough, in today's economic climate, to grow and develop a business and keep control. For example, firms in high-technology niche markets may well have competitors or customers trying to buy them out for their knowledge and expertise.[9] Alternatively, they may attract investors who offer development funds for a share in the firm. Thus the business may not exist for long enough to be passed down through the family. From the Boyd Partners Australian survey,[2] it was estimated that around 67 per cent of firms were family-owned businesses, with approximately 55 per cent surviving the first generation and 28 per cent the second. French data from the 1980s[10] showed that the proportion of managers at the second generation or beyond never exceeded 35 per cent. In part, this was seen as being caused by the difficulties in the transmission of ownership of the firm within the family group – that is, the succession of ownership.

Succession in the family firm can prove difficult for a number of reasons, including the different ambitions and attitudes of the second-generation family members. The literature on family-owned businesses (FOBs) discusses this issue at great length, indeed it dominates the literature on FOBs. A recent study featuring a sample of ethnic-minority business owners for the Scottish Executive, illustrated that first-generation immigrants may have started a business in sectors such as retailing and catering but problems now exist in transferring succession due to the different aspirations of the second generation. Their children were not willing to accept the long hours of work associated with running such businesses.[11]

An example of an intergenerational family firm, Bon Accord Glass, is provided in the accompanying 'Entrepreneurship in Action' box. Generational issues and family relationships are dealt with in the next section.

ENTREPRENEURSHIP IN ACTION

Bon Accord Glass

Bon Accord Glass is a second-generation family business based in Aberdeen, Scotland. The firm has gone through many changes and developments since its launch in 1974 and currently holds significant market share in the north-east of Scotland. Bon Accord concentrates on three main areas in home improvement:

1. glazing – including a schools and other property board-up service, replacement glazing and new double glazing
2. replacement windows and doors
3. conservatories and related work.

In 2000, Bryan Keith became chairman of the company and his son Martin became managing director after a spell as joint managing director. Ownership of the firm is held by the family, and the company has more than 70 employees.

The founder of the firm, Bryan Keith had previously run a small carpentry business in Aberdeenshire and, with the launch and growth of the oil and gas industry, he began to look at the growing opportunities as the region boomed. Large building firms moved in and a small business like Bryan's could not compete with the wages on offer. At one stage he lost almost all of his staff in a month. He studied the construction industry and decided that supplying and fitting windows would provide the opportunity in a niche market. His customer base included trade, the councils for their property and home owners. Specialising in glazing led to an opportunity in the emergency boarding-up of windows and damaged-window replacement. Linked to the construction industry, Bryan also formed a small company specialising in purchasing and renovating property for sale – including industrial properties.

With the slump in the oil industry in the 1980s, there was a fall-off in demand for new housing but the strategy for the firm meant that the replacement window business came to the fore and it was able to build on this and establish a local market. Investments came from profits put back into the business to replace equipment, premises, and keep up with new technologies and working methods.

The progression into supplying and installing conservatories was due to demand in the market and, although Bon Accord was late in moving into this area, it has made a success of it and it is a key growth area. One method it uses for competitive advantage is to recruit its own builders and this aids communication and control. This way, the service element is kept in-house, although other related services such as plumbing are contracted out to firms on an 'approved suppliers' schedule.

Bryan Keith could also be described as a serial entrepreneur as he has also moved into other areas of interest related to his core business knowledge, such as hotels, where, as well as renovating them, he has ended up owning and running them. This is one of the business activities outside Bon Accord Glass's scope. He and Martin have also been involved in running a junior football club, due to Bryan's interest as a keen footballer in his youth. Standing in the business community has also been seen as very important and Bryan has been awarded honours by the business community.

He also holds an honorary doctorate for his services to the Robert Gordon University, where he has supported student entrepreneurial events, taught in the classrooms and taken part in initiatives to encourage 'entrepreneurial spirit'.

Martin Keith has worked closely with his father since his teens and one objective for him was to learn about all aspects of the business – from the ground up.

In the 10 years to 2004, company turnover has doubled to £7 million and Martin is focusing on building the business – based on the principles established by his father (i.e. quality, service and efficiency). He is also working with staff to improve customer communication, and is keeping the company abreast of technological developments. Bryan has seen a lot of change since he launched Bon Accord Glass; his main role now is to investigate strategic opportunities and also act as an adviser as the company develops in the marketplace.

Points for Discussion

1. Compare and contrast the roles of Bryan and Martin in this example of an intergenerational entrepreneurial family firm.

2. What are the advantages and disadvantages that Martin faces as a second generation owner?

Family Relationships

If an owner-managed business develops such that family members and successive generations are employed by it, as with Bon Accord Glass, then major issues have to be dealt with. Many issues that can affect the family business stem from relationships within the family group. As well as the organisational structure,[12] issues of survival and/or success can depend on how individuals work together.[13] Lank mapped out the stakeholders with interests in the family business and it is apparent that these interested parties have key roles to play if their goal is aligned with the business.[14] The parties associated with the family may be fairly wide ranging, but one would expect that the group may include in the direct line parents, children and grandchildren. Also the group may include spouses, siblings and even cousins.[15] For example, in 1990 there were 300 members of the Cadbury family with shares through trusts set up by previous generations.[6]

Research by Birley et al. investigated the relationships in the family firm in relation to the founder and, from 208 respondents, 45 per cent were children of the founder and 27 per cent grandchildren.[16] Audrey Baxter, of the Baxter family, outlined the importance of the roles with her siblings[17] when she succeeded her father as CEO: 'We are three very different people but our reasons for being in the company are the same.' She also explained that they had to talk to each other in order to keep everyone informed about company activities.

Without good relationships, situations in the organisation can become difficult to deal with and, in the more public organisation, can become public knowledge and cause possible harm (for example, the relationship between Henry Ford and his son Edsel).[18] Sibling rivalry, can cause major areas of concern such as in-fighting, jealousy and power struggles.[19; 20]

Growing concerns associated with the business in its initial stage are likely to be dealt with by the founder and his/her immediate colleagues (family, siblings or partners) and, just as firms pass through stages similar to or the same as those identified by Churchill and Lewis[21] (see Chapter 8), the family firm may experience this 'loop' on a number of occasions through the generations. On the other hand, the firm may not grow under the leadership of the founding entrepreneur[22] and the founder may not remain as leader past the 'success stage', as defined by Churchill and Lewis, particularly if external investors are involved.

Problems of Management in Family Businesses

- *Family positions* – either their role in the business or the various stances they may take over decision-making. For example, they may find themselves in a proactive role when they feel they are not qualified for it or may not even want to take on the role. Situations like this can occur due to the death of a parent.
- *Politics within family factions* can arise. For example, due to the role given to a family member's heir (i.e. not the CEO) or in shareholding allocation to family members.
- *The decision-making process may prove difficult* because of the dominance of certain family members and a lack of objectivity, or because the business's best interests are not central. It may also be that family involvement is so broad that it is difficult to get consensus.
- *Sibling rivalry* can result from many things, including jealousy on almost any basis (e.g. company position, earnings, shareholding and potential prospects).
- *Conflict* can arise from the above, as well as from external sources such as a rival wishing to buy the business.
- *Nepotism* can occur through the appointment of family members over those outside the family who have greater experience and are better qualified for the position in question. This can give rise to discontent in the workforce and the loss of very able members of staff.
- *Flotation of the business* can bring many problems (as well as benefits) for family members. Initially they will lose the amount of shareholding and control they have, external directors will be appointed and some family members may be removed from their positions in favour of qualified individuals.

Start-up, Growth and Evolution

At the business start-up phase, dependence on family for support, particularly financial support, is a common occurrence and comes with advantages as well as disadvantages. The advantages include the fact that the family members know the would-be entrepreneur and their characteristics. They may also be prepared to make any loan at low or zero interest and the time limit for returning the funds may be elastic. There may also be advice and support from family members who have business experience. On the downside, there may be some interference regarding the way the business is run, funds may be needed elsewhere in the family before the entrepreneur is ready to return it and there is a major risk if the business does not succeed.

However, as the business grows and becomes established, there are a number of things that make family-owned businesses very different from non-family-owned businesses. These include the company culture, ownership involvement and succession issues. Advantages in the family-owned business, often mentioned, include the 'sense of future' that comes from passing the organisation through generations. Learning from past experiences also increases the store of knowledge and know-how, and the networks the family operates in. The family involvement may also influence the adoption of a long-term view for the organisation and the business it is in. As reputation grows over the long term so standards expected from the business and its employees also develop.

It is also accepted that a passion for the business started by an entrepreneur is passed down through the heirs. The culture of the business is heavily influenced by family involvement and may be seen as engendering loyalty from employees as well as family members. There may also be a caring attitude – for example, in the growth of Cadbury and the personal development of staff through education and training. There may also be a strong sharing ethos, such as the John Lewis Partnership, where an idea thought of before the First World War came to fruition in 1929 when John Spedan Lewis made staff partners in the family business.[6]

Writers on the subject of the family business tend to look at the advantages of family involvement in similar ways – for example, the long-term focus or orientation of the business. They may also mention family resilience in difficult times when family members can be relied on; they may include faster decision-making and greater flexibility, and the key issue of 'knowing' the business, its products, contacts and markets.

There are also disadvantages to family involvement. To a non-family member, who may well have much needed knowledge or skills, some aspects can cause great frustration. This includes nepotism, where the family may tolerate inept or less able family members in senior positions, or there may be inequitable reward systems and difficulties in attracting talented outsiders into the firm. Over and above this, there are well-documented cases of autocratic or paternalistic styles of management within the family dynasty (for example, Henry Ford).[18]

▪ ▪ ▪ ▪ Ownership and Succession

Succession in a business is not a simple issue and can occur for any number of valid reasons. In fact, evidence suggests that getting it wrong or ignoring the issue of succession can lead to the death of a business. This is not helped by the fact that there are many complex factors to consider,[23] including who will run the business, how to devolve control and how to keep the members of the management team functioning together over the transitional period. Such issues can be dealt with by proper and carefully considered succession planning. The transitional phase can be addressed by determining the qualities required from the successor and ensuring that they do not already exist either in the family or within the management team.

The succession question can come up as a direct consequence of various circumstances. For example, the report *SME Ownership Succession*, by Martin *et al.*[24] for the Small Business Service (SBS), points out that ownership succession issues arise if the owners wish to exit the business for harvesting, personal reasons or to retire. New owners of the business may come from external buyers or a continuation of the business from inside. The authors found that ownership succession tended to be linked primarily to age-related events and the owner's personal life journey. The report also points out that, according to labour-force survey statistics, more than one-third of SME owners were vulnerable to age-related failure during succession because of their age groups, as succession becomes critical for individuals in their late fifties or early sixties.

The research for the SBS report[24] was conducted in three regions of England and business advisers interviewed during the course of the research were concerned about the high proportion of ageing owners who were making no provision for the succession or continuity of their businesses when they withdrew. Owner-managed firms without a distinct management team and having between 10 and 50 employees were seen as being particularly vulnerable to succession failure. In the East Midlands, it was found that the rate for the region was higher than the national average with

45 per cent of the self-employed likely to be vulnerable to succession failure (in 2000). The SBS's statistics suggested that some 54,000 small firms in the UK (based on 35 per cent of owners exposed to age-related issues and providing around one million jobs) were at risk of succession failure.

From the SBS research, a number of conclusions were reached regarding the vulnerability of the businesses. Family-owned[24] businesses were in particular danger when business growth was personal to the owner rather than having strategic goals for the succession of the business; when managers were dependent upon the owner making decisions; where there was no natural internal successor and when the owner ignored the need for succession. In order to keep the business sustainable, the SBS report recommended that succession planning should be addressed by owners when still in their early fifties.

The report *Leadership in Family Business*,[25] by Nigel Nicholson of London Business School, found that family businesses faced special challenges and problems and that one key area of this relates to succession. From a sample of approximately 150 UK companies, it was found that the average age of the board members was over 50. Allied to this, 30 per cent of the sample had actually gone beyond the third generation, but more than half of the companies were unable to state what kind of succession they would be looking for in the future – that is, from a family member or from someone from outside the business. Nicholson highlighted that loyalty was ranked very highly in the top three of the important qualities sought by the boards. Perhaps significantly, 60 per cent of the sample did not have a non-executive director on their board, showing that these family businesses were still dominated by the family.

Over time, family ownership of the business may begin to move from total control to some degree of a diluted holding. This occurs through the introduction of private or public shareholders. The succession phase may well coincide with a change of business development and with a change in direction for the business. With the inflow of new partners or shareholders, a power transfer from the family through to professional management may be the result. This leads to a number of key questions relating to the personal qualities of CEOs – that is, the way to choose a successor and the involvement of the outgoing owner(s).

Succession can easily go wrong for all sorts of reasons and there are many examples, including the Ford Motor Company and the legendary decision-making of Henry Ford. Because of the early death of his son, Edsel, the company was inherited by his grandson, Henry Ford II.[18]

Robert Heller[26] outlines instances of disaster for family succession and he gives advice that fits all types of business, including promotion on merit and promoting talent in the organisation. He also suggests the use of elder statespeople to guide younger managers – similar to the use of mentoring in entrepreneurship. Crucially, like Tom Peters, he advocates keeping close to the customer base. A good example of a successful family business is the Wood Group where Sir Ian Wood developed what was essentially a family fishing business into a multinational engineering business in the energy sector.

Successful succession in a family business requires an understanding of the situation, appropriate training and experience of the successor. Failure to implement a successful succession may be due to reasons related to members of the family wishing to exit from the business – for example, where the immediate heirs are seeking to establish themselves in different careers. Planning for succession is vital and a number of approaches and guides are available from sources such as the ACCA's *Keeping it in the Family*.[1]

Family Businesses: Succession Planning

Harvey suggests that there are eight recognised models for the family business to change generations.[1]

1. Having one heir – 'the Crown Prince' – however chosen. A good example of this is Samsung where the founder chose his successor from the family (see the box entitled 'An Entrepreneurial Global Family Firm').

2. Having a 'sibling partnership', where roles are enacted according to the talents of the family (such as that at Baxters).

3. The 'cousin consortium', where family ownership means that some members are active at senior levels while others are working their way up the organisation. Some may also be passive shareholders.

4. The 'stop-gap manager', who holds the fort until the next generation is ready. In part this was the case at Fiat, but Vittorio Valletta was more than this and held the top position for 21 years.

5. Family ownership and professional managers. In this situation the family may not have anyone who could run the business, or who wants to run the business, so professionals are brought in while the family retains ownership.

6. A management buy-out.

7. Selling the business in the marketplace.

8. Disposing of the organisation as an asset sale – that is, liquidating assets to get cash.

An Entrepreneurial Global Family Firm: Samsung

The Samsung Commercial Company was incorporated by Byung-Chull Lee in 1938. He had moved to Taegu in south-eastern Korea in 1936 and established a rice mill using an inheritance to do so. Between 1936 and 1938 he traded in a wide range of products including wool and textiles. By 1938 the company employed 40 staff and began to expand into Manchuria and China. Today, Samsung's flagship Samsung Electronics division is one of world's largest makers of computer memory chips, after Samsung became involved in 1980 with the purchase of the Korea Telecommunications Company. The division also manufactures a wide range of commonly used electronic products such as mobile phones and microwave ovens. Other divisions in the group deal in heavy industries, life insurance, securities and trading. Before his death in 1987, Byung-Chull Lee chose his third son, Kun-Hee Lee, as his successor and gradually relinquished control to him. This is regarded as unusual as the eldest son is normally in this position but it is believed that Byung-Chull Lee felt that Kun-Hee Lee was most capable of operating the company.

Source: Derdak, T. (ed.) (1988) *International Directory of Company Histories*, St James Press, Chicago and London (vol. I; other references in vols II, III, IV, 7, 12, 13, 18, 29); see also www.samsung.com.

From research findings and guides, steps that help the succession process include starting to plan for succession early, developing a written succession plan, involving relevant family and business colleagues, making use of outside help and establishing a training process for the next generation. In the case of investment funding coming into an organisation, it may take three to five years to bring new things in, make new systems work and move the organisation forwards. At the end of a five-year cycle, the investors may well decide to sell their share on in the marketplace or within the organisation. The process to the investor is all about careful planning, business planned development, value creation and a good organisational structure.

■ ■ ■ ■ ■ Sustainability and Longevity

The importance of succession in business cannot be underestimated, particularly to incoming investors who not only wish to protect their investment but also want to see a successful business achieve its potential. The timing of succession and the departure by either the founder or chief executive of the company is not trivial. It is not just about age, as it is also associated with the individual's energy and their willingness to push ahead with the things they are attempting to achieve. Some executives may wish to retire at 40 having been highly successful, perhaps even as part of their personal plan, and others may want to continue that success even at the age of 75 or beyond.

In the case of family business changes, members of the family, even if they are qualified to do so, may not want to take the project forwards. This can be a difficult situation and it is normally suggested that there is a role for the outgoing CEO (or owner), and he or she may be asked to stay on as a mentor.

In the case of venture capital organisations, they may ask the outgoing CEO to stay on as a director and to invest in the new equity structure. Over and above this there is the question of their involvement in assisting the successor to be accepted into the organisation and embedded within it.[27; 28] The outgoing CEO does play a meaningful role. On the other hand, if there are family members who stay on the board but become non-executive directors, then any interference is deflected because they may not have day-to-day responsibility as this lies with the new executive team.

According to Nicholson's research, family business challenges and problems fall into three main areas:[25]

1. succession

2. insularity

3. family conflict and governance.

The change in governance can be difficult – for example, when an outgoing CEO cannot give up control. Reasons for this may include not feeling that their successor is good enough to do the job, and they may also take exception to the change in vision and direction of the organisation. This can present some difficulties, but diplomacy and discussion are essential in order to bring both visions into line for the future of the organisation.

Venture capital organisations, such as 3is, build databases of experienced, talented individuals who are potential CEOs. These people will have the solid track records, experience and qualifications necessary to fit the role of chief executive, with the prime purpose of continuing the success of the organisation. Qualities that the individuals must have include curiosity – as incoming chief manager in the organisation, they must be prepared to learn from people and ask questions. They must also listen to what people in the organisation are saying and be able to capture the knowledge of the previous owner. The original vision of the owner-manager may well be continued, but there should also be an independent approach to this in the new vision.

There are always different ways to organise a business, but it's very important to capture the best of what the organisation is doing when the new CEO and management team move in. The relationship that is developed with the second line management team is key to building the organisation. The incoming chief executive must have strong knowledge of the sector as this saves a lot of time – the new CEO will understand where the organisation lies within its particular niche and how it reacts within the business environment. The person selected as CEO must also be able to make rapid, effective decisions and will have good general management skills. Leadership and the motivation of staff are major aspects of any change in an organisation and it is important that these changes are made smoothly.

There are differences between the personal requirements of the CEO when dealing with large organisations. In a larger organisation an incoming CEO may have to have more strategic capabilities as the vision and the scale of the operation could be very different, as was the case with Fiat in the 1940s. The strategic capabilities of the individual also include intelligence of markets – not just at home but on an international level. Also, the CEO must have an understanding of strategic decisions and the ability to take them. The long-term view is essential and, as the organisation develops, the CEO must have the ability to move the organisation into position within the marketplace.[29] The CEO post in a large organisation may be less people-orientated than that of the CEO moving into a growing family business.

Putting the right people in place and making the organisation gel with the incoming new management is a special skill. For the business and the investor it is vital that relationships work and it is necessary to study requirements within the organisation before the CEO post is filled. The post is essentially a management executive-related job, but there may be difficult areas – particularly when a prior history is involved in the organisation.

It is interesting to note that there is a large requirement in many organisations for the identification of suitable successors – for large organisations as well as family businesses. The people question is vital for investors prior to investing in an organisation, and investors tend to adopt a management audit approach where they will look at the key management team, the individuals, what they have achieved, their education, and their background and experience. If some member of the team is not deemed suitable, then change recommendations may well be forthcoming. It is essential that the company has people with appropriate skills in place and, should individuals leave during the investment phase or decide to move on for some other reason such as retirement, then the investor will vet the suggested changes for the new posts.

Planning to keep the business going can be complex depending on the development of the business, its size and breadth of operations. Dealing with such issues requires common goals, a willingness to contribute and a determination to succeed. For many organisations things may just happen rather than a plan coming to fruition, and the initial vision of the founding entrepreneur may be far away from the position the business achieves.

Family Businesses: Planning for Change

According to Harvey there are some factors to take into consideration to ensure success,[1] including:

- recognising the need for change and planning for it
- using appropriate non-family board members
- optimising tax planning
- creating a 'family council'
- willingness of the leader and departing generation to foresee retirement.

As an essential ingredient in the planning process, the preparation of the next generation and heirs is vital to success, and includes:

- educating the heirs to as high a level as possible (e.g. a Master's degree in an appropriate area, or an MBA)
- ensuring that staff (and owners) are trained to do the job
- gathering work experience outside the business and gaining a wider perspective
- ensuring that heirs understand the business – in some instances from the bottom up
- developing competency, attitude and motivation in the running of the business.

Exit Strategies

There are many reasons for the family wishing to exit from the business. In the early stages this may be relatively straightforward through a failure of the business and the three-generation phenomenon of rags to riches, then back to rags, which holds good for many organisations. However, failure may also occur through the lack of innovation, a lack of investment or lack of interest on the part of the family. If the company stagnates, through lack of innovation in its products or services, it may become outmoded or outdated, and is likely to require substantial investment to rectify this. Other considerations include family members seeing new pastures and different areas in which to work. As stated in the example above, it may be that family members no longer wish to be involved in the family business and want to pursue their own business and careers instead. Most of us will have some knowledge of a business where the founder and owner-manager has developed, in some cases, a multi-million-pound business, only to find that family members do not wish to stay with the business and have hopes and aspirations for other careers they wish to pursue.

From the founder's point of view, succession may be the first option but there are other alternatives such as selling the business altogether – thus becoming a one-generation organisation. The founder may allow a management buy-out based on the workforce that has been built up, or a management buy-in where an external group of managers would take over the organisation. Other options include bringing in professional management while the family retain shareholding, or merging the organisation with others and acting on a consultancy basis. Yet another alternative is to sell the business to other relatives,[30] but however, or to whom, the business is sold, it will still affect the founder or his/her heirs.[31] However, the founder need not disappear from the business completely as he or she may take on an advisory role or even a more active one, dealing with key customers, say, or acting as a mentor for the new CEO.

■ ■ ■ ■ **Conclusions**

The importance of the family business cannot be understated. Although a great number of these organisations come and go there are still a vital few that achieve great growth, influence and contribution to the economy. The attrition rate is high and research from around the world indicates that few family-owned buinesses make it to the third generation and beyond.

Although family businesses may have problems, such as internal family politics and the normal rivalries that exist between siblings, they have played a major role in building the society in which we live. A great deal of support can come from the family, and company culture and values are seen as important. New generations of family members need to fill an appropriate role and situations can arise that warrant the inclusion of professional senior managers – for example, where family members are not experienced enough or underqualified to take on senior positions.

The question of succession in the business is vital and occupies a great deal of the research available on family-owned businesses. The obvious successor need not necessarily be the oldest family heir, and planning the succession process is vital for ensuring success. Planning early is important and ensuring that stakeholders are involved will aid the success of the plan – setting up a family group or council may be the best way forward. Formal education and training are vital ingredients for the execution of the plan. Although the succession issue can arise through death or retirement, there may be other reasons such as ill-health or the founding entrepreneur wishing to move on to some new project.

In some instances the heir to the business may not come from the family – for example, where a senior manager fills a stop-gap role until the family member is ready to assume a senior role. There may also be management buy-out situations where the family members will sell their shares to an experienced internal management group and, in this instance, venture capitalists may become involved by providing funds, expertise and even a new CEO.

The role of the outgoing CEO is important and he or she may act as an adviser or mentor to the new CEO. It may also be difficult for them to accept the position they are in, so part of the planning process has to include aspects of acceptance and change. At the heart of a business it is all about people, and family businesses also have to cope with the relationships, good and bad, that exist between family members.

A fictional case study, 'A Life in Toys', is provided at the end of this chapter to illustrate some of the key issues in family-owned businesses.

'A Life in Toys' (A Fictional Tale)

Introduction and Background

Martyn Roper has just turned 60. On his birthday he began to reflect on what he had achieved throughout his career. Although now a very wealthy man, it wasn't always so, and his company Wisdom Toys is now the most successful of its type in the UK. The company, based in Manchester, has around 150 employees, of which 100 are on the operational side of the business and the others are in management, marketing and design. Company turnover is running at around £16 million mainly due to export sales, and forecasts for the future see a 10 per cent increase in sales over the next few years. However, this isn't enough for his two sons, Paul and Tom, and they have just been made aware of an opportunity that could double sales in the next two years and triple current turnover by year four. Martyn is concerned about this.

Martyn has always had to struggle and he is a resilient, shrewd character who 'bucked the trend' in his family by becoming a tradesman instead of going into the family grocery business. At 15, and the youngest in his family, his passion for woodwork and woodcarving led him to leave school and start an apprenticeship as a carpenter. His father, George, was very upset because Martyn was extremely bright at school, and he disowned him. Martyn moved in with an aunt. He kept in touch with his three brothers and two sisters, and George Roper's grocery business grew successfully into a 10-store group.

After completing his apprenticeship, Martyn was offered a post working with the Northern Seas Lighthouse Board and he spent 15 years on maintenance, repairing lighthouses, ships and other assets. A lot happened to him during these 15 years including getting married, the birth of his children and making educational toys for his young relatives.

Wisdom Toys is Launched

His eldest sister, Jane, showed these early toys to friends and acquaintances and, before Martyn knew it, his remaining free time was spent producing even more innovative toys. Although he always believed that the business world was not for him, with the help of his wife Pam he explored the possibilities of starting his own business. With the birth of his children, a reconciliation had taken place with his father, and family funds, as well as savings, were used to launch Wisdom Toys. So, at the age of 36, Martyn found himself with a staff of six and Pam running the administration of the business.

The first three years were extremely tough for the business but by the end of year four, it had stimulated a lot of interest and the number of employees had increased to 25.

Business Growth

The real turning point was in year five, when Martyn employed another designer to assist him and he was fortunate to bring in a young product design engineer. That year, Martyn paid back the family loan and, although they said they did not want it back, it was much needed as aggressive competition from large chains had hit George Roper's business hard. Due to this situation, Jane joined Wisdom Toys and was bought in as a shareholder with 10 per cent of the business. This cash injection was used to develop new products and turnover grew rapidly as the company began to export. The designs won awards for innovation and sales were stimulated as Wisdom Toys was acknowledged as leader in its niche.

Martyn built his team of designers and researchers, and his educational toy sales created a high profit return that allowed him to start a division making antique replicas and taking commissions. To bring in capital to get this division started, Martyn sold a 20 per cent share in the firm to friends (they do not take part in the management of the business and are very happy with their returns). Paul, his eldest son, who had graduated as a design engineer, joined the firm and ran this division. Paul is generally quiet and unassuming, is happiest designing and creating prototypes, and doesn't really like the other aspects of the business.

The Family Makes the Difference

Laura

The person who really helped Martyn to build the business is his daughter Laura, who had qualified as a chartered accountant and was a natural leader as well as a good manager. Her training, after graduation, with a major international accountancy/consultancy firm was such that she gained a lot of valuable experience working with a large number of companies and a variety of industries. In the eight years that she has worked for Wisdom Toys there has been a huge increase in the turnover, profitability and value of the company. She became a natural ally of Jane and together they put in place human resource development policies to develop their employees and bring on new talent. She had also helped Martyn to stave off two potential bids for the firm from international buyers who wanted to snap up its unique product lines.

Paul

Since joining the business, Paul has wanted to develop educational toys in plastic; he sees this medium as flexible and complementary to the ranges on offer. Martyn has always resisted this idea as he feels that the company may not be able to compete effectively with others that are already well established and he does not see the company establishing uniqueness. The costs of moving into direct manufacture of this new line may be too high, requiring new premises as well as machinery and equipment. Martyn estimates this option at a cost of more than £2 million.

Tom

One problem for Martyn began in the last year when Tom, the youngest family member, joined the business. Tom graduated with a degree in marketing and gained experience in market research before becoming a junior product manager for a large organisation. Making the sale is Tom's key driver and he is exceptional at it. Even in the short time he has been in the business, he has had a major impact on the order book. Unfortunately, he is also impatient and intolerant of others who don't do things fast enough and the firm has lost a few members of staff through resignations after dealing with him. Paul tends not to argue with Tom, but Laura has had to keep him in check over staff issues.

Martyn has resisted becoming too involved as he's trying to allow Tom to 'carve a niche' for himself in the business. Despite this, people have always been important to Martyn and he has had a quiet word with Tom – who chose to ignore the advice. He is concerned that Tom is not leading well, nor is he getting the best out of the marketing and sales team.

A New Opportunity

Through contacts, Tom has been offered the possibility of a multi-million-dollar contract for an American firm specialising in educational and recreational toys for pre-school children. However, the toys will have to be plastic and profit margins per unit will be as low as 3 per cent on some lines, but volume should easily make this up. The US company will also take nearly four months to pay invoices and Wisdom Toys will have to pay for machine tools and recoup this from sales.

Martyn has always been careful with investment and is concerned that the project could over-extend the business by costing more than it makes. He is also worried that they will lose control of what they already have while setting up the new division. At present, the business does not have enough capital available to fund the investment. Paul is delighted by this turn of events and has been asked, through Laura, to investigate investment costs as well as the possibility of subcontracting manufacture elsewhere (while maintaining design control and project management).

Sell the Business or Keep it in the Family?

Added to all of this, Martyn has received a serious offer to buy the business for more than twice the value of annual sales, with the proviso that he retire and his children remain in the business. Laura is very much against this as she feels the company could develop and grow even more. Jane is delighted as her 10 per cent will be worth a lot to her and Pam is happy that Martyn would take time away from his hard work as CEO. The external investors would like the sale to go through. Paul is undecided but Tom wants to keep the business in the family with him as CEO. The situation is about to be discussed at the next board meeting.

Table 10.1: *Wisdom Toys Shareholding Allocation*

Family Member and Shareholder	Per cent
Martyn and Pam	50%
Jane	10%
Paul	5%
Tom	5%
Laura	5%
Mary (not in the family business)	5%
External investors	20%

Review Questions 10.1

1. What are the advantages of owning and developing a family business?

2. What are the drawbacks to owning and developing a family business?

3. How would you define a family firm?

Review Questions 10.2

1. Assume that your father was the founder of the family firm. What problems might you face in taking over as CEO?

2. What are the options available to the founder if no one in the family wishes to succeed him/her?

3. What are the key elements in managing succession?

Review Questions 10.3

1. What would you expect from the involvement of a venture capitalist in a family business?

2. What characteristics and attributes would you look for in a member of a management buy-out?

3. When do you think the family business is most vulnerable?

Suggested Assignments

1. Using the case study provided ('A Life in Toys'), discuss in groups the main issues that it illustrates in family-owned buinesses. How typical are these issues?

2. Complete a report for the CEO outlining the strengths and weaknesses of the individuals in the management team.

3. Make a recommendation to the CEO regarding succession in the business.

4. Explain potential problem areas to the CEO including the shareholding in the family.

Recommended Reading ■ ■ ■ ■ ■ ■ ■ ■ ■ ■

Churchill, N.C. and Lewis, V.L. (1983) 'The Five Stages of Small Business Growth', *Harvard Business Review*, May–June, pp. 30–50.

Ciampa, D. and Watkins, M. (1999) 'The Successor's Dilemma', *Harvard Business Review*, November–December, pp. 161–7.

Hamm, J. (2002) 'Why Entrepreneurs Don't Scale', *Harvard Business Review*, December, pp. 110–15.

Harvey, D. (2004) *Keeping it in the Family*, ACCA, London.

Martin, C., Martin, L. and Mabbett, A. (2002) *SME Ownership Succession*, Small Business Service, Sheffield.

References

1 Harvey, D. (2004) *Keeping it in the Family*, ACCA, London.
2 Smyrnios, K.X. and Walker, R.H. (2003) *The Boyd Partners Australian Family and Private Business Survey*, RMIT University, Melbourne.
3 Leach, P. and Bogod, T. (1999) *The Stoy Hayward Guide to Family Business*, Kogan Page, London.
4 Friedman, A. (1988) *Agnelli and the Network of Italian Power*, Harrap Limited, London.
5 Mantle, J. (1999) *Benetton: The Family, the Business and the Brand*, Little Brown & Company, London.
6 Kennedy, C. (2000) *The Merchant Princes*, Hutchinson, London.
7 Drucker, P. (1995) *Managing in a Time of Great Change*, BCA, London.
8 http://www.familybusinessmagazine.com.
9 Keogh, W., Stewart, V. and Taylor, J. (2001) 'Developing Strategies for Growth in HTSFs: Looking Beyond Survival in an Increasingly Competitive Marketplace', in W. During, and R. Oakey (eds), *New Technology-based Firms in the New Millennium*, Pergamon, London.
10 Lescure, M. (1999) 'Small and Medium Industrial Enterprises in France 1900–1975', in K. Odaka and M. Sawai (eds), *Small Firms, Large Concerns*, Oxford University Press, Oxford.
11 Deakins, D., Ishaq, M., Smallbone, D., Whittam, G. and Wyper, J. (2004) *Minority Ethnic Enterprise in Scotland: A National Scoping Study*, Scottish Executive, Edinburgh.
12 Barry, B. (1975) 'The Development of Organisation Structure in the Family Firm', *The Journal of General Management*, vol. 3, no. 1, pp. 42–60.
13 Alcorn, P.B. (1982) *Success and Survival in the Family-owned Business*, McGraw-Hill, London.
14 Lank, A. (1997) 'Making Sure the Dynasty does not Become a Dallas', in S. Birley and D.F. Muzyka (eds), *Mastering Enterprise: Your Single-source Guide to Becoming an Entrepreneur*, Pitman Publishing, London.
15 Poutziouris, P. (1994) 'The Development of the Family Business', in A. Gibb and M. Rebernick (eds), *Small Business Management in New Europe*, and Proceedings of 24th ESBS, Slovenia.
16 Birley, S., Ng, D. and Godfrey, A. (1999) 'The Family and the Business', *Long Range Planning*, vol. 32, no. 6, pp. 598–608.
17 Smith, M. (1996) *Great Scots in Family Business*, Lang Syne Publishers, Glasgow, Report for Scottish Enterprise.
18 Collier, P. and Horowitz, D. (1987) *The Fords*, Collins, London.
19 Levinson, H. (1971) 'Conflicts that Plague Family Businesses', *Harvard Business Review*, March–April, pp. 90–8.
20 Miller, W.D. (1998) 'Siblings and Succession in the Family Business' (case study), *Harvard Business Review*, January–February, pp. 22–9.
21 Churchill, N.C. and Lewis, V.L. (1983) 'The Five Stages of Small Business Growth', *Harvard Business Review*, May–June, pp. 30–50.
22 Hamm, J. (2002) 'Why Entrepreneurs Don't Scale', *Harvard Business Review*, December, pp. 110–15.
23 Fox, M., Nilikant, V. and Hamilton, R.T. (2004) 'Managing Succession in Family-owned Business', *International Small Business Journal*, vol. 15, no. 1, pp. 15–25.
24 Martin, C., Martin, L. and Mabbett, A. (2002) *SME Ownership Succession*, Small Business Service, Sheffield.
25 Nicholson, N. (2003) *Leadership in Family Business*, London Business School, London.
26 Heller, R. (1998) *Goldfinger: How Entrepreneurs Grow Rich by Starting Small*, HarperCollins Business, London.

27 Ciampa, D. and Watkins, M. (1999) 'The Successor's Dilemma', *Harvard Business Review*, November–December, pp. 161–7.

28 Bennis, W. and O'Toole, J. (2000) 'Don't Hire the Wrong CEO', *Harvard Business Review*, May–June, pp. 171–6.

29 Gedajlovic, E., Lubatkin, M.H. and Schulze, W.S. (2004) 'Crossing the Threshhold from Founder Management to Professional Management: A Governance Perspective', *Journal of Management Studies,* vol. 41, no. 5, pp. 899–912.

30 Grisanti, D.A. (1984) 'The Agony of Selling out to Relatives', in D.E. Gumpert (ed.), *Growing Concerns: Building and Managing the Smaller Business*, Harvard Business Review Executive Book Series, John Wiley & Sons, New York.

31 Berolzheimer, M.G. (1984) 'The Financial and Emotional Sides of Selling Your Company', in D.E. Gumpert (ed.), *Growing Concern: Building and Managing the Smaller Business,* Harvard Business Review Executive Book Series, John Wiley & Sons, New York.

CHAPTER 11

Issues in Business Start-up

Learning Outcomes

At the end of this chapter you should be able to:

1 discuss the importance of different factors that affect the business creation process

2 analyse the role and importance of education in creativity

3 identify factors that inhibit or block creativity and ideas formulation

4 describe the importance of developing, modifying and refining ideas over time

5 discuss the different paradigms involved with the start-up process in different types of new ventures

6 describe successful post-entry development marketing strategies in competitive sectors

7 discuss whether special issues apply to business start-up in rural areas.

■ ■ ■ ■ Introduction

In previous chapters we have reviewed the greater attention paid to entrepreneurship and entrepreneurial activity in modern economies; in this chapter, we return to focus on the process of entrepreneurship by exploring in greater detail some of the issues in business start-up. It is worth bearing in mind that this start-up and development process can occur over a considerable period of time. Initial business ideas take time to formulate, research, raise funding and find partners and may be considerably refined before the launch of the business. Every business start-up is a unique event; the circumstances that contribute to success are intangible and may be different for each individual entrepreneur. Thus we need to be careful about recommending 'paths to success'; what may work for one entrepreneur may not work for another. However, we suggest, later, that intervention and support still have a role in the start-up process. The business start-up process can be broken down into a number of stages, as listed in the accompanying box.

Stages in the Start-up Process

■ Formation of the idea
■ Opportunity recognition
■ Pre-start planning and preparation, including pilot testing
■ Entry into entrepreneurship
■ Launch and subsequent development

Each of these stages will have a number of factors that will impinge on the process. These may either encourage further development or have a negative influence, perhaps causing the individual nascent entrepreneur to terminate the process. These factors will include the nature of the local environment, culture, access to finance, local support networks, role models and enterprise support and encouragement. A representation and suggested paradigm of this process is illustrated in Figure 11.1. For the sake of simplicity the representation abstracts from reality. In practice a host of factors may affect each stage – for example, the psychology of the individual entrepreneur, mental processes and personal characteristics such as tenacity and perseverance in overcoming obstacles and barriers. Some of these factors will be brought out in the case study that is included in this chapter (and in other cases in other chapters of this book), but for this part of the chapter we discuss some of the more 'external' factors that can impinge upon the different stages. Again, we don't attempt to capture all of these but some of the most important are represented in Figure 11.1 and discussed below. It is also worth noting that:

■ the nature of the process outlined in Figure 11.1 could apply to entrepreneurial teams rather than entrepreneurial individuals seeking to start a new business

■ the nature of the process will be affected by feedback at different stages – for example, the nature of the business idea will be modified over time as a result of feedback from different stages in the process.

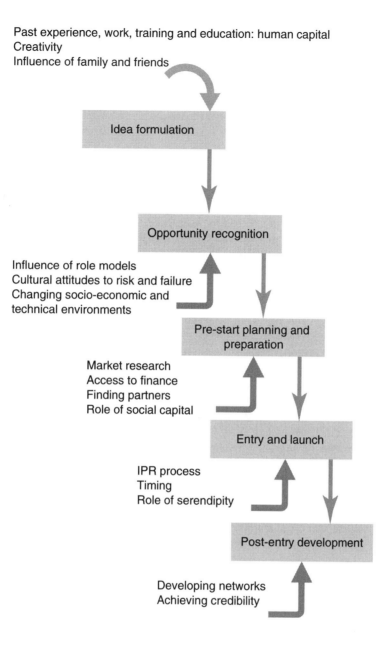

Past experience, work, training and education: human capital
Creativity
Influence of family and friends

Idea formulation

Opportunity recognition

Influence of role models
Cultural attitudes to risk and failure
Changing socio-economic and
technical environments

Pre-start planning and
preparation

Market research
Access to finance
Finding partners
Role of social capital

Entry and launch

IPR process
Timing
Role of serendipity

Post-entry development

Developing networks
Achieving credibility

Figure 11.1: *Business Creation and the Start-up Process:
A Suggested Paradigm*

■ ■ ■ ■ Idea Formulation

The formation of business ideas will be affected by a nascent entrepreneur's past experience, training, education and skill development. This accumulation of knowledge, skills and experience is termed 'human capital', a concept used particularly in the context of labour markets by economists following the pioneering work of Gary Becker.[1] Formulation of business ideas may be influenced by work experience, by individual training and recognition that a particular product or process 'could be done better'. Recognising that a process or product could be done in a superior way has been the spur behind many new businesses. For example, in the case study of Aquamotive (available from the online resources for Chapter 6), the entrepreneurs in question developed an innovative new product after identifying a problem and realising that they could provide a better solution. The majority of new business ventures are known to be in sectors or industries where the new business owners have had previous experience. For example, Cressy[2] has argued that human capital is an important determining factor in new business creation. The importance of human capital tends to be reinforced by external financial institutions, since research has shown that bank managers rate previous experience as an important factor in lending to new-venture entrepreneurs.[3]

For younger entrepreneurs, who will have limited human capital, it can be argued that education can have an important role in providing a conducive environment for idea formulation. It has been suggested that younger entrepreneurs (up to the age of 30) are under-represented in entrepreneurship because of limited personal capital and limited access to finance.[4] The limited experience (or human capital) that potential entrepreneurs in this age range can draw upon will limit the scope of opportunities for developing ideas. Youth, however, can also be an advantage. Young entrepreneurs may be more willing to test different ideas and bring a different perspective to trading opportunities. For example, recent research undertaken by the author with ethnic-minority entrepreneurs in Scotland has suggested that, in some cases, young second-generation entrepreneurs are more willing to take on the risks and strategies associated with innovation and business growth than first-generation entrepreneurs, partly because of the greater ambition of second-generation entrepreneurs when succeeding their first-generation parents.[5] Idea formulation here will be affected by educational experience and early training. It is arguable that education should provide scenarios that encourage creativity, lateral thinking and problem-solving. However, there can be a conflict in providing sufficient scope within a curriculum for the development of such transferable and 'core' skills. There are indications that greater importance is being placed on 'enterprise' abilities including problem-solving, group work and ideas generation. The Enterprise Insight initiative[6] has been mentioned in a previous chapter and, in Scotland, a comprehensive strategy, Determined to Succeed,[7] has recently been introduced, aimed at introducing enterprise-related skills at all levels of primary and secondary education. Other examples of attempts to widen the curriculum, such as Young Enterprise,[8] can unfortunately be 'add-ons' rather than developments that are embedded in the curriculum.

Enterprise Education Initiatives: Some Examples

- *Young Enterprise*: a programme encouraging young people to form a trading company.
- *Enterprise Insight*: a campaign to raise awareness of entrepreneurship and encourage positive attitudes.
- *Determined to Succeed*: a Scottish programme aimed at introducing enterprise in the curriculum to all primary and secondary school children.
- *Science Enterprise*: a programme aimed at science and technology students in universities to encourage commercialisation of student business ideas.

Education systems are important in the development of creativity and idea formulation. For example, Timmons[9] comments, 'The notion that creativity can be learned or enhanced holds important implications for entrepreneurs who need to be creative in their thinking' (p. 43). Thus, education is an important conditioning experience. Creative thinking can be enhanced or constrained by the education system and this will affect the way we view opportunities, not just in our formative years but later in life as well.

Creativity

Figure 11.1 indicates that creativity will affect idea formulation. The process of creative thinking is now recognised as an important element in management. It has spawned a literature in its own right,[10] so we can only recognise and comment on its importance here. Such literature suggests that obtaining the right environment and the right team of individuals is important for creative thinking and hence idea formulation.[11] According to Clegg, creativity is the ability to connect previously unrelated things or ideas.[12] A creative individual will think laterally rather than vertically (defining a problem in one way), perceive many possible divergent options rather than focus on a unique convergence, use imagination rather than apply logic. The alternative to creative thinking is analytical and logical reasoning; these different ways of thinking are appropriate in different circumstances, however, creative thinking is a necessary but not sufficient condition for idea formulation. Providing sufficient conditions implies providing the appropriate circumstances and environment for creativity. There are known techniques that can be employed to improve creative thinking and hence idea formulation, such as 'brainstorming' techniques, but equally important can be the removal of barriers.

Barriers to Creative Thinking

- Vertical thinking: defining a problem in only one way
- Stereotyping situations and compartmentalism
- Compressing information
- Complacency and non-inquisitiveness

Reacting and conforming to 'norms' often limits creative options. To encourage individuals to think creatively, it may be necessary to change the environment or employ different techniques. John Kao's 'Idea Factory' is one example of an attempt to provide an environment as an incubator of new business ideas and to nurture creativity, being designed to provide an environment that is safe, casual and liberating.[13]

Finally, it should be realised that idea formulation can take considerable time. The sudden breakthrough is comparatively rare. Ideas take time to refine; they benefit from discussion with others, from research, from information gathering and from feedback. Thus, being creative is only part of the process. Additional skills must be developed that can take basic ideas, then modify and refine them – perhaps involving considerable research – before ideas become viable business start-up ventures.

■ ■ ■ ■ Opportunity Recognition

Converting an idea into a business opportunity is the key element of the process of business creation. Moving from the idea stage to the exploitation of the opportunity requires many elements to be in place. The economic environment has to be conducive, the culture must be appropriate for risk-taking and the nascent entrepreneur must have the confidence to take an idea suggested by opportunities through to fulfilment. Opportunities are generated by change. Change may be political, economic, social, demographic or technical. For example, economic change may be characterised by a period of economic growth and expanding demand, which may create opportunities for new business ideas that take advantage of increased affluence, leisure time and spending power of the population. The growth in the leisure industry has spawned many new developments and opened niche markets in areas such as sports, holidays and travel. The increased pace of technological change has created opportunities for new business ventures in new technologies, in new developments in information technology such as the Internet and in new applications in bio-technology. Social and demographic change may provide opportunities through changing attitudes or through creation of new markets in ageing population structures.

These factors are the engines of change, but harnessing such change to create new business ventures requires entrepreneurs to formulate ideas and fit them to the opportunity. It is this combination that is important. The idea has to be right for the opportunity. For example, in the Aquamotive case the entrepreneur recognised an opportunity to develop a new fish-farming application service, but the market required considerable development. The market was not ready or receptive to the new technology. Thus the correct timing of the idea with the opportunity, created by forces of change, can be critical.

Cultural attitudes to risk and failure can also impinge at this stage. For example, it has been suggested that, in the UK, we have lower tolerance levels of failure than other nations, such as the USA, and different attitudes to risk-taking.[14] Cultural factors are obviously intangible and difficult to gauge, but they help to determine whether the entrepreneur that has a business idea – that is, has recognised an opportunity – will be encouraged or discouraged from attempting to exploit that opportunity. If failure is heavily punished, as we have suggested it is in the UK, then fear of failure may act as a significant constraint on this process.[15] We suggest that the existence (or otherwise) of role models will also affect such a process. In Scotland a deliberate attempt has been made to provide more role models of new and recently successful entrepreneurs through the publication of *Local Heroes*.[16] Other developments to provide more role models and 'surface' examples of under-represented groups have also been advanced in the UK – for instance, with successful black female entrepreneurs.[17] Role models remove one of the stumbling blocks in the process of new business creation – they help to identify with success and encourage the next step of developing the business idea and identifying the right opportunity. Such role models should not be too successful, though: potential nascent entrepreneurs need to be able to identify with them, where they came from and how they were successful, and more publications that help to identify entrepreneurs from many different ethnic and cultural backgrounds are needed as source material.[18]

Habitual and Portfolio Entrepreneurs

The phenomenon of the habitual entrepreneur – an entrepreneur who repeatedly starts new businesses through the development of new ideas and exploitation of opportunity – has been identified by several writers.[18; 19] The recognition of opportunity does not have to come from new entrepreneurs; existing entrepreneurs will be in a position to recognise new opportunities, buy other businesses and use previous success to develop new ideas. New opportunities will arise just from being in business. These may be exploited by setting up additional businesses (portfolio entrepreneurs); or perhaps through selling an existing businesses, perhaps to a large firm competitor, and using the harvested capital resulting from the business sale to launch another (new) business; a process that may be repeated several times by the same entrepreneur (habitual entrepreneurship). Richard Branson and Stelios Haji-Ioannou (see the 'Entrepreneurship in Action' box) are classic examples of the former. Examples of the latter, which are more common but less well known, include Sir Clive Sinclair (ZX computers) and Tom Hunter (Sports Division).

ENTREPRENEURSHIP IN ACTION

Stelios Haji-Ioannou and the 'easy Group'

The son of a Greek-Cypriot shipping tycoon, Stelios Haji-Ioannou is well known as the entrepreneur responsible for starting easyJet, yet he has also started other ventures, including easyCar, easyInternetcafe and easyCinema. These qualify him as a portfolio entrepreneur or, as he describes himself, a 'serial entrepreneur'. He founded easyJet in 1995 with a £5 million loan from his father. The company has achieved spectacular growth in nine years by exploiting a successful model from the USA of a low-cost airline, South-West Airlines. By 2001 easyJet was carrying 8.25 million passengers on 40 routes. Far from being affected by the events of 9/11, easyJet has continued to expand, thrive and increase profits, while the major airlines have, of course, struggled to survive, with famous names such as Sabena in bankruptcy. Adopting an aggressive price-cutting strategy with Internet bookings and ticket distribution, easyJet seeks to fill seats at the lowest cost. As a result in 2004 easyJet was continuing to expand and was handling more passengers than ever. The airline illustrates how a successful and high-profile entrepreneur has achieved success by copying a business model from elsewhere.

In April 2002, however, after floating easyJet on the London Stock Exchange, Stelios Haji-Ioannou found himself up against City institutional shareholders concerned about corporate governance practices and was forced to resign as chairman of the company. He was quoted as saying his skills lay in 'starting new ventures, taking risks and being a serial entrepreneur' and has turned his attentions to launching yet more new ventures, such as easyHotel and easyCruise.

This case illustrates how some portfolio entrepreneurs may be (more) suited to starting early-stage development of ventures rather than their subsequent development.

The reader should also consider this example alongside the entrepreneurial growth theories discussed in Chapter 8.

■ ■ ■ ■ Pre-start Planning and Preparation

A further combination of factors will be important to the eventual success of new business creation. Among the most important are research, obtaining information (to determine entry strategy), raising sufficient finance, and the role and influence of social capital. For obvious reasons, little research has been done on new business ventures that subsequently fail, but it is commonly asserted that one of the main reasons for the reported high failure rates of such new ventures is under-capitalisation.[20] Researching the market and the competition is dealt with in more detail in Chapter 12, but in addition search activity will be required in raising finance. Previous research into the causes of small firm failure rates, however, has been with third parties. A recent study by Benson,[21] with directors of small companies that had failed, suggests that the reasons for failure are more complex, with under-capitalisation only one of a number of factors that were more reflective of real-world complexity, including the importance and quality of professional advice.

The length and time of the search activity will depend on the opportunity and the characteristics of the new venture. If formal venture capital is required, raising such finance may take some time, because of due diligence procedures (12 months), as well as research and preparation. Although, for certain businesses, such as Internet start-ups, such time periods may be compressed into a matter of weeks or even days. Research undertaken by the author with entrepreneurs using non-executive directors, produced a number of cases where the entrepreneurs had spent some time researching opportunities in preparation for a management buy-in (MBI).[22] In these cases the entrepreneurs had researched a large number of potential candidate companies (up to 100) as a target for an MBI. If informal, or business angel, finance is sought, this will still involve a search and matching process by the entrepreneur before a suitable investor may be found.[23] Even raising bank finance can involve a search procedure and time to find sufficient bank finance, and the best terms and conditions.[24]

Preparation means finding the right management team with complementary skills. Evidence on team starts suggests that they have advantages over individual entrepreneurs because of the match of skills brought together within the team.[25] However, the evidence is far from conclusive. Oakey concluded that, with new-technology small firms, the best performers were those with a single founder.[26] Team starts have been the focus of policy 'best practice',[27] but it must be remembered that it is important to get the right 'mix' of skills in the proposed entrepreneurial team. Our research with entrepreneurs that had appointed non-executive directors demonstrated that the matching process was crucial to the success of the relationship and affected the growth and performance of the firm.[28] Chapter 12 discusses in more detail the process of business planning, focusing on designing, writing and implementing business plans. Therefore, we do not go into the planning process in detail in this chapter but, as indicated in Chapter 12, the importance of pre-start preparation through market research, competitor analysis and careful planning of entry strategy cannot be underestimated for determining the success of the business start-up process.

The Role of Social Capital

It is arguable that the role of social capital (the experience and advice available from extended family and social networks) is of key importance in start-up and entrepreneurial development. Its role is complementary to that of sources of financial capital, yet it has received relatively limited attention in research with start-up and nascent entrepreneurs, although this is beginning to change. For example, Daviddson and Honig[29] have commented that, 'From an entrepreneurial perspective, social capital provides networks that facilitate the discovery of opportunities, as well as the identification, collection and allocation of scarce resources' (p. 309). They conclude in their study that sources of social capital are important for predicting start-up entrepreneurial activity.[29] The author's recent research with ethnic-minority entrepreneurs in Scotland has highlighted the complementary role of social capital.[5] Social capital replaces the role of institutional sources of advice in the same way that informal finance can replace and substitute for the role of institutional sources of formal finance. The complementary nature of its role was revealed through the involvement of family, relatives and the general local community as sources of advice. In addition, it was found that ethnic-minority entrepreneurs might also rely on access to business advice through a network of business contacts via their own community.

■ ■ ■ ■ Entry and Launch

As suggested before, the timing of entry is important. While advantages exist for first movers, moving too early can result in insufficient customers to make heavy investment worthwhile. The issue of timing becomes crucial if the protection of intellectual property rights (IPR) is involved. The entrepreneur with a new product or process needs to decide whether and when to patent. The process of patenting is expensive and time consuming, but obtaining patents may be a necessary prerequisite for formal or informal venture capital. Developing the entry strategy is an important part of the launch of the new business; attention will need to be paid to marketing, a factor that is sometimes neglected by the technology-based entrepreneur.[30] The important relationship between marketing and entrepreneurship has been noted by a number of writers,[31] but the concept of the development of the idea and formulating strategies has been explored by only a few. The issue of developing entry and early-stage strategy has been illustrated with a number of cases in this book and, later in this chapter, we also suggest an alternative paradigm for high-technology-based firms.

The role of serendipity is often an underplayed factor in the business creation process. To the casual observer, the entrepreneurial and marketing strategies developed in the case study firms may appear to contain a strong element of chance, yet precursor developments can be highly important as preparation for exploitation of the business opportunity. With high-technology-based cases, non-high-technology development beforehand, in different cases, was an important preparation for the development of entrepreneurial and marketing strategies concerned with the technology-based ventures. The role of serendipity has scarcely been acknowledged, let alone researched, in entrepreneurial development and strategies,[32] yet our evidence demonstrates that chance is only one element; the entrepreneur must be prepared to exploit opportunities, recognise and take advantage of them. The role of the non-technology phase of development lies in learning to deal with customers, with suppliers and bank managers, and in gaining general business experience.

■ ■ ■ ■ Post-entry Development

Early-stage development is a crucial phase for the novice entrepreneur. The entrepreneur is naive and must learn quickly to understand customers, suppliers, cash flow and how to deal with other stakeholders in the new business, which may include the bank manager or other financiers. For businesses in a team start, it is only the post-entry stage that leads to the testing of relationships between individuals, confirmation of their role and the value that each of them can bring. One of the most important issues that a new business faces is credibility. Being new, especially if markets are competitive, means that customers have to take quality on trust, that suppliers will be unwilling to give trade credit and that banks will be unwilling to extend significant credit facilities. One strategy that can overcome this lack of credibility is to include an experienced entrepreneur as a part-time director in early-stage development. From our research with small companies that employed non-executive directors, we isolated a subsample of start-up companies only; in this subsample the most important reason for employing a non-executive director was to achieve credibility.[33] Alternatively, the use of an experienced entrepreneur as a mentor may also lead to introductions to key customers, to achieving credibility with suppliers and to bringing invaluable experience that overcomes the relative naivety of the start-up entrepreneur.

In addition to achieving credibility, the establishment of early-stage networks can be important in the development of new ventures. Part of the reason for bringing in experienced entrepreneurs will be to access their extensive networks of contacts. Where this is not possible, new entrepreneurs need to establish their own network of contacts that may help them to break into new markets during the crucial early-stage development of the new business. There is now an extensive literature and evidence on the importance of networks, especially in a competitive sector.[34]

There are a number of factors in the post-entry development stage that new start-up entrepreneurs may not prepare for, or may underestimate in importance. Through naivety, inadequate approaches may be taken to cash flow, dealing with late payers, payment of VAT, cost and stock control, putting in place employment contracts for staff – to name just a few examples of common areas that may be neglected by early-stage entrepreneurs. The Ace Cleaning case study, available in the online resources for this chapter, provides one example of how an entrepreneur has dealt with such issues in early-stage development.

Marketing: a Neglected Function in Post-entry Development?

Early-stage entrepreneurs may suffer from a form of myopia through too much focus on the product or service, rather than attention to entry and subsequent marketing strategy. This may be particularly true with new-technology-based entrepreneurs and we discuss their situation as a special case below. However, any entrepreneur may take a mere reactive approach to customers, rather than a proactive marketing strategy.

In marketing terms, products or services may be seen to have an efficiency dimension. Customers will buy products and services because they do what they are meant to do and often entrepreneurs will focus on ensuring that their product or service is as good or better than their competitors', or that it provides something that is different. However, this is not the only explanation for purchase. Customers also may buy products due to 'reputation effects' or 'symbolic effects'.

During early-stage development new entrepreneurs may have to compete with established firms that have established reputations and find ways of attracting and retaining customers. This may mean that the early-stage entrepreneur has to find novel ways of delivering the service or product. Two examples are given from material in the text.

1. Adopting a direct marketing strategy, as was the case with Laskarina (see the separate 'Entrepreneurship in Action' box). Although Laskarina focused on ensuring that its service was of high value it also adopted a direct marketing strategy to maintain value.

2. In the case of Ace Cleaning (given in the online resources) the entrepreneur purchases an existing contracts list to 'buy-out' a previous owner. In a competitive industry, such a move saves an initial expensive marketing campaign to attract customers and, instead, the focus can be on retaining customers rather than winning new customers. Although such a strategy may appear expensive, in reality this was less expensive than establishing a new company and trying to win new customers.

Laskarina Direct Marketing Post-Entry

An example of how a small firm can use its flexibility and small size to advantage, even in a competitive sector, by focusing on niche markets and specialisation, is provided by the story of Laskarina, a travel company specialising in holidays for UK customers to unspoilt Greek islands. Laskarina was started by Kate Murdoch, together with her husband Ian, back in 1976 when travel to Greece was dominated by the big package-holiday operators. Kate recognised an opportunity to cater for people who wished to holiday in the 'real Greece' and started with holidays on just one Greek island, Spetes. Kate took the name of Laskarina from that of the heroine and native of the island of Spetes, Laskarina Bouboulina. So important did the company become for the island that the people of Spetes gave Kate Murdoch a special award for helping its tourism industry. The company also brought some wealth and tourism to a number of other less visited Greek islands such as Symi, Halki and Lipsi, which otherwise would have remained relatively backward.

The company has been highly successful, winning 'best travel company' awards from the *Observer* for an amazing eight years on the run from 1996 to 2003; it also won the 2001, 2003 and 2005 *Holiday Which?* award for best tour operator; yet the company has remained small. It eschews marketing through travel agents and instead markets its holidays direct from a small office in Wirksworth, Derbyshire. It focuses on a specialised, niche market by supplying good-quality accommodation and ensuring that customers are well looked after while they are in Greece. It is a formula that has been highly successful, illustrating that a small firm can use its flexible and specialised nature to advantage against much larger operators. It is also a formula that has been copied by many other small travel operators specialising in niche holiday markets.

The Murdochs still described Laskarina as 'a very small family company employing 13 UK staff – and 15 British Island managers in Greece'.

New-technology-based Entrepreneurs: a Special Case?

It is generally accepted that start-up for a technology-based entrepreneur may not involve a product on the market during the post-entry and early-stage development stage. For example, such entrepreneurs can decide to start trading while still undertaking R&D or still developing a prototype, perhaps funded by grant aid to overcome negative cash flow. A standard paradigm for such a start-up is shown in Figure 11.2, where the technology-based entrepreneur comes from one of two sources: a public-sector research institution or the R&D department of a larger private-sector firm. For such entrepreneurs, obtaining patents (to secure markets and funding) may be more important than achieving credibility. Also, because the market may still have to be developed, such entrepreneurs are generally seen to face special marketing problems.[35]

New-Technology-based Entrepreneurs: an Alternative Paradigm

Figure 11.3 presents an alternative paradigm for early-stage development of such entrepreneurs. Drawn from case-study evidence, it suggests that high-technology development can occur after an initial non-technical start-up. The non-technical start-up provides an important preparation for the entrepreneur through the learning experience, providing the basis for the development of more advanced strategies concerned with marketing, finance and risk management for the technology-based development. The importance of this preparation should not be underestimated. It provides the novice entrepreneur with a valuable window of development when potential mistakes can be overcome, lessons can be learned, and contacts and networking can be developed. The entrepreneur, during this period, learns to recognise the importance of marketing

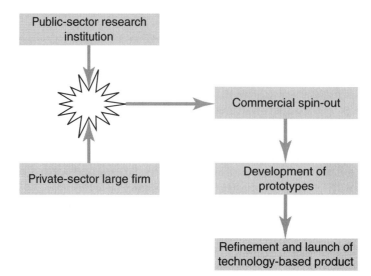

Figure 11.2: *Technology-based Start-up*

strategies, while moving away from ad hoc developments. The traditional view normally sees the technology-based entrepreneur as a technical expert, in a high-technology environment, and lacking commercial expertise. We suggest that an alternative paradigm can be presented; that a precursor non-technical period of development can be valuable and necessary in the preparation of entrepreneurial strategies appropriate for the technology-related development.

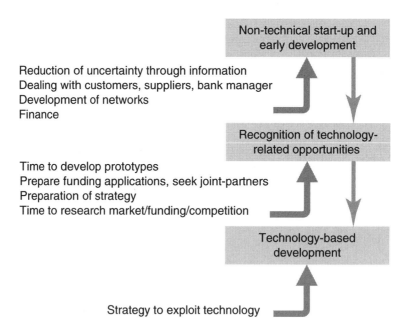

Figure 11.3: *An Alternative Representation of Start-up and Early-Stage Development for the High-Technology Small Firm*

■ ■ ■ ■ Management Buy-outs and Management Buy-ins

Both management buy-outs (MBOs) and management buy-ins (MBIs) have not been regarded traditionally as examples of entrepreneurship and business creation. MBOs involve the buy-out of the equity of a company by the existing management team, often funded by a venture capital institution. Although this can lead to changes in management style and strategy, it can be argued that little new is created. MBIs involve an outside entrepreneur or management team buying into the equity of an existing company, again often funded by a venture capital institution. As stated before, our research with small companies that employed non-executive directors, revealed MBIs where a single outside entrepreneur was often involved in the processes of new business creation, thus entailing considerable pre-MBI planning, research and search activity.

MBOs, by their nature, do not lead to new business creation per se and have been regarded as very different from new-start business creation. This may well be the case where an existing management team is given an opportunity to 'buy out' the equity of previous owners, a situation that does not lead to new business creation. However, some MBOs can be much closer to entrepreneurship, where either a team or an individual can virtually transform an old company and its associated way of doing business. In addition, where an MBO is undertaken by an individual, rather than, say, the previous management team, this can be virtually equivalent to new business creation. The Ace Cleaning case study (see the online resource material) is an example of this type of transformation and 'new' business creation and it does illustrate some of the management issues in early-stage development and a management 'crisis'.

■ ■ ■ ■ Franchising

Another entry route, again not always associated with entrepreneurship, is to take on, or take over, a franchise. Franchising still involves new business creation and also, therefore, all the aspects of the process that have been identified in this chapter. The difference, of course, is that the franchisor, rather than the franchisee, undertakes much of this process, including idea formulation, opportunity recognition, pre-start planning and market research. The interested reader might like to note that franchising can cover a range of self-employment activities; for a discussion and typology see Brodie et al.[36] Franchising has become a growth industry in its own right, with 50 per cent of franchise systems less than five years old,[37] although the rapid growth of the previous decade seems to have levelled off since the turn of the century.[38] Although the large franchises are well known and are present on almost every high street, the vast majority of franchises are much smaller with 43 per cent having fewer than 10 outlets.[39]

Buying a franchise, rather than undertaking *de novo* entrepreneurship, can have advantages as well as disadvantages for the individual. The main advantages and disadvantages are illustrated in Table 11.1.

Despite the considerable disadvantages shown in Table 11.1, arising from the loss of control in a franchise, their popularity, as noted above, has mirrored the importance and growth of small firms in the economy as discussed in earlier chapters. The appeal of the reduced risk, while still retaining elements of entrepreneurship, has obviously been a powerful motivating factor for many people, and the growth of franchising seems likely to continue unabated in the twenty-first century.

Table 11.1: *The Main Advantages and Disadvantages of Buying a Franchise as a Means of Business Start-up*

Advantages	Disadvantages
The franchise is usually based on a proven and tried and tested recipe for business success.	Proven track records have their price – successful franchise systems require very large investments by the franchisee.
The franchisee can benefit from economies of scale, e.g., in marketing, advertising and buying supplies.	Although you can sell on to someone taking over your role as franchisee, this may be less than could be achieved with *de novo* entrepreneurship.
Market research may be undertaken by the franchisor.	Trading is limited by geographical area and location, hence growth of the business will be finite and limited.
Training is provided by the franchisor.	Problems may exist in the relationship with the franchisor, leading to financial disputes.
The franchisor may act as a business mentor providing early stage advice.	Innovation may be limited because the franchise operates to a strict formula for production and sales and marketing.
Stationery and other business systems may be provided as part of the franchise package.	
Benefits from the strong brand name.	
Franchise systems are often favoured by banks due to an established track record.	

The Environment and Business Creation

Chapter 3 examined diversity in entrepreneurship and the role of ethnic-minority entrepreneurs who have created new ventures in inner-city environments; by operating in ethnic enclaves, such entrepreneurs have achieved remarkable success in a difficult environment. Similarly, it is arguable that rural environments provide environmental problems associated with limited access and limited (or peripheral) markets, and should be treated as a special case.

Business Creation in a Rural Context

It is arguable that business creation in a rural environment is distinctive from that in an urban environment, although precisely what is defined as 'rural' as opposed to 'urban' has been the subject of some academic discussion.[40] It is arguable that business creation can be more difficult in rural environments.[41] For example, the more scattered population may mean that business opportunities are more limited and the nature of the infrastructure may mean that resources, such as a skilled labour, are scarcer. In addition, demographic features of rural areas are different from urban areas. In the UK, as in most European countries, rural areas suffer from emigration of younger people, increasing the scarcity of resources such as a trained and skilled labour force. However, rural areas may offer attractions to entrepreneurs seeking to establish businesses in such areas due to a perceived (higher) quality of life in a rural environment. Therefore, business creation will be affected by the nature of individual entrepreneurs that may be attracted to the rural environment.[42]

There are further distinctive features of business creation in a rural environment – for example, networks are more difficult to establish in rural environments.[43] This affects the nature of entrepreneurial development, greater emphasis for entrepreneurial growth may be placed on global rather than local networks. Entrepreneurs in urban areas may have the luxury of achieving early growth through local markets; for entrepreneurs in rural environments, local markets are rarely sufficient to sustain substantial growth, but this may force rural entrepreneurs at an early stage to develop distinctive and resourceful growth strategies.[42]

It is also claimed that creativity and innovation are more limited and develop at a slower pace in rural environments.[44] This is because of the more limited pace of technological and infrastructure developments, but it has also been claimed that there is a lower speed of technological take-up by rural entrepreneurs.[44] For example, a lack of competition and local monopolies may result in producing more inertia and technological lock-in than may occur in urban environments.[42] A further implication of lower creativity and innovation is that it is reasonable to hypothesise that entrepreneurial learning may be more restricted.[45] An example of the nature of technological change and rural environments is provided in the accompanying box.

Technology and Rural Environments: Broadband

The recently announced rollout of broadband to rural areas by BT (announced in 2004, but will reach more remote rural areas over a three-year period) has highlighted some of the features of rural environments. Until recently, broadband has been available only in the main urban areas. A widely held perception has been that this would hold business development back in rural areas, indeed it was expected to cause further migration of new businesses to urban areas.[45]

However, the story so far has been either that business owners were sufficiently adjusted to rural environments not to need the enhanced capability of broadband, or that there have been sufficient incentives to increase demand.[46] For example, the Highlands and Islands region of Scotland has been enjoying record start-up figures for new business creation with increasing numbers of people seeking alternative lifestyles.[47] This phenomenon is also noticeable in other rural areas of the UK, partly affecting the approach of BT and its decision to roll out broadband to a greater number of rural areas.

The role of in-migrants for the development of entrepreneurial activity is an issue that has been identified in a number of studies.[42; 44] It has been suggested that in-migrants, in rural environments, can be more receptive to new opportunities, opportunity recognition and entrepreneurial growth.[42] As with other aspects of rural entrepreneurship, this is an area where the research agenda is still developing. The role of in-migrants adds to the distinctive diversity and characteristics of rural entrepreneurship.

Lifestyle or Growth Businesses

From the discussion so far we can see that environments are dissimilar, each possesses distinct advantages and disadvantages, and the entrepreneur has to engage with his/her environment in order to survive and prosper. This environmental dissimilarity is another reason why there is a wide variation in the kinds of new ventures. Since environments vary, different kinds of entrepreneur exist and many influences may interact to cause a particular individual to form a particular business at a particular time and place.[48] Two specific factors have been highlighted as determining the level of new business creation.[48] First, the perception of environmental munificence – that is, the extent to which the entrepreneur perceives the availability of critical resources. Second, resource acquisition self-efficacy, where the small business owner's ability to mobilise and gather the required resources from his/her environment becomes vital.

The rural environment is perceived as being disadvantaged, but it also offers the ideal circumstances in which to study business creation. First, rural areas, by most definitions, are less concentrated in terms of business activity than urban areas, and this means it is easier to trace out patterns of activities. Second, rural areas are viewed as being lean in terms of those resources associated with business start-up. As discussed earlier, they may be perceived as being distanced from main markets and main centres of business activity, have a lower and more dispersed population, a weaker infrastructure, more limited local markets, higher cost of both obtaining and having raw materials due to the remoteness of location, and, as indicated earlier, suffer from shortages of skills within the local labour market. Therefore, rural areas are perceived to be scarce in terms of environmental munificence and the critical resources associated with the entrepreneurial process. Consequently, examining the process within the context of rurality is interesting, since it enables us to see how entrepreneurs overcome what could be viewed as being potential difficulties and hindrances to growth and development. The associated discussion, in the student's online learning resources, uses the rural context to investigate what entrepreneurs do and develops this into a working definition and description of entrepreneurial actions, together with additional case examples.

The level of growth in business creation in rural areas reported earlier has been attributed, at least in part, to the attraction of the quality of life that the countryside was perceived to provide, drawing people to rural areas.[49] These were often lifestyle businesses. It has also been suggested that the flexibility associated with rurality, the need to be more innovative and competitive, has meant that the more dynamic expansionist firms have tended to be concentrated in smaller towns and rural areas.[50]

Further discussion of the impact of rural environments is given in the student's online learning resources, which also includes two case studies of business creation in a rural environment. Despite the problems of peripherality and limited local markets, these examples demonstrate that entrepreneurship associated with business creation in rural areas can be successful, with growth rather than lifestyle businesses. This supports some evidence that rural firms are more profitable and enjoy greater business growth (in certain size ranges) than their urban counterparts, possibly because rural environments have compensating factors such as a high-quality and loyal labour force.[51] Thus, although the environment may be a limiting factor, in practice, if sufficient pre-start preparation, planning and research is undertaken, an opportunity for business creation can still be exploited successfully.

The nature of rural entrepreneurship means that there are distinctive policy implications.[44] Governments cannot assume that policies to encourage entrepreneurship will have similar impacts in urban as in rural areas; for example, a number of writers have suggested that there is a premium associated with support programmes in rural areas.[44] In the final section of this chapter, we consider in greater detail whether enterprise support can influence the nature of business creation.

■ ■ ■ ■ ■ The Role of Enterprise Support and Business Start-up

Introduction

In the UK, it is arguable that the role of enterprise support has evolved in an ad hoc manner, but for reference purposes a simplified version of the framework of support agencies that will be referred to in this chapter is shown, for England and Wales, in Figure 11.4; for Scotland, which has different support agencies, the equivalent structure is shown in Figure 11.5. These illustrations do not attempt to show all the agencies involved in providing start-up advice and support to entrepreneurs and small firms, but show the relative funding links between different agencies. The general relationship that might exist between the entrepreneur and the enterprise support agency, via a business adviser or mentor is shown in Figure 11.6.

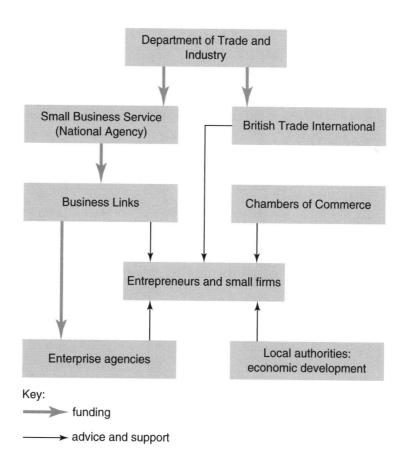

Figure 11.4: *Support Agencies for England and Wales*

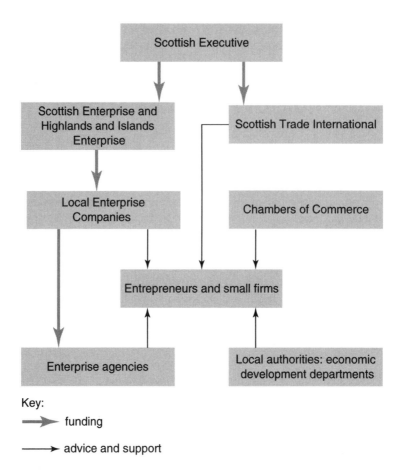

Key:

⟹ funding

⟶ advice and support

Figure 11.5: *Support Agencies for Scotland*

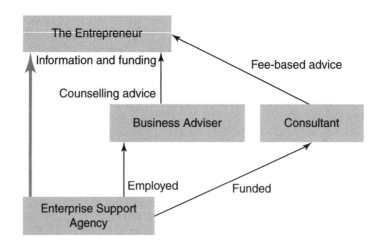

Figure 11.6: *Enterprise Support: The Entrepreneur–Adviser Relationship*

This evolution of enterprise support has meant varying importance placed upon supporting start-ups. However, the publication in 2004 of the SBS Action Plan[52] re-emphasises a government policy commitment to 'making the UK the best place in the world to start and grow a business' (p. 4). However, it is not possible to support all new start-up enterpreneurs and one of the principles of enterprise support that has enjoyed varying importance is the concept of selectivity.

Selectivity

It is too expensive to provide business advice to all new business owners on a one-to-one basis. Business advisers have to meet their clients frequently and may have intensive periods of counselling sessions; in many areas this has led to segmentation of support. For example, in Scotland local support agencies will provide a basic level of advice to most start-ups, but have specialist high-growth programmes for selected perceived high-growth start-ups. It should be noted, following our discussion of rural environments, that segmentation is difficult to achieve in rural areas, due to the smaller pool of start-up business owners.

Continuity

It is arguable that some businesses will need continuity of pre-start, start-up, aftercare and business development adviser support. In the same way that start-up support has varied across areas and, historically, practice has varied: not only has the extent and length of aftercare varied, but also the continuity of support has varied. In principle, early-stage clients may be passed on to general business development adviser support, but in practice there has been a sharp division in support, with different agencies focusing on different types of support and, in some cases, overlapping areas of responsibility.[53] Many early-stage business clients, perhaps at a critical stage in their development, however, will not have access to further support. Segmentation, driven by public and ERDF European funding, has meant that only higher-growth-potential clients have received intensive and proactive aftercare support in a limited number of areas in England and Wales.

Integrated Model: the Business Link Model

Business Links (introduced in the early 1990s) were meant to be an integrated model of business support: a one-stop shop. This has some attractions since resources, information and delivery can all be provided in the one location. Advisers can easily speak to each other and with trainers, managers and specialist advisers. The Business Links were also meant to combine different initiatives under one roof, such as the DTI Information Society Initiative to provide, for example, an IT centre for training, advice and consultation. However, as reviewed by a number of writers, the provision of such an integrated one-stop shop has been highly variable.[54; 55]

Special Needs Groups

The provision of volume adviser support, where limited start-up advice is given, can ignore the needs of special groups where there is a case for more targeted and more specialised support. For example, in Birmingham, specialised agencies such as Black Business in Birmingham (3bs) aim to cater for the needs of ethnic minorities in business. In Glasgow, the Wellpark Enterprise Centre has been promoted as an example of specialised support for women from socially excluded groups by a Bank of England Report.[56] Other cities have similar targeted support agencies. The advantage of providing specialised, targeted support for special needs groups is that it can integrate business development with economic inclusion and establish business forums that maintain links with such business groups.

It is arguable that technology-based start-ups should receive specialised start-up support and longer aftercare provision, given their special requirements for funding and, in some cases, R&D. The current focus on exploiting commercialisation is important for the UK's economy, and some Business Links and LECs have integrated support linked to HEIs. For example, in the east of Scotland, Dundee Technopole combined with BioDundee has established a partnership linking world-class expertise at the University of Dundee in bio-sciences to an incubator and Medipark, and a successful bio-science cluster.

The complexity of the support picture across the UK, however, is illustrated by the confusing range of specialist support agencies that may provide advice to technology-based start-up firms, women in business, ethnic-minority firms and other categories of firm, which may qualify for a range of support, funding and specialised advice.

Providing Start-up Support: a Review of Evidence

Storey[57] has compared the provision of start-up support to 'a lottery in which the odds of winning are not good' (p. 16). The basis for this view has been that the blanket coverage of start-up support programmes, such as the Enterprise Allowance Scheme (EAS), have not resulted in a noticeable impact on the quality of firm starts and may have encouraged low-quality firm start-ups, even though Storey considered the EAS to be one of the 'better schemes'. The vast majority of new firm starts are known to be poor job creators.[57] Thus, it has been argued that the opportunity cost of such start-up enterprise support is high, since the careful targeting of public funds, in the form of enterprise support, at the small number of high-performing growth firms that are new starters, should result in a more cost-effective way of supporting new venture development.

However, research by the author and colleagues with local area programmes has found evidence that mentoring and business adviser support had beneficial effects on the subsequent business development and the development of entrepreneurial learning with start-up owners involved in business creation.[58] More recent research by the author, with a local area targeted support programme with new-start ethnic-minority entrepreneurs, also found that adviser support had beneficial effects, in particular enabling new-start ethnic-minority entrepreneurs to link into a wider network of mainstream funding and further training.[59]

One of the problems with evaluations of such assistance is that the benefits of support are difficult to measure and quantify objectively. Without going into details, benefits tend to be subjective, related to the quality of advice, in areas such as managing change, problem-solving or accessing finance. Thus, support that attempts to improve the quality of new business creation may be difficult to evaluate.

Initiatives to improve the quantity of new business creation are a different matter and have proved to be much more problematical. For example, an evaluation of the seven years of a Business Birth Rate Strategy in Scotland concluded that the strategy had made little impact on business creation or the nation's business birth rate.[60] A recent study by Mole et al.[61] comparing three English counties – Cleveland, Buckinghamshire and Shropshire – concluded that: 'policies to boost new firm founding rates would lead to more firms in low-income elasticity demand sectors, such as hairdressing and motor vehicle repair', the implication of the authors being that support that is designed to increase the rate of business creation would merely lead to more firms in competitive sectors; the disadvantage being that such business creation is likely to have both displacement (where established firms close down) and deadweight (zero impacts on the beneficiaries of public funding) effects.

We suggest that there is a need to make a distinction between support to address the quality of new business creation, where interventions with good-quality advice can make a critical difference, and support that seeks to address the rate or quantity of new business creation, where there is little evidence that such support makes a perceivable or measurable impact. In addition, there is emerging evidence that targeted support programmes such as those geared to women entrepreneurs, ethnic-minority entrepreneurs and young people, who may face additional barriers, are beneficial in contributing to the diversity of business creation, to increasing the quality and quantity, and therefore to local economic development.

■ ■ ■ ■ Conclusions

This chapter has considered the process of business creation, often regarded as the distinguishing feature of entrepreneurship. We have seen that the entrepreneur is required not just to generate ideas, but more importantly to recognise the correct opportunity for exploiting them. Although chance may be involved, pre-start preparation and planning is also crucial. For example, case evidence, drawn from research undertaken for this text, has demonstrated that precursor preparation before launching new technology-based products was an important factor, allowing development of networks, learning and appropriate marketing strategies by the entrepreneurs concerned. This evidence was drawn from cases used in this text, including Alternative Publishing and Aquamotive (see the online learning resources).

Although each new business start-up is a unique creative event, we have noted that start-up is diverse and complex; it may involve serial and portfolio entrepreneurs, it may involve new franchise systems and franchisees, it may involve MBIs and MBOs, and it may be different in nature in rural and urban environments. It is arguable that intervention in the start-up and business-creation process may not be valuable or productive. However, we have also argued that targeted support can be beneficial and that it is possible to improve the quality, if not the quantity, of new business creation.

Review Questions 11.1 ■ ■ ■ ■ ■ ■ ■ ■ ■ ■ ■ ■ ■

Thinking Creatively

1. Why is the environment important for creativity?

2. List barriers to creativity in your organisation/university.

3. How can group dynamics affect creativity?

4. Give an example of an enterprise education intiative. Why might an emphasis on creativity be an important part of such an initiative?

Review Questions 11.2 ■ ■ ■ ■ ■ ■ ■ ■ ■ ■ ■ ■ ■

1. What are the start-up stages before market entry and launch?

2. Why should creativity be encouraged in young people with potential business ideas?

3. Discuss, either individually or in a group, whether the traditional education system encourages creativity.

4. Why does change affect the formation of business ideas? Can this explain the explosion of dotcom business ideas with the growth of Internet use and trading?

5. What are the research and search procedures necessary in the pre-start and planning stage?

Review Questions 11.3

1. Suggest ways in which new-start entrepreneurs can overcome the credibility problem?

2. What is the difference between an MBO and an MBI? Would you consider MBOs and MBIs as valid entrepreneurial activity?

3. Why can timing be crucial to the business entry decision?

4. Describe why a rural or urban environment can affect the business-creation process.

5. How might mentors/business advisers help new start-up entrepreneurs?

6. What start-up assistance is provided in your locality for new start-up entrepreneurs?

Suggested Assignments

The following assignments are based on the case of Ace Cleaning Ltd, which can be found in the online student resource centre.

1. Students discuss the case of Ace Cleaning Ltd in a small group. They are required to identify the options available to Mary Anderson, and recommend and present a course of action.

2. Students are required to consider the Ace Cleaning case as consultants, discuss how Mary should change her management style and practices, and make recommendations as consultants to Ace Cleaning Ltd.

3. Compare the Ace Cleaning case to the Alternative Publishing case (see Chapter 3). What are the similarities and differences between the two cases? How does the business-creation process differ in each case?

Additional questions

4. Argue the case for and against intervention in the start-up process by public-sector enterprise development agencies.

5. Why might the use of previous entrepreneurs as mentors to new-start entrepreneurs be beneficial in terms of impact and development of such new-start businesses.

Recommended Reading

Daviddson, P. and Honig, B. (2003) 'The Role of Social and Human Capital Among Nascent Entrepreneurs', *Journal of Business Venturing*, vol. 18, no. 3, pp. 301–31.

Kao, J.J. (1991) *Managing Creativity*, Prentice-Hall, London.

Kao, J.J. (1997) *Jamming: The Art and Discipline of Business Creativity*, HarperCollins, London.

Reynolds, P.D. and White, S.B. (1997) *The Entrepreneurial Process: Economic Growth, Men, Women and Minorities,* Quorom, Westport.

Small Business Service (2004) *A Government Aciton Plan for Small Businesses: The Evidence Base*, SBS, DTI, London.

References

1 Becker, G.S. (1962) 'Investment in Human Capital', *Journal of Political Economy*, vol. 70, pp. 9–49.

2 Cressy, R. (1996) *Small Business Failure: Failure to Fund or Failure to Learn*?, Centre for SMEs, University of Warwick, Coventry.

3 Deakins, D. and Hussain, G. (1994) 'Risk Assessment with Asymmetric Information', *International Journal of Bank Marketing*, vol. 12, no. 1, pp. 24–31.

4 Scottish Enterprise (1993) *Scotland's Business Birth Rate: A National Enquiry*, Scottish Enterprise, Glasgow.

5 Deakins, D., Ishaq, M., Whittam, G. and Wyper, J. (2004) unpublished Interim Progress Report for the Scottish Executive, Scottish Executive, Edinburgh.

6 Enterprise Insight (2001) *Enterprise Insight*, DTI, London.

7 Scottish Executive (2003) *Determined to Succeed – Enterprise in Education: Scottish Executive Response*, Scottish Executive, Edinburgh.

8 Gavron, R., Cowling, M., Holtham, G. and Westall, A. (1998) *The Entrepreneurial Society*, IPPR, London.

9 Timmons, J.A. (1994) *New Venture Creation: Entrepreneurship for the 21st Century*, 4th edn, Irwin, Illinois.

10 Goodman, M. (1995) *Creative Management*, Prentice-Hall, London.

11 Proctor, T. (1998) *Creative Problem Solving for Managers*, Routledge, London.

12 Clegg, B. (1999) *Creativity and Innovation for Managers*, Butterworth-Heinemann, Oxford.

13 Kao, J.J. (1997) *Jamming: The Art and Discipline of Business Creativity*, HarperCollins, London.

14 Birley, S. and Macmillan, I. (eds) (1995) *International Entrepreneurship*, Routledge, London.

15 Reynolds, P. and White, S. (1997) *The Entrepreneurial Process: Economic Growth, Men, Women and Minorities*, Quorum, Westport.

16 Scottish Enterprise (1997) *Local Heroes*, Scottish Enterprise, Glasgow.

17 Wanogho, E. (1997) *Black Women Taking Charge*, E.W. International, London.

18 Westhead, P. and Wright, M. (1999) 'Contributions of Novice, Portfolio and Serial Founders Located in Rural and Urban Areas', *Regional Studies*, vol. 33, no. 2. pp. 157–74.

19 Carter, S. (1999) 'The Economic Potential of Portfolio Entrepreneurship: Enterprise and Employment Contributions of Multiple Business Ownership', *Journal of Small Business and Enterprise Development*, vol. 5, no. 4, pp. 297–306.

20 Cressy, R. (1996) *Small Business Failure: Failure to Fund or Failure to Learn*?, Centre for SMEs, University of Warwick, Coventry.

21 Benson, A. (2004) 'Reasons for Cessation of Trading of Incorporated SMEs in Manufacturing and Engineering in the Humber Sub-region 1998–2000', unpublished DBA thesis, University of Hull, Humberside.

22 Deakins, D., Mileham, P. and O'Neill, E. (1998) 'The Role and Influence of Non-executive Directors in Growing Small Firms', paper presented to Babson Entrepreneurship Research Conference, Ghent, Belgium.

23 Mason, C.M. and Harrison, R.T. (1995) 'Informal Venture Capital and the Financing of Small and Medium Sized Enterprises', *Small Enterprise Research*, vol. 3, no. 1, pp. 33–56.

24 Deakins, D. and Hussain, G. (1991) *Risk Assessment by Bank Managers*, Small Business Research Centre, University of Central England, Birmingham.

25 Vyakarnaram, S., Jacobs, R. and Handleberg, J. (1997) 'The Formation and Development of Entrepreneurial Teams in Rapid Growth Businesses', paper presented to Babson Entrepreneurship Research Conference, Babson College, Boston.

26 Oakey, R.P. (1995) *High Technology New Firms: Variable Barriers to Growth*, Paul Chapman Publishing, London.

27 DTI (1996) *Small Firms in Britain Report 1996*, DTI, London.

28 Deakins, D., Mileham, P. and O'Neill, E. (1998) The Role and Influence of Non-executive Directors in Growing Small Firms, ACCA research report, ACCA, London.

29 Daviddson, P. and Honig, B. (2003) 'The Role of Social and Human Capital Among Nascent Entrepreneurs', *Journal of Business Venturing*, vol. 18, no. 3, pp. 301–31.

30 Oakey, R.P. (1995) *High Technology New Firms: Variable Barriers to Growth*, Paul Chapman Publishing, London.

31 For example, Carson, D., Cromie, S., McGowan, P. and Hill, J. (1995) *Marketing and Entrepreneurship in SMEs: An Innovative Approach*, Prentice-Hall, London.

32 Martello, W.E. (1994) 'Developing Creative Business Insights: Serendipity and its Potential', *Entrepreneurship and Regional Development*, vol. 6, no. 2, pp. 239–58.

33 Deakins, D., Mileham, P. and O'Neill, E. (1998) The Role and Influence of Non-executive Directors in Growing Small Firms, ACCA research report, ACCA, London.

34 Shaw, E. (1997) 'The Real Networks of Small Firms', in D. Deakins, P. Jennings and C. Mason (eds), *Small Firms: Entrepreneurship in the Nineties*, Paul Chapman Publishing, London, pp. 7–17.

35 Jones-Evans, D. (1997) 'Technology Entrepreneurship, Experience and the Management of Small Technology-based Firms – Exploratory Evidence from the UK', *Entrepreneurship and Regional Development*, vol. 9, no. 1, pp. 65–90.

36 Brodie, S., Stanworth, J. and Wotruba, T.R. (2002) 'Direct Sales Franchises in the UK', *International Small Business Journal*, vol. 20, no. 1, pp. 53–76.

37 Tikoo, S. (1996) 'Assessing the Franchise Option', *Business Horizons*, vol. 9, no. 3, p. 78.

38 Watson, A. and Kirby, D.A. (2004) 'Public Perceptions of Franchising in Britain: Releasing the Potential', *Journal of Small Business and Enterprise Development*, vol. 11, no. 1, pp. 75–83.

39 Dickie, S. (1993) *Franchising in America: The Development of a Business Method*, University of North Carolina Press, North Carolina.

40 Deakins, D., Galloway, L. and Mochrie, R. (2003) 'The Use and Effect of ICT on Scotland's Rural Business Community', Research Report for Scottish Economists' Network, University of Stirling, Stirling.

41 Anderson, A.R. (1997) 'Entrepreneurial Marketing Patterns in a Rural Environment', paper presented at the Special Interest Group Symposium on the Marketing and Entrepreneurship Interface, Dublin, January.

42 McKain, R. (2003) 'Social Constructions of Environmental Quality and Opportunities for Enterprise in Rural Scotland', unpublished PhD thesis, University of Highlands and Islands, Perth College, Perth.

43 Vaessen, P. and Keeble, D. (1995) 'Growth-oriented SMEs in Unfavourable Regional Environments', *Regional Studies*, vol. 29, no. 4, pp. 489–505.

44 Smallbone, D., North, D., Baldock, R. and Ekanem, I. (2002) 'Encouraging and Supporting Enterprise in Rural Areas', Research Report for the DTI's Small Business Service, London.

45 Deakins, D., Galloway, L. and Mochrie, R. (2004) 'Rural Business Use of ICT: A Study of the Relative Impact of Collective Activity in Rural Scotland', *Journal of Strategic Change*, vol. 13, no. 2, pp. 139–50.

46 Galloway, L., Mochrie, R. and Deakins, D. (2004) 'ICT-enabled Collectivity as a Positive Rural Business Strategy', *International Journal of Entrepreneurial Behaviour and Research*, vol. 10, no. 4, pp. 247–59.

47 Highlands and Islands Enterprise (2004) *HIE Annual Report*, HIE, Inverness.

48 Cooper, A.C. and Dunkelberg, W.C. (1981) 'A New Look at Business Entry: Experiences of 1805 Entrepreneurs', in K.H. Vesper, *Frontiers of Entrepreneurship Research*, Babson College, USA.

49 Curran, J. and Storey, D. (1993) 'The Location of Small and Medium Enterprises: Are there Urban–Rural Differences?', in J. Curran and D. Storey (eds), *Small Firms in Urban and Rural Locations*, Routledge, London.

50 Anderson, A.R. (1995) 'The Arcadian Enterprise: An Enquiry into the Nature and Conditions of Rural Small Business', unpublished PhD thesis, University of Stirling.

51 Smallbone, D., North, D. and Kalantardis, C. (1996) 'The Survival and Growth of Manufacturing SMEs in Remote Rural Areas in the 1990s', paper presented to the 19th ISBA National Small Firms Policy and Research Conference, Birmingham.

52 Small Business Service (2004) *A Government Aciton Plan for Small Businesses: The Evidence Base*, SBS, DTI, London.

53 Ram, M. (1996) 'Supporting Ethnic Minority Enterprise: Views from the Providers', paper presented to the 19th ISBA National Small Firms Policy and Research Conference, Birmingham, November.

54 Bennett, R., Robson, P. and Bratton, W. (2000) 'Government Advice Networks for SMEs: An Assessment of the Influence of Local Context on Business Link Use, Impact and Satisfaction', working paper no. 182, Centre for Business Research, University of Cambridge, Cambridge.

55 Mole, K. (1999) 'Heuristics of Personal Business Advisers', unpublished PhD thesis, University of Wolverhampton.

56 Bank of England (2000) *Finance for Small Businesses in Deprived Communities*, Bank of England, London.

57 Storey, D.J. (1993) 'Should we Abandon Support to Start-up Businesses', in F. Chittenden and M. Robertson (eds), *Small Firms: Recession and Recovery*, Paul Chapman Publishing, London, pp. 1–26.

58 Deakins, D., Sullivan, R. and Whittam, G. (2002) 'Developing Support for Entrepreneurial Learning: Evidence from Start-up Support Programmes', *International Journal of Entrepreneurship and Innovation Management*, vol. 2, nos 4/5, pp. 323–38.

59 Paisley Enterprise Research Centre (2002; 2004) *Interim Evaluations of the Ethnic Minority Business Support Programme*, Glasgow City Council, Glasgow.

60 Scottish Enterprise (2001) *Review of the Business Birth Rate Strategy*, Fraser of Allander, Scottish Enterprise, Glasgow.

61 Mole, K., Greene, F. and Storey, D. (2002) 'Entrepreneurship in Three English Counties', paper presented at the 25th ISBA National Small Firms Policy and Research Conference, Brighton, November.

Preparation for Business Start-up:
Research, Design and Implementation of Business Plans

CHAPTER

12

Learning Outcomes

At the end of this chapter you should be able to:

1 describe different sources of information

2 discuss the potential of online databases for information gathering

3 evaluate the potential of primary and secondary sources of information for entrepreneurs

4 describe the importance of different sources of information for carrying out a feasibility study

5 describe the importance of qualitative research for the business plan

6 construct cash-flow forecasts in the light of research undertaken

7 construct the main sections of a business plan

8 describe the importance of strategic planning for the successful development of a business

9 appreciate the importance of careful research for the accuracy of forecasts in the business plan

10 construct a cash-flow forecast from some income and expense assumptions

11 discuss the advantages and limitations of business plans for the adequate monitoring of business performance

12 discuss the wide variety and flexibility of business plans and the need for a coherent national standard.

■ ■ ■ ■ **Introduction**

In this chapter, we examine the steps required for researching, developing and designing business plans in relation to the business start-up process. References to sources of advice and support are also included.

Designing and writing the business plan should be seen as the outcome of a careful research process and subsequent planning procedure as illustrated in Figure 12.1. We will discuss some of the stages of this research process in more detail; however, the business plan should be regarded as part of that procedure but not as the end of that process.

The business plan is part of the ongoing process of strategic planning for the entrepreneur and small business, whether produced for a start-up business or for an existing business. The business plan can have several purposes (see box).

Purposes of a Business Plan

■ It may be produced to raise funding from banks or venture capitalists, or it may be required to obtain grant funding from an agency such as a Business Link or a Local Enterprise Company

■ It may serve as a strategic planning document for entrepreneurs, a plan to guide the business and as a basis for taking strategic decisions

■ It may serve as a subsequent monitoring device

Nowadays there are many guides produced by banks, enterprise agencies and accountants, as well as books published on this ongoing planning process.[1] These are often also available on CD with a business plan format already provided. This chapter does not attempt to replicate these guides, which are often excellent summaries of the essential first steps in starting in business for new entrepreneurs. These guides are often a framework for organising ideas and formulating a draft business plan. Many agencies and bankers would say that most new business start-ups are now required to produce an elementary business plan. This is a major advance on what might have existed in the not so distant past, when a person with a business idea could talk it over with their bank manager, produce some rough 'back of the envelope' calculations and walk out of the bank with a start-up overdraft. The majority of start-ups and even expansions of existing businesses are still planned on the basis of some cash-flow forecasts with a few introductory pages of explanation. Although there have been major improvements, partly as a result of the development of agency and other professional sources of advice and support, there remains tremendous variety in the standard of business plans that are produced, with many that are severely limited in scope. There is, as yet, no research into the quality and effectiveness of many business plans that are produced. There is an often-quoted statement that a business plan is 'out of date as soon as it is produced'; yet, if a business plan is to be effective, this should not be the case. This chapter aims to explain how a business plan can be used effectively as an ongoing monitoring and strategic planning document, which, although it may need revision, should be effective for several years. After all, if considerable effort has been expended on research, as recommended in this chapter, then this should have some pay-off in the future planning and monitoring of the business.

One problem when designing and writing a business plan is that different funding bodies can have different requirements. We have seen in Chapter 4 that even among

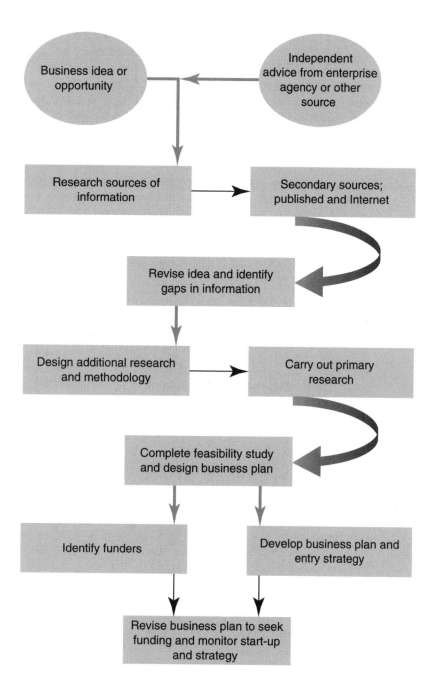

Figure 12.1: *Business Start-up: the Strategic Planning Process*

different bank managers there were considerably different expectations in terms of what was expected and required from entrepreneurs when producing a business plan for a start-up business.[2] In addition, venture capitalists will require a much more detailed business plan and perhaps more market analysis than a bank manager will, for the obvious reason that the venture capitalist will not be able to take security to safeguard his/her investment. Mason and Stark have found that there are significant differences in what is expected in a business plan between bankers, business angels and venture capitalists.[3] An enterprise or development agency will also vary in its requirements if a business plan is required to secure grant-aided funding. Thus, the advice to potential and existing entrepreneurs before writing the business plan is to seek to determine what format is preferred by the potential funder in terms of presentation and content. In the case of banks, this is usually obtainable from their own start-up guides and suggested formats on CD. This will avoid unnecessary rewrites or changes to the presentation. It is best to have a full business plan that you are satisfied with and that will serve you as the entrepreneur when taking strategic decisions for the business. Remember that the business plan should be produced for yourself, not for the potential funder; it can be modified, shortened, summarised or extended for different potential funders (or users), and you should be prepared to make these changes. Some additional hints on the presentation of business plans are given later in this chapter.

Following the process illustrated in Figure 12.1, we discuss sources of information and research methods before moving on to look in more detail at the design and implementation of business plans.

■ ■ ■ ■ ■ Sources of Information

A business is often at its most vulnerable when launching because it will not have the same knowledge or information as its competitors. It will need to establish a range of contacts with suppliers and buyers, its credit rating will inevitably be low and it may not be aware of what credit it can take advantage of, or what are the best sources of advice. There may also be shortages of skilled labour and it will still have its reputation to establish. These problems can at least be reduced if a new business takes advantage of the wide range of sources of information that are now available.

Secondary Data Sources

Sources of information are conveniently classified as either primary or secondary information sources. All secondary information sources include officially published data, provided by the government or its agencies or by other institutions, such as banks, the CBI, trades unions, local authorities and Chambers of Commerce. In addition, institutions have online web pages that may provide access to sources of information. For example, national data provided by the Office for National Statistics (ONS) is available from its website at http://www.statistics.gov.uk.

It is likely that, in the future, printed sources of statistical data will become redundant as online access methods are developed further. However, at present these (official) sources are still being developed, and reference to published sources is still necessary. The main sources of published data are illustrated in Table 12.1, with some comments provided on the relevance and value of each source.

Online and CD-ROM Databases

The development of online and CD-ROM databases has meant that it is possible to gain direct access to some databases, giving an advantage in terms of direct access and downloading data. These can be powerful packages, providing additional graphical illustrations and analysis. Libraries have databases that store basic statistical data as a database on a CD. These may be databases of literature, journal articles or statistical and financial information. The development of these databases has made 'literature searches' far easier, and there is nowadays an increasing amount of information and basic data that is available on CD-ROM. Some examples are given in Table 12.2.

Table 12.1: *Secondary Data: Published Sources of Information*

Source	Type of data	Comment
National Income and Expenditure Year Book	Main components of national income and expenditure	Provides national or regional data on output, incomes, wages or prices
Annual Abstract of Statistics	Summary tables on population, national income and the labour force	More comprehensive than the Year Book
2001 Census	Demographic and socio-economic data	Data analysis and trends often published separately
Monthly Digest of Statistics	Components of national income	
Economic Trends	Data on economic indicators	Useful indicator of major economic trends
Regional Trends	Regional economic indicators	
Population Trends	Demographic indicators	Useful predicator of future market trends
Financial Statistics	Data on financial indicators	Gives indications of credit activity
Bank of England Quarterly Bulletin	Gives detailed money supply and lending data	
New Earnings Survey	Income and hours worked of the labour force	Useful source on wage rates
Business Monitors	Data on specific industries	Useful indicator of trends in industry
Census of Production	National output data	
Labour Market Trends	Data on earnings and employment rates	Useful source of data with occasional articles
MINTEL	Market intelligence reports	Valuable source of intelligence and market data if available (fee-based)
Trade and industry journals	Qualitative data	Occasional articles can be useful
Patent office	Information on existing patents	Provides a search facility
Euro-information centres	Various information on EU funding	Selected localities

Table 12.2: *Examples of Online and CD-based Databases*

Source	Type of data	Comment
EXSTAT	Micro-level data on companies	Brief summaries of trading records
FAME	Financial data on all companies	Powerful package including graphical illustration and financial ratios
DATASTREAM	Financial data	Financial analysis
KOMPASS	European database	Details on companies throughout Europe
Patent Office	Existing patents	Fee-based service
Local industrial directories (usually produced by local authorities)	Information on local companies	Quality of information and source varies

The Internet

Increasingly, an alternative approach to gathering information on competitors may exist through the Internet. All large firms have their own web page, and with the search engines that now exist, information on potential competitors can be obtained and downloaded. For suggestions of search engines in this area see the discussion of use of the Internet for business in Chapter 7. Obviously, the importance of the Internet will increase in the future as an increasing range of secondary sources of information becomes available through this medium. At present, however, printed versions of secondary sources are still in demand, because of the time taken to search the Internet and the variation in quality on web pages. For example, until a web address is accessed, at present the researcher is unlikely to know the extent and quality of information that is made available. Table 12.3 gives some useful web addresses that can be valuable sources of secondary data and information.

Primary Data Sources

Although there is a vast range of secondary sources of information, it will be appreciated that they often do not provide the right combination of data or perhaps the data is incomplete. There are many situations when this is going to be a problem, particularly with the requirements of entrepreneurs for specific information regarding products and potential demand. As an entrepreneurial student, you may be preparing for entrepreneurship. As a potential entrepreneur, who is considering launching a new product, the only way to obtain information concerning potential demand is to carry out your own market research using survey techniques and questionnaires. For these reasons, we will concentrate on some of these survey techniques.

There are a number of ways that primary information can be obtained, the most obvious being through the use of questionnaires using an alternative variety of methods, including postal or telephone surveys, focus groups and face-to-face interviews. However, data may also be obtained by observation, traffic surveys, by interview over a longer period of time (longitudinal research) to establish whether, say, there are changes in social attitudes, by records of respondents (e.g. purchases of

Table 12.3: *Sources of Information on the Web*

Web address	Type of information	Comment
www.statistics.gov.uk	Range of national data	The Office for National Statistics website. Variable quality of information. Summary articles
www.sbs.gov.uk	A range of research reports and sources of advice with links to sources of advice	The Small Business Service website, a growing and improving range of research information
www.dti.gov.uk	Range of industry information and Govt initiatives	Useful for links to other sites
www.britishchambers.org.uk	Detail of reports and information on Chambers of Commerce	Useful source for occasional reports
www.newbusiness.org	Information on business start-up and advice provided by the Scottish Enterprise network	Up-dated information on the Business Birth Rate Strategy of Scottish Enterprise
www.scotent.co.uk	Information on support agencies in Scotland	Links to Local Enterprise Companies
www.cabinet-office.gov.uk	Up-to-date information on areas of Govt priority	Occasional reports available; employment reports, social inclusion reports
www.hm-treasury.gov.uk	Occasional reports. Tax information	Useful for up-dates on the Budget and taxation changes

families recorded by the Family Household Expenditure Survey). A brief overview of some of the methods that can be used to obtain primary data is given below.

Survey Methods

In a feasibility study and/or a subsequent business plan, you may wish to organise a survey of potential customers using a survey method. There is a danger that these surveys will be done superficially, often containing questions that reveal only the most basic information. You will need to aim for high-quality information and that can only be achieved if your questionnaire and survey is well designed. Since the information obtained from any survey is going to form the basis of conclusions and recommendations in the final business plan, the quality of this final business plan is going to depend crucially on the research techniques used and the design of your questionnaire. Past experience has revealed that student entrepreneurs who carry out their own research pay insufficient attention to the design of questions and the survey method to be used. Giving careful consideration to the design of questions and survey method will improve the quality of analysis that can subsequently be carried out in either a feasibility study or a business plan.

Survey methods include questionnaire-based surveys, which are normally postal, telephone or interview-based surveys that may be more open-ended. Their main advantages and disadvantages are summarised in Table 12.4.

253

Table 12.4: *Advantages and Disadvantages of the Main Survey Methods*

Method	Advantages	Disadvantages
Postal Survey Questionnaires	Sample size can be large if response is adequate	Low response rates unless incentives are used
	Relatively quick	Difficult to control for respondent
	Inexpensive	Responses may be unreliable
	Can provide useful basic data	Sample is self-selecting and may be biased
	May be the only option for some data	Only limited information can be obtained
	Responses can be completely confidential	Responses may be incomplete
	Structured questionnaires make for easy analysis	Questionnaire needs careful construction
Telephone Survey Questionnaires	Saves time over postal survey	Questions may be more limited
	Response rates are often much higher than postal survey	Respondent has little time to consider question
	Control over respondent and responses	Data may not be available easily
	Sample less likely to be biased	
Face-to-face Interviews	Provide qualitative, in-depth information	Relatively expensive and time-consuming
	Complete control for researcher	May be difficult to analyse
	Flexible, allowing additional issues to be pursued	Subject to personal bias of researcher
	Most reliable method in terms of validity of responses	
Focus Groups	Group-based interviews to give synergy and encourage greater response	Requires a trained facilitator to get best results
	Can save time and expense	Group needs to be carefully balanced
	Well-tried method in market research	Difficult to record outcomes in a coherent manner

Any survey method will depend for accurate and coherent subsequent analysis on the research design, which includes questionnaire design. It may be acceptable to combine these different survey methods (for example, short interviews of a reasonable sample may be combined with more in-depth material with a small number of respondents). In-depth interviews are designed to obtain qualitative information whereas larger surveys are designed to obtain quantitative information.

Research Design

The research design and survey method used will depend on the aims and objectives of the research. For example, a full feasibility study undertaken in advance of a business plan will aim to provide both quantitative data and analysis and more in-depth qualitative information so that a combination of methods will be appropriate. Research design involves the selection of the appropriate survey method(s), the sample and the design of appropriate questions. The design involves matching the survey method or combination of methods to the aims of the study and research. Good research design and some thought given to the survey method used will pay dividends later in analysis and the production of the final business plan. This is shown in diagrammatic form in Figure 12.2.

Sampling Method

Some attention should be paid to how you are going to choose your sample. The sampling frame may be provided, such as the provision of a membership list of an

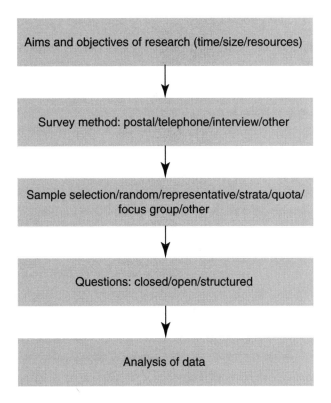

Figure 12.2: *Research Design*

association; you may then decide to survey the whole membership, the population, or choose a sample. How this sample is chosen will affect the interpretation that can be placed on the final results. The sample will be drawn from some sampling frame, such as *Yellow Pages*, a membership list or perhaps the electoral roll in a local area. Samples may be of the following types.

Purely Random To select a true random sample, each member of the population must have the same chance of being selected. One way to choose a random sample is to generate random numbers using a computer program. You then use these numbers to select respondents from your sampling frame.

Representative Sample A representative sample contains a microcosm of the features of the population in their appropriate proportions. Thus if you are surveying firms, you may wish to have representations of different firm sizes in true proportions to their numbers in the population of all firms. That is, say, 97 per cent of your sample should employ fewer than 20 employees. The extent to which your sample can be representative will depend on having information about the population. Samples can only be representative if features of the full population are known, such as the proportion that earn less than '£X' per week, or the proportion that are male/female, married/not married, and so on.

Stratified Sample A stratified sample attempts to break down the population in a coherent manner, using one or two criteria. One example might be the industrial sector of businesses that are respondents. The sample is not representative in having true proportions but you use the criteria of, say, industrial sector as a way of ensuring some representation is included from each group, or 'strata', of the population. Samples may be chosen randomly from each strata if the sampling frame permits this.

Quota Sample Quota sampling is a commonly used technique in market research where a characteristic of the population (often age/gender) is used to provide quota numbers for interviewers to ensure a minimum number of respondents is identified in each category. In contrast to stratified sampling, this method is often used where no sampling frame is available.

The Importance of Research

Given limited resources and time, the potential entrepreneur may have little scientific basis for the selection of the sample. A small amount of research will pay dividends, however, and prevent the business plan appearing as though it has been 'thrown together'. A short methodology section in the business plan (or feasibility study) will indicate that some thought has gone into the research behind the plan and that assumptions are well founded, have a good basis, and that the strategic plans and projections are not haphazard or just 'dreamt up' by the potential entrepreneur. This can make a tremendous difference and also affects the confidence with which you can present a business plan to any potential funders. Good research will not leave any 'holes' that can be picked up on by potential backers of the proposition.

Question Design

As noted before, some care devoted to question design will pay dividends when analysing the results of any research. Some simple rules regarding good question design are recommended and these are listed in the accompanying box.

Question Design: Some Simple Rules

Questions should:

- be unambiguous
- be relatively short
- not be biased or leading in some way
- be designed to achieve the objectives of the research
- be structured (semi-structured or open-ended, but open-ended are generally best avoided with postal questionnaires).

New Developments

There are now software packages available that offer a full business-planning package. These will provide the essential sections and help you to produce financial forecasts. Of course, any amount of software cannot replace the basic planning process, which requires adequate research. A business plan, however well produced and presented, will be only as good as the quality of data and information input into the software that is being used. Obtaining impressive software should not blind the entrepreneur or user to the need to provide good-quality research and reliable data that will be processed by the software into a business plan that will serve the business as a valuable planning tool for a number of years.

■ ■ ■ ■ Designing the Business Plan

There are a number of standard sections that would normally be included in any business plan. These should include sections on aims and objectives, competitive analysis, marketing strategy and SWOT analysis. However, the sections required for the business plan will vary depending on the nature and sector of the business. A manufacturing business requires a different business plan from a service sector-based business. An exporting firm requires a different business plan from a components supplier that relies on large UK customers. A small start-up concern requires a different business plan from a medium-sized firm that is planning an expansion into different products. This is one of the problems faced by software packages that aim to provide a standard package that can be used by any business. A business plan has to be flexible and it is impossible to be prescriptive since every business plan will be different and will be produced for different requirements. Having said that it is impossible to be prescriptive, there are certain sections and guidelines that can be discussed and we attempt to do this below. We look at what might be expected from any business plan; you may not wish to include all of the sections – not everyone will have the time or resources to produce a full and detailed business plan. However, some thought given to the following suggestions will help the entrepreneur to plan for the possible different scenarios, competition and future changes that he/she may face. Putting in this effort at the research and design stage will improve the process of decision-making, which is one of the main purposes of any business plan.

The following sections are recommended when designing the content of the business plan. As emphasised above, these sections are not prescriptive and can be modified to suit the purposes of individual entrepreneurs and business plans.

Executive Summary

If your plan is carefully researched, constructed and written, then an executive summary will be very useful to the users of the business plan, who may be potential funders or partner entrepreneurs in the business. Although the executive summary should be the first section of the plan, it is likely to be the last to be written and can be the most difficult because you have to summarise the main contents of the business plan. You will find it useful to build the executive summary around the competitive strategy.

Introduction

A short introduction should give some background to the business, the key people, and an introduction to the nature of the business and the industrial sector. This section can be used to give the main aims and objectives of the business. In this section you will need to explain the purpose of the business plan. Is it to map out an expansion plan for the business? Or is it to provide a strategy for the launch of a new business? The aims and objectives could be placed in a separate section. You can also use this section to explain the rationale for the business and the business plan. Deciding how to differentiate between what are aims and what are objectives of your business can be difficult. A general guide is that aims can be considered to be quite broad and less specific than objectives. Objectives should be written in terms of specific outcomes. For example, an *aim* of, say, a five-year business plan would be to:

■ provide a strategic planning process to become a major competitor in the industry.

Whereas an *objective* of the same business plan might be to:

■ achieve a fourfold growth in sales within five years.

In the introduction you can provide additional information such as the nature of incorporation if a start-up, whether the company is registered, whether you have registered for VAT, in which case a VAT number should be quoted, starting employment levels, resources and whether there is a need for recruitment of staff and personnel.

Market Analysis and Research

In this section you can report the findings of market research that might have been undertaken, if primary research has been completed, along the lines suggested for this section. You should avoid the temptation to give too much information although, as suggested before, illustrations of the main findings can be quite useful for presentation purposes and for potential readers of the plan. However, those readers will not want to wade through a large amount of information and data. If the questionnaire that has been used as the basis for the research has been well designed, then it should be possible to present the information and analysis in the form of summary tables with brief comments on the significance and importance of market analysis, and summaries of the potential total market and market share.

Some of the software packages that were mentioned above will give a market opportunity analysis. Additional analysis provided by such software can be a useful way of impressing any potential funder.

This section should be used to explain the assumptions behind income generation in the cash-flow statements. Are the income levels based on the market research findings, or perhaps on other factors, such as seasonality or state of economic levels of activity, or capacity levels if a manufacturing concern? Other factors should also be included, such as the basis of payment; income may be generated on the basis of commission, fees or sales. If sales of products and services are involved, then some form of normal credit period will be assumed. Standard practice is, of course, 30-day credit periods between the sale taking place and income shown in the cash flow. If your business is subject to strong seasonal factors, such as high sales in the Christmas period, then this should be shown in the income statement of the cash flow, with allowance made for any credit period.

You may wish to consider outlining a brief marketing and distribution plan. This can be contained within the business plan, or if distribution is a major part of the firm's operations, then it is recommended that a separate document is produced. The marketing plan effectively sets out how sales are to be achieved. It may include all aspects of the 'marketing mix' (see box).

The Marketing Mix

- Pricing policy
- Promotion (advertising and other forms of promotion)
- Production (the outlets and marketing strategy should reflect the production capabilities of the business)
- Place (the location of the business and outlets used)

It is important to get these aspects of the business integrated, so that distribution channels and outlets do not overburden the production process and capabilities and the outlets are appropriate to cope with production capacities. An example is used to illustrate such concepts below (see box).

Example: Matching Marketing with Production

A small firm had produced a new form of hanging-basket bracket that was produced to a new design and to a high quality. Yet the marketing strategy adopted bore no relation to production capabilities. The bracket was marketed through a major chain gardening store and as soon as one large order was placed, the firm could not cope with the production quantities required by a major multiple retailer.

This problem of matching production to outlets and distribution channels cannot always be resolved, but planning for different outcomes in the business plan can help to resolve this problem if it does arise, and a separate marketing plan can be a valuable planning tool for any business.

Access to retail outlets can be a problem for some businesses. You should demonstrate that you have given some thought to this and that you have secured retail outlets if the product is new.

Production Strategy

If your business is concerned with manufacturing and production, a separate section should be devoted to the planning of production. If the business is concerned merely with expanding using existing production facilities, through perhaps obtaining new market outlets, then a separate production plan will not be necessary. However, you may need to plan for additional production facilities, new machinery and increased capacity. You will need to identify the additional resources and capabilities that will be required for new production levels. Additional skilled staff may be required and recruitment policies should be explained.

For a new start-up business that requires production facilities, the business plan will obviously need to describe how these are to be obtained and how staff are to be recruited.

The assumptions described in this section will form the basis behind the projections in the expenses of the cash-flow statements. There may be some research necessary in order to predict these forecasts accurately. You should not rely on your own estimates but obtain, as far as possible, quotations for ordering the supplies and equipment required.

Timing

An important element of any manufacturing business is timing production to co-ordinate with sales orders and matching supply of materials with production capabilities and sales orders. This is the importance of integrating market predictions and sales back through the production process and ensuring that the supply of materials and components is of the quality required to ensure that your customers are satisfied with the product. It must be stressed that orders can be lost if insufficient attention is paid to quality in the production process and quality obtaining from suppliers. This can be a particular problem for a new (producing) firm, which can be vulnerable if certain specifications have been laid down to suppliers with no guarantee that these are going to be met. If possible, although this may use up some resources, it is worth trying to get some prototypes made to check quality. Of course, this will be a particular problem where new technology or new production techniques are being employed, which is one of the reasons why financing technology-based firms gives rise to different and special issues from other types of start-up.

Timing is important because resources and finance will be required before products are made, before sales are made and certainly well before income is received. This should be reflected in the cash-flow statements. Any manufacturing and producing firm is certain to have a negative balance in the first part of the cash flow. It is better to plan properly for this, so that financial resources can either be set aside, if internal resources are available, or funding requirements can be made clear in the business plan.

Action Plans

To aid the planning process it is worth providing an action plan. The purpose of this is to map actions against time and the production process. This will allow you to plan different requirements into the production and marketing stages as they are required over time.

An action plan can be produced for any type of business and modified to produce a Gantt chart, which maps out the sequential timing of decisions against production/sales levels, and can serve as an action plan for the business.

SWOT Analysis

A section on SWOT analysis involves the identification of strengths, weaknesses, opportunities and threats (SWOT) for the business. There can be some dispute over how SWOT analysis can be presented and explained. To some extent, a SWOT analysis should consist of a series of short bullet points so that the reader can see quickly the main strengths and weaknesses of the business and the opportunity. However, the statements that comprise the bullet points should not be so short that they become perfunctory statements, leaving the reader wishing for further explanation or elaboration. Again, a balance has to be struck between the need to keep the statements short (and preferably punchy) and the need to provide an adequate statement that the reader or user of the business plan can understand and comprehend.

A long list of strengths and weaknesses is not necessary; the list should be relatively short, perhaps half a dozen bullet points under each heading. It is also better to be honest. A long list of strengths followed by short list of weaknesses is more likely to raise suspicions from potential funders than it is to impress them.

The SWOT analysis should 'fit' the business plan. If many strengths are shown but other aspects of the business plan are perhaps weak (such as limited analysis of market projections), then the SWOT analysis will look out of place in the context of the rest of the business plan.

There are few guidelines that can be given for the SWOT analysis. You as the entrepreneur(s) is/are the best person/people to write the SWOT analysis but, bearing in mind the points raised above, you should not be afraid to note down your strengths. These may include extensive experience in the industry, a reputation for quality, a sound knowledge of working practices and employment conditions in the industry, existing contacts with potential customers, and knowledge of new techniques/technologies that can be applied to existing production processes.

A SWOT analysis will always remain subject to personal preferences and views. The reader of the business plan should be aware of this and will make some allowances for this. A different individual could interpret strengths and weaknesses in different ways. Unless a business plan is put together by an independent consultant, a SWOT analysis will remain a personal statement by the entrepreneur(s) of their view of the strengths and weaknesses of the business, and the opportunities provided by the business creation or development.

Competition

The competition and a section dealing with competitive analysis will follow from the identification of threats in the SWOT analysis. The extent of knowledge of competitors will probably vary, but it should be possible to identify the major competitors and what their relative strengths are. It is also useful to identify what strategies they have used to establish their market position. For example, have they used market-nicheing strategies, or perhaps more aggressive market-penetration strategies? Or have they established their position merely by reputation and word of mouth?

In Chapter 2, we have discussed the increased importance of small firms across European economies and some of the reasons for this increased importance. Often the reason for the start-up of a new firm by an entrepreneur is that they have recognised a market niche in an industry that is not being catered for by existing (large) firms. A small firm/entrepreneur will have the flexibility to respond to new market opportunities and market niches. While it is likely that the competition may consist of well-established firms, these may not have the flexibility to respond quickly to new market opportunities and challenges.

The analysis of competition should match the market analysis that is presented in the business plan as discussed above. If you are predicting a relatively large market share, this will not fit with a competitor analysis which suggests that the major competitors are strong, well established and that the market is difficult to penetrate. This analysis should also fit the marketing strategy. A market-nicheing strategy will probably aim for high-quality services or products, and likely outlets should have been identified that are willing to take your products, or potential customers should have been identified if a service is being marketed.

You should also give some thought to potential competition. As opportunities develop, it could be that you may face competition either from additional entrepreneurs who start up or as a result of retaliation on the part of the existing competition. If the business plan is to be a valuable document over a three- or five-year planning period, then some thought must be given to future competition and the likely sources of that competition.

It is possible to provide contingency plans. However, given that the number of different possible scenarios is infinite, you will not be able to provide a contingency plan to cope with all possible eventualities, possible reactions and strategies of the competition. All that can be done is to recognise that the outcomes that are predicted in the business plan can change and that the business plan should be used to monitor operations and then adjust predictions and/or strategy as circumstances change. As we will see later, it is desirable to conduct a limited amount of sensitivity analysis, which will demonstrate to potential funders that you have thought about different outcomes and the reaction of existing and potential competitors.

Competitive Strategy

In some ways this is the most important section of the business plan, since it should map out the strategy for the survival, development and growth of your business. A strategy should be identified that will enable the business to meet the aims and objectives that will have been set out in the early part or sections of the business plan. The development of competitive strategy will be the natural outcome of the process of researching the market opportunity, the nature of the product or service, the SWOT analysis and the competitive analysis. Porter has provided a well-known taxonomy of generic market strategies, which are outlined below.[4] It is likely that your strategy will fall into one of these three categories. Porter shows that competitive strategies are a response to the environment in which the business operates; in other words, they are generic to the environment and the nature of competition faced by the business. Porter's three generic strategies are described below.

Cost Leadership

Under this strategy, the emphasis is on maintaining a competitive edge through a cost advantage over competitors. It may, but does not necessarily, involve undercutting competitors on price and maintaining a competitive edge on price. Undercutting through price does contain disadvantage: it may lead to some form of price war and, even if competitors are at a cost disadvantage, they may be better placed to sustain losses that might be incurred through any price-cutting war to gain customers. The advantage of cost leadership for entrepreneurs will lie in the generation of additional income that may result from cost reduction and that may be reinvested to provide new production techniques or new products.

Differentiation

This strategy may follow from a need to diversify production or services. It should not be confused with the third (focus) strategy. It is a strategy that is more likely to apply to existing and well-established producers where, perhaps, products have entered a maturity stage of their life cycle and there is a need to diversify production to maintain growth in the firm.

Focus

This third strategy is the one that is most likely to be adopted by new firm entrepreneurs. It recognises that many market opportunities result from specialisation. Small firms have the advantage that they can be flexible as well as specialised. The development of a focus strategy involves the identification of a market niche that has not been exploited by existing producers. The firm should quickly be able to gain a reputation for satisfying this market niche. Identifying the correct time to launch and exploit the market opportunity can be crucial. Thus there are market 'windows of opportunity' that appear at different times. Launching too early or too late can result in missing this opportunity.

Although Porter's categories have been very influential, they may be seen as a bit limiting. Kay has produced a useful alternative analysis of competitive strategy that focuses on the importance of value added that a firm can bring to the industry.[5] The extent to which a firm will produce value added to its costs of production will determine its success. For example, in an analysis of the retail food industry Kay shows that the strategies adopted by Tesco have been very successful at adding value to its operations. Since Kay's analysis, Tesco has proceeded to be the dominant retailer, despite increased competition, by focusing on quality and value added.

These analyses stress the importance of getting the strategy right for the type of market that you are in. There is no right or wrong strategy, but it must be appropriate for the business, the operation, the market and the business development plan.

Critical Success Factors

The identification of critical success factors is a useful section that should be included in the final business plan. It can serve as a useful summary and checklist of factors that have been identified in other sections of the business plan, and is best placed towards the end of the business plan. Like the SWOT analysis, it will tend to be a personal reflection on the most important factors that are going to be critical to the success of the business. Thus, again, it is impossible to be at all prescriptive about this section, but you may like to think about the following factors.

■ What factors does the success of the business hinge upon? Are they factors concerned with gaining orders or are they concerned with securing quality from suppliers?

■ How important are the key personnel to the success of the business? If a key member of staff leaves, how will this affect the performance of the business? Can they be replaced?

■ How important is the recruitment strategy of the business? Does the success of the business depend on obtaining appropriate skilled staff?

■ Does the success of the strategy adopted depend on how competitors react?

It is worth considering each section of the business plan and identifying just one or two key factors from each section that will be critical to the performance of your business and to its success. As an entrepreneur, this will help you to identify key and critical success factors and, at later stages, to monitor performance. Having identified such factors, you can adopt strategies that can ensure success or lead to alternative arrangements. For example, if a supplier is identified as a critical factor, you may wish to investigate alternative arrangements for ensuring supply.

Cash-flow Statement

The cash-flow statement contains the projected income from sales and other sources, and all the expenses concerned with the launch and operation of the business. It is best prepared on a computer spreadsheet package, although business-planning software, as mentioned before, will have its own spreadsheet and financial analysis built in.

The importance of the cash-flow statement is that it shows the timing of income and expenses, and should show all these figures for 12-monthly periods of up to three or perhaps five years, depending on the potential users of the business plan. It shows the liquidity of the business at any one time and reflects the need or otherwise to raise funds and credit. If the business plan is being prepared for a bank manager then it is unlikely that cash-flow forecasts will be required beyond three years. If, on the other hand, it is being prepared for a venture capitalist then it is more likely that five years' cash-flow forecasts will be required.

A pro forma cash-flow statement is shown as an example in Figure 12.3, but the detail of the cash-flow will obviously depend on the individual business. The notes given in the pro forma are referred to below.

1. Income will consist of sales, fees and commission. It may include income from grants or loans. The timing of the receipt of this income should be as accurate as possible. A small adjustment to the timing of the income can affect the extent of any negative or positive net cash flow.

2. Total income just calculates the total for each month. On a spreadsheet this is easily calculated by inserting the appropriate formula to sum cells and then copying across different cells.

3. Expenses can either be summarised under different headings or shown individually, but they should identify all expenses from the operations of the business. These will include equipment, materials, computing equipment, staffing, car leasing, insurance and promotional expenses. Again, timing is important and should be as accurate as possible since a small adjustment will affect the extent of the positive or negative cash flow.

4. Staffing should include National Insurance (NI) contributions, although NI payments can be shown separately.

5. It is important to consider and include items such as insurance. If you are a producer you will need products' liability, public liability and employers' liability insurance. If insurance is a relatively small part of sales, perhaps only 2 per cent, it can be paid in just one annual premium.

6. If the business is registered for VAT, then it will be entitled to a VAT rebate on VAT payments. These can be claimed every three months. Registering for VAT becomes mandatory over a threshold turnover of £52,000, but registration is advisable at levels below this to claim VAT rebates.

7. Total expenses merely add up the expenses in each column and this is easily done on a spreadsheet.

8. Subtracting the total expenses from the total income shows the net cash flow for each month. A general point to consider is that you will want to take advantage of any credit. This will be reflected in the liquidity of the business as shown in the net cash flow.

9. The opening balance for the first month is normally shown as zero, although it is possible to have reserves (from previous operations) shown in the opening balance.

HYPOTHETICAL COMPANY YEAR 1

	JAN	FEB	MARCH	APRIL	MAY	JUNE	JULY	AUGUST	SEPT	OCTOBER	NOV	DECEMBER	TOTALS (11)
INCOME (1)													
SALES		3500	4000	5000	5500	5000	6000	3000	6500	6500	7000	10000	62000
FEES	2025	2025	2700	2025	2700	2700		1350	3375	2700	3375	2025	27000
GRANT													0
ENTERPRISE AGENCY	7000												7000
													0
TOTAL INCOME (2)	9025	5525	6700	7025	8200	7700	6000	4350	9875	9200	10375	12025	96000
EXPENSES (3)													
MATERIALS	3500	3000	3000	3500	3000	3000	3500	3000	5000	4000	4000	3000	41500
EQUIPMENT													
MACHINERY	5000	5000	5000	5000									20000
COMPUTERS		3600											3600
PRINTER		1000											1000
VIDEO			750										750
TABLES			600										600
CHAIRS		600											600
BOOKCASES			300										300
WAGES (4)													0
PRODUCTION	2893.75	2315	2893.75	2315	2315	2315	2893.75	2315	2893.75	2315	2315	2315	30095
OFFICE	607.5	607.5	810	607.5	810	810		405	1012.5	810	1012.5	607.5	8100
HEAT AND LIGHT			1000			1000			800			1200	4000
RATES				1000						1000			2000
INSURANCE (5)				1500						1500			3000
TELEPHONE		200	200			200			150			250	800
CONSUMABLES													0
PRODUCTION	200	200	200	200	200	200		200	200	200	200	200	2200
OFFICE STATIONERY	300	100	100	100	100	100		100	100	100	100	100	1300
VAT (REBATE) (6)						-1575			-1500			-1500	-4575
TOTAL EXPENSES (7)	12501.25	16422.5	14853.75	14222.5	6425	6050	6393.75	6020	8656.25	9925	7627.5	6172.5	115270
NET CASHFLOW (8)	-3476.25	-10897.5	-8153.75	-7197.5	1775	1650	-393.75	-1670	1218.75	-725	2747.5	5852.5	-19270
OPENING BALANCE (9)	0	-3476.25	-14373.8	-22527.5	-29725	-27950	-26300	-26693.8	-28363.8	-27145	-27870	-25122.5	
CLOSING BALANCE (10)	-3476.25	-14373.8	-22527.5	-29725	-27950	-26300	-26693.8	-28363.8	-27145	-27870	-25122.5	-19270 (12)	

Figure 12.3: *Cashflow Forecast for a Hypothetical Company and Pro-forma*

10. The closing balance adds the opening balance to the net cash flow. The closing balance is automatically carried forward to become the opening balance in the next month (period).

11. The totals are added horizontally. They need not be shown, but they are a useful check on calculations and can show the total income and expenses for the year.

12. The last closing balance for the year will become the opening balance for the next year, and should be carried forward as in previous months.

If drawings are made by the owner/entrepreneur, perhaps as a sole trader, then these are best shown as part of the expenses concerned with the operation of the business. These are likely to be regular withdrawals and they should be shown monthly rather than a total figure at the end of the year. Note too that the cash-flow statement is not the same as profit and loss.

As stated before, the net cash flow reflects the liquidity of the business. The cash-flow statement can show additional income, say borrowings, that are not part of the profit and loss account.

Forecasted Profit and Loss Account

It is advisable, but not essential, to forecast an end-of-year profit and loss account. This involves adding up all the trading income, subtracting cost of goods sold, to get the trading profit and loss. General expenses for the year can be totalled, including depreciation subtracted from the trading profit to get the net profit.

Forecasted Balance Sheet

A forecasted balance sheet is sometimes required, particularly by bank managers, and this can be relatively easily calculated from the projections for the end of year.

The balance sheet is a statement of assets and liabilities at any particular time period. As a planning tool it is not very useful since it provides only a snapshot at any one time, but it may be required by bank managers.[6]

A number of financial ratios can be calculated and included in terms of profitability and liquidity. It is not necessary to go into detail on the calculation and usefulness of these but standard business-planning software will calculate these automatically.

Sensitivity Analysis

The purpose of the sensitivity analysis is to provide a test of the susceptibility of the business to changes, or a test of the robustness of the business proposition to cope with unforeseen changes. We can assume that most of the expense forecasts will be accurate. Despite careful research, income forecasts will still contain some uncertainty and the purpose of sensitivity analysis is to examine the consequences of changing some of the income forecasts on the net cash flow.

There is little point in developing any sensitivity analysis beyond the first year of operation, but it is worth formulating for the first year with what may be called an optimistic and a pessimistic scenario.

The optimistic scenario might *increase* sales and other income by 10 per cent. Expenses will need to be adjusted to allow for this – for example, through increased cost of materials, and perhaps through increased salary costs. The pessimistic scenario might *decrease* sales and other income by 10 per cent with appropriate adjustments of expenses.

A further purpose of sensitivity analysis is to examine the effects of changes in timing on the next cash flow and funding requirements. For example, a delay in securing orders can be as important as a fall in income and will increase the funding requirements for the business plan. Therefore, a full sensitivity analysis would examine changes in timing of income flows as well as changes in their level.

Note that examples are not provided in the text of additional financial statements, such as the forecasted profit and loss account and forecast income statement, but can be found in the student online learning resources.

■ ■ ■ ■ ■ Writing the Business Plan

As indicated before, the business plan is best prepared using a computer package that incorporates a standard word-processing program combined with a spreadsheet program for preparing the cash-flow and additional financial statements. Alternatively, the business-planning software that is now available will integrate a spreadsheet with a word-processing package that contains the main sections of the business plan.

Some hints and guidelines are given below in terms of the actual writing and presentation of the final business plan.

1. The construction of the cash-flow statement should be undertaken at a relatively early stage, perhaps after the analysis of the market research. This has the advantage of deciding what information and forecasts need to be justified and explained in the written parts of the business plan. It also allows you to consider whether you have done sufficient research and whether there any additional expenses that need to be calculated.

2. It helps presentation if you use relatively wide margins (e.g. we would recommend at least one-inch-wide margins on either side and generous top and bottom margins). This avoids presenting too much information on one page and allows the potential user or funder to make notes.

3. Start each section on a fresh page. Again this improves presentation and enables the user to find sections quickly.

4. Avoid the use of appendices where possible. If appendices are used to provide market research data, it can be difficult for the reader/user to refer to data while reading the appropriate section in the business plan. Appendices may be used *sparingly* (e.g. to give CVs). These may be left out of some versions of the same business plan.

5. Do use illustrations, although do not overdo this. Comments have been made on the illustration of research data in the previous chapter. Illustrations are useful and can help the user assimilate data quickly. Ability to do this, however, may depend on the sophistication of the software being used.

6. Do include a contents page at the beginning. This will enable the reader to locate different sections easily and navigate around the business plan document quickly.

7. Presentation is improved by the inclusion of headers and footers. By allowing for generous top and bottom margins, this will allow either a header or footer to be inserted on each page of the business plan. This could be the name of the business.

8. Do include some notes to the accounts, whether you are providing a cash-flow statement only or a more detailed set of accounts that may include profit

and loss and a forecasted balance sheet. Even though assumptions will have been given in different sections in the business plan, it will still be necessary to provide some notes on certain figures in the cash flow to explain what additional assumptions have been made or the basis of calculation.

9. Do put contact names on the front or inside page of the business plan.

10. The business plan should not be too long, perhaps 30 pages including appendices is a rough maximum (or 10,000 words as a maximum). There is no ideal length, although there is little point in producing a very detailed plan if its only aim is to raise a small overdraft at the bank.

11. Bind the business plan securely (not stapled) and provide a cover that will stand up to some wear and tear. If you wish, you can go to the expense of getting the business plan properly bound by a printer. However, we do not recommend this since you may wish to change certain sections or add pages. Generally this will provide you with less flexibility than a loosely ring-bound document, which will allow you to modify and produce different versions of the same business plan for different users and funders.

12. Finally an over-used phrase is that the business plan should 'stack up'. We would defy anyone to explain exactly what this phrase means but it is best expressed by saying, in principle, that different sections should integrate and support the findings. Assumptions should underpin the forecasts. If different sections are out of line this will be transmitted as an unbalanced plan. A strategy section that emphasises small scale and quality should match other sections such as the market research and marketing strategy and the cash-flow forecasts.

Implementation

As emphasised above, the business plan should not become out of date as soon as the business begins operations. Before operation and trading the business plan is a document that can be read and used by a number of different people, perhaps other partners in the business, perhaps analysed by potential funders. It should itself enable planning of the launch and operation of the first stage of the business.

After start-up or launch of the new product/diversification, the business plan can be used to monitor performance against the projections. It can be used to signal better (or worse) performance, dangers and critical success factors. Timing can be crucial and, if properly planned for, production and marketing plans can be matched against business plan, forecasts to give some guide to the performance of the business. Income and expense forecasts can be matched against real outcomes to give an indicator of performance. During the first year any change in performance can be matched against the sensitivity analysis carried out in the business plan, and this will give some indication of the extent to which the business is out-performing or under-performing according to forecasts in the business plan.

It must be remembered that the business plan is a strategy document as much as anything else. It is not there merely to provide a financial forecast, but to provide the strategy for the survival, development and growth of the business. If forecasts do prove to be substantially different from real outcomes, then the strategy will need to be reviewed, and possibly changed and adapted to different circumstances.

Assuming that the business plan has been produced for at least three years, it will need to be reviewed at the end of the first year. If there have been substantially different outcomes, it will be worth revising the business plan, perhaps by revising cash-flow outcomes. Assuming that a spreadsheet has been used, this should be achieved relatively easily. The strategy and details provided in the business plan should still be appropriate and should be used (perhaps with some modifications) for the remainder of the planning period. Forecasts should now be more accurate and more reliable. As the business plan is reviewed in subsequent years the advantages of forward planning should become apparent. The business plan should serve to guide planning throughout the life of the business.

Business Planning: Further Hints

1. *Be confident in your presentation of the business plan.* Careful research should increase confidence. Potential funders will still need to be impressed by your own confidence and knowledge behind the forecasts that are in the business plan. No matter how well the business plan is prepared, potential backers are still influenced by presentation.

2. *Prepare for questions on the business plan.* Has anything been missed out? If profit and loss is not presented some rough calculations will give a potential backer an indication and may prepare for questions on this.

3. *Talk to different people.* Take the business plan to different agencies and backers and get their opinion on how it 'stacks up'.

4. *Don't give up if you can't raise funding at the first attempt.* For example, our own research has shown that different bank managers can have quite different interpretations of the same business plan, despite the advent of expert systems and credit scoring.[2]

5. *If you can afford it, get the comments of a qualified accountant to verify the contents of the business plan.* Again, research has shown that bank managers are more (positively) influenced by business plans that have been authorised by accountants.

6. *Be patient.* Be prepared to accept a long process of vetting if you are seeking funding from a venture capitalist. The due diligence procedure of a venture capitalist can take six months or more before a decision is made on whether to back a proposition.

7. *Be prepared.* A venture capitalist will also be looking for exit routes. If you are seeking this form of funding you will need to be prepared for the eventual Initial Public Offering (IPO) (share issue) of the business, which is the normal exit route for a venture capitalist.

8. *Investigate.* Try to find out what potential funders are looking for. Many agencies that might provide funding have very specific criteria – for example, that you attend enterprise training sessions (if a new entrepreneur). Whether you need these or not, you will have to attend to qualify for the funding. There can be an assumption on the part of existing managers (in large firms) that they do not need enterprise training. Yet the management of a start-up concern such as a small firm needs different management skills from that of a large firm.

■ ■ ■ ■ Sources of Advice and Support

There are a number of free sources of start-up advice and support; these have benefited from a higher profile recently with the UK government's stated desire[7] to make the UK 'the best place in the world to start and grow a new business' (p. 4). As a key part of this aim, the UK government is seeking to build an 'Enterprise Culture' in which access to enterprise start-up advice is promoted and easily available. Although the nature and meaning of an 'enterprise culture' has been questioned previously by a number of studies,[8; 9] it appears that greater emphasis is again being placed on individuals having the ability to choose entrepreneurial and business start-up career choices as well as other employment and careers.[7] An important part of this policy is aimed at young people, where greater emphasis is being placed on the development of enterprise skills with young people at all levels of the education system.[10] In England, the expansion of the Enterprise Pathfinder project will make enterprise activities available in over 500 schools. In Scotland a review of Enterprise and Education has led to the development of a comprehensive strategy in primary and secondary levels: Determined to Succeed.[11]

These recent developments have meant that sources of advice have become more important and closer links have been established between educational institutions and agencies, although such links are still in need of development.[12] Links may be established with a number of sources of advice and support and some of these are listed with comments in Table 12.5. Recent research has indicated that satisfaction levels with public-sector agencies have recently improved,[13] but in the past the publicly funded support system has been criticised for being confusing and duplicative of resources.[14] The ad hoc development of the support agency movement over time has meant that provision of support, spatially and vertically, is the result of chance and accidents of geography, and the economic mix of the environment that happened to exist at the time that different agencies were formed. Despite the considerable framework of support that now exists (established in the 1990s), the delivery of small business advice can still vary considerably from agency to agency. There can be large asymmetries in the size, staffing and operation of individual agencies. However, the launch of the Small Business Service in 2000–01 in England has provided greater consistency in the deliverers of support advice, the Business Link Operators. In Scotland, a comprehensive overhaul of the support network has led to a consistent service delivered by the Business Gateways, funded by Scottish Enterprise, and in Wales the Welsh Development Agency provides support through its own funded agencies.

Overall there is certainly much consistency and accessibility to a range of sources of advice and support, some of which are listed in Table 12.5. When added to the list of sources of information and secondary data and a number of independent websites, the prospective entrepreneur now has a large range of sources of advice and support to turn to. It is important to consult as many sources as possible, to talk through ideas and development plans; the more this is done, the better and more reliable will be the final business plan.

■ ■ ■ ■ Conclusions

The research, design and implementation of the business plan is part of the ongoing planning process within any firm. If, as a start-up entrepreneur, you adopt planning policies that are based on sound research and careful consideration of strategy, this will have benefits throughout the life of the business. We have already indicated that, during the 1990s, there were high birth rates of new small firms and entrepreneurs but, at the same time, these were accompanied by high death rates. One of the reasons for these high death rates has been insufficient thought and time given to proper and adequate planning of the strategy of the new firm.

We started this chapter by commenting that, nowadays, business plans are much more common and much more detailed than they used to be. Even relatively recently,

Table 12.5: *Sources of Advice and Support*

Agency/organisation	Type of information	Comment
Business Link Operators (BLOs)	Range of start-up and business management development advice Training	Funded by contract from Small Business Service, some have closed and merged Have to meet SBS targets
Business Gateway	Range of start-up and business management development advice Training	Funded directly by Scottish Enterprise and the Enterprise Network in Scotland In Highlands replaced by Highlands and Islands Enterprise
Regional Development Agency	May have projects or centres that employ and deliver support and advice	Nine in England, equivalent bodies in Wales and Scotland
Chambers of Commerce	Fee-based membership	Can be valuable source through contacts and intelligence held for members Often provide specialist advice such as exporting Gives access to network of Chambers and the British Association of Chambers
Specialist Enterprise Agencies	Specialised advice and training	May operate in specialised locations on special schemes funded by BLOs
PYBT (PSYBT in Scotland)	Advice to young people under 26	Detailed aftercare support, can provide grants and loans and are therefore a source of funding for young people.
Federation of Small Businesses (FSB)	Fee-based membership, a source of advice especially on legal and taxation issues	Largest association of small businesses In the UK
Other small business and entrepreneurial associations	Examples: Forum of Private Businesses (FPB) Entrepreneurial Exchange	Of variable value and all fee-based membership usually on a sliding scale Websites can be valuable source of free information
Confederation of British Industry	May provide specialist technical advice	Fee-based membership
Patent Office	Specialist advice and searches (fee-based)	Can be a valuable source of advice for those seeking to patent
Professional bodies	Lawyers, accountants	Some may have special low rates for start-up businesses Expensive but often the most valuable source
Banks	May provide 'free information'	Useful for start-up guides and business planning documents
Other bodies	A number of other bodies may provide specialist sources which will vary in quality, e.g. local authorities	

properly researched business plans were relatively rare. One of the reasons for the growth in the use of business plans has been the spread of the agency movement and the requirement of banks (sometimes working in co-operation with agencies) for business plans if any funding is required. However, another reason is that it has become accepted that a carefully constructed business plan is important to the survival and successful performance of any business, whether large or small.

Business plans are very flexible. They can be used for both large and small firms, for start-ups or for expansion, for private- or public-sector organisations; they can be a few pages or a substantial document running to 10,000 words or more supported by appendices. Despite the recent evolution of national standards, prompted by bodies such as support agencies, business plans are still very variable in quality, so it can be difficult to determine whether a business plan is of good quality. We are still left with that over-used phrase mentioned before that a good business plan should 'stack up' or 'hang together'. We have indicated that what this really means is that the different sections should be interconnected, that it should be underpinned by careful research, by knowledge of the market opportunity, and that the assumptions and research should underpin the financial forecasts.

Review Questions 12.1

1. What are the different purposes for which we might need to develop a business plan?

2. What is the difference between primary and secondary sources of data?

3. You have been asked to advise a start-up entrepreneur on the most important sources of secondary data information. What advice will you give?

4. An entrepreneur wishes to research a new service. What advice could you give on different survey methods that might be used to identify customer needs?

Review Questions 12.2

1. Why is research design important for the collection of primary data?

2. In conducting surveys what would be wrong with just stopping people in the street to ask them questions?

3. What are the advantages of postal surveys (over other survey methods)?

4. What are the disadvantages of interview-based surveys?

Review Questions 12.3

1. What different competitive strategies could be adopted by a start-up entrepreneur?

2. What is the difference between a cash-flow forecast and a forecast profit and loss account?

3. How does a business plan differ from a feasibility study?

4. Assuming that the business plan has been completed, you have raised funding and you have started the business, what should you now do with the business plan:

   (a) throw it away

   (b) file it in case the funder needs to see it

(c) continue to use it?

Explain your answer.

Suggested Assignments ■ ■ ■ ■ ■ ■ ■ ■ ■ ■ ■ ■ ■

1. Feasibility study

Students are divided into groups to research and produce a feasibility study for an existing firm/entrepreneur. The feasibility study may involve a new market opportunity or a change of strategy, perhaps involving diversification from existing markets. The firm will be local and identified as a potential client by the university/college. Students work as consultants to the client entrepreneur and are required to:

(a) negotiate and agree terms of reference with the entrepreneur

(b) use appropriate research methods, including market research with an appropriate questionnaire

(c) identify and analyse existing and potential competition

(d) identify the additional costs/resources that will be required to exploit the opportunity

(e) examine the local labour market as appropriate if additional staff are required

(f) produce a feasibility study as a written report with sections that include introduction/terms of reference, research methods, findings, conclusions and recommendations

(g) present the findings to the entrepreneur and obtain feedback

2. Business plan

Students are required to complete a business plan through the development of research work carried out for the feasibility study. The business plan should follow the guidelines given in this chapter and include the following sections:

■ executive summary

■ introduction

■ market analysis and assumptions for cash flow

■ SWOT analysis

■ competition analysis

■ competitive strategy

■ required resources with budget

■ cash-flow forecast

■ profit and loss forecast, if required by client

■ notes to the accounts

■ conclusions

■ appendices, if required.

The business plan will be produced by the students working in small groups and working as consultants for a client entrepreneur/firm. The completed written business plan will need to be of high quality.

Students should complete a final presentation to the entrepreneur/client.

Recommended Reading ■ ■ ■ ■ ■ ■ ■ ■ ■ ■ ■

Barrow, C., Burke, G., Molian, D. and Brown, R. (2004) *Enterprise Development: The Challenges of Starting, Growing and Selling Businesses*, Thomson, London.

Butler, D. (2000) *Business Planning: A Guide to Business Start-up*, Butterworth-Heinemann, Oxford.

Williams, S. (2000) *The Business Start-up Guide*, Lloyds/TSB Bank, Bristol.

References

1 For example, Barrow, C., Barrow, P. and Brown, R. (2000) *The Business Plan Workbook*, 4th edn, Kogan Page, London, or any of the commercial banks' own guides.

2 Deakins, D. and Hussain, G. (1994) Financial Information the Banker and Small Business: A Comment, *The British Accounting Review*, vol. 26, pp. 323–35.

3 Mason, C. and Stark, M. (2004) 'What do Investors Look for in a Business Plan? A Comparison of the Investment Criteria of Bankers, Venture Capitalists and Business Angels', *International Small Business Journal*, vol. 22, no. 3, pp. 227–48.

4 Porter, M. (1980) *Competitive Strategy: Techniques for Analysing Industries and Competitors*, Collier Macmillan.

5 Kay, J. (1993) *Foundations of Corporate Success: How Business Strategies Add Value*, Oxford University Press, Oxford.

6 Fletcher, M. (1994) *Bank Managers' Lending Decisions to Small Firms*, Department of Entrepreneurship, University of Stirling, Stirling.

7 Small Business Service (2004) *A Government Action Plan for Small Business*, DTI, London.

8 Curran, J. (2000) 'What is Small Business Policy in the UK For? Evaluating and Assessing Small Business Support Policies', *International Small Business Journal*, vol. 18, no. 3, pp. 36–50.

9 Gray, C. (1998) *Enterprise and Culture*, Routledge, London.

10 Davies, H. (2002) *A Review of Enterprise and the Economy in Education*, DfES, London.

11 Scottish Executive (2003) *Determined to Succeed; Enterprise in Education – Scottish Executive Response*, Scottish Executive, Edinburgh.

12 Deakins, D., Glancey, K., Menter, I. and Wyper, J. (2004) *Columba 1400: Creating Enterprise Culture*, Final Research Report for Scottish Executive and the Hunter Foundation, Scottish Executive, Glasgow.

13 Bennett, R. and Robson, P. (2003) 'External Advice and Business Link', in Cosh, A. and Hughes, M. (eds) *Enterprise Challenged: Policy and Performance in the British SME Sector, 1999–2002*, CCBR, University of Cambridge.

14 Deakins, D. (1993) 'What Role for Support Agencies? A Case Study of UK Enterprise Agencies', *Local Economy*, vol. 8, no. 1, pp. 57–6.

Index

(note: Figures in brackets following page numbers refer to chapter-end notes.)

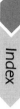

Index